The Structures
of the Life-World

Alfred Schutz
and
Thomas Luckmann

Translated by

The Structures
of the Life-World

RICHARD M. ZANER

and

H. TRISTRAM ENGELHARDT, Jʀ.

HEINEMANN · LONDON

Heinemann Educational Books Ltd

LONDON EDINBURGH MELBOURNE AUCKLAND TORONTO
HONG KONG SINGAPORE KUALA LUMPUR
IBADAN NAIROBI JOHANNESBURG
NEW DELHI

ISBN 0 435 82818 5
Paperback ISBN 0 435 82819 3

Published by Heinemann Educational Books Ltd
48 Charles Street, London W1X 8AH

Printed in Great Britain by Fletcher & Son Ltd
Norwich

Contents

Preface

ALFRED SCHUTZ died in the spring of 1959 in his sixty-first year. Death struck in the midst of preparations for the book which he had planned for some time and on which he had started to do intensive preliminary work in the summer and fall of the year before his death. The intention that motivated him in this project was to bring together the results of his investigations into the structure of the world of everyday life and to present in one connected argument what was still scattered among various publications.

This book, then, *The Structures of the Life-World*, was written in unusual circumstances. The plans that Schutz had drawn by the time of his death were sufficiently mature to include a general outline of the contents, detailed references to his published work and how it was to be integrated into the book, as well as drafts and *aide-mémoires* on analyses that still had to be carried out. When his widow discussed these materials with me, we agreed that their publication would be of considerable use to students of Schutz and eventually indispensable to scholars interested in an exact reconstruction and interpretation of Schutz's philosophical and sociological *opus*. We also realized, however, that such a posthumous publication could never achieve, even approximately, the intentions that had guided Schutz in his own conception of the book. But as a former student of Schutz's and as someone whose own thinking had been decisively influenced by him, I agreed to take up the task where Schutz had left off. I suspected that I had embarked on a difficult enterprise but could not yet know how difficult it would turn out to be. The completion of the *Strukturen der Lebenswelt* combined the difficulties of the posthumous editing of the manuscripts of a great teacher by his student with the problems of collaboration between two unequal authors: one dead, the other living; one looking back at the results of many years of singularly concentrated efforts devoted to the resolution of the problems that were to be dealt with in the book, the other the beneficiary of these efforts; one a master, always ready to revise his analyses but now incapable of doing so, the other a pupil, hesitant to revise what the master had written but forced by the exigencies of the analyses that he continued in the direction indicated by the master to go back, occasionally, to the beginnings.

In a sense this book is the *Summa* of Schutz's life, and as such it is his book alone. In another sense it is the culmination of the work of many authors, among whom Schutz is the most important and I am merely the last. The analysis of the structures of everyday life, however, is not completed in this book. It is an unending task of a *philosophia perennis* and of a historical theory of society.

Schutz had continued with his studies on the frontier between philosophy and social science ever since his first major work, *Der sinnhafte Aufbau der sozialen Welt*, was published by Springer in Austria in 1932. Austria was the country of his birth, childhood, youth, military service in World War I, legal, economic, and philosophical studies, and early occupational life in law and banking. Between his first book (and also the only one published in his lifetime) and the plan for a second, a quarter of a century elapsed. During this time he met Husserl, who had read his book with great appreciation and invited Schutz to become his assistant in Freiburg—an offer Schutz had to decline. These were the early years of Fascism and Nazism. Schutz went to Paris before Hitler's occupation of Austria. In 1939 he emigrated to the United States of America, accompanied by his wife, with whom he started a new existence under unfamiliar conditions. In this he shared the fate of many other European scholars. What was unusual, however, was that he rebuilt a career in law and business in his new country, continued with his investigations, *and* began lecturing: at the Graduate Faculty of the New School for Social Research in New York, an institution that under the presidency of Alvin W. Johnson had become a haven for many refugee scholars. It was only during the last years of his life that Schutz curtailed his other activities in order to accept, in 1952, a professorship at that institution.

This quarter of a century of much external turbulence in Schutz's life was filled, nevertheless, with intensive research into the foundations of the social sciences. He became increasingly certain that an adequate solution to the basic methodological problems of the sciences of man could only be found in a precise description of the peculiar human constitution of the "subject matter" of these sciences. He was confirmed in his early conviction that a rigorous method for the descriptive analysis of the constitution of the world of everyday life in human experience was available in Husserl's phenomenology. But he saw that what remained to be done was to apply the phenomenological method to the social world, the product of human symbolic action and material work. Schutz thus built on the thought of Husserl. But his effort to clarify the relation between social science methods and theories and their empirical basis, the world of everyday life, anticipated and applied to the social sciences ideas of the late Husserl that became fully known only after publication of the most important *Krisis*-manuscripts in *Die Krisis der europäischen Wissenschaften und die transzendentale Phänomenologie* (1954). However, Schutz was not only a phenomenological philosopher. He was also a social scientist trained in law, economics, and sociology. He shared Max Weber's *methodological individualism* and realized the strategic importance of an adequate theory of human action for the methodology of social science. In this regard Schutz's work is an impressive continuation of a central concern of Weber's. Yet there can be no doubt that Schutz's original thinking and systematic investigations led him into new territory, where neither Husserl, whose acquaintance with the social sciences did not match his knowledge of the physical sciences (and his mastery of mathematics and logic), nor Weber, whose thinking never entirely dissociated itself from conventional Neo-Kantian philosophical premises, might have wanted to follow him. In this territory Schutz was a pioneer, and a generation of younger scholars are following trails that were blazed by him.

The more than thirty essays and articles that followed the *Sinnhafte Aufbau* and that appeared during his lifetime were published in English (except for a few in German, French, and Spanish) in various philosophical and sociological journals and volumes of symposia.[1] They deal with a wide variety of problems,

1. Most of these publications were reprinted after his death, between 1962 and 1966, by Nijhoff, The Hague, in the three volumes of Schutz's *Collected Papers* which were edited, successively, by his student Maurice Natanson, his colleague Arvid Brodersen, and his

ranging from intersubjectivity, signs and symbols, language, typification and knowledge, "multiple" realities, and social action, to
the methodology of the social sciences and to critical discussions
of William James, Max Scheler, Jean-Paul Sartre, and, of course,
Husserl. The scope and variety of topics show the interests of a
far-ranging mind, though the scattered form of publication may
give the superficial impression of a fragmentary *opus*.

This impression is misleading. The basic pattern of Schutz's
thought, as it appears in the *Sinnhafte Aufbau*, was enriched but
not basically changed by new intellectual influences, as, for example, by his encounter with American pragmatism and especially with William James and George Herbert Mead. The careful reader of his various essays will note that the work of Schutz
continued in the direction to which his first book may well serve
as a signpost. But the unity of his thought shows up most clearly
in a comparison of the *Sinnhafte Aufbau* with the plan for the
Strukturen der Lebenswelt. The investigations Schutz undertook
in the quarter of the century between his first book and the plan
for his second can be seen as variations on the main theme of the
former, perhaps as transpositions into a different key or occasionally as developments of themes that were originally subordinate. Schutz's research in this period, if one looks back at it with
the sketch for the latter work before one's eyes, also can be seen
as the probing of a singularly consistent mind into problems that
were already raised or touched upon in his early work. The final
summing up of his thought and work, conceived as a systematic
description of *the common-sense world as social reality*,[2] was
clearly intended to rest firmly on the resolution of these problems. The painstaking analyses of the objectivating activities of
human consciousness and of their most important results, typifications, and signs and symbols in intersubjective communica-

widow Ilse Schutz. For a detailed bibliography, see the appendix to the
second volume of this book, or consult the bibliographies of the
selections of Schutz's work, *On Phenomenology and Social Relations*,
edited by another of his former students, Helmut Wagner, for the
Heritage of Sociology Series of the University of Chicago Press and
published in 1970, or the bibliography attached to the essays in
memory of Alfred Schutz, *Phenomenology and Social Reality*, edited
by Maurice Natanson and published by Nijhoff, The Hague, 1970.

2. This is, incidentally, the title of a brief and highly perceptive
discussion of Schutz's thought by his friend Aron Gurwitsch in *Social
Research*, XXIX, no. 1 (Spring, 1962), 50–72.

tion, were evidently felt to be necessary presuppositions for this *Summa*. Building on Husserl's and his own analysis of human orientation in space and time and on his investigations of the experience of fellow-men in face-to-face situations, he successively uncovered the layers of those elementary structures of everyday life which provide the foundation of social experience, language, and social action, and thus of the complex historical world of human life.

It is to be regretted that Schutz could not carry out the plans for what, with some slight exaggeration, one may call the *terminus ad quem* of his life as a philosopher and social scientist. It is probably futile to speculate on what precisely the definitive shape and the final formulations of the book would have been if he had been allotted the time to complete it. But it is perhaps necessary to emphasize something that should be evident. This book cannot be the book as Schutz would have written it. It is not even the book I *think* he would have written: a complete submersion of my own thought and work in his plan was neither possible nor, I am sure, was it something that Schutz would have wished under the circumstances. On the other hand, I have tried to be as faithful as possible to the basic intention of the project: the analysis of the structures of everyday life.

The following is the original plan for chapters and sections:

Chapter I: The Life-World of the Natural Attitude
  A. As unquestioned ground of the natural attitude
  B. The taken-for-granted and the problematic
  C. A state of structure for the subject of lived experience
  D. Plans and practicalities
Chapter II: Stratifications of the Life-World
  A. Spatial
  B. Temporal
  C. Social
  D. Provinces of reality with finite meaning-structure
  E. Systems of signs and symbols
  F. ? Provinces of relevance
Chapter III: Knowledge of the Life-World. Relevance and Typicality
  A. The stock of knowledge at hand and its structure
  B. The situation
  C. Plan-determined interest
  D. Relevance
  E. Typification
  F. Typicality, stock of experience, and knowledge of the future

I have followed the general structure of Schutz's plan, with two major exceptions. The third chapter on the subjective stock of knowledge has a somewhat different internal structure than Schutz had projected; more important, two relatively subordinate sections of the original plan for this chapter, on the typifications of social reality and on the socialization of types, have been more fully developed. Additional analyses of the problems raised in these sections soon demonstrated the need for systematic treatment. The result is an entirely new chapter: the present Chapter 4 on knowledge and society. The other major change results from my decision to abandon the projected final chapter on the methodology of the social sciences. Schutz's plans do not seem to go far beyond what is systematically developed in the essay on common sense and scientific interpretation of human action; nor do they give sufficient details on how he intended to proceed. Thus I did not think that I could successfully develop the analysis of *this* problem in a manner fully consistent with Schutz's ideas (I have formulated my own thoughts on the subject elsewhere).

But in many instances I have followed the details of Schutz's plans for the individual chapters. When I did not, the change was dictated by the intrinsic requirements of the analysis and the systematization of presentation. I should like to add that I am fairly certain that Schutz himself would not have hesitated to make changes of this kind. As a kind of junior author, of course, I had to think twice where he would have thought once.

These changes cannot be listed here one by one. In some instances, I would find it difficult myself to reconstruct the degree of literal fidelity to the details of the original plan. The appendixes to the second volume will reproduce the original plans by Schutz, his working papers, and all other relevant manuscripts. Readers interested in these matters, scholars who may want to have precise knowledge of Schutz's writings, and, indeed, anyone who wishes to weigh faithfulness to intentions against deviations in details must be referred to the appendixes.

For the general orientation of the reader it will be useful, however, to give here an over-all idea of the nature of Schutz's plan and to characterize briefly the working papers and manuscripts. The plan consists of file cards in different colors (the colors are used to indicate differences between chapter-heading cards, section and subsection cards, and numbered reference cards referring to different papers). The working papers and manuscripts consist of references to and excerpts from Husserl MSS in Louvain (Series A: 6001–6073), Buffalo (B I 15: 6100–6159 and B 16: 6160–6186), and to excerpts from Husserl's *Krisis* (7001–7076). There is another reference to the *Brief Boehm*. Furthermore, a number of cards worked into the general plan contain references to the *Grosses Relevanzmanuskript* (which was later edited by Richard Zaner and published posthumously in English under the title *Reflections on the Problem of*

Relevance [New Haven: Yale University Press, 1970] and in German as *Das Problem der Relevanz* [Frankfurt, 1971]), as well as to section X of the manuscript on relevance, and the manuscript on the "Leerstelle," i.e., vacancies, that is attached to it. The manuscripts expressly written in preparation of the *Strukturen* consist of six notebooks, written in German. Schutz planned to write the book in German, and this is probably the reason why he also chose this language for the preparatory work for the book. Incidentally, this is the reason why I used German in the writing of the book.

The notebooks contain materials of varied degrees of importance. In part they consist of German translations of terms and passages from Schutz's English articles, brief excerpts from, and *aide-mémoires* on, writers dealing with the problems with which Schutz was concerned, and some detailed plans for the restructuring of analyses from his published work, evidently in order to integrate them better into the over-all scheme of the book project. These plans were apparently followed in part in the detailed outline for the chapters and sections which he wrote down later on the index cards mentioned above. More importantly, the notebooks contain revisions of some lines of analysis in his published work that sometimes go beyond matters of style. Most importantly, they also contain sketches for new lines of analysis and explicit recognition of open problems left for resolution later. MS. I (Bar Harbor, Me., 1957) is primarily concerned with the theory of relevance; MS. II (Seelisberg, Switzerland, August 12–16, 1958) deals mainly with the theory of action and is based on *Common Sense and the Scientific Interpretation of Human Action, Choosing Among Projects of Action,* and *Concept and Theory Formation in the Social Sciences;* MS. III (Seelisberg, August 17–18, 1958) deals with the same problem and is also primarily based on the articles mentioned; MS. IV (Seelisberg, August 19–27, 1958) is mainly devoted to the problems of the theory of communication and is based on *Symbol, Reality and Society;* MS. V (Minnewaska, N. Y., October 26–November 9, 1958) is based primarily on the same article and deals with the same problem but moves into problems of multiple realities, "transcendence," and again, the theory of relevance; MS. VI (New York, November 9–14, 1958) is a continuation of V. The notebooks were transcribed by Mrs. Schutz.

The story of my own involvement in the *Strukturen der Lebenswelt* covers the major part of my adult life but is easily

told. After several years of studies elsewhere in linguistics, literature, psychology, and philosophy, I came to New York in the early
fifties to do work in philosophy and later in sociology at the
Graduate Faculty of the New School for Social Research. Among
my teachers were Karl Löwith, Kurt Riezler, Kurt Goldstein,
Dorion Cairns, and three scholars who influenced my later thinking most directly. One was Carl Mayer, a foremost expert on Max
Weber and a sociologist of religion, whose great influence was
exercised mainly through his teaching. Another was Albert Salo-
mon, whose enormous knowledge of and great passion for the
history of political and social ideas inspired students of most
varied backgrounds. The third was Alfred Schutz.

I learned much from these men, and I find it impossible to
assess separately the degree to which I am indebted to each one.
There is, perhaps, one point of difference. Since I sat in Schutz's
seminars for several years, corresponded with him on drafts of
some of my own work, read his work again and again, adapted,
for English publication, a key chapter from his *Sinnhafte Aufbau,*
wrote introductions to and discussions of his work, incorporated
the results of his analyses in various of my own writings, and,
finally, worked for years on the *Strukturen der Lebenswelt,* there
are whole areas of my thinking, especially in the theory of action
and communication, where I find it most difficult to say with
certainty what is *not* his.

It is appropriate, in recounting the story of those years, that
I use the occasion here to thank Aron Gurwitsch, who was never
formally my teacher but from whom I learned much, especially
when we were colleagues at the Graduate Faculty of the New
School for Social Research in the first half of the sixties (I remember with pleasure a joint seminar on Schutz), for his careful
reading of early drafts of large portions of this book. It was on
his advice that I removed from the manuscript an entire section
on the boundaries of the social world. Originally, I did write it
for inclusion in the *Strukturen,* but I was led to conclusions with
which, as Gurwitsch pointed out, Schutz would have been unlikely to agree. It was published, however, in *Phenomenology and
Social Reality: Essays in Memory of Alfred Schutz,* edited by
Maurice Natanson (The Hague: Nijhoff, 1970).

I have also removed another section from this first volume.
It deals with language in everyday life and was meant to form a
key part of the analysis of the connection between various finite
provinces of meaning, at the end of the second chapter. In the

writing it grew out of all proportion and developed into an analysis of the constitution of language in everyday life. I shall incorporate it into the sixth chapter of the *Strukturen*, in Volume II, where it more logically belongs in its present form. Placed in a somewhat different context, it constitutes the core of my contribution to *Life-World and Consciousness: Essays for Aron Gurwitsch*, edited by Lester E. Embree (Evanston, Ill.: Northwestern University Press, 1972). Unfortunately, this leaves incomplete the analysis of the links between the finite provinces of meaning and thereby of the concluding part of the second chapter. The reader is referred to the second volume.

I shall *not* use the occasion to thank Mrs. Schutz, for that would be gratuitous. She is much too intimately a part of Schutz's life, also of his life as a scholar, and much too inextricably part of the efforts to bring his legacy to fruition, for anyone, even someone closely connected with these efforts, to be permitted to thank her for what is now part of *her* life.

In 1960, a year after Schutz's death, I came back to my alma mater. I taught there until 1965 in the department which had been Schutz's and returned there again for one term in 1966. The original draft for the first four chapters of the *Strukturen* was written during this period, most of the first three chapters during a term's leave of absence (which I spent in the Black Forest) in 1963/64. After this time I taught in Frankfurt till 1970. During this period I revised the original draft. The final draft was sent to Richard Zaner and H. Tristram Engelhardt, Jr., whom I am fortunate enough to have as translators.

Finally, the reader may want to know when the second volume—which will contain the two chapters on social action and on signs, symbols, and communication, and the appendixes with Schutz's original materials for the book—is likely to appear. It is probably foolhardy to make predictions. Yet I think that I shall have completed the final draft for these chapters this spring and that the second volume should appear within a year.

THOMAS LUCKMANN

Translators' Introduction

As Professor Luckmann's preface indicates, *The Structures of the Life-World* is the final focus of twenty-seven years of Alfred Schutz's labor, encompassing the fruits of his work between 1932 and his death in 1959. It represents Schutz's seminal attempt to achieve a comprehensive grasp of the nature of social reality. In contrast to his first book, *Der sinnhafte Aufbau der sozialen Welt*,[1] this study is a more detailed and basic analysis of the foundations of social structures. Moreover, the initial critique of Weber and the appropriation of insights from Husserl's phenomenology had had over a quarter of a century to develop into a thoroughly original view of these phenomena. *The Structures of the Life-World* presents an elaboration of themes that had only been sketched in Schutz's first book and elsewhere in his papers.[2] More importantly, it presents an integration of his theory of relevance within his analysis of social structures. The analysis of the role of relevance in structuring the life-world appeared in somewhat incomplete form in his posthumously published *Reflections on the Problem of Relevance*,[3] where for the first time systematic treatment of the phenomenon was available, if only in outline. In the present book that treatment is

1. Alfred Schutz, *Der sinnhafte Aufbau der sozialen Welt* (Vienna: Springer, 1932; 2d ed., 1960). [English translation by George Walsh and Frederick Lehnert, *The Phenomenology of the Social World* (London: Heinemann Educational Books, 1972), pp. 45–96.]

2. Alfred Schutz, *Collected Papers* (The Hague: Nijhoff, 1962–), Vol. I: *The Problem of Social Reality*, ed. Maurice Natanson (1962); Vol. II: *Studies in Social Theory*, ed. Arvid Brodersen (1964); Vol. III: *Studies in Phenomenological Philosophy*, ed. Ilse Schutz, introd. Aron Gurwitsch (1966).

3. Alfred Schutz, *Reflections on the Problem of Relevance*, ed. Richard M. Zaner (New Haven, Conn.: Yale University Press, 1970).

amplified and placed within the full scope of Schutz's fundamental project of giving a phenomenological description of the life-world.

In many respects the book is also a brilliant summation of his thought. Because of the depth and breadth of the analyses, it touches most of the themes to which Schutz addressed himself during his lifetime, such as: the spatial and temporal dimension of the life-world, structures of fantasy and dreaming, the origin of uniqueness in individual biographies, the stock of knowledge, type and typicality, the origin and development of the earliest social relations, and so on. The final vision of a major philosopher, the book develops the notions of the "accent of reality" and "the style of lived experience or cognition" in characterizing the various provinces of meaning, the worlds of dream, fantasy, and everyday life. Such fundamental concepts as the "course of life" (i.e., the stream of everyday living), the "thou- and they-orientations" (immediate and mediate social relations), and the like, are elaborated and integrated in the context of Schutz's account of the structures of the world taken for granted in everyday life.

As Schutz emphasized many times, everyday life intrinsically involves the suspension of doubts concerning the reality of the world. It invokes a kind of epochē, the bracketing out of a critical attitude. As a phenomenological endeavor, Schutz's study is an explicit focusing on that implicit epochē, which is tantamount to adopting a second epochē and establishing a critical phenomenological attitude. This epochē of the ("natural") epochē has the force of making it possible to undertake the description of the world as taken for granted in everyday life. The structures of the life-world become apprehended as the fabric of meaning taken for granted in the natural attitude, the basic context of "what is unquestioned"—and in this sense what is "taken as self-evident"—that undergirds all social life and action. In projecting a comprehensive analysis of these structures, Schutz hoped to offer a developed phenomenology of social reality and thereby give an account of the foundations of the social sciences.

This goal is pursued in a series of steps. The first chapter concisely examines the life-world as the province of the natural attitude, as the realm within which the world is taken for granted as "self-evidently" ("unquestionably") real. Schutz appreciated that this "reality" is experienced as social; this is indeed the central thrust of the work. Hence, the analysis of the structures of the life-world provides the foundations for a comprehensive social theory.

The second chapter demonstrates that an understanding of the compass of the life-world reveals a central social dimension. Spatial and temporal relations, thus, are also social relations that help structure the world in terms of the face-to-face encounter with fellow-men ("consociates"), mere contemporaries, and then our predecessors and successors. The basic strata of the life-world underlie (in Husserlian terminology, they "found") ever more social strata of meaning, and in so doing they become increasingly socialized. Schutz thus succeeds in showing not only that the spatial and temporal relations are social but also that the very style of lived experience and cognition in the everyday world is social. The world with its multiple items is accepted as a theater where knowledge and action are fundamentally intersubjective.

The third and fourth chapters, which constitute the bulk of the volume, develop this theme. In particular, they demonstrate the social and contextual character of knowledge. First, the contextual, situation-bound character of everyday life is examined. Every moment of conscious life occurs within a specific situation, so that the categories of every determination of every situation have a predominantly social origin. We are always in a situation and the situation is always socially conditioned. The concept of "situation" is adroitly developed in terms of one of Schutz's most crucial notions: the thematic, interpretational, and motivational relevance structures which ground "all experience and all acts." Schutz brings his account of the situation and of relevance structures to bear on his accounts of types and typicality. The latter are to be understood only in terms of the situation in which they arose and the relevance structures that conditioned their development. A type is produced in a situation and arises as a solution (or attempted solution) to concrete problems. Every type thus contains an implicit reference back to the problem situation of its constitution, to "the 'originary' problem-state." That state, however, owes its constitution in turn to the three relevance structures. But then, all of the analyses of relevance implicitly refer back to social structures determining the situation. In short, context and social reality are interwoven, and it is only in terms of this interdependence that relevance and typicality are to be understood. This is in fact a sweeping and novel *epistemology*: a phenomenological account of knowledge as basically social. It is *ab initio* proof against solipsism.

Further, knowledge and society are recognized by Schutz as deeply interwoven. Knowledge, both specialized and general, occurs in a matrix of action and experience shared and conditioned by others. Indeed, since the reality of the everyday life-world is a social reality, it possesses social structures of relevance into which everyone is born, and in which he lives, and "grows older" with his fellow-man. The child in his first interaction with others is included in a reciprocal motivational context with structures of relevance (goals, means, attitudes) that have been socially delineated and are "taken for granted." As motivational and interpretative relevances emerge socially, a social stock of knowledge is developed and made objective in signs, marks, and language. A further consequence of this analysis of the socialization of knowledge is that one is offered the basis not only for a *social theory of knowledge* but also for a *sociology of knowledge*. And, the structures basic to such a sociology suggest that the social stock of knowledge has some striking properties, including one of the most fundamental and important of social differentiations: viz., the social distribution of knowledge. The differentiation ranges from the dissimilar knowledge possessed by the two sexes (e.g., a mother tells her daughter about the problem of menstruation) to the knowledge possessed by specialists that is not in the hands of laymen. The difference between the layman, the well-informed, and the specialist is a fundamental epistemological "division of labor" that has broad and important consequences for the structure of society. The social distribution of knowledge structures society and social roles; it constitutes a profound separation and inequality within any society. Among other things, it is basic to an understanding of the nature of sexual roles and differences in the distribution of power in society. As Schutz puts it, "groups of 'experts' form one of the institutional catalysts of power concentration" (p. 315; this and subsequent parenthetical paginations refer to the present book). Further, the social distribution of knowledge is important in understanding the status of subcultures that often possess different "versions" of general knowledge and form "societies within society."

It should also be noted that Schutz's work is highly suggestive of numerous other issues with which he concerned himself very little or not at all. To indicate but one such area, it should prove to be most fruitful for developing new ways of appreciating individual deviations from the everyday reality of the normal person. For example, what is the style of lived experience or cognition of the schizophrenic? Or, in what meaning-context does the "accent of reality" fail to fall on the paramount province of wide-awake life and fall instead upon the waking dream of a hallucination? Schutz suggests this problem when he analyzes Don Quixote's interrelations with the windmill (see Chapter 2, A, 3). He adds the provocative suggestion that hallucinations, unlike dreams, can be social, as in the case of *folie à deux* (p. 32). But the further one retreats from an intersubjective reality, the further one leaves the everyday life-world behind—this being not a private world, but rather "the world of our common experience." If one leaves that world, one then approaches autism, the withdrawal from everyday life described by Eugen Bleuler in the first full characterization of schizophrenia,[4] and the severe break with reality characteristic of that disease. Other forms of deviation appear as "careers" determined by particular biographies— e.g., pederasty (p. 96). A typology of mental illnesses focusing on the relevance structures and situations peculiar to them should provide a way of understanding the meaning-contexts of insanity and offer a philosophical basis for an interpersonal theory of psychiatry. (One thinks of Harry Stack Sullivan's work by that title, *The Interpersonal Theory of Psychiatry*, and his reliance on such bases as G. H. Mead's "social psychology." [5] *The Structures of the Life-World,* with its greater details and more fundamental insights, would be a far more adequate basis.) Other kinds of issues that are still far from being fully understood and which might be illuminated by Schutz's work could be mentioned—e.g., value theory (which Schutz himself suggested was one of the important consequences of his work), philosophy of history, what might be termed the "logic of actual use" (or the rationality of everyday life), and the like. Space does not permit more than a mere mention of some of these, however.

IN TRANSLATING THIS TEXT we have attempted to render the manuscript into an English commensurate with Schutz's own terminology and phraseology. Since in this text Schutz employed

4. *Dementia Praecox oder Gruppe der Schizophrenien* (Leipzig: Deuticke, 1911). [English translation by J. Ziskin, *Dementia Praecox or the Group of Schizophrenias* (New York: International Universities Press, 1966).] It might also be mentioned that Gerhard Bosch's fine study of infantile autism (*Infantile Autism* [New York: Springer, 1970]), which draws a great deal from the work of Husserl, has many close parallels with some of Schutz's notions.

5. Harry Stack Sullivan, *The Interpersonal Theory of Psychiatry* (New York: Norton, 1953), pp. 16–17.

distinctions in the German unavailable in English, various devices have been used to preserve their meaning. For the most
part, these devices have been used previously, either in other
translations of works by Schutz or by Schutz himself when he
wrote in English. A short glossary lists words which have received a somewhat unique translation. In general, though, readers familiar with English translations of Schutz and Edmund
Husserl will find nothing new. Indeed, there are for the most part
very few technical usages, so that the choice of terms is self-
explanatory to anyone acquainted with phenomenology. It is
worth noting in advance, however, that certain terms have a
translation peculiar to Schutz. For example, John Macquarrie's
and Edward Robinson's translation of Heidegger's *Being and
Time* has given wide currency to rendering *vorhanden* and *zuhanden* as "present at hand" and "ready to hand," respectively.
Schutz's use of the English phrases "on hand" and "at hand" corresponds to his own use of *vorhanden* and *zuhanden,* which have
been translated accordingly. The same holds for the translation
of *Einstellung* in some contexts as "orientation" (and not "attitude"), though its translation as "attitude" in such phrases as
"natural attitude" has been well established and is maintained
here. In general, we have tried where possible to capture the
exact meaning of the original without undue violence to English
style. But since the development of Schutz's program of analysis
demands careful appreciation of his meaning, we have judged
that this places the need for precision above that of style.

The reader will notice that Volume I ends somewhat abruptly.
This is due to the need for publishing Chapters 5 and 6 separately. As a result, the first volume breaks off where another
chapter was intended to continue the analysis. Nevertheless, the
first volume has a unity of theme that follows the examination
of the structures of the life-world through the analysis of the role
of knowledge in the life-world. The analysis of action and language in the second volume continues the examination without
supplanting the results of the first. The latter is thus a work in
its own right. It may even profit from the accident of its isolation
and allow the student of Schutz to study these analyses separately.

Neither this seminal study, nor other work of Schutz's, could
have appeared without the remarkable devotion and persistence
of his wife, Ilse Schutz, and the translators gratefully acknowl-

edge her substantial part in the publication of this work. We want as well to express our particular debt to Susan Malloy Engelhardt for her considerable assistance and guidance in the translation and preparation of the manuscript. Without her many contributions this translation would surely have faltered.

RICHARD M. ZANER
H. TRISTRAM ENGELHARDT, JR.

Glossary

Anzeichen	indication
ausgezeichnet	paramount
auslegen	explicate
Bereich	province
Bewusstseinsspannung	tension of consciousness
Du-Einstellung	thou-orientation
Durchführbarkeiten	practicabilities
Erfahrung	experience
Erlebnis	lived experience
erreichbar	within reach
Folgewelt	world of successors, subsequent world
fraglos gegeben	taken for granted
Gegenstand	object
geschlossene Sinngebiete	finite provinces of meaning
Handeln	action
Handlung	act
Handlungsentwurf	project for an act
Ihr-Einstellung	they-orientation
Lebensplan	life-plan
Lebenswelt	life-world
Leiblichkeit	live corporeality
Nachwelt	world of successors
Objekt	Object
Objektivierung	objectivation
Reichweite	reach (e.g., world within actual ——)
Sinn	meaning

Sinnzusammenhang	meaning-context
Typ, Typus	type
Typik	typicality, set of types
Umwelt	environs, surrounding world
ursprünglich	original, originary
vorhanden	on hand
Vorwelt	world of predecessors, precedent world
wiederherstellbar	restorable (e.g., world within ——— reach)
Wissensvorrat	stock of knowledge
Zeichen	sign
zuhanden	at hand
Zusammenhang	context, connection

The Structures
of the Life-World

1 / The Everyday Life-World
and the Natural Attitude

[A] THE LIFE-WORLD AS THE UNEXAMINED GROUND
OF THE NATURAL WORLD VIEW

THE SCIENCES that would interpret and explain human
action and thought must begin with a description of the foundational structures of what is prescientific, the reality which seems
self-evident to men remaining within the natural attitude. This
reality is the everyday life-world. It is the province of reality in
which man continuously participates in ways which are at once
inevitable and patterned. The everyday life-world is the region
of reality in which man can engage himself and which he can
change while he operates in it by means of his animate organism.
At the same time, the objectivities and events which are already
found in this realm (including the acts and the results of actions
of other men) limit his free possibilities of action. They place
him up against obstacles that can be surmounted, as well as
barriers that are insurmountable. Furthermore, only within this
realm can one be understood by his fellow-men, and only in it
can he work together with them. Only in the world of everyday
life can a common, communicative, surrounding world be constituted.[1] The world of everyday life is consequently man's fundamental and paramount reality.

By the everyday life-world is to be understood that province
of reality which the wide-awake and normal adult simply takes
for granted in the attitude of common sense. By this taken-for-

1. In Husserl's sense. See his *Ideen*, Vol. II: *Phänomenologische
Untersuchungen zur Konstitution* (The Hague: Nijhoff, 1952), §§
50, 51, and esp. 185, 193.

grantedness, we designate everything which we experience as unquestionable; every state of affairs is for us unproblematic until further notice. The circumstance that what has up until now been taken for granted can be brought into question, is a point with which, of course, we will still have to deal.

In the natural attitude, I always find myself in a world which is for me taken for granted and self-evidently "real." I was born into it and I assume that it existed before me. It is the unexamined ground of everything given in my experience, as it were, the taken-for-granted frame in which all the problems which I must overcome are placed. This world appears to me in coherent arrangements of well-circumscribed Objects having determinate properties. For men in the natural attitude the world is never a mere aggregation of colored spots, incoherent noises, or centers of cold and warmth. The possibility of a reduction of experience to such as these, and the consequent question of how they become reconstituted into objects of experience, does not confront me in the natural attitude. It rather expresses a problem pertaining to specifically philosophical and scientific thinking.

Moreover, I simply take it for granted that other men also exist in this my world, and indeed not only in a bodily manner like and among other objects, but rather as endowed with a consciousness that is essentially the same as mine. Thus from the outset, my life-world is not my private world but, rather, is intersubjective; the fundamental structure of its reality is that it is shared by us. Just as it is self-evident to me, within the natural attitude, that I can, up to a certain point, obtain knowledge of the lived experiences of my fellow-men—for example, the motives of their acts—so, too, I also assume that the same holds reciprocally for them with respect to me. How this commonness of the life-world is constituted, what structure it has, and what its significance is for social action must be carefully examined. For the time being it is enough to establish that in the natural attitude I assume that the objects of the outer world are in the main the same for my fellow-men as they are for me. In the same way, "nature," the province of things in the outer world, purely as such, is intersubjective. Furthermore, I take for granted that the significance of this "natural world" (which was already experienced, mastered, and named by our predecessors) is fundamentally the same for my fellow-men as for me, since it is brought into a common frame of interpretation. In this sense, the province of things belonging in the outer world is also social for me.

To be sure, my life-world consists not only of this province (although it is already related to my fellow-men), but also of a province experienced as "nature." But I find not only "nature" but also fellow-men as elements of my situational circumstances. It is self-evident to me in the natural attitude not only that I can act upon my fellow-men but also that they can act upon me. I know that I can enter into manifold social relations with them. This knowledge also contains the implicit assumption that they, my fellow-men, experience their relations which reciprocally include me in a way that is similar, for all practical purposes, to the way in which I experience them.

Since we cannot here enter into the phenomenological problem of the constitution of intersubjectivity, we must be content with the statement that in the natural attitude of everyday life the following is taken for granted without question: (a) the corporeal existence of other men; (b) that these bodies are endowed with consciousness essentially similar to my own; (c) that the things in the outer world included in my environs and that of my fellow-men are the same for us and have fundamentally the same meaning; (d) that I can enter into interrelations and reciprocal actions with my fellow-men; (e) that I can make myself understood to them (which follows from the preceding assumptions); (f) that a stratified social and cultural world is historically pregiven as a frame of reference for me and my fellow-men, indeed in a manner as taken for granted as the "natural world"; (g) that therefore the situation in which I find myself at any moment is only to a small extent purely created by me.

The everyday reality of the life-world includes, therefore, not only the "nature" experienced by me but also the social (and therefore the cultural) world in which I find myself; the life-world is not created out of the merely material objects and events which I encounter in my environment. Certainly these are together one component of my surrounding world; nevertheless, there also belong to this all the meaning-strata which transform natural things into cultural Objects, human bodies into fellow-men, and the movements of fellow-men into acts, gestures, and communications. Now, to be sure, William James does call the subuniverse of the sensorily perceivable, physical world the "paramount reality."[2] It follows from the preceding remarks, however, that there are compelling grounds for positing the entire world of everyday life as our pre-eminent reality. What is plainly given to us in the natural attitude under no circumstances merely includes the objects of external perception (understood purely as such), but rather includes also the lower-order meaning strata thanks to which natural things are experienced as cultural Objects. Indeed, since these meaning strata attain reality only through Objects, matters of fact, and events in the outer world, we believe that our definition is not incompatible with that of James. We agree with Santayana, "that the mind never has ideas, much less ideas which it can communicate, without a material means and a material occasion. The tongue must be moved, the audible conventional word must pass the lips and reach a willing ear. The hands holding tools or plans must intervene in order to carry out the project."[3] The life-world, understood in its totality as natural and social world, is the arena, as well as what sets the limits, of my and our reciprocal action. In order to actualize our goals, we must master what is present in them and transform them. Accordingly, we act and operate not only within the life-world but also upon it. Our bodily movements gear into the life-world and transform its objects and their reciprocal relations. At the same time, these objects offer to our actions a resistance which we must either subdue or to which we must yield. The life-world is thus a reality which we modify through our acts and which, on the other hand, modifies our actions. We can say that our natural attitude of daily life is pervasively determined by a *pragmatic motive*.

Nevertheless, in the natural attitude the world is already given to me for my explication. I must understand my life-world to the degree necessary in order to be able to act in it and operate upon it. Likewise, thinking in the attitude of the life-world is also pragmatically motivated. We have already pointed to the main "self-evidences" that lie at the basis of the natural attitude. We now turn to a brief description of the structure of thinking within the natural attitude.

2. [William James, *Principles of Psychology*, 2 vols. (New York: Henry, 1890), Vol. II, Chap. 21. Hereafter, footnote additions and interpolations that have been made by the translators will be enclosed in square brackets.]

3. [George Santayana, *Dominations and Powers* (New York: Scribner, 1951), p. 146.]

Each step of my explication and understanding of the world is based at any given time on a stock of previous experience, my own immediate experiences as well as such experiences as are transmitted to me from my fellow-men and above all from my parents, teachers, and so on. All of these communicated and immediate experiences are included in a certain unity having the form of my stock of knowledge, which serves me as the reference schema for the actual step of my explication of the world. All of my experiences in the life-world are brought into relation to this schema, so that the objects and events in the life-world confront me from the outset in their typical character—in general as mountains and stones, trees and animals, more specifically as a ridge, as oaks, birds, fish, and so on.

How the typifications are constituted in the stock of knowledge is a problem which is still to be investigated in detail. In any case, it is "self-evident" to me in the natural attitude that these trees "really" are trees, for you and for me, these birds "really" are birds, and so on. Every explication within the life-world goes on within the milieu of affairs which have already been explicated, within a reality that is fundamentally and typically familiar. I trust that the world as it has been known by me up until now will continue further and that consequently the stock of knowledge obtained from my fellow-men and formed from my own experiences will continue to preserve its fundamental validity. We would like to designate this (in accord with Husserl) the "and so forth" idealization. From this assumption follows the further and fundamental one: that I can repeat my past successful acts. So long as the structure of the world can be taken to be constant, as long as my previous experience is valid, my ability to operate upon the world in this and that manner remains in principle preserved. As Husserl has shown, the further ideality of the "I can always do it again" is developed correlative to the ideality of the "and so forth."[4] Both idealizations and the assumptions of the constancy of the world's structure which are

4. [Edmund Husserl, *Formale und transzendentale Logik* (Halle: Nijhoff, 1929), § 74. English translation by Dorion Cairns (The Hague: Nijhoff, 1969). *Erfahrung und Urteil* (Prague: Academia, 1939; 2d ed., Hamburg: Claassen & Goverts, 1948), §§ 24, 51b, 58, 61. English translation by James S. Churchill and Karl Ameriks, *Experience and Judgment: Investigations in a Genealogy of Logic* (Evanston, Ill.: Northwestern University Press, 1973). A new German edition is soon to be published by Felix Meiner, Hamburg.]

grounded on them—the validity of my previous experience and, on the other hand, my ability to operate upon the world—are essential aspects of thinking within the natural attitude.

[B] THE PROBLEMATIC AND THAT WHICH IS TAKEN FOR GRANTED

WE HAVE NOW DESCRIBED the most important structural characteristics of thinking within the life-world as well as the self-evidencies pertaining to the natural attitude. This description coincides in all essentials with the concept of the relative-natural world view developed by Max Scheler,[5] who sees the fact that it is given as unquestionable to be its determinative characteristic. It is the sedimented group experience that has passed the test and which does not need to be examined by individuals as regards its validity.

Now, however, the typical experiences, maxims, and intuitions contained in the relative-natural world view do not constitute a closed, logically articulated system—as do the higher forms of knowledge that are placed by Scheler in opposition to the relative-natural intuition. This holds all the more for my own stock of knowledge within the life-world—which for the most part is taken over from group experience and includes beyond that my own previous experiences. The deficient agreement of the components of my stock of knowledge does not fundamentally compromise its self-evidency, its validity "until further notice"; this again contrasts with the higher forms of knowledge, for example, science with its postulate of logical congruence as regards valid theories. In the natural attitude, I only become aware of the deficient tone of my stock of knowledge if a novel experience does not fit into what has up until now been taken as the taken-for-granted valid reference schema. We thereby come again to a problem which we have already noted at the beginning and to which we must now turn our attention: what does it mean to take something for granted as simply given "until further notice"? And how is that which has become questionable transformed into something taken for granted?

5. See Max Scheler, *Die Wissensformen und die Gesellschaft* (Leipzig: Der Neue Geist, 1926), pp. 58 ff.

In order to answer these questions, we must next describe in more detail how what is taken for granted is experienced. Then we must direct our attention to a more precise analysis of the inducements through which we are motivated to regard an experience as in need of explication. From this point, we will examine under what typical circumstances a problem is considered as solved or an explication as adequate.

What is taken for granted does not form a closed, unequivocally articulated, and clearly arranged province. What is taken for granted within the prevailing lifeworldly situation is surrounded by uncertainty. One experiences that which is taken for granted as a kernel of determinate and straightforward content to which is cogiven a horizon which is indeterminate and consequently not given with the same straightforwardness. This horizon, however, is experienced at the same time as fundamentally determinable, as capable of explication. It is, to be sure, on hand from the outset not as questionable (in the sense of doubtful) but rather as able to be questioned. As a result, accordingly, what is taken for granted has its explicatory horizons—horizons therefore of determinable indeterminacy. The stock of knowledge pertaining to thinking within the life-world is to be understood not as a context transparent in its totality, but rather as a totality of "self-evidencies" changing from situation to situation, being set into relief at any given time by a background of indeterminacy. This totality is not graspable as such but is cogiven in the flow of experience as a certain reliable ground of every situationally determined explication.

On the other hand, viewed from the prevailing "kernel" of self-evidency the (still) undetermined horizon is a *possible* problem whereby I expect, within the natural attitude (fundamentally through my abilities), to solve this problem. How the transformation of a possible problem into an actual one comes about, how I become motivated to an explication of the horizon, is a question whose solution must now concern us, so far as possible before we have undertaken a precise analysis of relevance structures and the formation of typicalities.[6]

That which is taken for granted is the province of the familiar: it presents solutions to problems of my previous experiences and acts. My stock of knowledge consists of such solutions to problems. These became constituted in interpretations of ex-

6. See Chap. 3, B and C.

perience (that is to say, explications of the horizon). In such explications the perceptions, experiences, and alternatives of action that became questionable were classified into the reference schemata at hand; the latter are, in turn, under certain circumstances modified by them. The explication (which is in principle never "finally" completed) was only pushed as far as was necessary for the mastery (determined through the pragmatic motive) of the lifeworldly situation. If an actual new experience in a similar lifeworldly situation can without contradiction be classified into a type formed out of previous experiences (and thus if it "fits" into a relevant reference schema) then it, for its part, confirms the validity of the stock of experience. What is merely given as questionable in the novelty of each current experience is, in the routine flow of experiences in the natural attitude, routinely made into something taken for granted. What is questionable in this way is, of course, not intrinsically problematic; and neither is the "solution" brought out as such in consciousness. In general, the current experience, on the contrary, appears to me as at the outset reliable, according to its type; this all the more when it is concerned with a genuine positing of identity, for example with a previously perceived object. For the most part, the current experience appears to me as something that is in its kernel taken for granted, although it is naturally in principle "new." The succession of experiences in the natural attitude typically forms a chain of self-evidencies.

Now, our question is how this routine succession of unproblematic experiences becomes interrupted and how a problem is set off against a background of self-evidency. In the first place, the current experience may not simply be classifiable into a typical reference schema conforming to the situationally relevant level of types. Thus, for example, it may not be enough for me to recognize a plant as a mushroom if I anticipate picking it, for the subordinate typifications "palatable" or "poisonous" are relevant for me. On the other hand, I may, while taking a walk, simply perceive "mushrooms," without my being motivated to an explication of "edible mushroom," "poisonous mushroom." However, without a situationally conditioned motivation for explication of that kind, an actual experience may contradict a type (given as relevant). How does this occur? When I pass by the object taken for granted in perception as a mushroom, its back enters with immediate evidence into my field of vision. Let us now suppose that the back of the mushroom reveals itself as in no way capable of being inserted into any typical previous experience. The routine classification of my experience that has already occurred in a habitual reference schema meets with opposition. The taken-for-granted flow of my experience is interrupted; expressed generally: the most important element of my experience is indeed what I have with immediate evidence in the direct grasp of my consciousness. However, there also belong to every experience, in addition to the retention of previous phases of consciousness, anticipations of further phases which are more or less determined in respect to their types. Such immediately evident aspects are not, however, also cogiven at the time in the immediate perception; a typical back side, for example, is apprepresented for the front of the mushroom.[7] Now, a formally apprepresented aspect may itself become evident in the future flow of my experience. But it may appear in contrast to the now remembered apprepresentation; that is, it may contradict the anticipated phase (if it now becomes actual) of the anticipation. If the apprepresented aspects of an object (that is, anticipated phases of my consciousness), when they come to self-presentedness, are incongruent with the previous experience, we can say that the taken-for-granted nature of my experience "explodes." What has until then been taken for granted is in consequence brought into question. The reality of the life-world demands of me, so to speak, the re-explication of my experience and interrupts the course of the chain of self-evidency.

The core of my experience, which on the basis of my stock of knowledge I admit as self-evident "until further notice," has become problematic to me. I must now turn my attention to it. That means, however, that the explication of the kernel of experience sedimented in my stock of experience can no longer be considered as adequate in the depth of a horizon that is adequate "until further notice," and that I must again take up the explication of the horizon. The fundamental motivation for this is thereby already given so that the discrepancy between my stock of experience and the actual experience in any case in principle places in question a partial province of my stock of knowledge. (The fact that under certain conditions my stock of knowledge

7. For the analysis of apprepresentation, consult Edmund Husserl, above all: *Cartesianische Meditationen und Pariser Vorträge* (The Hague: Nijhoff, 1950), §§ 49–54 [English translation by Dorion Cairns, *Cartesian Meditations* (The Hague: Nijhoff, 1960)] and *Ideen*, Vol. II, §§ 44–47.

as such can become questionable, together with the sedimentation processes through which typifications generally are formed, and thus the fact of a radical "crisis," are facts that need not be discussed by us here.)

When, therefore, I approach a re-explication of the horizon of the kernel of experience which has become questionable, the depth and breadth of the explication is conditioned through the setting of the problem. Let us again consider the example of the mushroom whose back does not fit into any set of typical mushroom backs. If the re-explication is motivated only through the discrepancy of the current experience with my stock of knowledge, and if, besides this, it has no other motivated significance for me, then I must modify my entire mushroom type. Through more careful handling, inspection, and so on, I can come to the conclusion, for example, that it is still a mushroom. From now on, my modified type "mushroom" will therefore have to include an *up until now* atypical mushroom back. Or rather, I may find, with further explication of the front of the mushroomlike object lying before me, that its other qualities are incompatible with the type "mushroom." In this case, my modified mushroom-type will to that extent be narrower, since it excludes from the type "mushroom" the qualification *up until now* pertaining to the typical front sides of mushrooms, which are conjoined with what will henceforth be atypical mushroom backs. In both cases, the problem that lies before us is solved, and that which became questionable during the early type-modification is once again taken for granted "until further notice." If my setting of the problem contains still other motivations, I would naturally wish to press the explication of the horizon further before I find a solution that is satisfying "until further notice."

Up until now, we have discussed cases in which the actual experience cannot be inserted without qualification into a situationally relevant set of types. An important motivation for the explication of horizons is, however, also directly given—namely, that an experience fit without further difficulty into the reference schemata and into the set of types belonging to my stock of knowledge. But for all that, it is not simply "passed by," but rather becomes questionable in the new situation because the *level* of the set of types is exposed as insufficient. Familiarity is familiarity solely with reference to the typical, while the atypical aspects of the horizon remain undetermined, since in relation to them a typification has been shown to be superfluous (that is, in the actual past explicative situation). Our knowledge is taken for granted; that is, what was questionable became explicated, the problem solved—in a manner and to a degree that was sufficient for the actual, situationally conditioned problematic. But this also means that the process of explication was interrupted somewhere (fundamentally it could always be driven further!), so that the solution was partial; in other words, it was a solution "until further notice." Our stock of knowledge and its correlative schemata of typification results from the discontinuance of processes of explication, and exhibits the sedimentation of past situational problematics.

Now, however, every new situation may have ontologically, biographically, and socially determined aspects which let the hitherto sufficient typification appear insufficient to me as regards some actual experience and motivate me to advance, by means of the actual experience, to new explications. We have already enlarged on a simple example. Up to now I may not have eaten a mushroom, and the level of typification of "mushroom" was sufficient for me. Through famine (having been caused by whatever sort of natural, social, or specifically biographical circumstances) I am now interested in eating mushrooms. If I now see one (that is, if an actual experience gets without question in the reference schema "mushroom"), the inaccessibility of the type "mushroom" enters into consciousness for my now situationally conditioned experiences and acts. If at some earlier time, I had already learned to distinguish between edible and inedible mushrooms, I may now attempt to call to mind the horizons belonging to them that have been obscured. If not, I will only make use of conjecture, which is also anchored in my stock of knowledge and which just like many other problems is already explicated by my predecessors or fellow-men: I can take the mushroom home and buy a book on mushrooms; or (assuming that I am completely left to my own resources) I may undertake various experiments, for example, with animals. The design of the experiments will depend upon my stock of knowledge (for example, my body and the bodies of certain animals have in this and that respect been taken as similar; therefore, I may posit for the experiment that they are the same in these respects, if it occurs to me that, if I do not eat any mushrooms, then I will in any event starve; but in the event that I eat the mushrooms that are not injurious to other animals, then, with a certain probability, I may survive).

In all these cases, it is a question of a further explication of the horizon. It has turned out that the previous explications stored in my stock of experience (determined by earlier situations and regarded as adequate solutions for these previous situations) do not suffice for the solution of that which is problematic in the current situation. I am now motivated to proceed with the explication until the solution appears to be sufficient as well for the actual problem under consideration.

There is a further circumstance through which an experience can become problematic in relation to my stock of knowledge. As has been said, my stock of knowledge is not a logically integrated system, but rather only the totality of my sedimented and situationally conditioned explications, which are composed in part from individual and in part from socially transmitted "traditional" solutions of problems. From every novel situation there accrues to me new knowledge, which is *not* examined in regard to its compatibility with reference schemata that appear irrelevant for the problematic under consideration. Such reference schemata do not at all come within the grasp of my consciousness. Now, the inadequacy of the explications relevant up until now, and indeed the inadequacy of whole provinces of reference schemata, can be given to consciousness by means of many actual experiences. With the help of other schemata, I then turn to an explication of the reference schemata that have not up until now appeared to be immediately relevant. Only then can a possible incompatibility of two or more provinces of reference schemata come into consciousness. This incompatibility for its part motivates me to a new explication of the current experience and of the horizons surrounding it that have now become questionable, or of the schemata which have up until now been regarded as sufficient. Thus, even in practical problems as they confront me in everyday life, I can find a tendency to "theoretical" thinking, or in any case to an, at least partial, integration of incompatible reference schemata in my stock of knowledge. Obviously, a logical articulation of my stock of knowledge is not in any way reached through this. The composite provinces of presuppositions remain for me, as always, more or less opaque.

While this general opacity of the stock of knowledge within the life-world appears as a deficiency from the standpoint of theoretical knowledge, one must nevertheless remember that, within the natural attitude, I am governed by the pragmatic motive. My stock of experience serves me for the solution to practical problems. In theoretical thinking, I can make doubt a methodological principle. In the world of everyday life, I am interested, in contrast, in being able to orient myself in my action in routine ways. The explications sedimented in my stock of knowledge have the status of actional directions: if things are thus and so, then I will act thus and so. Because of the successful employment of these directions, I do not need at every moment to go to new solutions of problems, horizonal explications, and the like, but rather I can act as I have already acted "in such circumstances." Thus, while the directions may therefore be opaque throughout their "theoretical" horizons, they appear to me in "practical" situations as obviously applicable. Their continuous "practical" success guarantees their reliability for me, and they become habitualized as recipes. Naturally, it is to be further observed that my stock of experience is to a considerable extent transmitted socially. The recipes have already "proven" themselves elsewhere. The first guarantee of the recipe is social.

[C] THE STRUCTUREDNESS OF THE LIFE-WORLD FOR THE LIVING SUBJECT

AS WE HAVE ALREADY SAID, the life-world is intersubjective from the very beginning. It presents itself to me as a subjective meaning-context; it appears meaningful in the explicative acts of my consciousness. The life-world is something to be mastered according to my particular interests. I project my own plans into the life-world, and it resists the realization of my goals, in terms of which some things become feasible for me and others do not. From the outset, however, I find in my life-world fellowmen who appear not merely as organisms but rather as bodies endowed with consciousness, as men "like me." A fellow-man's behavior is not, if you will, a spatiotemporal event, but rather action "like mine." That is to say, it is imbedded for them in meaning-contexts and is subjectively motivated and articulated purposefully according to their particular interests and according to what is feasible for them. Normally, in the natural attitude we "know" what it is that another is doing, why he does it, and why he does it now and under these circumstances.

Meaning is not a quality of certain lived experiences emerging distinctively in the stream of consciousness—that is to say,

of the objectivities constituted within it. It is rather the result of
my explication of past lived experiences which are grasped reflectively from an actual now and from an actually valid reference schema. As long as I am engaged in lived experiences and
directed toward the Objects that are intended in them, these
experiences have no sense for me (apart from the particular
meaning- and time-structure of action!). Lived experiences first
become meaningful, then, when they are explicated *post hoc* and
become comprehensible to me as well-circumscribed experiences.
Thus only those lived experiences are subjectively meaningful
which are memorially brought forth in their actuality, which are
examined as regards their constitution, and which are explicated
in respect to their position in a reference schema that is at hand.[8]

Accordingly, it is only in explication that my own behavior
becomes meaningful for me. But again too, the behavior of my
fellow-man becomes "intelligible" to me through the interpretation in my stock of knowledge of his bodily performances, of his
expressive movements, and so on, whereby I simply accept as
given the possibility of his meaningful behavior. Further, I know
that my behavior can correspondingly be explicated by him as
meaningful in his acts of interpretation, and "I know he knows
that I know." The everyday life-world is therefore fundamentally
intersubjective; it is a social world. All acts whatever refer to
meaning that is explicable by me and must be explicated by me
if I wish to find my way about in the life-world. Interpretation
of meaning, "understanding," is a fundamental principle of the
natural attitude with regard to my fellow-men.

But it is not only the currently comprehended action of my
fellow-men (or of myself) that is subjectively experienced as
motivated and purposeful behavior, that is as meaningful; it is
also the institutionalizations of action in social settings. These
refer in principle to the action of my fellow-men, my predecessors, whether these are explicated as anonymous (as "one does
it that way"), as individualized lawgivers, as founders of religion,
and so on. Their action once again refers to the meaning that
they have connected with their action.

This holds analogously for objectifications of human inten-

8. See *Der sinnhafte Aufbau der sozialen Welt* (Vienna: Springer,
1932; 2d ed., Vienna: Springer, 1960), § 2. [English translation by
George Walsh and Frederick Lehnert, *The Phenomenology of the
Social World* (London: Heinemann Educational Books, 1972), pp. 45–96.]

tions in sign systems and language, and also for the objectivated results of human acts, such as works of art. They all refer to original meaning-bestowing acts of reflective explications, subsequent acts of re-explication, and their habitualization in what my predecessors and colleagues in tradition and the relative-natural world view [9] take as meaningful and self-evident.

But even tools are experienced not just as things in the external world (which of course they also are), but rather in a subjective reference schema of interests and contexts of plans. They are for me "pliers" or a "hammer," with which I can attain certain results. At the same time, however, they refer to a more or less anonymous reference schema of their usefulness "for everyone," or for a "workman," and so on. And surely, a reference is possible in principle to the original meaning-bestowing acts of "someone," or of a certain historical or mythological figure who "invented" the tool. In the natural attitude, these diverse cultural strata of meaning always adhere to the object, even when I do not reflectively hold the meaning-bestowing acts in front of me.

Finally, as already mentioned, the natural Objects as such are also included in the province of meaning pertaining to culture. My experiences in the life-world of natural objectivities always adhere to the meaning of their fundamental experience-ability by fellow-men, and they appear to me in linguistic typifications, recipes for behavior, and the like, in which the explications of my predecessors are always present to me. In the natural attitude I am already cognizant of the historicity of the social and cultural world. The questionableness of the social and cultural world is of a historical character. Its objectivations are traceable back to human doings, which can be explicated as regards their meaning. By means of the latter, I "understand" the purpose of the tool, I grasp what a sign stands for, and I understand how a man orients himself in his relation to a social setting.

Now, in the natural attitude it is self-evident to me that in principle my fellow-man, "everyone" just like me, subjectively experiences, in subjective meaning-contexts, the resistances and limitations on projects, as well as the "obvious" motives of acts, and so on, imposed on us by the natural and social world. Just so, it is also self-evident to me that this articulation of nature and society that transcends me and him is the same, and conse-

9. The expression is used here in Max Scheler's sense.

quently that his subjective meaning-contexts as well as my subjectively experienced adumbrations and modes of apprehension are of an "Objective" order.

Everyone lives through his individual life cycle of birth, old age, and death; he is subject to the vicissitudes of health and sickness; he alternates back and forth between hope and grief. Every man takes part in the rhythm of nature, sees the movement of the sun, the moon, and the stars, lives through the change of day and night, and is situated in the succession of seasons. Every man stands in mutual relations to other men. He is a member of a social structure into which he is born or which he has joined, and which existed before him and will exist after him. Every total social system has structures of familial relationships, age groups, and generations; it has divisions of labor and differentiation according to occupations; it has balances of power and dominion, leaders and those led; and it has these with all the associated hierarchies. Thus for every man, the social world can also be lived through as a system of order with determinate relation-constants, although his perspectival apprehensions, his subjective explications of order, are for me as well as for him dependent on his position or standpoint, which in part is forced upon him and in part is determined by the biographical chain of his decisions. But again, it is in principle "understandable" to me in another manner.

[D] PLANS AND PRACTICABILITIES

WE SAID THAT thinking in the natural attitude is determined by the pragmatic motive. We must find our way about in the life-world and while acting and being acted upon must come to terms with the data imposed on us by nature and society. Now, however, it is through my action, through my somatic and somatically mediated activity, that I seek to modify what is imposed upon me. Every step stands under the same precept. The life-world is above all the province of practice, of action. The problems of action and choice must, therefore, have a central place in the analysis of the life-world.[10] At this point, only a few observations need be brought out in order to characterize in

10. See Chap. 5 [in Vol. II of this study, to be published later].

general the role of the pragmatic motive in the natural attitude.

In our thinking in the life-world, we are, above all, directed toward the future. What has already happened can still be reinterpreted but does not allow itself to be changed. What is still to come, however, is (as we know through our own previous experience) in part uninfluenceable by us, but in part modifiable through our possible acts. This knowledge, of course, rests upon the idealizations of the "and so forth" and the "I can always do it again." As regards the future events which cannot be influenced, we are indeed only spectators. However, we are not therefore nonparticipants, but rather are motivated through grief and hope. In respect to those future events, which we assume are modifiable through our actions, we must decide whether or not we want to act, and if the occasion arises, how to act. Now, however, in every specific biographical situation (to which, naturally, my stock of experience also belongs), we find that many elements of this life-world are unalterable, while others are modifiable through my action. I find myself in a spatiotemporal and social situation, in a naturally and socially articulated surrounding world. From that, there accrue to me relevance structures that (by means of memory and of my past, of past decision, of acts undertaken, of incompleted projects) are combined together into a plan system that is indeed not homogeneous but which appears to me as uniform. There may at times be a plan in the foreground of my consciousness that is determined by a governing interest. However, it is always surrounded with a horizon of meaning to which I can again explicatively advert. If I do so, I will discover that the governing interest is connected with other interests, that a goal that is to be actualized is a partial step toward the actualization of higher goals, that decisions have resulted from previous decisions. In daily life, acts are components within a higher-order system of plans: for a specific province within the life-world, for the day, for the year, for work and leisure—which in turn have their place in a more or less determined life-plan. If for the moment I actualize my design to write a letter to my friend, then I could say without further explanation: today I only have a few hours—for this and that reason; I intend soon to visit the town where my friend lives—for this and that reason; in the next few days I must overcome a problem which my friend knows about—and so forth and so on.

The fact that my acts, which I am able to apprehend as typical acts, will have typical consequences, is at the same time presented to me in my stock of experience. I have written letters with similar contents to other friends, and they have reacted thus and so. I have written letters with different contents to the same friend, and he has reacted thus and so. And still more simply: I have succeeded in bringing forth by means of my writing an irrevocable alteration in my surrounding world, even if it be ever so slight. Every action in my surrounding world changes it.

It is, furthermore, also obvious to me that (in order to write my friend) I must undertake a whole series of component actions which are subordinate ends toward a higher goal. I must write down specific marks; I cannot merely imagine the letter. I have the choice of only a few possibilities, which I know about through my previous experience: pen, pencil, typewriter, each of which has in turn a horizon of meaning which has already been explicated, such as impersonability, carelessness, etc. These possibilities will for their part, each according to my particular interests, my relations to my friend and to the limitation of the situation (I write more or less on the line and only have a pencil handy), force upon me decisions within a hierarchy of plans. If I choose the pen, I cannot on the other hand write the same letter with the pencil. If I "ask" my friend for certain information, then I cannot "beg" for it, etc. If my time is very limited, then I can only write my friend X, but not also Y and Z.

In short, within the natural attitude I do not act only within a biographically determined hierarchy of plans. Rather, I also see typical consequences of my acts which are apprehended as typical, and I insert myself into a structure of incompatibilities that is lived through as being obvious. They are partially ontological in character (I cannot write letters with my eyes), partially historical (it would never "have occurred to me," in the fifteenth century, to write other than with a pen), and partially biographical (I have never learned to write legibly; I have to write with a typewriter). Thus the purely conceivable hierarchies of plans confront specific and partially unalterable spheres of incompatibilities; the result is a system of motivations for *practicable* goals.

2 / The Stratifications of the Life-World

WE HAVE OCCUPIED OURSELVES up until now with the life-world of everyday life, which we defined as that reality the wide-awake, normal, mature person finds given straightforwardly in the natural attitude. Thus the concept of the everyday life-world already embraces more than William James's concept of the "paramount reality," [1] which refers to the sensibly perceivable physical world. As we have shown, both the cultural meaning-stratum that first makes physical Objects into objects of naïve experience and also the everyday social world belong to the everyday life-world. Nevertheless, the life-world embraces still more than the everyday reality. Man sinks into sleep, day after day. He relinquishes the everyday natural attitude in order to lapse into fictive worlds, into fantasies. He is able to transcend everydayness by means of symbols. Finally, as a special case, he may consciously modify the natural attitude. Now, we can conceive the concept of the life-world so broadly that it includes all modifications of attitude and alertness—viz., the tension of consciousness present with the normal adult. We can also contrast the world of scientific thought with the life-world of natural experience. That is ultimately a terminological question. It is materially important, though, to describe the structure of the quasi-ontological provinces of reality as they are lived through by the normal, wide-awake adult. In doing so, we must neglect the special problems of the child's world and of pathological realities. It must again be established that the everyday life-world is the paramount province of reality, and that the natural attitude is

1. [William James, *Principles of Psychology*, 2 vols. (New York: Henry, 1890), Vol. II, Chap. 21.]

the fundamental attitude of the normal adult. The following section of our investigation will concentrate upon describing this province that is of singular importance for the social sciences. In the second section of this chapter we wish to analyze the temporal, spatial, and social stratification of this province. But above all, the quasi-ontological structure of the life-world, understood in the broader sense, must be investigated.

[A] PROVINCES OF REALITY WITH FINITE MEANING-STRUCTURE

I. ACCENT OF REALITY

IN A WELL-KNOWN CHAPTER of his work *The Principles of Psychology*,[2] William James maintained that reality was nothing else than a relatedness to our active and emotional life. The source of all reality is subjective; everything that evokes our interest is real: to call an object real signifies that this object stands in a definite relation to us. "In short, the word 'real' is a fringe of meaning." Our first impulse is to take as immediately real all that is meant, as long as it remains uncontradicted. Nevertheless, there should be several, indeed probably infinitely many, different orders of reality that at any given time have a special style of being that is characteristic of them alone. James called them "subuniverses." [3] As examples he cites the world of meaning —viz., the world of physical objects (which is for him the principal order of reality)—the world of science, the world of ideal relations, the world of idols, the various supernatural worlds of mythology and religion, the various subuniverses of individual meanings, the worlds of visionaries and of the insane. As long as one is attentive to it, each of these worlds is, in its own fashion, real. But as soon as one withdraws attention from it, the world disappears as a reality. According to James, all propositions, whether attributive or existential, are believed by the mere fact that they are thought, so long as they do not thereby conflict with other propositions believed at the same time (they claim that their terms are identical with those of other propositions). Thus

2. *Ibid.*, pp. 282–322.
3. *Ibid.*, Chap. 21.

for example, the play world of a little girl is "real" so long as it remains undisturbed. The girl is "actually" the mother, her doll "actually" the child. In the world of artistic production, for example, knight, death, and devil have "real" existence on Dürer's engraving, namely, as existents in the province of meaning for artistic fantasy. In the reality of the external world, they are pictorial "representations." During the play, Hamlet is real for us as Hamlet, not as the actor X who "represents" Hamlet.

With these insights concerning the character of reality, James touches upon essential problems that are also important for our considerations. In any case, James consciously moved within the limits of a psychological line of inquiry; now, his beginning will be developed in another direction. It is important above all to stress that the orders of reality do not become constituted through the ontological structure of their Objects, but rather through the meaning of our experience.[4] For this reason we prefer to speak not (as does James) of subuniverses of reality, but rather of finite provinces of meaning, upon each of which we could confer the accent of reality. A finite province of meaning thus consists of meaning-compatible experiences. Otherwise put, all experiences that belong to a finite province of meaning point to a particular style of lived experience—viz., a cognitive style. *In regard to this style*, they are all in mutual harmony and are compatible with one another. The emphasized restriction is important. Inconsistencies and incompatibilities that some isolated experiences have *in relation to their partially asserted meaning* can appear throughout the same provinces of meaning without the accent of reality being withdrawn. Rather, this may have as its consequence only the invalidity of just these respective experiences within the finite province of meaning.

The finite character of a province of meaning (of the everyday life-world, of the world of dreams, of the world of science,

4. See Edmund Husserl, *Ideen*, Vol. I: *Allgemeine Einführung in die reine Phänomenologie* (The Hague: Nijhoff, 1950), § 55, p. 134. [English translation by W. Boyce Gibson, *Ideas: General Introduction to Pure Phenomenology* (London: Allen & Unwin, 1931), p. 168.] "In a certain sense and with proper care in the use of words we may even say that *all real unities are 'unities of meaning'* . . . *an absolute reality is just as valid as a round square*. Reality and world, here used, are just the titles for certain valid *unities of meaning*, namely, unities of 'meaning' related to certain organizations of pure absolute consciousness which dispense meaning and show forth its validity in certain *essentially* fixed, specific ways" (Husserl's italics).

of the world of religious experience) rests upon the character of the unity of its own peculiar lived experience—viz., its cognitive style. Harmony and compatibility, with regard to this style, are consequently restricted to a given province of meaning. In no case is that which is compatible within the finite province of meaning P also compatible within the finite province of meaning Q. On the contrary, seen from the P that has been established as real, Q appears, together with the particular experiences belonging to Q, as purely fictive, inconsistent, and inverted. For this reason we are justified in speaking of *finite* provinces of meaning. There is no possibility of reducing one finite province of meaning to another with the help of a conversion formula. The transition from one province of meaning to another can only be accomplished by means of a "leap" (in Kierkegaard's sense). This "leap" is nothing other than the exchange of one style of lived experience for another. Since, as we shall soon see, a specific tension of consciousness belongs essentially to the style of lived experience, such a "leap" is accompanied by shock experience that is brought about by the radical alteration of the tension of consciousness. When we speak of finite provinces of meaning, then, the finite character is based solely upon the corresponding structure of meaning. For in the course of a day, indeed of an hour, we can, through the modifications of the tension of consciousness, traverse a whole series of such provinces.[5] There are just as many shock experiences as there are finite provinces of meaning able to receive the accent of reality through changes of attitude. Here we will cite only a few examples: going to sleep as a leap into a dream, awaking, the theater curtain rising, "being absorbed" in a painting. Still further examples are: the shifting of consciousness when one begins to play, the lived experience of the "numinous," the jolt by which, for instance, the scientist shifts after dinner to the theoretical attitude, and also laughter as a reaction to the displacement of reality which is the basis of a joke.

As long as our experiences participate in the same lived experience—viz., cognitive style—as long therefore as they remain in a finite province of meaning, the reality of these experiences continues for us. Only when we are motivated by our life-plan to

5. Further, there still remains the problem of "enclaves": every project of an act in the everyday life-world, for example, calls for a sort of reflective attitude, even if it is not scientific.

accept another attitude ("I must not keep on daydreaming, I must get down to work"), or when we are disturbed by a "foreign inter-ference" (e.g., by a bang when we are looking at a picture, stum-bling during a daydream, sudden hunger during scientific con-templation, etc.—one also thinks of religious "illumination"), only when we experience a specific shock that bursts the limits of that which is for us a momentarily "real," finite province of meaning, must we transfer (or "wish" to) the accent of reality to another province of meaning. According to the examples, it appears as if the everyday life-world had a certain pre-eminence. In fact the life-world presents the primal types of our experience of reality. In the course of daily life we are continually held within the life-world and we can, with a certain restriction, con-strue the other provinces of meaning as modifications of it. Cer-tainly one may not forget that the accent of reality can be be-stowed on each province of meaning, so that indeed from the perspective of the everyday life-world the other provinces of meaning may appear only as quasi-realities, but so that at the same time, from the scientific attitude, or from religious experi-ence, the everyday life-world can be seen as a quasi-reality.

2. THE STYLE OF LIVED EXPERIENCE: NAMELY, THE COGNITIVE STYLE AND THE TENSION OF CONSCIOUSNESS

We have said that the accent of reality rests upon the har-mony between experiences and a specific style of lived experience —viz., a cognitive style. What then is a style of lived experience, or a cognitive style? It is founded upon the *specific tension of consciousness*. As Bergson realized, tensions of consciousness are functions of our "attention to life" [*attention à la vie*].[6] Ac-tivity is united with the highest tension of consciousness and manifests the strongest interest for encountering reality, while the dream is linked with complete lack of such interest and pre-sents the lowest degree of the tension of consciousness. This in-terest is the fundamental regulative principle of our conscious

6. See Henri Bergson, *Essai sur les données immédiates de la conscience* (Paris: Alcan, 1938), pp. 20 ff., pp. 94–106; *Matière et mémoire* (Paris: Alcan, 1889), pp. 189–95, 224–33; *L'Energie spiri-tuelle* (Paris: Alcan, 1919), pp. 15–18, 80–84, 108–11, 129–37, 164–71; *La Pensée et la mouvant* (Paris: Alcan, 1934), 91 ff., 171–75, 190–93, 233–38.

life. It defines the province of the world that is relevant for us. It motivates us so that we merge into our present lived experiences and are directed immediately to their Objects. Or it motivates us to turn our attention to our past (perhaps also our just-past) lived experiences and interrogate them concerning their meaning, or rather to devote ourselves, in a corresponding attitude, to the project of future acts.

Let us now concern ourselves in more detail with that degree of conscious tension which is of special importance for us, namely, that of *wide-awakeness*. Consciousness is itself under the greatest tension, which originates from the attitude of full attentiveness to life and its necessities. In acts and doings that are directed toward the surrounding world, the ego is fully interested in life and is therefore wide-awake. The ego lives in its acts. Its attentiveness is concentrated upon the realization of its projects. One is here concerned with an active, not a merely passive, attentiveness. In passive attentiveness I experience, for example, the "surge" of *petites perceptions,* the (merely passive) lived experiences and not-significant manifestations of spontaneity. Significant spontaneity (in Leibniz' sense) can be defined as the effort to attain always-new perceptions. In its lowest form it leads to the enclosure of perceptions and their transformation in apperceptions. In its highest form it leads to acts, in particular those that gear into the external world and alter it; thus it leads to performing. The condition of wide-awakeness outlines every pragmatically relevant province of the world. This relevance for its part determines the form and content of our life of consciousness. It determines form because it determines the tension of our recollections and thereby the span of our remembrances of past lived experiences, while at the same time determining the span of our expectations. It determines content because all of our actual lived experiences are modified through previously sketched projecting and its realization.[7]

A further aspect of the style of lived experience, or the cognitive style, which is immediately connected with the tension of consciousness, is a *dominant form of spontaneity.* Daydreaming, for example, transpires in passivity, scientific work in acts of

7. Here, of course, from the analysis of the tension of consciousness as such we arrived at the analysis of the dimension of time, in which the acting ego lives through his own acts as well as arriving at other problems of a theory of action. (For these questions, see Chap. 5 [in Vol. II of this study, to be published later].)

thought, everyday life in acts of performing (that is, in meaningful spontaneity that rests upon a plan and is thereby characterized so that the projected state can be brought about through movements of the animate organism which gear into the external world), etc.

Further, a *special epochē* belongs to the cognitive style. The phenomenological suspension of acceptance of the world's reality is essentially different from the various epochēs that underlie the mythology of empirical science. But also the natural attitude of daily life has a special form of epochē. In the natural attitude a man surely does not suspend his beliefs in the existence of the outer world and its Objects. On the contrary, he suspends every doubt concerning their existence. What he brackets is the doubt whether the world and its Objects could be otherwise than just as they appear to him.[8]

The style of lived experience, or the cognitive style, contains as well a *specific form of sociality*. Here again there are various possibilities: from solitude (that loses itself in dreams, for example) to the various forms of the experience of others; of their communications and "products" in the intersubjective everyday life-world that is shared by us, in which communication and intersubjectively related action are the rule.

Just as a specific form of sociality belongs to the style of lived experience, or to the cognitive style, so also does an appropriate *specific form of self-experience*. In a dream, or in fantasy, one can subjectively experience oneself as endowed with completely different attributes of a different biography from those which one "has" in daily life. In the scientific attitude one subjectively experiences oneself as scientist; one thinks within a problem situation predetermined by the scientific viewpoint, thus, so to speak, anonymously. One can in religious experience subjectively experience oneself in the totality of one's self, or one can in everyday social relations experience oneself only under various aspects of roles.

Moreover, a special *time perspective* belongs to the style of subjective experience, or cognitive style. The inner time of dreams and of the solitary ego differs from the homogeneous space / time of natural science. And it differs also from the social standard time which has its origin in the point of intersection of

8. See H. Spiegelberg, "The Reality Phenomenon and Reality," in *Philosophical Essays in Memory of Edmund Husserl,* ed. Marvin Farber (Cambridge: Harvard University Press, 1940).

inner time with world time, and which serves as the basis of the universal time structure of the intersubjective life-world. Furthermore, to attempt a systematic typology of the various provinces of meaning and their own styles of subjective experience (cognitive styles) would be an important exercise. It would have to be shown exactly how, with waning tension of consciousness and withdrawal from daily life, larger and larger segments and strata of the everyday life-world lose their "self-evidency" and the accent of reality. It would have to be indicated how the epoché of the natural attitude, which suspends doubt concerning the existence of the everyday life-world, is replaced by other forms of epoché which "bracket" belief in determinate provinces of the everyday life-world. Such a typology cannot be displayed here in all completeness, since our chief problem is the analysis of the daily life-world, which indeed may, with some emendation, be characterized as the primary reality. In the following section we will devote ourselves to the description of the stratification of this most eminent province of meaning. And in this connection we will have to characterize the style of lived experience, or the cognitive style, of this province. But first of all we want to say something concerning other provinces of meaning with finite meaning-structure, in order to procure a background against which this description should stand out forcibly. We take as an example the world of dreams and the worlds of fantasy.

3. FANTASY WORLDS

We speak of "fantasy worlds," since it is a question not of a single but rather of several finite provinces of meaning. Although, in direct contrast to the life-world, they appear to be closely related to one another, since they all bracket determinate strata of the everyday life-world, they are nevertheless heterogeneous and not mutually reducible. This becomes clear if we consider as examples the internally consistent meaning-structures of the worlds of daydreams, games, fairy tales, jokes, poetry. Nevertheless, sundry essential elements of the style of lived experience, or of the cognitive style, are common to these fantasy worlds as such.

a) When my attention becomes absorbed in one of the several fantasy worlds, I no longer need to master the external world. There is no resistance by Objects surrounding me which have to be subdued. I am exempted from the urgency of the pragmatic motive under which I stand in the everyday natural attitude. The intersubjective standard time of the everyday life-world no longer governs me. The world is still limited through what is present in my perception, memory, and knowledge. Events and situations over which I have no control do not force alternatives upon me between which I must choose. My productive ability is not circumscribed by external circumstances. But also, as long as I live in fantasy worlds, I cannot "produce," in the sense of an act which gears into the external world and alters it. As long as I tarry in the world of fantasy I cannot accomplish anything, save just to engage in fantasy. However, under certain circumstances I can sketch out in advance the course of fantasy as such (I will imagine the fairy gives me three wishes), and I can then fulfill this project. It is still uncertain whether this falls under a broadly conceived definition of the concept "action." It is important that fantasying remains secluded by itself, that the intention to act is absent—in contrast to the plan of an act in the everyday life-world which (strictly as a plan) is also in a certain sense "merely thinking." [9]

But then does not Don Quixote act? Does he not gear into the external world, when he charges against the windmill? Moreover, it must be said that Don Quixote does not step out of the bounds of fantasy's province of meaning, to which he imparts the accent of reality. For him, the "fantasyer" confronted with the realities of everyday life (just as, conversely, for the realist who encounters Eulenspiegel's phantasmagoria), the giants are actual giants, not imaginary creations. In the episode of the windmills he must indeed recognize that his interpretation of the Object already given to him has been brought into question by the subsequent event. In the natural attitude, of course, we experience the same thing when it turns out that the distant something that we took to be a tree, is a man.[10] But Don Quixote behaves dif-

9. In the words of Husserl, *Ideen*, Vol. I, and *Ideen*, Vol. III: *Die Phänomenologie und die Fundamente der Wissenschaften* (The Hague, Nijhoff, 1952), we could say that all fantasying is "neutral," i.e., it lacks the specific positionality of thetic consciousness.

10. For a precise analysis of this problem, see Husserl, *Ideen*, Vol. I, § 103, and *Erfahrung und Urteil* (Prague: Academia, 1939; 2d ed., Hamburg: Claassen & Goverts, 1948), pp. 99 ff., 370 ff. [English translation by James S. Churchill and Karl Ameriks, *Experience and Judgment: Investigations in a Genealogy of Logic* (Evanston, Ill.: Northwestern University Press, 1973). A new German edition is soon to be published by Felix Meiner, Hamburg.]

ferently than we do: nothing is capable of bringing him out of his fantasy world's province of meaning. He does not admit that the objects that he took to be giants were windmills all along and that he just must have been mistaken. Certainly, he has to admit that the objects now, at this moment, are windmills. He does not dispute the reality of the actual experience: it was the vanes of the windmills that violently lifted him out of the saddle. But the actual experience obtains its sense only in the fantasy world's province of meaning. The shock which he experiences is a physical one; it does not force him to shift the accent of reality, but only to find an explanation for the event suited to the province of meaning of the specific fantasy world.

And Don Quixote finds it: in the last moment his archenemy, the sorcerer, must have transformed the giants into windmills, since it cannot be doubted that they previously were giants. With this explanation Don Quixote conclusively encloses himself in the world of his fantasy and removes the possibility of changing over into the reality of the everyday, since he has universally removed the accent of reality from it. The giants are actual, the windmills are mere appearance, phantasmagoria.

We again recall William James's dictum that *"any object which remains uncontradicted is ipso facto believed and posited as absolute reality."* [11] Husserl also comes to the same conclusion. [12] He distinguishes between existential predicates (whose opposites are negations of existence) and predicates of reality (whose opposites are predicates of unreality, of fiction). He writes, *"In the natural attitude, there is at first (prior to reflection) no predicate 'real,' no genus 'reality'"* [Husserl's italics]. Only when we fantasy and go from the attitude of living in fantasy (thus of quasi-experience in all its modes) over to the given realities, and when we thereby go beyond the contingent particular fantasy and that which it fantasies (taking this as an example for possible fantasies in general, and fictions in general), does there accrue to us the concept "fiction" (viz., fantasy) and on the other hand the concepts "possible experience in general" and "actuality." Husserl then writes:

Of the imaginer (the "dreamer"), who lives in the world of imagination, we cannot say that he posits fictions as fictions; rather, he has modified actualities, actualities as-if. . . . *Only he who*

11. [James, *Principles of Psychology*, II, 289.]
12. *Erfahrung und Urteil*, § 74a, pp. 359 ff.

lives in experience and from there "dips into" imagination,
whereby what is imagined contrasts with what is experienced, *can
have the concepts of fiction and actuality* [Husserl's italics].[13]

From the previous considerations we infer that the contexts
of compatibility in everyday life are not in the province of fantasy. The logical structures of harmony, on the other hand (in
Husserl's terminology: the predicates of existence and nonexist-
ence), maintain their validity. I can fantasy giants, magicians,
winged horses, centaurs, and indeed perpetual motion, but not a
regular decahedron—it would then be the case that I was juxta-
posing empty concepts. In fantasy's finite province of meaning
only factual, not logical, incompatibilities can be overcome.

b) Add to this that the valid boundaries and conditions of
our spontaneity in the life-world are not valid in the same sense
for our fantasying. One who fantasies can fantasy *what* he wants
(even if not *how* he wants). He can fill the empty expectation of
his fantasying with any conceivable content whatever. If one can
at all designate fantasying as action in the pregnant sense, then
it is an action taken freely.

c) Also, the *time perspective* of the fantasy worlds differs
fundamentally from the time perspective of the everyday life-
world. According to Husserl [14] fantasmata lack stable temporal
loci in Objective time. Therefore they are not individualized, and
the category of self-identity is not applicable to them. "The same"
fantasma may recur within a single continual activity of fantasying, where the unity of this activity is guaranteed by means
of the continuity of inner time, in which it is produced for attentive perceiving. But fantasmata that belong to various fantasy
series (or those, in our terminology, which belong to various
provinces of finite meaning-structure) cannot be compared with
one another in respect to their self-identity or likeness. It is senseless to ask whether the witch of one fairy tale is identical with
that of another. The fantasying ego can in its fantasies fictively
change all distinctive traits of standard time, with the exception
of its irreversibility. I can fantasy the course of events, so to
speak, through a temporal magnifying glass or a time snatcher.
The irreversibility, though, resists any variation through fantasy
because it springs from the duration of inner time itself, which
is itself constitutive for our fantasies and the fantasmata pro-

13. [*Ibid.*, p. 360.]
14. *Ibid.*, §§ 39–42.

duced therein. While I fantasy (and also while I dream), I become older. I can indeed fictively change my past in a present fantasy, but the present fantasy itself becomes constituted in the duration of the stream of consciousness and bears its characteristic traits.

d) If I take my own *self as the object of fantasying*, then I can insert myself in every merely conceivable role. But the self which I imagine is experienced only as a part of my complete personality, as an aspect of the self that exists only due to me. In my fantasying I can also fictively change my live corporeality, but within the bounds that are posited through the primordial experience of the limits of my animate organism. I can fantasy myself to be a dwarf or a giant, but always as an internality that is delimited outward.

e) *The social structure of fantasy worlds* is complex. One can fantasy by oneself or with others; with a fellow-man or with many to whom one is related socially; and en masse. The daydream is solitary; communal fantasying extends from *folie à deux* (to give one extreme example), through reciprocally oriented intersubjective child's play, to the phenomena investigated by group psychology.

On the other hand, fellow-men, predecessors as well as successors, and all possible sorts of social relations, acts, and reactions, can become contents of my fantasying. Here the freedom of the fantasying ego has a wider latitude. It is, for example, possible for the fantasy to include the imagined cooperation of a fictitious fellow-man to such an extent that the fictitious conduct of this fellow-man can either confirm or annul my own fantasma.

4. THE DREAM WORLD

a) Sleep is complete *relaxation of consciousness* and is combined with complete *withdrawal from life*. The sleeping ego does not have any pragmatically conditioned interest to translate its confused perceptions into clarity and distinctness; that is, to convert them into apperceptions. But it continues to perceive, to remember, to think. Thus there are perceptions of its own animate organism, of its position, of its weight, of its limits; perceptions of light, sound, warmth. All these perceptions are passive; they are without any advertence, without the activities of hearing, looking, that would form the perceptions into apperceptions;

the *petites perceptions* are lived through, but they escape the selective and formative activity that originates from the attention to life (*attention à la vie*). Although they do not become clear and distinct but remain in a state of confusion, they are not further hidden, or implicitly contained within the higher-level formations of an active, pragmatically motivated attention. It is rather the passive attention, and consequently the totality of the *petites perceptions* in their influence on the intimate personal center of the dreamer, that determine his interest and the themes of his dream.

b) The typical form of *spontaneity* in the dream world has a certain similarity with that of the fantasy worlds. But the dreaming ego does not once *act* in the loose sense of this concept. Fantasy worlds are characterized by freedom of consideration, while there is no such freedom in the dream world. The fantasying ego can "volitionally" fill its empty anticipations with whatever contents it wishes; and it is just these contents to which it grants the accent of reality. It can, if it pleases, fantasy its possibilities to be facticities. The dreamer, on the other hand, can neither fulfill empty anticipations as he would, nor "actualize" his possibilities. The nightmare clearly shows the inescapability of the happenings of dreams and the impotence of the dreamer.

Still the dream is not exclusively restricted to passive consciousness. It just does not have any projects that require actualizing. I can, though, dream of myself as acting, even if the dream is often accompanied by knowledge that I do not "actually" act. In this case my dreamed action has in fact its apparent projects, apparent plans, that all originate from the sedimented prior experiences of daily life. But the voluntative fiat is lacking.

c) The *time structure* of the dream world is extraordinarily complex. Earlier and later, present, past, and future appear to be confounded. The dreaming person observes future events as if they were past; past events are dreamed of as open and modifiable and thereby bear a clear, future character; successions can be simultaneously transformed, and so forth. It appears as if the subjective processes of dreams elapse independently of the inner duration, the temporality of the stream of consciousness. This (of course deceptive) appearance begins this way so that the subjective processes of dreams are set free of the fixed categories of standard time. They are not inserted in the Objective temporal order. But since the subjective processes of dreams transpire in inner time, the subjective processes that arise out of the awake life of the dreaming person (and which are based on the categories of standard time, whose categorical context, though, is dissolved in the dream world) become involved in the duration of the dream. The irreversibility of this duration remains unaltered even in the dream world. Only the awake person who attempts to remember his dream may at times have the illusion of a possible inversion.

d) It must be said in regard to *sociality* that the state of dreaming is, in contrast to that of fantasying, *essentially* solitary. We cannot dream together. The other person always remains only the Object of my dreams, incapable of sharing them. The other of whom I dream does not appear in a common living present, but rather in a quasi-social relation. The other, even if I dream of him in aspects of his live corporeality and in strict relation to my intimate self, appears as a type, which is presented but with which I do not live. In the dream state the monad, with all its reflections of the universe, inclusive of the social world, is in reality solitary.

This brings us to a point which was just touched upon in the discussion of the temporal structure of the dream world: only the awake person can communicate. This conceals a serious difficulty for the description of dream phenomena. Only in the awakened state can I "consciously" turn to the dream. In this turning toward the dream I make use of the concepts and categories (above all of the language structure) of the everyday life-world, which are subject to the fundamental principles concerning the compatibility of this province of meaning. In dreams there is, for the dreaming person, no possibility of communication. This first becomes possible when one leaves the finite province of meaning of the dream. We can only grasp the sphere of dreams by means of "indirect communication," to use an expression of Kierkegaard's. That means, though, that the subjective processes of dreams can only be communicated, so to speak, by way of a "negative" contrast, i.e., in their difference from the meaning-structures of the lived experiences of everyday life. The poet, or the artist, is far closer to a description adequate to the meaning of the dream world than the scientist and philosopher, since his means of communication attempt to transcend the everyday meaning-structure and language.

[B] STRATIFICATIONS OF THE EVERYDAY LIFE-WORLD

I. THE STYLE OF LIVED EXPERIENCE IN THE EVERYDAY LIFE-WORLD

IN RELATION to other provinces of reality with finite meaning-structure, the everyday life-world is the primary reality. We have already thoroughly discussed why this is so: the life-world is the province of my live corporeal acts; it offers opposition, and it requires exertion to overcome it. Everyday reality introduces me to tasks, and I must realize my plans within it. It allows me to be successful or frustrated in my attempts to actualize my goals. By means of my performances I gear into everyday reality and alter it. I can test the results of my performances as occurrences within an intersubjective and therefore "Objective" world. I can let them be tested by others, detached from the subjective generative process, independent of circumstances, so that everyday reality may be produced through my performings. I share this reality with other men, with whom I have in common not only goals but means for the actualization of these goals. I influence other men and they influence me. We can act together. The everyday life-world is that reality in which reciprocal understanding is possible.

The world of daily life is given to us in a taken-for-granted way. We have also thoroughly discussed this circumstance. The province of meaning of this world retains the accent of reality as long as our practical experiences confirm its unity and harmony. It appears to us as "natural" reality, and we are not prepared to give up the attitude that is based upon it unless a special shock experience breaks through the meaning-structure of everyday reality and induces us to transfer the accent of reality to another province of meaning. Now, what are the essential traits of the style of lived experience, or the style of cognition, which characterizes the world of daily life? We will begin with a concise characterization summarizing the preceding more exhaustive explanation and referring to more precise analyses that must still be undertaken.

a) Wide-awakeness is the form of the tension of consciousness which characterizes daily life—it originates from the interests of full attentiveness (*attention à la vie*).[15]

b) The characteristic epochē is the epochē of the natural attitude, in which doubt concerning the existence of the outer world and its Objects is suspended. The possibility that the world could be otherwise than as it appears to me in everyday experience is bracketed.[16]

c) The dominant form of spontaneity is meaningful action that gears into the external world by means of live corporeal movements.[17]

d) The specific form of sociality is based on the experience of another fellow-man as endowed with consciousness, sharing with me a common intersubjective world of understanding and action.[18]

e) The characteristic form of self-experience is doubly grounded. It consists of the socially "bound" possession of individuality under various aspects of roles, and of the action of the "free" ego.[19]

f) The temporal perspective is that of the standard time that originates in the point of intersection of internal duration and world time, as the temporal structure of the intersubjective world.[20]

Now we can describe the spatial, temporal, and social structures of everyday experience that become constituted in this style of lived experience.

2. SPATIAL ARRANGEMENT OF THE EVERYDAY LIFE-WORLD

a. *The world within actual reach*

The wide-awake person in the natural attitude is interested above all in that sector of his everyday world which lies within his reach and which arranges itself spatially and temporally around him as its center. The place in which I find myself, my actual "here," is the starting point for my orientation in space. It is the zero-point of the system of coordinates within which the

15. See Chap. 2, A, 2.
16. *Ibid.*
17. See Chap. 5 [Vol. II].
18. See Chap. 2, B, 5.
19. See Chap. 2, B, 6, and Chap. 3, B, 4.
20. See Chap. 2, B, 4.

dimensions of orientation, the distances and perspectives of objects, become determined in the field that surrounds me. Relative to my animate organism, I classify the elements of my surroundings under the categories right, left, above, below, in front of, behind, near, far, etc.

The sector of the world which is accessible to my immediate experience, we will term *the world within actual reach*. It embraces not only actually perceived objects but also objects that can be perceived through attentive advertence. The world in my actual reach contains, apart from this sector's orientation to proximity and distance, which is centered upon me, an arrangement according to the modalities of meaning. Through this the Objects of this sector are given to me. This arrangement in visual range, in auditory range, indeed in the field of reach, is certainly overlaid by the identity (which is taken for granted in the natural attitude) of things as seen, heard, etc. Nevertheless, the modalities of perception are of still greater subjective significance within the world in actual reach. For though they progressively fade in our memory, the objects grasped memorially through these modalities become more and more vivid through typifications embedded in contexts of significations that are socially objectivated or made linguistic. The latter, though, extensively idealize and render anonymous the meaning-modalities and apprehensional perspectives still active in current experience.[21]

b. *The world within potential reach*

i. *Restorable reach*

The world in my actual reach, the sector of the world that is accessible in immediate experience, has a fixed structure in a coordinate system, and receives its reference point through an orientation to my animate organism. The content of this sector is therefore subject to constant change, due to my animate organism's movements. By means of these, near strata of the field sink away into the distance, while distant strata come closer. After all, there is no distinction between the world within my actual reach and the sector that was just now in my actual reach. I leave my room and start moving away. I turn away from this sector that was just now in my actual reach. In the street I remember a book that I left lying on my table. The book was previ-

21. See Chap. 3, C, 2.

ously in my reach; now it is no longer in it. It transcends my actual reach, but, in this case, it belongs to my experience of this transcendence and thus lies within my restorable reach. I need only return to my room, and then I will have a high probability (for most practical purposes of daily life, we can say certainty) of finding this room again with the table and book from which I have just departed; indeed I will find it just as I left it. The house in which I live will be standing (unless a fire has consumed it), the table will be standing by the window (unless someone has moved it), the book will be lying on it (unless someone has taken it away). These assumptions are, naturally, examples of the basic assumption of constancy in the world-structure, or the lifeworldly idealization of the "and so forth." [22] Therefore, *ceteris paribus*, I establish the sector which was previously in my actual reach as constant or constantly changeable. Further, I know that I must carry out only these and those movements, take these and those steps, in order to bring this sector into my actual reach again. *That* I can carry out such movements, such steps, is taken for granted by me on the basis of the second lifeworldly idealization: "I can always do it again." [23] The experiences sedimented in my stock of knowledge account for the empirical cumulations of restorability: I need only turn around and in five minutes I will be home again; I must undergo a long, painstaking training in order to be able again to climb a 3000-meter high mountain.

Sectors of the world that were only once within my reach arrange themselves by overlapping imperceptibly with the universal province of the world lying within my restorable reach. I am more or less acquainted through my own experience with the universal province. Indeed, it transcends the sector that actually lies within my present reach. But this experience of transcendence presents an everyday lifeworldly experience of the transcendence of an acquaintance, of a confidant.

ii. Attainable reach

As the zone of restorability in the world within potential reach bears the temporal character of the (remembered) past, so another zone is characterized by the temporal character of the future. A world which was never in my reach, but which can be

22. See Chap. 1, B.
23. *Ibid.*

brought within it, will be termed *the world within my attainable reach*. My assumption that in principle I can bring the world, including the sectors that are still unknown to me, into my reach, also rests (in general) upon the idealization of the "and so forth" and "I can always do it again." Certainly various problems arise here. The fundamental expectation that I can bring whatever sectors of the world I please into my reach is empirically arranged not only according to *subjective degrees of probability* but also according to *grades of ability* that are physical, technical, etc. My position in a particular time and society is part of the latter limitation. (A citizen of the Middle Ages could travel to China only with the very greatest difficulties and with the greatest loss of time. Today I can fly to Hong Kong in a day. My children may be able to take a trip to the moon. I cannot scale the north slope of Mount Eiger, yet someone else can. But perhaps I could also, if . . . , etc. All these are examples of variations of technical possibilities.) In addition, there is still, however, my biographical situation and the plans and hierarchies of plans that follow from it and the subjective probabilities that are conjoined therewith. (I could fly to Hong Kong, but that I will do it is, for *me*, improbable.)

Also, I am to various degrees familiar with the world within attainable reach. I am in any case familiar with the set of applicable types from my previous experiences that have sedimented in my stock of knowledge. I know the Dolomites but not the Mexican Sierra Madre. Still, I read somewhere that there are definite similarities. I know the subtropical river landscape in the southern United States, but not that of the Amazon, etc., etc.

From what has been said, it can be concluded that the prospects of restorability (or attainability) which belong to the two zones of potential reach are in no way equivalent. Let us make this precise in regard to the temporal dimension of spatial arrangement. As far as what concerns the former zone of potentiality, we must bear in mind that that which now has the prospect of being an easily reinstatable reach for me was previously in my actual reach. My previous acts and experiences belonged to the world within my previous reach. They are on the other hand joined with my present state of consciousness, which is what it is only because the now-past reality was once my actually present one. The expectation of reactualizing, within my reach, a world that was once actually present is founded upon the memories of my own "successful" lived experiences that I have already accomplished. The prospects of restorability are therefore, *ceteris paribus*, maximal.

Through anticipation, the second zone of potentiality is based on my future states of consciousness. This zone is joined with my past lived experiences not directly, but only in such a manner that my expectations originate from my stock of knowledge, which contains sedimented past lived experiences. With this basis I can consider the prospects for planned acts, estimate my ability to attain this or that goal. It is clear that this second zone of potentiality is in no way homogeneous but is arranged into sublevels that have various prospects of attainability. The chances typically decrease in relation to the increasing spatial, temporal, and social distance of the respective sublevel from the center of my actually present world.

iii. An indication of the social dimension of spatial arrangement

The world that is in actual reach of my fellow-man is extensively but not completely different from the world that is in my actual reach. On the basis of my stock of knowledge it is, in the natural attitude, taken for granted by me that the entire sector of the world in another's actual reach can be brought into my actual reach through an exchange of locations. Here also special problems of ability arise: even though I could "naturally" see from his location that which he sees just now, I still cannot do it because I, for example, am nearsighted. Even though, therefore, strictly speaking, the worlds in my actual reach are not identical with his, the sectors still overlap so much that I can in the natural attitude, for all practical purposes, speak of a common surrounding world.

Our biographies, though, are different. Sectors of the world that are in his previous, yet now restorable, reach may be in a merely attainable reach for me, and vice versa. That which is attainable for me may also be attainable in principle for him, but (considering the gradations of subjective probability and of ability) will probably not be attained by him. The same naturally holds for me.

Further, these gradations of the actual, restorable, and attainable reach point not only to my and his world, but also to the world of a third person and finally to "everyman's." Thus a system of spatial arrangements extends over the various strata of the social world. This system is an important aspect of social relations. It enters into the differentiation of intimacy and anonymity, of strangeness and familiarity, of *social* proximity and distance (my wife and I, who do not share the same childhood landscapes; my boyhood friend, who was my neighbor for ten years; a person in an American small town with whom I am unacquainted, but with whom I share a homeland, whom I meet in Budapest, etc.). At the same time, on the other hand, the social differentiation according to intimacy and anonymity, etc., is an important aspect of the subjective experience of the spatial organization of the life-world, whatever may be evident from a further explication even of the examples just mentioned (homeland, foreign land). At the highest level of social anonymity and, at the same time, "objectivity," a world becomes constituted which is potentially accessible to every man who is "willing, fit, and able."

And finally it must be said, in anticipation, that the formal structure of attainability and restorability is valid in general for subjective lived-experiencing of the social world, completely irrespective of the aspects of spatial arrangement. Thus there are, for example, specific more or less good chances for the restorability of a relation of friendship with a boyhood friend, whom I haven't seen for such and such a period of time. There are more or less good chances for the attainability of a certain relation with my friend's friend whom I do not know, specific chances for the attainability of certain relations with a farmer, when I myself am a farmer, with historians, when I myself am a sociologist, etc.

3. ZONES OF OPERATION

This analysis has brought us to problems that concern spatial arrangement as such and affect not only the temporal but also the social stratification of the life-world. These are stratifications which we will treat in the subsequent sections of this chapter. First of all, however, we will turn to the description of a zone that is constituted originarily in the world within reach. This description leads us still further to the problems of action which will not be fully examined until a later chapter.[24]

In the world within reach there is a zone which I can influence through *direct* action. We term this zone *the zone of opera-*

24. [Chap. 5 (Vol. II)].

tion. G. H. Mead is to be given credit for having analyzed the reality structure of physical Objects in relation to human action, above all the manipulation of them. What he termed the *manipulative zone* presents the kernel of reality. It embraces those Objects which can be touched as well as seen, in contrast to the zone of distant things, which cannot be experienced via live corporeal contact but which lie within the field of vision. Only the experience of physical objects in the manipulative zone gives us the "fundamental test of all reality," namely, the experience of resistance. Only this defines the "standard size" of things which outside of the manipulative zone appear in the distortions of optical perspectives.[25]

Mead's theory that the manipulative zone presents the kernel of the reality of the life-world agrees with our interpretation.[26] Of course, Mead's distinction between the manipulative and the distant zones should not be overstressed. This distinction is indeed of great importance for the analysis of the origin of Objective experience, but not for us. In the description of the natural attitude of the normal, fully awake adult, we are concerned with Objective experience. This is so because such a person already has at his disposal a stock of experience to which there also belongs the category of distance, and the taken-for-granted knowledge that distance can be overcome through acts, namely, changes of locations that are directed to a goal. Within the natural attitude the visual perception of a distant thing is immediately connected with the expectation that the distant thing can be brought into manipulative proximity through a change of location. To this there belongs also the expectation that the distorted perspectives of Objects will thereby disappear and their standard size be established. This automatic expectation subsequently may or may not be fulfilled (a child may, for example, attempt to grasp the stars with his hand). But for adults within the natural attitude, expectations of this kind are only an inversion of the process by which objects from the zone of operation become distant through being inspected and felt from all sides. This experience is extended to objects of a "similar sort," which have not yet

25. See G. H. Mead, *Philosophy of the Present* (Chicago: Open Court, 1932), pp. 124 ff.; *Philosophy of the Act* (Chicago: Open Court, 1938), pp. 103–6, 121 ff., 151 ff., 190–92, 196–97, 282–84.

26. [Alfred Schutz, *Collected Papers*, Vol. I: *The Problem of Social Reality*, ed. Maurice Natanson (The Hague: Nijhoff, 1962), pp. 306–8.]

been inspected and felt, and which confront one initially as distant things. Naturally, false typifications occur even with adults, even according to the previous experiences stored in one's stock of knowledge. Reaching for the stars is of course a false typification by the child (more or less of the sort: I can grasp twinkling things, as for example those that hang on the Christmas tree).

It is clear that the world within my reach, inclusive of my zone of operation, changes because of my changes in location. By means of the movements of my animate organism, I transfer the center, O, of my system of coordination to O', and this circumstance alone is sufficient to alter the coordinate values belonging to this system. A distinction should be noted here: the displacements of the world in my range are typically not fixed. This circumstance is in part to be ascribed to the peculiarities of visual perception: what was a background becomes a figure; I turn my head and a panorama rolls by me. But in part it must be ascribed to compartmentalization by the modalities of perception through which the world within reach is presented to me: I cross the bridge and see the wood in front of me becoming "larger" while I hear the noise of the brook diminish, etc. In comparison, my zone of operation proper is more narrowly circumscribed and becomes constituted in the interlacing of kinesthesias and locomotions. If I move away, after one pace I can no longer grasp the book (the glass, the safety cable, etc.). If a ball slips away from me on a slope, then I must run after it. If I fight an enemy, a few steps place him out of reach of my hands, my knife, my spear, my bow. Thus the limits of the zone of operation proper are, within subjective lived-experiencing, so to speak, more graspable, more sharply outlined, "more important." But the last example points to a certain artificiality in the definition of the zone of operation, and we had to assure ourselves that we were speaking about a zone of operation proper. Of course we did not want by means of this adjective to separate a true from an untrue zone of operation, but rather to point to a genetically (biographically) originary zone in which action occurs without mediation and is confirmed in immediate results (including false results). But when, in the example we mentioned, we spoke first of hands, and then of a knife, etc., we had already gone beyond, perhaps imperceptibly, the limits of such an originary province of operation. For soon after the child has mastered his locomotion and learned to coordinate his hands in purposeful behavior, he also learns to utilize tools, to include spoons, chairs, etc., in his attempts to reach the top of the chest of drawers. The narrowly limited primordial zone of operation of the child broadens by leaps and bounds until it reaches the technological limits that are laid out in society's prevailing stock of knowledge.

This observation brings us to the next, a problem closely related to the previous one and following from our first definition of the zone of operation as the province of unmediated action. We live in a time in which, for example, ICBM's have enormously extended our possibilities of action in respect to distance, quantity, and results. Moreover, this is correspondingly valid for the world within reach: I can telephone, pursue events on the television screen while they occur on other continents, etc. Obviously, through technological development there has entered here a qualitative leap in the range of experience and an enlargement of the zone of operation. It is a leap indeed, one connected to the line of inventions of bow and arrow, smoke signal, gunpowder, etc. In the end, this concerns the questions of the nonmediated and the mediated character of action and experience in general. But we do not want to go into these matters yet. It is of course useful to introduce a distinction between the *primary zone of operation* (the province of nonmediated action, and correspondingly the primary world within reach) and the *secondary zone of operation* (and the corresponding secondary reach), which is built upon the primary zone and which finds its limits in the prevailing technological conditions of a society. With regard to secondary zones of operation (and reaches), one must still further distinguish between that which is possible due to the condition, of technological knowledge in the society, and that which is due to the factor of the extension of operation (and of reach) that is typically accessible and employable by typical persons in daily life. Social structures will have a typical distribution of the prospects of access to the taken-for-granted, the occasional, to what in exceptional cases is the strict institutional control of the use of the extensional factor. This factor must be considered in the empirical analysis of the life-world of the Eskimo, of the modern American, etc., even if it need not be considered in the formal analysis of the structure of the life-world in general.

It can now be said that those parts of the world in my primary reach that do not belong to the primary zone of operation, transcend it. They present a province of my possible operation in connection with which possibility is typically greater than that for the world presently outside my reach. Further, gradations of ability that are conjoined with gradations of restorability and attainability belong here. In contrast, the relationship between secondary zones of operation and secondary reaches is less simple. There are intersections and overlappings (that also must be understood historically) between the secondary zone of operation and the secondary reach, while the primary zone of operation is always inserted within the primary world in reach. We can with rockets bombard the moon, which we can see every night, but we cannot yet bombard the fixed stars which we can see "just the same."

4. THE TEMPORAL ARRANGEMENT OF THE EVERYDAY LIFE-WORLD

a. World time

i. Finitude and the duration of the world

When we described the transcendence of the world in actual reach by the world in potential reach, we were primarily interested in the spatial aspect of this transcendence.[27] But even there we could not avoid anticipating its temporal aspects, because it is basically a temporal problem of turning away and turning toward: the world previously in actual reach (the book on the table at home), from which I have turned away (as I went away), transcends the world in actual reach (the street I'm walking on) to which I've turned (I look at the showcases). But I can at any time and from various motivations turn back toward the world which was in my formerly actual reach (I see a bookstore's showcase and remember that I wanted to take a book to my friend, and in my memory I locate the book as still at home lying on the table). Now the world in my formerly actual reach is indeed no longer in my present reach. It is, though, the theme of my current conscious activity in the form of remembrance and anticipation: the book as *still* lying on the table. We have already discussed the idealizations which ground this anticipation. In such motivated turning away and toward, I fasten onto segments of the world which transcend my actual reach (and whose simultaneity with my inner duration I do not directly experience) as being permanent. Thus, this everyday lived experience of tran-

27. See Chap. 2, B, 2, b, i.

scendence already concerns not only the world as extension, but also the world as duration.

The lived experience of transcendence involved in sleep possesses a still more unequivocal temporal foundation. Through a radical alteration in the tension of consciousness, I withdraw from the intersubjective everyday world. I focus on the activities of consciousness that are directed to the "world," and the stream of consciousness flows on in passivity (the problem of dream activities, which we raised in the analysis of provinces of finite meaning-structure, remains undecided here). Upon awaking, my activities of consciousness begin where they left off before I went to sleep. We will not concern ourselves here with the modifications by which processes are carried out passively in inner duration. Before sleeping I made up my mind to jump out of bed early tomorrow immediately upon awaking. Now I confront this resolution (no matter what I may have dreamt in the interim). In this sense, I "find" myself in the morning as I "left" myself last evening. It at first appears that I am again connected with the time of my waking life which was "broken off" that evening. But between my withdrawal from the everyday life-world and my recent return to it, "time has not stood still." It has become morning. I experience the world as having become older (yesterday was Sunday, today is Monday). I live through world time as transcending "my" time. This lived experience of transcendence, although an everyday one, concerns the world in general in its temporal structure.

The transcendence of world time can be experienced in the withdrawal into sleep and the return to being awake, without reference to the existence of fellow-men. This is not so in the otherwise similar experience of the transcendence of world time, which originates essentially from reflection within the intersubjective world. Just because I can follow well-circumscribed, lived experiences back into my stream of consciousness, and remember a first "this," a first "that," I do not thereby reflectively grasp an "absolute beginning." I have been told that I was born. I "know" this. I can also locate my birth on the basis of a syllogism which is dependent on my knowledge (all men are born, I am a man; therefore, I was born). I cannot locate my birth in my inner duration—quite apart from the antinomies which would then result. I can deduce it only as an original "return" to a world transcending and independent of it. I can do this with myself, as with my fellow-men, nations, fixed stars, etc., and indeed, according to knowledge having more or less certainty. In the natural attitude, within which I do not reflect on the conditions of my knowledge, it is obvious to me that the world existed before my birth, just as I know that it existed before the birth of my children and as I do not doubt that it had existed prior to the birth of my great-grandfather.

The expectation of my death as a definitive departure (from the life-world) also arises out of my existence in the intersubjective world. Others become older, die, and the world continues on (and I in it). It is indeed one of my basic experiences that I become older. I become older; thus I know that I will die and I know that the world will continue. I know that there are limits to my duration. The relevance system of the natural attitude is derived from this: the manifold, mutually interwoven systems of hope and fear, wants and satisfactions, chances and risks that induce men to master their life-world, to overcome obstacles, to project plans, and to carry them out.

ii. The fixed course of world time and "first things first"

Knowledge of finitude stands out against the experience of the world's continuance. This knowledge is the fundamental moment of all projects within the framework of a life-plan, and is itself determined by the time of the life-world. Still other moments connected with the structure of lifeworldly time enter into the realization of concrete projects, into the everyday conduct of life, as determinate factors. The structure of lifeworldly time is built up where the subjective time of the stream of consciousness (of inner duration) intersects with the rhythm of the body as "biological time" in general, and with the seasons as world time in general, or as calendar or "social time." We live in all these dimensions simultaneously. But since there exists no absolute congruence (so to speak, simultaneity) between events in these dimensions, we have as an inevitable consequence of this incongruence the phenomenon of waiting. This significant phenomenon, largely overlooked in philosophy, psychology and social sciences, was investigated by Bergson.[28] If I want to prepare sugar water, then I must wait until the cube dissolves. My stream of consciousness flows on independently of the succession of natural events upon whose results I must wait. Carrel and Lecomte de

28. [Henri Bergson, *Creative Evolution*, trans. Arthur Mitchell (New York: Modern Library, 1944), pp. 12–13.]

Noüy have analyzed an aspect of biological time: the healing process pertaining to wounds.[29] Again, one must wait. The pregnant woman must wait until the time of the delivery. The farmer must wait until the right time comes for sowing, or for the harvest. In waiting we encounter a time structure that is imposed on us.

Not only is the incongruence of the various temporal dimensions (which has waiting as its subjective correlate) imposed on us, but so also is an Objective structure of simultaneity and succession that lies beyond our influence. The possibility of actualizing a number of plans, of undertaking acts, having experiences, is already very limited by time alone. I can do one thing, perhaps another, but not a third in addition all at the same time. The succession of events in the outer world is imposed on me in my corporeal rhythm and in the social calendar. I must postpone one thing and give another temporal priority. Not only must I plan out my acts, decide between alternatives according to a hierarchy of values, but also I must arrange the temporal course of my affairs according to their degrees of urgency. Since these value hierarchies receive a status subordinated to the course of the day (as indeed they are conditioned by finitude generally), the degrees of urgency are then aspects of the realizability of value decisions within the imposed everyday structure of temporality. *First* I must take care of this (in other respects unimportant, subordinate) matter, so that I can then turn to a more significant concern (I have to shave, and so I must first wait until the water is hot before I go to a conference whose result may be a turning point in my life). All of the "unimportant" interludes, partial acts, etc., which for example I can pass over in my daydreams, are necessary elements of my life in everyday situations in which nature and society, including their temporal structure, give me "resistance." I cannot jump over my shadow even though I can jump over the place where my shadow *lay*. I cannot speak clearly with my mouth full. Before I get to the place where I had mentally hurried ahead, I must get into the car, start the engine, and make a hundred or more movements. I must shave and tie my tie. The imposed, fixed course of temporal structure affords a plan for the day alongside the life-plan determined by my

29. [See Alexis Carrel, *Man the Unknown* (New York: Harper, 1939; repr., New York: MacFadden-Bartell, 1961), and Lecomte du Noüy, *Human Destiny* (New York: McKay, 1947).]

finitude. This plan for the day is only mediately determined by the hierarchy of plans conditioned by finitude. But it depends immediately upon the principle of "first things first," the fixed courses of events in everyday existence.

iii. World time and situation

We could say that world time is experienced as the transcendence of my finitude and that this experience becomes the fundamental motive of the life-plan. We could say further that the fixed course of world time expresses itself in the structural laws of succession and simultaneity in the everyday reality of the life-world, and becomes the fundamental motive of the plan of the day. Obviously, finitude and the fixed course of time, the life-plan and the daily plan, are connected. In the natural attitude one experiences finitude and the fixed course of time as imposed upon one and inevitable. One experiences it as the limit within which one's action is possible, as the fundamental temporal structure of one's reality, of the reality of one's ancestors, of one's fellow-men, of one's successors.

World time, though, is experienced as irreversible. I become older and cannot become younger. The French Revolution can never occur again. "The same," when it occurs for the second time, is no longer a first but a second occurrence of "the same." Indeed, the natural attitude contains a distinction between the historicality of nature and that of the world of men. With reference to this, the relative-natural world views differ in other respects from each other. Indeed, they can be stamped with the certainty of the eternal return even of human events. Nevertheless, the social world is fundamentally experienced as historical in every linguistically and culturally given degree of difference between the world of men and the world of nature. This is so solely on the basis of the subjective experience of the succession of generations (grandfather, father, children). It need hardly be mentioned that this need not in any way be connected with a reflective consciousness of history, as is more or less determinant in occidental (relative-natural) thought. Born into a family, I know that my grandfather lived in "another time"; I know that the "Golden Age," the time of the founders of the race, of the Fall of man, the "Middle Ages," etc., lie far in the past. I also live through this as imposed on me: that I was born into this time and into no other. I live through this also as a fundamental temporal moment of my historical situation. I know also that my fellow-men are coaffected by it: not only are they mortal as I am and unable to be in two locations simultaneously, but also they are born into a particular historical situation. All of these are unmodifiable temporal elements of the factual existence of the life-world, but with an important difference. Finitude and the fixed course of temporality are as much unmodifiable as invariable; but, whereas the historical situation of the individual particular existence as such is unalterable, there is a different one for me, another for my great-grandfather, and another for my children.

We have, then, described three aspects of the temporality of the life-world: permanence/finitude, the fixed course of temporality/"first things first," and historicality/situation. We have emphasized that finitude and the fixed course of temporality and situation are unalterable elements imposed on factual existence in the life-world. Within the fundamental structure imposed on me, within the unalterable "limits" of my experience and action, and finally, motivated by my finitude, I exert myself, I overcome opposing forces, I act. For me the unalterable "limits" (about which I hardly ever reflect in the natural attitude, since in everyday happenings one generally lacks a motive for it) are the taken-for-granted basis of my dealings. In describing the zone of operation we have already discussed the structure of my gearing into the surrounding world, and of its alteration by my action, though from the viewpoint of the zone into which I can actually and actively gear. Now we can broaden the concept and speak of a *province of the practicable* in general, which has been built up in the stock of my knowledge from my experiences in previously actual zones of operation. This province of the practicable meets its absolute limitation in the unmodifiable ontological structure of the life-world, especially in its temporal structure. This province is also relatively limited by the technologically practical (also somewhat indirectly by the theoretical, scientific) state of knowledge of the society into which I was born, and by my own previous experiences. The province of the practicable is thus also limited immediately through my historical and biographical situation.

b. *The temporal structure of the sphere of reach*

In the analysis of the sphere of reach we have already said something about its temporal structure, and we can satisfy ourselves here with a summary statement.

The world in actual reach has essentially the temporal character of the present. The actual experiences refer first to the prevailing, at-hand stock of knowledge which has for its part been built up through sedimentations of the past. Secondly, actual experiences refer to their horizons, which can for their part be actualized in future steps of explication.

The world in potential reach has a much more complicated temporal structure. The world in restorable reach is based upon the past, upon that which was previously in my reach and upon that which (as I assume on the grounds of the idealizations of the "and so forth" and "I can always do it again") can once again be brought into my actual reach. The shift in the point of intersection in my coordinate system has transformed my previous here into a there. With the idealizations just mentioned, I assume that the actual there (the former here) can again be retransformed into an actual here. The world in my past reach has thus the character of a world that can be actualized. Thus, for example, my previous zone of operation also functions further in my present as a potential zone of operation in the mode of a there. And it has as such a specific prospect of restorability, which likewise has a temporal dimension.

Just as the first zone of potentiality is dominated by the past, so the second depends on anticipations of the future. In my potential reach there is also the world which never was in my actual reach, but which is posited under the idealization of the "and so forth" as attainable sooner or later. The most important instance of this second zone is my fellow-man's zone of operation. Though we are situated in a common (spatial-temporal-social) situation, his zone of operation coincides only partially, or perhaps not even at all, with mine. For me his zone of operation is one in the mode of a there. But it would also be an attainable zone (in the mode of a here) if I were in his position, a circumstance I can in turn effect by an appropriate change of location. G. H. Mead comes to a similar conclusion: "Present reality is a possibility. It is what would be if I were there rather than here." [30]

Consequently, we can with a certain simplification say that the structure of the sphere of reach has the following subjective temporal correlates: the actual reach—the present phase of the

30. "The Objective Reality of Perspectives," in *Philosophy of the Present*, p. 173.

stream of consciousness with its actually present theme and the explicable horizons founded upon the stock of experience; the restorable reach—the memory; the attainable reach—expectation.

c. Subjective time

i. The temporal actualization of the stream of consciousness

We have up till now spoken of the subjective correlates of world time. Now we must deal with that which is properly subjective time—inner duration and its articulation. Are there, then, any temporally structured "unities" of the stream of consciousness? And if so, how are they articulated? The problem which is to be handled here is most intimately connected with the problem of the temporal structure (given in inner duration) of the meaning of experiences. This connection has been independently seen and examined by three philosophers who have decisively influenced the style and mode of questioning in modern philosophy (Bergson, William James, and Husserl). We can occupy ourselves with this here only insofar as it is of direct importance for the description of the temporal structure of the natural attitude; beyond that, we refer to the work of these three philosophers.[31]

The unity of the stream of consciousness rests, as Husserl has brought out, upon time's character as the form of lived experiences. In the fixed succession, a Now is transformed into a just-past-Now and becomes a past-Now. The actual impressional phase of an experience is nothing but a limiting phase of continuous retentions and protensions. Every actual lived experience necessarily carries a horizon of the past and a horizon of the future. The last is filled with typifying anticipated lived experiences. The anticipations are either confirmed or disappointed in the course of being transformed into the impressional phase. As such they carry new anticipations and forthwith become retentions, since new impressional phases succeed them.[32]

31. See also Alfred Schutz, "William James's Concept of the Stream of Thought Phenomenologically Interpreted," in Collected Papers, Vol. III: Studies in Phenomenological Philosophy, ed. Ilse Schutz, with an introduction by Aron Gurwitsch (The Hague: Nijhoff, 1966), pp. 1–14.

32. One should compare this with W. James's concept of the "specious present," Principles of Psychology, I, 608 ff.

It is, as Husserl has shown, a universal principle of consciousness that in my conscious acts I "live" attentive to their intentional Objects, not to the acts themselves. Thus, in order to grasp these acts I must attend to them reflectively; that is, of necessity *post hoc*. I must, as Dewey put it, "stop and think." [33] Reflecting, I am no longer drawn along by the stream of consciousness; I do not "live" in the actually present phases as such. Rather I place myself "outside of them" and look "back." This manner of expression could perhaps be misunderstood. There is no extratemporal "shore" upon which I could save myself from the stream. While I reflectively attend to the past phases or even the phases just become present, I remain "in" the stream of consciousness. The inner duration is continuous, and the reflective acts themselves have a temporal structure within the stream of consciousness. Every attempt to translate the phenomena of inner time into spatial expressions is, as Bergson has clearly shown, misleading. [34] With this reservation, though, Dewey's phrase may yet help to elucidate the temporal structure of the meaning-constitution of experiences. The meaning of an experience does not inhere within the experiences "as such," but rather is conferred in a reflective advertence.

There are two different modes in which the sense of past experiences can be "grasped." All experiences become originarily constituted step by step in inner duration (polythetically, as Husserl termed this process). [35] In reflective advertence I may, then, set about executing in actually present consciousness this polythetic process of building up. Since all experiences are characterized by a polythetic constitution, I can, therefore, in principle (in order to grasp the sense of any experience) reflectively realize the polythetic building up of this experience in reflections after the fact. I *can* do that, at least under ideal conditions. On the other hand, I *must* do it, if I want to attempt to grasp the meaning of those experiences whose meaning is *essentially* contained in the polythetic structure of its elements in inner duration, that

33. [Schutz, *Collected Papers*, I, 214–15.]

34. [*Essai sur les données immédiates de la conscience*, pp. 136 ff., 142 ff., 174–80.]

35. Edmund Husserl, *Vorlesungen zur Phänomenologie des inneren Zeitbewusstseins* (Halle: Niemeyer, 1928), § 11. [English translation by James S. Churchill, *The Phenomenology of Internal Time-Consciousness* (Bloomington: Indiana University Press, 1964).]

is, experiences of so-called temporal Objects. When it concerns the meaning of a musical theme, of a poem, etc., I must carry out polythetically, after the fact, what has been built up polythetically. I can indeed state the "content" of a poem in a few (or in many) words. But I cannot grasp its true meaning without actually now running through the polythetic phases. In order to grasp the sense of a composition, I must reproduce it, at least internally, from the beginning to the last measure.

With the experiences, though, that do not refer to temporal Objects, I can indeed proceed in the same fashion, but I need not. I can grasp the meaning of polythetically structured experiences in one single grasp (as Husserl says, monothetically). Experiences concerned with formal knowledge such as thinking, especially in its strict sense, provide important examples.[36] The distinction between polythetically and monothetically grasping the meaning of experiences will, moreover, be of great importance for the description of the constitution of the stock of knowledge, and its transmission by society, as well as for the analysis of the understanding of the acts of fellow-men.[37]

However, the distinction is already important at this juncture, since it brings us to an essential point concerning the temporal articulation of consciousness. There are limits to the possibility of continually resolving the meaning of an experience which can be grasped monothetically, into single polythetic steps. It is a peculiarity of our consciousness that its lived experiences are not divisible without limit. As Bergson has shown, inner duration cannot be partitioned into quantitatively homogeneous unities. Indeed, certain spatiotemporal phenomena resist a spatialized analysis. If we posit that an essentially unitary movement is the same as a measured space, then the arrow in fact will never reach its target, Achilles will never pass the tortoise. The "unities" of inner duration are not homogeneous units of measure, as they are construed when applied to extension and, analogously, to the "extension" of world time. They are rather unities of temporal articulation that are describable with difficulty in a language imprisoned in spatial modes of expression. The problem was also seen by William James, who employed the fortunate comparison with the flight of birds and spoke of "plans of flight and resting places" [38] for consciousness.

36. [*Ibid.*]
37. See Chap. 3, esp. § 2; and Chap. 4, esp. §§ 2, 3.
38. James, *Principles of Psychology*, Vol. I, Chap. IX.

The question of temporal articulation thus cannot concern the homogeneous structural unities of a temporal "extension." Rather, it is concerned with exhibiting the temporal frames of reference which are the basis of the constitution in consciousness of well-circumscribed experience and of our grasping of its meaning. The "unities" of inner duration are, concisely formulated, not homogeneous "quantitative" units of meaning. As already mentioned, there are no isolated self-contained experiences. Every present experience relates to a context of experience, which consists of past, already "separated" experiences and of more or less open expectations of future experiences. The experience which is now actually being built up in the stream of consciousness was therefore in a certain sense already anticipated in past phases of this same stream of consciousness. Naturally, it is not anticipated as this specific experience transpiring in all its uniqueness, but is nevertheless anticipated as an experience of this or that sort. Whether besides this the past anticipations are actually confirmed or disappointed is of no consequence. Also, the meaning of an "unexpected" experience (that is, of an experience which disappoints past anticipation) is built up in contrast to the experience that was anticipated but which did not occur. The original meaning-context of my experience, the context in which an experience becomes constituted as such and not otherwise, presupposes the temporal relation between actual experience, past experience, and anticipated experience. The idealizations of the "and so forth and so on" and of the "I can do it again," which have already been discussed, belong to the structure of this temporal meaning-context.

Experiences cannot be pressed into unities that do not take this context into account. When I observe a bird in flight I do not see separately now phase a_1 and then phase a_2, etc. Every actual phase contains retentions of the just-past phases; and the retentions of these retentions in turn contain retentions of the phases that have become just-past in relation to them. Further, every actually present phase contains anticipations of typical continuing phases. Bergson termed this *the kinematographic function of consciousness*.[39] An artificial separation of the flow of phases into "unities" isolated from one another, photographs of moments, so to speak, dismembers the meaning-context. This Bergsonian example is relatively simple. One can, though, il-

39. [Bergson, *Creative Evolution*, pp. 340–43.]

lustrate this temporal relation in even more complex meaning-structures. The description of the meaning of a musical theme or of a simple conversation could serve as an example. Characteristic of both is the flowing succession of impressional phases, in which the beginning (of the theme, of the sentence) is held retentively and becomes united with anticipations of completion.

What we have discussed concerns a universal characterization of the life of consciousness, which does not contain uniform homogeneous spatiotemporal elements (as many schools of psychology would have it). Rather, it is articulated into "unities" of inner duration which are relational unities. The "quanta" of inner duration are dependent upon retention, impression, and anticipation. These arrange themselves one after the other in characteristic rhythms, which are determined by the tension of consciousness that happens to be prevailing at that time. They form the basis by which the reflective advertences to past experiences become possible. That reflective advertences are, on the one hand, motivated and that the motivation, on the other hand, determines the span of retrospection, as well as the "unities" of meaning that thus arise, are facts which demand further discussion. For the time being, it is enough to establish that various grades of the tension of consciousness (and, correlatively, various provinces of reality with finite meaning-structure) have their characteristic rhythm, their characteristic "tempo," so that these determine the "orders of magnitude" for subjective lived experiences of time.

ii. Concerning biographical articulation

The temporal articulation of the stream of consciousness is determined by the tension of consciousness, which alters with transitions from one province of reality with finite meaning-structure to another, as well as, to a lesser extent, with transitions from one situation to another within the everyday life-world. But that tells us something only about the articulations of the course of the day. Certainly, it thus concerns the basic temporal structures of inner duration, in which the meaning of such experiences becomes constituted. Now we must nevertheless ask whether there is not a superimposed significational level of temporal articulation. How does the course of the day, together with its temporal articulations, get into the course of life? How does this meaning, with its broader scope, become constituted, and how does it become temporally stratified upon the meaning-structures of everyday life? A satisfactory answer to these questions is not available within this section because it cannot be derived from the analysis of the subjective flow of duration as such. Rather, the answer involves problems which we will attend to only in the following chapters: the structure of the complete intersubjective world, and the social-biographical situation of the individual with its involved complex of relevance structures, hierarchies of plans, and scopes of acts. The categories of biographical articulation are not really categories of inner duration as such, but rather are categories which are formed intersubjectively and established within the relative-natural world view. They are basically imposed upon the individual and become interiorized by him. The formal structures of childhood, youth, maturity, old age, etc., point to global social fluctuations in scope as well as great variations in content. These different historical formations of biographically meaning-bestowing categories are indeed experienced in the natural attitude as taken-for-granted articulations of the course of life. Despite this basic restriction, which we leave to later expositions,[40] there is still something we can say about biographical articulation.

The temporal articulation of the course of the day, and the temporal articulation of the course of life, exist together in a reciprocal relation. *On the one hand,* the biographical articulation is *superimposed* over the rhythm of the day. If I reflectively attend to past periods of life, summarily to survey them and examine their meaning, then I obtain monothetically within my grasp, in such *post hoc* interpretations of the greatest span, huge stretches of polythetically built up courses of days (how has it "come about" that I am a drunkard?). Similarly, when I project plans of greater scope, I, typifying, anticipate great stretches of days elapsing "as a means to the end." (I intend to write a comparative investigation of proverbs.) How I am motivated to such interpretations and projects, is a question which we cannot answer here.[41]

But, *on the other hand,* interpretations and projects (whose scope of meaning is the course of life) are *inserted* into the inner duration's course of the day. They are not only determined by the current situation but also are subjected in a very general fashion

40. See above all Chap. 2, B, 6; also Chap. 3, A, 1, d, and Chap. 4, A, 2.
41. See the analysis of relevance structures, Chap. 3, B, 2, d.

to the articulations of inner duration (which is fundamentally what obtains, for example, in the observation of a bird's flight). Thus, in this respect they are not a separate problem as yet untreated.

A further aspect of biographical articulation concerns the unique flow and sedimentation of my experiences in inner duration. As we have brought out, my situation in the life-world is determined by the general structure of world time and my finitude in it, by the fixed course of world time and the principle of "first things first," as well as by the historicality of my situation. But my present situation is also "historical" in still another sense. My situation consists of the history of *my* experiences. Autobiographically determined elements are also among the structurally determined elements of my situation. Among these there are in turn many elements which can be deduced from the social embedding of my experiences. There are in addition essentially private, incommunicable lived experiences, or in any case essentially private aspects of my experiences. The most important and absolutely unique autobiographical aspect (insofar as it can be "standardized" by the social superstructure of biographical categories) is the flow of experiences in my inner duration. Since every situation and every experience has a horizon of the past, every current situation and experience is necessarily codetermined by the uniqueness of the course of experience, of its autobiography. The sequence in which experiences successively order themselves and, correlatively, the "place" in the course of life where certain experiences occur, is most significant. When we as adults turn to past segments of our life, we can discover very "decisive" experiences that subsequently determined our life. These experiences repeatedly play such a role, less from an inherent quality than from the special point in time in which they occur. We read a book at a particular phase of our intellectual development, became acquainted with a person at a "decisive" point in time, became ill at a certain time, became satisfied or disappointed "too early" or "too late" by one or another experience, etc. These are experiences and are subject to the same structural laws as all my other experiences, just as the experiences of my fellow-men are. They are typical experiences of this or that sort, but they have a unique biographical articulation and consequently a specific meaning because they fit into a particular place in the flow of our duration.

5. THE SOCIAL ARRANGEMENT OF THE LIFE-WORLD
OF EVERYDAY EXISTENCE

a. The pregivenness of the Other and the intersubjectivity of the world taken for granted

We have already established that the life-world is at the outset intersubjective. We brought out [42] that in the natural attitude of everyday existence, one accepts the existence of other men as taken for granted. The human bodies that I can find in my surrounding world are for me obviously endowed with consciousness; that is, in principle they are similar to mine. Further, it is obvious to me that the things of the external world are fundamentally the same for Others and for me. And, in addition, it is obvious that I can enter into relations with my fellow-men, that I can communicate with them, and, finally, that a structured social and cultural world is historically already given to me and my fellow-men. We want now to examine these aspects of the natural attitude in greater detail, beginning with the prior givenness of fellow-men.

The *fundamental axioms* of the social, natural attitude are, first, the existence of intelligent (endowed with consciousness) fellow-men and, second, the experienceability (in principle similar to mine) by my fellow-men of the objects in the life-world. The second must include modifying moments because of the experience of the spatial arrangement of the life-world,[43] the experience of one's individual zone of operation,[44] and the experience of one's biographical articulation.[45] It is from the experience of these structures that I know that "the same" Object must necessarily show different aspects to each of us. First, because the world in my reach cannot be identical with the world in your reach, his reach, etc.; because my here is your there; and because my zone of operation is not the same as yours. And, second, because my biographical situation with its relevance systems, hierarchies of plans, etc., is not yours and, consequently, the explications of the horizon of objects in my case and yours could take entirely different directions: the modifications of the

42. See Chap. 1, A.
43. See Chap. 2, B, 2.
44. See Chap. 2, B, 3.
45. See Chap. 2, B, 4, c, ii.

second fundamental axiom rest upon the first. More precisely, they follow from the explication of my experience of other men in my surrounding world. But in the fully social, natural attitude these modifications are then (for all practical purposes of everyday existence) set aside through the following pragmatically motivated basic constructions, or idealizations:

First, the idealization of the *interchangeability of standpoints*. If I were there, where he is now, then I would experience things in the same perspective, distance, and reach as he does. And, if he were here where I am now, he would experience things from the same perspective as I.

Second, the idealization of the *congruence of relevance systems*. He and I learn to accept as given that the variances in apprehension and explication which result from differences between my and his biographical situations are irrelevant for my and his, our, present practical goals. Thus, I and he, we, can act and understand each other as if we had experienced in an identical way, and explicated the Objects and their properties lying actually or potentially in our reach. And (this is added to and combined with the idealizations of the "and so forth" and of the "I can always do it again"), we learn to accept as given that we can in principle proceed in this manner, that is, we learn that not only is the world that we have experienced in common socialized, but also the world which I have still to experience is in principle socializable.

The idealizations of the interchangeability of standpoints and the congruence of relevance systems together form the *general thesis of the reciprocity of perspectives*. This thesis is for its part the foundation for the social formation and linguistic fixation of Objects of thought (Whitehead's "objects of thought") [46] which replace, or better, which substitute for the Objects of thought present in my presocial world. To prevent one from mistaking these Objects of thought as results of a *contrat social*, it must be emphasized that they are already encountered in language by every individual born into a historical situation. The fact that individuals can acquire the life-world's linguistic (that is, social) formation as the basis of their world view, rests on the general thesis of reciprocal perspectives. This general thesis, though, as we mentioned, assumes the existence of fellow-men

46. [See Alfred N. Whitehead, *Process and Reality* (New York: Free Press, 1969), p. 67.]

as unquestionably given. This characterizes the natural attitude from beginning to end. In the fully social, natural attitude it is taken for granted that the life-world which is accepted as given by me is also accepted as given by you, indeed by us, fundamentally by everyone.

At this point, the possibility of a further differentiation arises. The *we*, which in principle signifies everyone, can be restricted in scope. In reflective explication of a social encounter, of a conversation, I may experience that you have never, for the practical considerations of the present situation, experienced the world (in particular a specific sector of the world) as I have and as others, with whom I have shared similar situations, have. In order to maintain the general thesis of the reciprocity of perspectives (especially the idealization of the congruence of relevance systems), I come to the conclusion that you do not take my relevance systems into consideration at all. You are therefore not like "everyone," but rather something else. Thus, there are basically two possibilities: either I recognize that we are indeed not like everyone (i.e., that everyone is not like everyone else), but that rather there are various kinds of men—for example, us and you; or, it is also possible, as is to be gathered from ethnological material, that I might maintain the identity of us and everyone. In that case, you cannot be a ("normal") man. But with these observations, we anticipate questions that can only be handled later on. Here we will just mention that it is the relative-natural world view that makes one or the other of these solutions the "natural" one.

b. *The immediate experience of the Other*

i. *The thou-orientation and the we-relation*

All experience of social reality is founded on the fundamental axiom positing the existence of other beings "like me." The forms into which my experience of social reality is placed are in contrast very diverse. I experience other men in various perspectives, and my relation to them is arranged according to various levels of proximity, depth, and anonymity in lived experience. The breadth of variations in my experience of the social world extends from the encounter with another man to vague attitudes, institutions, cultural structures, and "humanity in general." We must now describe the structures in which the social world becomes built up in experience. We can first of all effect a rough distinction between the immediate experience of an Other and the mediate experience of the social world. Since we intend in due course to show that mediate experience is in essence derivable from immediate experience, we will begin with an analysis of the latter.

I immediately perceive another man only when he shares a sector of the life-world's space and of world time in common with me. Only under those conditions does the Other appear to me in his live corporeality: his body is for me a perceivable and explicable field of expression which makes his conscious life accessible to me. It is possible only then for my stream of consciousness and his to flow in true simultaneity: he and I grow older together. The encounter (the face-to-face situation) is the only social situation characterized by temporal and spatial immediacy. This essentially determines not only the style but also the structure of social relations and acts occurring in this situation.

How does such a situation become constituted? It is presupposed that I turn my attention to the Other. This advertence, which we designate with the expression *thou-orientation,* is a universal form in which an Other is experienced "in person." We will subsequently term such an Other a fellow-man. The thou-orientation arises simply through the fact that I experience something in the world within my reach as "like me." It must, however, be stressed that we are not here concerned with a judgment based on analogy. The thou-orientation is originarily prepredicative. I do not just reflect polythetically: "this here is a man, as I"; rather, I actually grasp the man in his existence before me, in temporal and spatial immediacy. But the concept of the thou-orientation does as a consequence require that I also *know* what sort of a man (that is, in his "being-thus-and-so") is standing in front of me. It is clear that we are concerned here with a formal concept. Empirically, there is no "pure" thou-orientation. When I meet a fellow-man it is always also a particular man, or in any case a particular type of man with his particularities. The thou-orientation is thus continuously articulated in various stages of the concrete apprehension and typification of the thou.

The thou-orientation can either be unilateral or reciprocal. It is possible that I turn to you [47] while you do not pay attention

47. [Schutz uses the second person familiar in this passage, in conformity with his main concept: *Du-Einstellung* (thou-orientation). We translate with the less distinctive "you" to conform with standard English usage, as this concept does not invoke, for Schutz, the special sense of intimacy commonly attached to the second per-

to my existence. It can, though, also be the case that I turn to you as you do to me. In the case of a reciprocal thou-orientation, a social relation becomes constituted. We will designate this with the expression, *we-relation*. Analogous to what was said about the thou-orientation, we can again speak formally about a "pure" we-relation—which is constituted in a "pure," reciprocal thou-orientation. One must not forget, however, that the we-relation is also actualized only in various stages of concrete apprehension and typification of the Other.

I can, then, only share in the conscious life of another man when we encounter each other in a *concrete* we-relation. When you talk to me, for example, I can explicate the Objective significance of your words (make them explicit in a highly anonymous system of signs). Besides, I participate in the step-by-step constitution of your speaking in the genuine simultaneity of the we-relation. As a consequence, I can (more or less adequately or inadequately) grasp the subjective meaning-configuration that your speaking and your words have for you. The processes of explication through which I grasp my consociate's subjective meaning-configuration do not, precisely considered, belong to the we-relation. My fellow-man's words are above all signs in an Objective context of significance. Further, they are also indications ("symptoms") of the subjective meaning that all his experiences, including his actually present speaking, have for him. It is I, though, who explicate the signs in Objective and eventually subjective meaning-contexts. The process of explication consequently does not belong to the we-relation, though it presupposes it.

The flow of concrete experiences in which the we-relation is actualized exhibits thoroughgoing similarities "in content" with my inner flow of lived experiences. A fundamental difference, though, remains: my flow of lived experiences is a flow within the inner time of my own stream of consciousness. There is, indeed, genuine simultaneity of the flow of lived experiences in the we-relation, although I meet a fellow-man whose here is a there for me. Although we speak of the "immediate" experience of a fellow-man, this experience is internally, also in the precise meaning of the word, "mediated." I grasp my fellow-man's flow of lived experiences only "mediately," in that I explicate his

son familiar by, for instance, existential philosophers. Thou-orientation is, as Schutz says, a formal concept for him.]

movements, his expression, his communications as indications of the subjectively meaningful experiences of an alter ego. But among all my experiences of the other I, what is mediated least is the encounter of the fellow-man in the simultaneity of the we-relation. Thus we will continue to speak, even though it is not completely accurate, of an immediate experience of the fellow-man.

This immediacy is preserved only as long as I live in the we-relation, that is as long as I participate in the joint flow of *our* experiences. When I turn *reflectively* to our experiences, then I have, so to speak, placed myself outside of the we-relation. Before I can consider a we-relation, its living phases of lived experience must be broken off or have faded away. I live in a we-relation and subjectively experience it only when I am absorbed in our common experiences. I can reflect upon them, but only ex post facto. Then, past common experiences can be grasped in great clarity, exactly, as well as in unclarity and confusion. The more I give myself over to reflection, the less I live in the common experience and the more distant and mediate is my consociate. The Other whom I experienced immediately in the we-relation becomes in reflection the Object of my thought. We will pursue this point later.[48] It is granted that I can also decide during a social encounter to "step out of" the we-relation. In this situation I can also decide to transform my fellow-man into a typical consociate.

ii. The social encounter

The "pure" we-relation, which is constituted in a reciprocal thou-orientation, consists of the bare consciousness of the existence of an Other. It does not necessarily include the apprehension of his specific characteristics. But just such an apprehension belongs to all concrete social relations. The extent of my knowledge of the Other can naturally be quite varied. That means, therefore, that the concrete social relations which have the character of an encounter are indeed founded on a "pure" we-relation. But it is not sufficient that I am sympathetic toward my fellow-man and that I see that he is sympathetic toward me. In addition, I must grasp more or less exactly *how* he is sympathetic to me. In the community of space and time, in the vivid presence of the fellow-man, I succeed at this through immediate observation. In contrast to the reflective grasping of the essential fea-

48. See Chap. 2, B, 5, c, i and ii.

tures of the "pure" we-relation, I actually grasp the Other in a certain determinacy. I also experience *us* only in the determinacy of our reciprocal relation. Thus, for example, I experience us in a friendly relation between me the younger person, and him the older; or the well-established superficial relation between me the customer, and him the salesman. These two examples show that the we-relation can become actualized in various ways. My social partner appears to me in spatially, temporally, and sociobiographically differentiated perspectives of apprehension that exercise a certain control over my experience of Others. Further, I do not subjectively experience partners in we-relations in the same nearness and depth of lived experience. Finally, I may in a we-relation attentively follow the experiences of my partner. That is, I may "livingly enter into" the processes of his consciousness and into his subjective motivations (as, for example, is the case when a third party observes the meaningless conversation between two lovers). Or I may only be indirectly interested and instead concentrate on his acts and their Objective consequences (as when the two of us saw through a tree trunk, it can be all the same to me "what he's thinking while he does it" as long as he keeps the rhythm of our sawing). Or I may concentrate on the Objective meaning of his communication (as, e.g., in a scientific discussion). The we-relations always become actualized in the dimensions cited. The gradations of immediacy are developed in various connections between these dimensions, within the (formal) we-relation, constituted via a reciprocal thou-orientation in spatial and temporal community. We will illustrate this conclusion by an example.

The act of love, as well as a superficial conversation between two strangers, is an example of the we-relation. In both cases, fellow-men meet each other in a *face-to-face situation,* as it is termed in sociological terminology. However, what a difference in the "immediacy" of the relation! But completely apart from this, that at one time a complete synchronization of inner time is achieved by means of the prevailing respective meaning-modalities and at another time it is not, there are further large differences in the perspectives of interpretation, in the proximity and depth of the lived experience. But it is not only my experiences of Others that vary in these dimensions, but rather (as I experience through "mirroring" in an Other) his also. We may say that variations in the degree of immediacy characterize the we-relation as such. This involves us in another problem which is of great importance for the subjective experience of the social world, and with which we will have to deal more closely in the analysis of the transition from immediate to mediate experience of social reality.

In an encounter, the conscious life of the Other is accessible to me through a maximal abundance of symptoms. Since he stands bodily before me, I can apprehend the processes in his consciousness not only by means of what he deliberately shares with me, but also through observation and interpretation of his movements, his facial expression, his gestures, the rhythm and intonation of his speech, etc. Every phase of my inner duration is coordinated with a phase of the conscious life of the Other. Since I perceive without interruption the continual manifestations of the subjective occurrences in my fellow-man, I remain tuned in to them without interruption. An especially important consequence of this circumstance is the fact that my fellow-man is in a certain sense presented to me as more "alive" and more "immediate" than I am to myself. Naturally I "know" myself much better than him: my biography is recallable by me in an infinitely more detailed fashion than it is by someone else. But this is knowledge about me, memory of my past, and demands a reflective attitude. Because, however, I unreflectively live and merge in the actual experience, my fellow-man is before me in his relation to me with a greater abundance of symptoms than I am to myself—as long as we remain just in the temporal and spatial communality of the we-relation.

Until now we stressed the immediacy of my experience of my fellow-man. But to every concrete situation in which I meet an Other, I bring with me my stock of knowledge, i.e., the sedimentation of past experiences. This stock of knowledge naturally includes as well a network of typifications of men in general, their typically human motivations, patterns of action, hierarchies of plans, etc. It includes my knowledge about schemata of expression and interpretation, and my knowledge of Objective sign systems, especially of a language. Subordinated to this general knowledge, there is further the detailed cognizance of motivations, acts, schemata of expression, etc., of certain types of men, e.g., of men and women, young and old, healthy and sick, farmers and city dwellers, fathers and mothers, friends and enemies, Americans and Chinese, etc. Finally, my stock of knowledge may also include prior experiences of this completely determined fellow-man. In the course of the we-relation I use my knowledge, test it, modify it, and acquire new experiences. My whole stock of knowledge is in any case subject to change, sometimes a negligibly small one, but sometimes a decisive one. My experience of my fellow-man in the we-relation is thus in a complex meaning- and interpretational-context: it is the experience of a man, it is the experience of a typical actor on the stage of the social world, it is the experience of this completely determined, unique fellow-man in this completely determined situation.

We have until now described a stratum of my experience of the fellow-man. A further essential component of this experience is that I also grasp *his* attitude to me. He also experiences my action not simply in an Objective interpretative context, but also as an expression of my conscious life. Further, I apprehend the fact that he experiences me as someone who experiences his conduct as an expression of his subjectivity. In the we-relation our experiences are not only coordinated with one another, but are also reciprocally determined and related to one another. I experience myself through my consociate, and he experiences himself through me. The mirroring of self in the experience of the stranger (more exactly, in my grasp of the Other's experience of me) is a constitutive element of the we-relation. As Charles H. Cooley has already shown in a penetrating fashion, the reciprocal mirroring is of fundamental import for the process of socialization.[49] It must still be noted that the complex refractions of the processes of mirroring do not, like individual rays, come into the grip of consciousness. Indeed, neither the we-relation nor the fellow-man are reflectively grasped in it, but are rather immediately experienced. My experience of my own course of lived experience and of the coordinated course of the lived experience of my fellow-man is unitary: experiences in the we-relation are common experiences.

In anticipation of the analysis of the structure of action, it is worth noting that this is important not only for the structure of social relations but also for the structure of social action in an encounter.[50] I can observe the success or failure of the concrete plans of my fellow-man in the course of his action. On the other hand, outside the we-relation on the basis of my stock of knowledge, I can calculate the Objective chances for the success of certain goals or acts, planned by typical actors, and I can associ-

49. [*Human Nature and the Social Order,* rev. ed. (New York: Schocken Books, 1964), pp. 152–63.]
50. See Chap. 4.

ate typical results of acts. But I can immediately grasp the result of the act of a fellow-man only in the course of common experiences, and in relation to his conscious life, since there I coexperience the course of the action.

We said [51] that the natural attitude is characterized by the assumption that the life-world accepted by me as given is also accepted by my fellow-men as given. We also demonstrated that this "obviousness," touching on the basic thesis of the reciprocity of perspectives, has its origin in the experience of the Other within the world in my reach, and becomes a component of that which is taken for granted in the fully socialized natural attitude. This obviousness is continually confirmed as the result of we-relations in which Others become fellow-men whose world in reach for the most part comes to coincide with mine. This circumstance is of great import for the construction of my stock of knowledge as such. I can always test the adequacy of my interpretative schemata, which are used in apprehending the expression schemata of my fellow-man by referring to the objects in our common surrounding world. When it is established that he interprets his experiences, or at least such objects as are before us, in a similar fashion to the way I do, I have a point of departure in that his expressive schemata sufficiently agree with my interpretative schemata, in any case for all practical purposes.

In general, it is thus in the we-relation that the intersubjectivity of the life-world is developed and continually confirmed. The life-world is not my private world nor your private world, nor yours and mine added together, but rather the world of our *common experience*. Furthermore, as just a marginal note, a breaking off, or even just a radical restriction, of the continual confirmation of this character of the world has grave consequences for the normal development of its intersubjectivity. The component of self-evidencies which is the underpinning for the life-world to which we are accustomed is, for instance, endangered in solitary confinement, even often demolished. The technique of brainwashing appears very probably to turn this circumstance to good account.

c. *The mediate experience of the social world*

i. *From immediate to mediate experience of the Other*
The encounter is only one relation, even if in its immediacy it

51. See Chap. 2, B, 5, a.

is the most originary and genetically important social relation. But we have found that within the temporal and spatial immediacy of the we-relation, differences in the immediacy of my experience of the Other already stand out; these are determined by the perspectives of interpretation, by depth, nearness, and intensity of lived experience. This gradation extends in general into my experience of the social world, the main sphere of which, not immediately experienced, consists of contemporaries. We wish this to characterize those other men with whom I do not actually have a we-relation, but whose life falls in the same present span of world time as mine. We can best pursue the gradations of immediacy by a simple example of the change of a person into a mere contemporary. I find myself face to face with an acquaintance. He excuses himself, shakes my hand, and departs. He turns around and calls out something to me. He is still farther, waves to me once more, and disappears around the corner. It would be difficult, if at all meaningful, to determine exactly when the we-relation came to an end, when the fellow-man who was given to me in immediate experience became simply a contemporary, of whom I can presume or maintain one thing or another on the basis of my stock of knowledge with greater or lesser probability ("in the meantime he has probably gotten home"). A qualitative change in my experience of him has entered in, no matter when one would want to fix its point in time. One could illustrate the gradations of immediacy in other ways, for example by describing typical forms of communication, ranging from a conversation during an encounter to a telephone conversation, to the exchange of letters, to news transmitted via a third person, etc. In all these cases there is manifested a decrease in the abundance of symptoms through which the conscious life of another is accessible to me. While we may establish the differentiation between immediate and mediate experience of the Other, because it involves more than merely quantitative differences, we may not forget that it involves two poles between which there are many empirically transitional forms. This statement will now be further substantiated.

The transition from direct to indirect experience of the Other seldom intrudes upon us in the natural attitude of daily life. In the routine of everyday life we unite both our own conduct and that of other men in meaning-contexts which are relatively independent of the *hic et nunc* of actual experience. This is one reason why the immediacy or mediacy of an experience (viz., the social relation) does not become a problem and does not require interpretation in the world of work. But the deeper reason for this is the fact that the immediate experience of the fellow-man would retain its constitutive characteristics, even if he became a mere contemporary. The actual immediate experience becomes a past, but then again a remembered, immediate experience.

We realize without further ado why the fellow-man with whom we spoke, whom we loved or hated, who was thus and not otherwise, should suddenly have become "different," only because he is not there at the moment. We still love or hate him, and nothing in the everyday course of events forces us to notice that our experience of him has been essentially changed in its structure. That this is the case, however, can be proven only by a careful description. Memory of the fellow-man does in fact include the constitutively essential characteristics of the (past) we-relation, which are fundamentally distinct from the features of an attitude (and from conscious acts in general) concerning mere contemporaries. In the we-relation the fellow-man was bodily present; I could grasp his conscious life in the greatest abundance of symptoms. We were tuned in to one another in temporal and spatial community. I was mirrored in him, he in me; his experiences and my experiences formed a common course: we aged together. But as soon as he leaves me, a change takes place. I know that he is in one sector of the world, which is now in history and not in my present reach. I know that his period of duration is inserted in the same world time as mine, but our conscious processes are not bound in genuine simultaneity. I also know that he must have become older, and, when I reflect on it, I also know that strictly speaking he must have changed with every new experience. But in the everyday natural attitude, without reflection I leave all this out of consideration and hold fast to the familiar representation of my fellow-man. Until I revoke it, I will credit those components of my stock of knowledge which concern this fellow-man and which have been sedimented in living we-relations, with invariability—and, indeed, until revoked, that is, until I acquire conflicting knowledge. This is knowledge about a contemporary with whom I do not empathize within a thou-orientation. He is in any case a contemporary who was at one time my fellow-man and concerning whom I have firsthand experience, and therefore experience that is fundamentally different from knowledge which I have about men who were never more than mere contemporaries.

This brings us to a point which we already indicated when we said that the formal structure of attainability and restorability, which characterizes the spatial experience of the everyday life-world, can also be transferred to the subjective experience of the social world.[52] The immediately surrounding social world, the living we-relation, can be taken as analogous to the world in actual reach; the restorable we-relation as analogous to the world in restorable reach; the social world of my contemporaries with their subdivision according to different probabilities for attainability as analogous to the world in attainable reach. In order to interpret this analogy, we must go into the essence of those social relations in which (to speak through Max Weber)[53] "there is an opportunity for the continuous *repetition* of behavior appropriate to a sense (that is, holding good for it and accordingly anticipating it." We are in the habit of viewing a marriage or a friendship primarily as a social relation belonging to a type of encounter that has a certain intimacy of lived experience. The reason for this lies in a fact already discussed: we tend to understand courses of acts as unities within larger (and more lasting) meaning-contexts, irrespective of whether this unity is also subjectively constituted in this way, in the plans and interpretations of the persons concerned. With a closer examination, the unity (of the meaning) of a marriage or a friendship which is thus established is resolved into multifaceted relations situated in social time ("golden wedding," "childhood friendship"), which partly consist of living we-relations, partly of relations among contemporaries. Strictly speaking, these social relations are not continuous but rather "repeatable."

What, then, is meant, for instance, when two friends speak of friendship? First, A, who stands in the relation of friend to B, may think of past we-relations with B. These we-relations, above all, form not an unbroken course but rather a series, broken by "lonely" sequences of lived experience and by different sorts of we-relations with Others. Second, A, when he speaks of his friendship with B, may not only think of past concrete we-relations but may also mean the fact that his conduct as such, or certain

52. See Chap. 2, B, 2, b, iii.
53. See *Wirtschaft und Gesellschaft* (Tübingen: J. C. B. Mohr [Siebeck], 1925), p. 14, topic 4.

aspects of certain types of his conduct, are oriented to B, and indeed to the simple factual existence of B, or to certain attributes of B, or even to certain alternatives of action taken as possible for B. That means that A stands in a certain orientation to his contemporary B (a "he-orientation"), which is from time to time detached from an immediate thou-orientation, which is then followed by phases fulfilled by a pure he-orientation. Finally, A may also mean that the we-relation with B is fundamentally (ignoring technical obstacles) restorable and that with subjective certainty he expects as well that the depths of lived experience, the perspectives of apprehension, etc., which distinguished past we-relations to B, are restorable in future we-relations with B.

From the above, a general conclusion follows: there are social relations that essentially can be constituted only in the immediacy of living we-relations. Obviously, there are in addition certain conditions which are biographically imposed on me and which involve biosocial roles, such as children-parents (I can, at least in a legal sense, be the son of a man whom I have never seen). And there are also chosen relations for which a certain intimacy and depth of lived experience are constitutive: for example, an amorous relation, a friendship (phenomena like the intellectual epistolary "friendships" of the Renaissance, or the—albeit one-sided—infatuation with film stars, etc., would require a specialized examination). Thus, apart from the originary structure of such social relations, the opportunities for the restorability of a living we-relation play an important role. How long can one, for instance, be a father, a husband, a friend at a distance? Here, undoubtedly, the social transformation of time is also of great importance.

But then there are also social relations, which need not necessarily be formed first in living we-relations, as for example the relation between master and servant (here one should note the historical variation: the vassal relation, for instance, until the decline of feudalism, demanded an original—and basically restorable—we-relation; producer-consumer, etc.). It should be pointed out here that this raises a difficulty, which has not up to now been defined with sufficient precision by empirical sociology, an ambiguity in the conceptual pairs, "community and society," "mechanical and organic solidarity," "primary and secondary groups." To what extent personal structure is influenced by long-term sociohistorical changes in the predominance of one or another type of social relations, or by the regular repetition of living we-relations in contrast to other sequences of social relations, is a question that must be left open at this point.

Above, we were concerned with the transitions of living we-relations to social relations between contemporaries. In doing so, we examined a border area lying between the immediate and mediate experience of the Other. The more we approach the latter, the smaller is the degree of immediacy and the higher the degree of anonymity characterizing my experience of the Other. We can divide the world of my contemporaries into various levels: fellow-men in earlier we-relations, who are now only contemporaries but with whom a living we-relation is restorable (with greater or lesser probability); those with whom a we-relation is no longer restorable (they are dead); contemporaries who were previously fellow-men of my present partner in a we-relation, who are for him so to speak "restorable" and for me "achievable" fellow-men (your friend X as yet unknown to me); contemporaries of whose personal existence I know, whom I will shortly meet face to face (Mr. Y, whose book I've read and with whom I have an appointment next week); contemporaries of whose existence I know "in general," that is, whose existence I can infer on the basis of my knowledge of the social world as reference points of typical social functions (postal officials, who dispatch *my* letter); institutional realities, about whose structure I have been instructed and whose staff is anonymous to me, although I could find out about the latter (the Parliament); institutional realities that are essentially anonymous and which I could therefore never encounter (the capitalistic economic system); socially formed Objective meaning-contexts (French grammar); and, finally, artifacts in the broadest sense, which like witnesses refer back to subjective meaning-contexts of an unknown manufacturer, consumer, spectator. All of these are examples of the increasingly anonymous strata of the social world of contemporaries, and the transitions of immediate experience of the Other into mediate experience of the social world.

ii. The contemporary as type and the they-orientation

Spatial and temporal immediacy, a presupposition for the thou-orientation and the we-relation, is absent in my experience of contemporaries. Contemporaries are not bodily present; therefore they are not given to me in prepredicative experience as this particular unique person. Nor do I have direct experience of their factual existence alone. I only know that certain contemporaries, or even a certain contemporary, coexist with me in world time. I also only know that these contemporaries or this contemporary exhibit certain characteristics. I know this on the basis of my prior experience and my stock of knowledge, through the help of various lifeworldly idealizations, but only with more or less certainty and probability. While I thus concretely experience a fellow-man immediately in his factual existence and his being-thus-and-so in the social encounter, I grasp the factual existence and being-thus-and-so of a contemporary only by means of derived typifications. Although the general problem of typification is more exactly examined below,[54] the experience of the social world cannot be described without anticipation of this analysis. Therefore it is within certain limitations that we turn to the investigation of those typifications which make it possible to grasp contemporaries.

One of the ways in which I can experience contemporaries is constituted in inferences from the previous direct experiences of fellow-men. We have already described this constitutional mode and have thus found that knowledge built up in immediate experience of the Other is constantly held, waiting recall, and is considered to be valid, even after the fellow-man has become a contemporary. Another way in which I experience contemporaries is similar to the first. The previous fellow-men of my actually present fellow-man are themselves grasped, insofar as I follow the example of my partner in the we-relation and take over from him the knowledge of an Other that he has acquired by direct experience and now holds constant. In this case, I cannot refer to my own immediate (or even to my past) experiences, but rather must first learn his information concerning the third person before I can accept as valid the knowledge contained in the communication.

In both cases the experience of a contemporary is based either on my own *past* experiences, both my immediate as well as my mediate experiences of Others, or on the transmitted remarks of an Other concerning a third. It is obvious that all knowledge thus transmitted refers back to an originary direct experience of fellow-men and is based on this. But I can also acquire knowledge of contemporaries in another way. My experiences of things and events in the life-world, of tools and artifacts in the broadest sense, contain references to the social world—to the

54. See Chap. 3, C.

world of my contemporaries and my forefathers. I can always interpret them as proofs of the conscious life of other beings "like me," as signs, marks, results of acts. But, indeed, such interpretations are in any case also inferred from my experiences of particular fellow-men. In the encounter with a fellow-man I was, in genuine simultaneity with my inner duration, witness to how his conduct was polythetically constructed, how he, step by step, realized his plans for acts, how he produced and used a tool, how he created and observed an artifact, and how he posited signs. I can interpret the finished tool, the artifact, the engraved or written sign, or the sign otherwise established in the outer world, as an indication of the stepwise subjective processes that have gone into them. Without the possibility of such a reference back to an originary basis, the tools, signs, etc., would be nothing but mere objects in the natural world.

My experience of contemporaries thus points to a necessarily indirect, mediated reference back to originary experiences. But that does not mean that I cannot focus on contemporaries with whom I am in social relations, in order to deal with them. The problem of social action will have to concern us later on. In the meantime we only want, by analogy to the thou-orientation (related to fellow-men in a social relation), to determine the concept of the *they-orientation* (i.e., he-orientation related to one or several contemporaries); we want to describe the essential characteristics of such an orientation and finally investigate the social relations founded on it.

In contrast to the way I grasp the conscious life of a fellow-man, the experiences of mere contemporaries appear to me as more or less anonymous events. The reference point of the they-orientation is a type for the conscious processes of typical contemporaries. It is not the factual existence of a concretely and immediately experienced alter ego, not his conscious life together with his subjective, step-by-step, constituted meaning-contexts. The reference point of the they-orientation is inferred from my knowledge and from the social world in general, and is necessarily in an Objective meaning-context. Only *post hoc* can I add interpretations referring to the subjective meaning-contexts of an individual, as is shown in the analysis of personal types. My knowledge of the social world is typical knowledge concerning typical processes. In whose consciousness these typical processes transpire, with whose factual existence they are bound—these are questions that I can basically leave open. Through their detachment from the subjective processes in inner duration, these processes ("typical experiences of someone") come to contain the idealizations of "and so forth" and "again and again," that is, assumptions of typical anonymous repeatability.

The unity of the contemporary is originarily constituted in the unity of my experiences—more precisely, in the synthesis of my explication of the stock of knowledge concerning the social world. In this synthesis I can coordinate typical conscious processes within a single consciousness; I form an individualized type. The more easily I can associate this type with my experiences of a former fellow-man, the simpler this becomes. But the more that Objective meaning-contexts (stratified on one another and dependent on one another) replace subjective meaning-contexts, the more anonymous will be the reference point of my they-orientation. An individualized type is fundamentally a representation, not an experience of a concrete Other. Typical attributes are held to be invariable, so that the modifications of this attribute in the inner duration of a concrete Other are not adverted to. We will illustrate this point with a few examples.

When I put a letter in the mailbox, I expect certain contemporaries to interpret my wish (which I express by means of addressing and putting a stamp on the letter in the socially approved fashion, in a way adapted to this practical end) and to conduct themselves accordingly. My expectation, as we said first, referred to certain contemporaries. But it is clear that the reference point was not certain persons, but rather certain types of contemporaries (postal employees). The acceptance of money depends, in the words of Max Weber, on the subjective chance that contemporaries will accept these small physical objects as payment. Both are examples of a they-orientation referring to the typical behavior of typical contemporaries. When I conduct myself in a certain way and fashion, or omit the performance of certain acts, to introduce another example used by Weber, I do so in order to avoid the typically established conduct of typical contemporaries (policemen, judges).[55]

In these examples my behavior is determined by the expectation that certain behavior is probable on the part of certain con-

---

55. [Alfred Schutz, *Collected Papers*, Vol. II: *Studies in Social Theory*, ed., with an introduction, by Arvid Brodersen (The Hague: Nijhoff, 1964), pp. 44–45.]

temporaries (mailmen, merchants, policemen). In relation to all these contemporaries I have a certain orientation. I include these contemporaries in my own behavior; in short, I have a social relation with them, which we characterize with the expression they-orientation. It must be stressed that these relations concern not concrete and specific other persons but rather types to which I ascribe certain attributes, certain functions, certain behavior. They are relevant for me only insofar as they conform to these typifications (probably more or less "well"). In the they-orientation I conduct myself on the basis of my knowledge of the social world: there are men who are "typical" postal employees, policemen, etc. Their behavior really stands for me in an Objective meaning-context. What they "think about it" is all the same to me, that is, the subjective meaning-contexts are for me (and for the they-relation) irrelevant, as long as they conduct themselves factually as postal employees, policemen, etc. My partners in they-relations are types.

At this juncture an important point must be added to the analysis of the thou-orientation and the we-relation. Typicality is a characteristic feature of the they-orientation and the they-relation. But that does not mean that it remains limited to this. Indeed, I cannot experience mere contemporaries other than in typification, but the same holds good, as we will see, for descendants and ancestors. Most important of all, my stock of knowledge of the social world consists of typifications. Since I already bring a stock of knowledge to every immediate encounter with a fellow-man, typifications also will necessarily play a role in the thou-orientation and we-relation. I also grasp the unique fellow-man who stands across from me face to face, with the help of typifications. Basically, there still remains an essential difference. My typifications of my fellow-man are brought into his uniqueness, which is immediately grasped in the living we-relation, and they are modified by this uniqueness. The typifications are "enlivened" in application to my fellow-man, are arranged and subordinated to the living reality. It should be noted in passing that the possibility arises that, even when one meets his fellow-man, one may "hold back" from the living we-relation and replace it, so to speak, with a they-relation. To a certain degree, this is the case reciprocally with examples of institutionalized acts, such as between buyers and sellers. The extent to which this is the beginning of the reification of the other person is a question that cannot be investigated here.[56] We only want, with the aid of a single example, to follow this presupposition back to the origin of this problem in the lifeworldly experience of the Other.

Let us assume that I find myself face to face with several fellow-men. Our experiences appear to me as an unbroken and common flow. But I can also direct my attention to an individual; I can dissect the "we" into me and him. Let us assume that I am playing cards with three partners. I can turn my attention to one or the other. In the thou-orientation I grasp his conscious processes step by step, by means of his words, his facial expression, his hand gestures, etc. And, I submerge myself in the subjective contexts in which the game and his actions in the game appear to him. I can turn to all the card players, one after the other, in such an attitude. But as an unparticipating observer, I can also undertake a transposition: I transpose the observed situation from fellow-human immediacy into the typified world of contemporaries. I explicate the situation on the basis of my stock of knowledge: the three (or the four, for I can also "observe" myself in this sense) are playing bridge. Statements of this kind concern conscious life only insofar as the typical acts (playing bridge) are coupled with typical meaning-contexts for the player, and insofar as I can coordinate such meaning-contexts with the conscious life of the individual players. Then I can also assume that for each individual the process exists in a subjective meaning-context for him. But basically I only need to postulate that this behavior (somehow, subjectively) is oriented to the Objective meaning-context (rules for bridge). This postulate naturally holds good in general for "people who play bridge," whoever they may be, whenever and wherever they may be playing. It is thus a typifying and quite anonymous postulate, not at all limited to the players in front of me. It is indeed the case that no concrete experience by A can be identical with an experience by B, no matter how typical it might be in an Objective meaning-context, since it belongs to the conscious stream of an individual man in a specific biographical articulation. The concrete experi-

56. There is a steadily growing literature in this field, starting from the concept of alienation in Marx, as well as from the sociological concept of roles. [For a discussion see, for example, Istaván Mészáros, *Marx's Theory of Alienation* (London: Merlin Press, 1970). An especially clear discussion of Marx's theory of alienation is also found in *Die Marxische Theorie* by Klaus Hartmann (Berlin: de Gruyter, 1970), pp. 120–24, 149–54, 333–35, 570.]

ence cannot be repeated. Only the typical "in it" can be repeated. Only insofar as I bracket the concrete fellow-men A, B, and C, and say "they" play cards, can I grasp representatives of the type cardplayer in them. But with that I have undertaken an explication through which the fellow-men A, B, and C were rendered anonymous.

In contrast, it may be said finally that A, B, and C, even when they play cards, are "still" my friends Caspar, Melchior, and Balthasar. If the objection is addressed to the already constituted courses of lived experience in the natural attitude, then it is justified. Regarding the constitution of everyday experience (e.g., "my-friends-Caspar-Melchior-and-Balthasar-are-playing-bridge"), it must be said that an anonymization of the living process and its transposition into an Objective meaning-context is a presupposition of my coherent experience. The Objective meaning-context, which was built up on the basis of my stock of knowledge and of the axioms, idealizations, and typifications peculiar to it, can secondarily be transported back into subjective meaning-contexts: I also use my typical knowledge in situations involving fellow-men. I grasp fellow-men as "people like . . ." But at the same time, I experience them in the we-relation as unique fellow-men whose conscious life manifests itself before my eyes. They thus have a double character: they are "people like . . ." and they are "thou's." On the basis of this double character of fellow-men there then occurs a third transposition: the mere contemporary, experienced by me as a type, is endowed with a conscious life like a fellow-man. But it must be established that I do not immediately experience the conscious life of the contemporary, but as it were "breathe" consciousness into the reference point of the they-orientation, into the type through an act of explication of mine. As a result, this consciousness remains just a typical, anonymous consciousness. It is clear that we have here touched on an important problem of the social sciences, that of the life-worldly basis of the so-called ideal type. In the following, we want to investigate a point important for the analysis of the life-world: the significance of the relation of typification and anonymity for the experience of social reality.

iii. The levels of anonymity in the social world

The foundational moment of the they-orientation is that one imagines the Other, whose existence is assumed or suspected, as a reference point of typical virtues, characteristics, etc. In this orientation, apart from this basic moment, the specific experiences of Others are, in the they-orientation, differentiated into various aspects. The most important variable is the degree of anonymity. We can say that the world of contemporaries is stratified according to levels of anonymity. The more anonymous the type (by means of which a contemporary is experienced), the more strongly objectivated is the meaning-context that is foisted upon the Other.

The anonymity of a type (an individualized social type) must be commented on in greater detail. We have already said that the "pure" thou-orientation arises from the immediate attention directed to the mere existence of the fellow-man, and that the grasping of the being-thus-and-so of a fellow-man is founded on this orientation. This does not prove true for the they-orientation. Basically, the latter consists in the fact that one imagines certain typical properties. In such conceptions I indeed posit such properties as existent, as now or earlier on hand to men. I need not, though, posit the availability of such a property in a certain Other, at a certain point in time, and in a certain place. The typical property is anonymous with reference to each individual person. As a consequence, the contemporary who, as we have shown, can be grasped only by means of such typifications, is in any case in this sense anonymous. This *factual existence* of the contemporary is not immediately experienced, but only suspected, assumed, or, rather, posited as taken for granted. In my *actual* experience the contemporary only has the status of a point of intersection of typical properties; his factual existence has for me the character of a subjective chance. From this it follows that the risk involved in those acts of mine that are directed to contemporaries, even in social encounters, is much greater in comparison with the act structure which as such and fundamentally has a chance character. What consequences this circumstance has for the structure of social relations between contemporaries is still to be shown.

But we can still speak of anonymity of individualized social typifications in another sense. The anonymity of a typification is inversely proportional to its fullness of content. The fullness of content for its part depends on the degree of generality, viz., the detail and determinateness of my stock of knowledge in relation to the typical property posited as invariable. The interpretation schema lying at the basis of a they-orientation may be inferred from immediate experiences of an earlier fellow-man; but it can also be related to generalizations of social reality. In the first case the type, a personal type, will be relatively detailed and filled with content; in the second case, the typification will be relatively general and empty of content. We can say that the fullness of content of the individualized social type conforms to the relative immediacy of the experiences from which it was constituted.

But typifications are not in themselves secluded, isolated schemata of meaning but are rather bound to and built upon one another. The more typifications an individualized type is built on, the more anonymous it is, and the broader is the province of the schemata of meaning presupposed in the type as self-evident. The lower strata of the typifications (viz., the typifying schemata of meaning) do not come explicitly into the grasp of consciousness and are in a more or less vague way coposited as taken for granted and unproblematic. This can be easily illustrated. One need only consider how many "self-evident" and unclear schemata of interpretation underlie typifications like "citizen of the world," "vintager," "leftist intellectual liberal," "combatant," "American."

The degree of anonymity of an individualized social type thus depends, as we could say, on how easily the relation constituted through it (or the coconstituted relation) can be changed into a we-relation. The sooner I can immediately experience the typical characteristics of "someone" as properties of a fellow-man, as components of his conscious life, the less anonymous is the typification in question. This may be illustrated by two examples. Let us assume that I think of my absent friend Hans who faces a difficult decision. From sedimented immediate experiences of my friend, I have the individualized type "my friend Hans," who becomes the reference point of my present he-orientation. I may also formulate types of behavior: the observation "my friend Hans, before difficult decisions," becomes "people like Hans" are wont to conduct themselves thus and so under such circumstances. Although dealt with as typifications, these are minimally anonymous, their content is filled in considerably and inferred from past immediate experiences. Further, my contemporary Hans can at any time become fellow-man Hans. Let us take another example: my friend tells me about X, whom I do not know and whom he has recently met, and describes him; that is, he constructs typifications of X in which he fixes and posits as invariant his own experiences of the properties of X, by means of the speech categories of his stock of knowledge. The choice of properties and their linguistic determination is therefore dependent upon my friend's stock of knowledge, upon his biographical situation, his motivations and plans when he met X, as well as upon his motivations and plans when he told me about X. While I listen to the description of X, I explicate the description of "people like X" with the aid of my linguistic interpretational schemata, with the help of my stock of knowledge, and in connection with my interests in "people like X" as well as in relation to my knowledge of my friend. The individualized social type X cannot be completely identical for my friend and for me. I may even question the characterization, or parts of it, and bracket these out on the basis of my (typifying) knowledge of my friend (my friend is easily excited, with "people like X" he has a blind spot, etc.). What is common in these two examples is that they are derived from immediate experience of a fellow-man, at first or second hand, and are relatively filled with content and not yet very anonymous. The memory of living fellow-men still permeates the typifications actually taking the place of the fellow-man. Such individualized types we will call *personal types*.

Another type-formation, at the same time more weakly individualized, grasps contemporaries only in reference to certain typical functions. Let us again take the example of the postal employee. My relation to the postal employee is much more anonymous than my relation to a personal type, since it is not concerned with Others whom I experience, have experienced, or probably will experience as fellow-men. Even if we should meet, it is extremely probable that we will both conduct ourselves on the basis of they-orientations "imported" into this situation, as it typically involves the institutionalization of such situations. If I post a letter, I need not (strictly speaking) refer to an individualized type "postal employee." I could, though, at least reflectively interpolate that his behavior stands for him in specific subjective meaning-contexts (salary, the chief, the comptroller, stomach upset—all these refer to Hans Müller); even more, I may refer to pure *types of behavior* (standardized courses of dispatching a letter, canceling, transport, delivery). It is of subordinate importance that I then associate the behavior types with someone ("anyone") who conducts himself just so and not otherwise. Such typifications, which closely approach pure behavioral types and which already have reached a higher degree of anonymity, we will characterize with the expression *functionary type*.

In contrast to the personal, the functionary type is relatively anonymous. Both individualized types, including the latter, are relatively content-filled (and close to lived experience), if one contrasts them with the other typifying interpretational schemata for social reality. Typifications of so-called social collectives, although they still contain individualizations, are, for example, quite anonymous, since they can never be immediately experienced as such. The class of such typifications is again itself arranged according to levels of anonymity. "The Parliament," "the Board of Directors of the Rockefeller Foundation," "the bowling team" are typifications exhibiting relatively low anonymity within this class, since they are built on individualized functionary types or even personal types, which can at least in principle be converted into the immediate experience of fellow-men. Such a conversion is more difficult (even though it is subject to institutional manipulation) when it concerns collectives whose individualized substrata serve as the basis for unclear, fluctuating distinctions—as, for instance, "the enemies of our people." When the typifications are like *the* state," *the* economy," *the* social classes," etc., they are completely unamenable to conversion into the living reality of a fellow-man. Highly anonymous Objective meaning-contexts and behavior-contexts are grasped in these typifications.[57] We still have to examine the question of the extent to which collectives (viz., the Objective meaning-contexts

57. The view that these Objective meaning- and behavior-contexts could be coordinated in a stream of consciousness and changed into a subjective meaning-context is a historical or, as the sociologist would say, an ideological, construction. The functions "of the state," "the will of the people," etc., can perhaps be explicated in an Objective meaning-context (e.g., in that of the historical sciences), so that the dangers inherent in these terms are hidden. Otherwise, this can only mean that the various aspects of Objective meaning-contexts are typical moments of subjective, conscious processes of state functionaries, representatives of the people, etc. As to this last possibility, one can by means of functionary types, and in principle also by means of personal types, become oriented in a they-orientation. *The* functions of *the* state cannot adequately be the basis of a consciousness, of a subjective meaning-context. The problem of a more exact analysis of the substrata of collective social realities remains one to be solved by sociology, and above all by the theory of socialization. These disciplines must exhibit the origin of the substrata in immediate and mediate experience of Others. An investigation of the possibilities and limits of the transformation of the meaning-contexts of social collectives into the subjective meaning-contexts of their functionaries (and, therewith, into the responsibility of the functionaries) is a problem of special import for jurisprudence and political science.

ascribed to them) are embodied in symbols that operate by instituting communities, and the way in which these symbols become taken-for-granted data of the social and cultural world into which the individual is born.[58]

iv. Social relations between contemporaries

While social relations between fellow-men are founded on the thou-orientation, social relations between contemporaries are based on the they-orientation. Thus while social encounters proceed through the reciprocal mirroring of the immediate experience of the Other, social relations between contemporaries consist in grasping the Other as a (personal or functionary) type. As a consequence, social relations between contemporaries have in principle only a probable character. In such relations I must be satisfied with the chance and anticipation that the contemporary to whom I am oriented, for his part, is oriented to me, and indeed by means of a meaningfully adequate, complementary typification. We will illustrate this point with an example.

When I get on a train, my conduct is oriented to the anticipation that certain persons will undertake certain acts, which will in all likelihood bring me to my destination. With these persons I am in a social relation between contemporaries, or as we can also say, in a *they-relation*. This relation can occur, first, because my stock of knowledge contains the functionary type "railroad employee" ("people who do everything necessary so that people like me . . ."), and second, because under certain purpose- and situation-bound circumstances I *orient my conduct to this type*. Third, as a part of a factual lifeworldly relation between contemporaries, not only I orient my conduct to a certain type, but also others orient their own conduct to this type, viz., to a complementary type ("traveling person"). This means that I ascribe to my partner in the social relation an expectational and interpretational schema containing *me as type*. In this example, the relatively anonymous character of the functionary type becomes clear: I and my contemporary orient our conduct less to individualized types than to a typification of conduct, or as we can also say, to types of courses of acts. Social relations between contemporaries are determined through the subjective chances of the meaning-adequate complementarity of the typifications used by the partners. In place of the reciprocal confirmation (or modification or disconfirmation) of expectations in the immediate

58. See Chap. 6 [Vol. II].

experience of a we-relation, conscious acts (reflections, conceptions) concerning typifications enter into social relations between contemporaries, presumably orienting the behavior of the partner. The more standardized a typification schema is (under a circumstance of type X people of type A conduct themselves in the manner of type Z, as concerns people of type B), the greater is the subjective chance that the expectation of each of the partners in the relation will be confirmed. The subjective chances are graduated from mere conjecture (he could take me for X or Z; if for X, he could behave in the ways a, b, c; if for Z, in the ways d, e, f) to subjective certainty (he is listed in the address book as a stamp dealer; if I send him an order, he can conduct himself only thus and so). The typification schemata, to raise a point not yet discussed, can be standardized in various ways. Either the province of use and the kind of use are guaranteed by institutions (if I don't pay the fare, people of the type "railway police" will take typical actions oriented to the fact that I am a man of the legally determined type "fare-dodger," whether this typification is pleasing to me or not). Or the typification schemata are traditionally determined; that is, I know that their province of use and their kind of use have a general social distribution. Or the standardization refers to the fact that it concerns types of courses of acts, coordinated with a "rational" means-purpose schema.

These essential characteristics of social relations between contemporaries have several important consequences. First, in contrast to the continuing enrichment in a we-relation of my experience of my fellow-men, in a they-relation this obtains only with radical limitations. My experiences of contemporaries do indeed change my stock of knowledge of the social world, and the typifications underlying a they-relation can be modified. But this happens only to a negligibly small extent, as long as the sphere of interest, which determined the original use of the type, remains unchanged.[59]

Our analysis of the general thesis of reciprocal perspectives is indicated by the second noteworthy point. In the we-relation I can always (again and again) find confirmation that my experiences of the life-world are congruent with your experiences of it.

59. In some studies, a somewhat naïve surprise has accompanied the discovery of a small influence of "personal contacts" on social "stereotypes."

We have seen that the extension of this to other men has been taken to be self-evident. But a confirmation in reference to mere contemporaries is not possible. It can only be maintained in a roundabout way through contemporaries who are former fellow-men and are "restorable" as fellow-men. Here, reference should again be made to the consequences of complete and relative isolation.

From the structure of they-relations, two further points arise here, though they can only be indicated in anticipation of the analysis of social action and the analysis of sign systems. Whether the relations assumed by me have actually arisen between a certain contemporary and me can only be determined from the outside, since social relations have a subjective chance-character. In projecting my acts I can take account of his motivations only insofar as they expressly belong to the type ascribed to him, as typical motivations *sufficient for the expected courses of acts*. If I mail a letter, I am presumably (in this case with subjective assuredness) in a they-relation with postal employees, for whom I (once again presumably, viz., with subjective assuredness) function as a "sender." Along with this I take into account that "people who become postal employees" are sufficiently motivated to undertake the actions of postal employees, as they for their part figure (and indeed with subjective assuredness) that "people who put letters in mailboxes" pursue the purpose of having the letter dispatched on its course. In whatever subjective meaning-context the letterwriting is for me, or the career of a postal employee is for him, is irrelevant for us both. In this sense his motives have nothing to do with mine. We will see later [60] how this situation differs from the structure of social action in an encounter.

The second point refers to communication.[61] When I make myself understood to my partner in the social relation, I also use sign systems. In the they-relation, in contrast, I am almost exclusively referred to sign systems. In addition, there is the fact that the "more anonymous" my partner is, the "more Objective" must the use of sign systems be. This again makes clear how close the relation is between the degree of anonymity of the experience of social reality, and the replacement of subjective meaning-contexts by means of systematically objectivated mean-

60. See Chap. 5 [Vol. II].
61. See Chap. 6 [Vol. II].

ings. Thus I cannot presuppose that a contemporary, with whom I am in a they-relation, adequately grasps the nuances of my statement which are given by my intonation, by my facial expression, etc. (as well as by a "knowledge," won in immediate experiences, concerning how it all is to be interpreted, and what relation it has to my biographical situation, to my momentary mood, etc.). If I consciously want to share such nuances with him, I must transpose them into Objective categories of meaning, whereby they inevitably lose their nuanced character. In addition, communications with a contemporary must be posited as a totality. The risk that my preinterpretation of his reaction is inaccurate is consequently related to this totality, while I, step by step, immediately experience in the we-relation whether he has correctly or falsely understood me.

In concluding, the relation of the they-relation to the we-relation should be brought once more to mind. They-relations characterized by a relatively small degree of anonymity can be converted into we-relations, via various phases of transition. Conversely, we-relations of special immediacy and depth of lived experience are transformed into they-relations with a small degree of anonymity. This is an important factor in the development of a fixed meaning for social relations (e.g., of the depth of lived experience in a friendship), which is *relatively* independent of the structure of immediacy and mediacy. And finally, the transitions from immediate to mediate experiences, such as occur in the natural attitude of everyday life, are smooth and do not, for the reasons already discussed, force themselves on the consciousness.

v. The world of predecessors, history, generations

When I have lived through a we-relation or a they-relation, I can reproduce my experiences in them, step by step, in my memory, or I can grasp them monothetically in hindsight. In both cases the constitutive characteristics of these experiences, their immediacy or mediacy, remain preserved. But these experiences, which for their part were actual experiences of my conscious life, are essentially changed in one respect: they have received the place-value of historicality. That is, they are concluded, terminated. In the living phases of actual experience, there were horizons of open future; now there are no more. That which had a subjective character of chance in a social relation, for instance my expectations with regard to the future behavior of my partners, is now absolutely sure. The expectations have been fulfilled or were disappointed. The temporal structures of experience, thus for example the time-structure inherent in action,[62] can possibly be reproduced as such in memory; but the memory fulfilling my present conscious phase has another structure and has another position in my biographical situation. The present biographical situation is the present horizon of the remembered experience: "first I wanted this, then I looked for means to realize my goal, then I did this and that, etc."—but in *every one* of these remembered phases there is also the refrain: "I have actually only achieved this."

The dividing line between the world of my contemporaries and that of my predecessors is not sharp. I can surely view all memories of my own experiences of Others as experience of past social reality. Indeed, as we have just remarked, the constitutive characteristics of these experiences are preserved in such memories. These are experiences in which Others were present in simultaneity with my life. I can coordinate the past phases of the conscious life of these Others with past phases of my own conscious life. This means, above all, that in hindsight I can follow along in its inner duration the step-by-step construction of subjective meaning-contexts under my attention.

This is not applicable to the world of my predecessors in the narrow sense. This world is *definitively* concluded; not only have the experiences lived through by my ancestors come to an end; but also the biographical articulation in which the individual experiences were joined together is definitively completed. With regard to the world of my predecessors, nothing more can be expected. For this reason I cannot experience ancestors as free; they can no longer act. The "freedom" of my mere contemporaries, as I experience them, is also limited, since I grasp them by means of typifications fixing motives and courses of acts as constant. I also grasp ancestors only by means of typifications; but in this case nothing is held constant that is not already invariable anyhow. Invariability characterizes all of my predecessor's world.

I can orient myself by means of typifications to my predecessor's world (to my grandfather, to Napoleon), but I cannot act in relation to them. My attitude toward ancestors also has a character other than that of the thou-orientation and the they-orienta-

62. See Chap. 5 [Vol. II].

tion. My behavior can be oriented to the behavior of my ancestors only insofar as their acts can become because-motives [63] for my actions, but with regard to my ancestors I cannot effect anything more. Social relations that are essentially reciprocal cannot exist with ancestors. Acts of my ancestors which are oriented to me (as the quite anonymous type "descendant"), for instance a clause in my grandfather's will, I can meet only with an attitude directed to my grandfather—apart from the fact already mentioned, that the act can become a because-motive of my behavior (e.g., I study at a certain university of his choice).

The experiences of the preceding world are obviously indirect. They can be transmitted by means of communication from my fellow-men or contemporaries, based on their own immediate experiences (childhood memories of my father) or can themselves be inferred (my father tells me of the Civil War experiences of his great-uncle). These examples show again how indistinct in everyday experience is the dividing line between the worlds of contemporaries and ancestors. My father is presently in a we-relation with me; his own childhood experiences are related to a time before my birth; they are "history" for me. And yet they are the experiences of a fellow-man. I can therefore coordinate his experiences, including those which are "history" for me, with the subjective meaning-contexts of the fellow-man present to me.

Apart from the role that communication between fellow-men and contemporaries plays in my experience of the world of predecessors, the deeds of my ancestors are decisive. They are expressions of their conscious life. We can distinguish various possibilities here. The deeds could be communications directed to the contemporaries of ancestors; they can also have been directed to descendants. Those ancestors can be specific persons or completely anonymous types. Insofar as the deeds involve communications, they are in any case in an Objective meaning-context, the sign system, and are thus by their very essence anonymous. But the signs are also manifestations of the conscious life of the one who posited them, and I can try to expound them as such. Through this change in my attitude I put myself in a kind of pseudo-contemporaneity with the historical subject. Historical research is indeed seldom directly interested in the conscious life of the historical subject. But it should not be forgotten that historical sources, documents, etc., always allow a backward refer-

63. *Ibid.*

ence of such a kind, since they presuppose and pass on experiences of social reality on the part of the sign-positing subject. The world of predecessors was the contemporary world of ancestors; it contains the same fundamental arrangements of subjective experience of the social world, beyond immediacy, anonymity, etc., as does the world of contemporaries.

While the precedent world as well as the contemporary world is experienced by means of typifications, there exists, however, an important difference. The ancestor lived in a world radically divergent from mine. The general theory of the reciprocity of perspectives, lying at the basis of the socialization of the life-world, confirmed in the we-relation and expanded, with restrictions, into the world of contemporaries, is, strictly speaking, not applicable to the precedent world. Through linking the world of contemporaries with the world of predecessors by means of the overlapping of generations, we indeed try also to extend the general thesis to the past. In the natural attitude of everyday life, I am not reflectively-theoretically turned to the past; but *pragmatically* the task of extending the general thesis cannot be forcibly brought before my eyes (there are no ancient Teutons to confront me—as contemporary Chinese very probably can—and prove to me that not "everyone" experiences the world as you and I do). Furthermore (and completely ignoring the infiltration of a historical attitude into the modern relative-natural world view), it is probable that one also begins to suspect, in the natural attitude, that the meaning-contexts in which the experiences of the ancestors existed diverge decisively from those of contemporaries. The reason for this is found in the experience of difference between the world views of different *generations*.

It is indeed just through the transmission of my experience of elders that the precedent world is originally constituted as a social world "like mine." All experiences of my ancestors were experiences belonging to an inner duration, a subjective meaning-context, as well as being constituted in encounters with Others, and in mediate social relations. I am in we-relations with my father, he was in we-relations with his father and so forth, back to the darkest past no longer graspable by typifications having full content; but this is also perceived as social past. At the same time, however, it is precisely in my experience of the elder that perhaps the most important modification of the general thesis of reciprocal perspectives is developed. My elder is a fellow-man in whom the interchangeability of standpoints and the congruence of relevance systems is confirmed for me. But he is also a fellow-man in whom I experience the risk pertaining to the "self-evidencies" contained in the general thesis. He thinks otherwise about this and that than I. Through him I learn to have insight into the dependency of relevance systems upon the biographical situation. And even an intimate associate (*"my* father") "thinks differently." It is again precisely through my experience of elders that a biographical-historical difference *within* the contemporary world is forced upon me. Many of the horizons that for me, in my biographical situation, still are open, are for the elder, the fellow-man in our common situation, already closed (marriage, choice of profession, the first-born); what in my current experience is related to anticipations or expectations is already fulfilled for him, sedimented in his memory. He already was "in my position," namely, in a typical situation of a typical young man. He also went into this situation with expectations which were analogous to mine now, but he now already knows "how it turned out." He appeals to his "personal experience" and cannot comprehend that he cannot convey it to me.

No matter how static a society may be, there must of necessity be a disposition toward the experience of generations and thereby a disposition toward a naïve insight into the historicality of the social world. It is quite clear that this still does not tell us anything about the social conditions for the development of a historical consciousness (much less of a historical world view). But just as the world of predecessors is constituted for me through the chain of generations, so also a modification of the general thesis of reciprocal perspectives enters "after the fact." The "content" of the we-relations of my ancestors must have been different. They were in different meaning-contexts: the "same" experience in another meaning-context cannot have been "the same." With diminishing fullness of content and increasing anonymity of my typifications of the precedent world, I reach a point at which I can only say: the experiences of an ancestor were human experiences; they must have had "some kind" of subjective meaning. The risk of applying more or less content-filled typifications to ancestors is much greater than that regarding such an application to the contemporary social world. This even holds good for my interpretation of sign systems, which are Objective but deposited in the past. Sign systems are "self-evidently" invariable; they do not have the "open" horizons of a living, conscious process. However, I cannot *directly* test the

posited equivalency of my interpretational schemata for sign
systems with the corresponding expressional schemata of my
ancestors. This can be done only indirectly, with the help of
"internal" evidence, founded again on assumptions and interpretations that are built up one on another. How much more simple
is the evidence of assertions related to the world time (for example, the carbon dating of archaeological finds), than that of assertions related to the historical time of the social world.

vi. The world of successors

The world of successors is fundamentally "open" and indeterminate. My experience of it can only take place by means of
highly anonymous typifications. Strictly speaking, I cannot legiti-
mately apply individualized types to it—the nearest one can
come, and even here there is a high risk of inaccuracy, is to apply
functionary types. I have *one* point of contact with posterity,
again through the subjective experience of generations. I can
assume that this child, or if not this child then another, will live
on past my death, that the properties of his conscious life which
I presently immediately experience will be unfolded in the future.
Beyond that, I can only assume that as long as there is a posterity
my successors will unite a subjective meaning to their lived experiences, that they will live in a world. But in which? Surely
there are differences in historical life-worlds: this future-directed
question is unanswerable by us today, for even in the natural
attitude of a man from a static society, the applicability to this
succeeding world, of *typifications* pertinent to his contemporary
world, is at least in principle out of the question.

6. THE COURSE OF LIFE: ONTOLOGICAL LIMITS, SUBJECTIVE CONDITIONS OF BIOGRAPHICAL ARTICULATION AND SOCIAL CONSTRUCTION

In our description of the experience of the life-world we
stumbled onto the boundary conditions of this experience which
are imposed on everyone. They form the limits within which subjective experience of the life-world is arranged in certain structures. Subjectively, they can be experienced as transcendencies
of the everyday world. World time limits subjective duration; one
ages in it and it forms the absolute boundary of life-plans. The
fixed course of world time conditions subjective action; it forces

the principle of "first things first" on daily plans. The historicality of the world conditions the historicality of the subjective situation in the world.

In our description of the essential laws of inner duration we saw that, in conjunction with the determinations of the animate organism, these laws conditioned the structure of each experience of the life-world. Everyone is given to himself as the center of a coordinated system that exhibits an arrangement according to actual and potential reach, as well as according to the actual and potential zone of operation.

Finally, an unalterable condition of lifeworldly existence is that the individual encounters Others. We described how the Other is experienced, mediately and immediately, and how certain structures of social relations are constructed out of such experiences—and not only how a historical social world is constituted, but also how the total life-world is socialized.

Accordingly, we have described the boundary conditions of the individual course of life as well as the basic structures of each experience in it. We are still faced with the question of how a course of life is expressed within these boundary conditions in the structures of experience. We already raised this question when we spoke about biographical articulation.[64] But we had to limit ourselves to an inspection of subjectively conditioned aspects of biographical articulation, that is, such as resulted from the essential characteristics of inner duration. We found that the biographical articulation is superimposed on the plan for the day. In other words, the horizons of experience, interpretations, and projects (the scope of whose meaning is the course of life within its ontological limitations) mold the articulations of inner duration in the daily rhythm and determine the bestowing of meaning with regard to plans for the day. We also found that, on the other hand, the horizons of experience, interpretations, and plans necessarily fit into the daily rhythm of inner duration. The second essentially subjective aspect of the biographical articulation is, as we have seen, the unique sequence of experiences in the inner duration and the correspondingly unique order in the sedimentation of experience in the stock of knowledge.

But we also said that the categories of biographical articulation are not really categories of inner duration but are rather much more intersubjectively constructed categories handed down

64. See Chap. 2, B, 4, c, ii.

within the relative-natural world view. We are now in the position of freeing ourselves from the initial limitation upon the observation of the subjective aspects and of making up for what has been neglected. It is naturally the task of empirical ethnology and sociology to describe the concrete "contents" of the social construction of biographical categories, and to establish causal hypotheses about the connection of certain forms with certain ecological, demographic, and institutional factors. We must also consider whether general aspects of the social categorization of the course of life can be determined, whether there are any particular foundational relations between the social categories of biographical articulation and experience of the life-world.

First, it should be said that the social categories of the biographical articulation *are already given* to the individual, as a component of the relative-natural world view. That is, they belong to a system of typifications that is on hand historically and is imposed on the individual as an essential component of an Objective social reality, that comes into existence prior to him, and that is valid for him. They are thereby an *element of the unchangeable historicality of the situation* of an individual being. Here, though, one must make a differentiation: the historicality of the situation is imposed on the individual; it is an ontological boundary condition of his factual existence. The relative-natural world view, viz., the social categories of biographical articulation which are contained in it, are in contrast experienced by the individual as something in the life-world to be overcome, as belonging to the potential zone of operation surrounding his life. The categories of biographical articulation are thus not boundary conditions of the lifeworldly situation, but are the possibilities for leading life within this situation. Indeed, as a component of the relative-natural world view, they have the character of quite anonymous typifications. But since they operate as meaning-bestowing themes for subjective life-plans, they merge into what is concretely taken for granted in the apprehension of the self and others.

Second, the character of *typifications* relevant for biographical articulation must be more precisely described. We just said that they are a component of the relative-natural world view. The latter is a system of communicable typifications of the life-world as such, socially objectivated, and established in sign systems, above all in the mother tongue. For the social construction of biography, not only the typifications of biography itself are relevant, but also the valuing interpretations of the social world superimposed on them in the system of typifications; they are expressed in legitimatizations of social institutions, laws, and recipes for acts, and govern social action on various levels of anonymity. Also relevant are the evaluations of "social positions" contained in the typifications of the social structure. All these typifications fill the social world with historically quite specific contents, which the individual learns as possibilities, impossibilities, and taken-for-grantednesses for *his* course of life. The individual experiences the social world which is already given to him and objectivated in the relative-natural world view, as a scale of subjective probabilities related to him, as an ordering of duties, possibilities, and goals attainable with ease or with difficulty. In other words, the social structure is open to him in the form of typical biographies. Thus the social structure is the rigid boundary in which his age, his life-plans, and thus his priority structures and daily plans gain concrete form.

There is another observation to be added to this point. When we said that the social structure is open to the individual in the form of typical biographies, this "openness" is ambiguous. It may mean that in a certain society *a* certain course of life is open to a certain type of man. Among the Comanches, if one was born a man with a strong body, it was "obvious" that he could only become a horse-thief and warrior. It can also mean that several alternative biographies with various Objective degrees of attainability are subjectively open to choose from. One can remain a farmer or one can try to learn a trade. Finally, an almost incalculable series of possible typical biographies, varying in their Objective degree of attainability, can be open to choose from. This depends as much on the character of the social structure of a given historical situation as on their construction in the relative-natural world view. Social structures (e.g., feudalism in contrast to the industrial society) are to a great extent differentiated through their "degree of freedom" in the choice of various courses of life. Moreover, within a social structure the biographical "degrees of freedom" are distributed socially. The sons of the middle class may in a certain society have a higher degree of freedom in choosing careers than the sons of kings. What was said about typical biographies in the sense of "careers" holds true also for certain more narrowly restricted patterns of acts. Brahmans may have more circumscribed freedom of choice in sexual pleasures than members of lower castes.

The examples illustrate still a further point: typical biographies, both under the total aspect of "careers" as well as in relation to restricted patterns of action, are involved not only with the social situation of the individual, but also with certain foundational conditions of his life. Many careers (warrior) or models of action (pederasty) are only "open" to men, others only to women (mother, suffragette). Certain careers, like practicing certain patterns of action, are moreover only attainable and possible after a certain unchangeable, ontologically determined (one must live just long enough to be a wise old man), or prescribed, socially structured (doctorate only after bachelor's) sequence. Consequently, "changing jobs," "turning back," is possible in certain sequences, but not in others.

Yet with regard to these expositions, one notes that an unequivocal subjective correlate does not necessarily correspond to the mentioned "Objective degrees of freedom." Compliance with what is obvious need in no way be subjectively experienced as a compulsion. The development of the subjective consciousness of force and freedom itself depends on complex sociohistorical causes. The individual may have chosen a career in consciousness of complete autonomy or in the consciousness of having been forced to something by his parents. The career, though, would be one which an "Objective" expert of the social structure could have predicted with a very high degree of certainty. This circumstance can be seen in still another context when we observe the transmission of typical biographies through certain fellow-men.

But first another variable characteristic of typifications related to courses of life must be mentioned. Such typifications can be combined into unequivocal, coherent biographies (youth, warrior, old wise man; but also high school, technical college, hydraulic engineer), or can be relatively weakly defined, freely cohering life lines (rich man, gentleman). This variability depends as much on the social structure in its facticity (e.g., race of nomads, industrial society) as on certain elements of the relative-natural world view (e.g., ethics of a certain standpoint, professional ethics).

The *third* point concerns the socialization of the individual in certain typical biographies. At the outset, the social structure and, correspondingly, the relative-natural world view do not in their totality confront the individual as Objective, quite anonymous data. Rather they meet him selectively and are transmitted by certain fellow-men. At first, there are certain ancestors, by whose transmission certain aspects and segments of the relative-natural world view, valid for them and "lived" by them, are handed over to me.[65] The fellow-men who are crucial for the first encounters with Objective social reality are naturally the elders, among these, above all and typically, the socially defined (not necessarily "biological") parents. Which elders these are is a matter which naturally is an element of the unchangeable historical situation in which the individual finds himself. In the chain of earliest we-relations, the validity of the more or less anonymous typifications brought to the encounter by the elders is constructed for the individual ("good children don't do that"). In these we-relations the typifications applied to the individual by an Other become, in the course of the processes of mirroring,[66] self-typifications—surely with a certain choice and modification —and imprint the personal structure. Social temporal categories which, so to speak, cock the hat of the individual's inner duration, belong to the most important categories which are so conveyed and intensified. In this we-relation the intersubjective character of the life-world is originally developed. But the individual also meets the limits of his factual existence in social superstructures (*dolce pro patria mori*, reward in "another world," etc.), which are transmitted in the further chain of we-relations and then eventually also in they-relations. The individual also learns what is worth striving for in his life, as it is imposed on him through his situation. He learns *within* these limits (train engineer, military chief, a poor but honest man), what can be endured (a boy doesn't cry at that), what is "unbearable" (no gentleman need put up with that; one can understand if a man goes to pieces *under such circumstances*, etc.). In these connections, one learns more or less exactly not only the what but also the how (train-engineer apprentice course; riding, archery; clench the teeth; get crying fits, etc.). The individual learns life-plans, and daily plans for actualizing life-plans, within a certain range of selection essentially conditioned by their trans-

65. Further aspects of this problem are discussed in the analysis of the social transmission of knowledge and the socialization of the stocks of knowledge; see Chap. 4, esp. A, 1 and 2; B, 3, b and c.
66. Cooley's "looking-glass" effect, *Human Nature and the Social Order*.

mission to him. They are transmitted as well by certain other persons within the boundaries of the immediacy- and anonymity-structure of the social world which is contemporary for him.

Typical biographies are offered to everyone in every society. An unalterable condition of each course of life is that it be articulated in social categories.

3 / Knowledge of the Life-World*

[A] THE STOCK OF KNOWLEDGE: ITS SITUATION-RELATEDNESS, ITS GENESIS, AND ITS STRUCTURE

I. STOCK OF KNOWLEDGE AND SITUATION

a. The limitation of the situation as the first fundamental element of the stock of knowledge

THE LIFEWORLDLY STOCK OF KNOWLEDGE is related in many ways to the situation of the experiencing subject. It is built on sedimentations of formerly actually present experiences that were bound to situations. Inversely, every actually present experience is inserted into the flow of lived experience and into

* In the analysis of stratifications of the life-world, we have often spoken of the stock of experience, or stock of knowledge. The description of the structure of subjective experiences of the life-world had to be broken off at several points, i.e., we had to be content with only an allusion to the role of the stock of knowledge. But in important places, the analysis of the taken-for-granted and the problematic already involved questions that could be adequately answered only by means of an exact investigation of the structure and genesis of the stock of knowledge, relevance structures, and typification. The same holds true for the description of the flow of experience and (in anticipation) for the analysis of the constitution and role of language in connection with different provinces of reality. In that we are now turning to a systematic description of the stock of knowledge, of relevance structures, and of typicality, we can refer on the one hand to past analyses of subjective experience of the temporal, spatial, and social stratifications of the life-world. On the other hand, in those places where the analyses had to be interrupted, we can continue and expand the analyses according to the perspectives suggested by the analysis of the stock of knowledge.

a biography, according to the set of types and relevance found in the stock of knowledge. And finally, each situation is defined and mastered with the help of the stock of knowledge. The stock of knowledge is thus related to the situation (viz., experience as bound to the situation) as much genetically as it is structurally and functionally. Before we can turn to the description of the genesis and structure of the stock of knowledge, it is therefore necessary to investigate more thoroughly the situational relatedness of the stock of knowledge. Although we can refer extensively to the prior analyses of the stratifications of the life-world,[1] the present problem will be to summarize and evaluate the results of these analyses. It will be shown that the limited nature of the situation and the spatial, temporal, and social arrangements of subjective experience of the life-world are fundamental elements of the stock of knowledge. These elements play another, more basic role in construction of the stock of knowledge than do specific experiences, which become partial contents in it. It will be further shown that the biographical articulation of experiences is decisive in the construction of the stock of knowledge, just as, on the other hand, the present (thus biographically articulated) stock of knowledge enters into orientation with the situation; it allows mastery of these experiences.

In every moment of conscious life I find myself in a situation. In its concrete contents this situation is indeed endlessly variable: on the one hand, because it is biologically articulated, so to speak, as the "product" of all prior situations; on the other hand, because it is relatively "open," that is, it can be defined and mastered on the basis of an actual stock of knowledge. It is unalterably "delineated" by the embedding of inner duration in a transcending world time and as a consequence of the insertability of the body into a structure of the life-world which is imposed on the experiencing subject.[2]

The transcendence of world time has various subjective correlates.[3] Vis-à-vis the permanence of world time, I experience my finitude. I experience the necessity of world time in waiting and in the subordination of my actions to the principle of "first things first." The specific historicality of my situation is contrasted to the authenticity of world time. In concrete experience these sub-

1. See Chap. 2.
2. See, in reference to this and the following, Chap. 2, B, esp. 2, 3, and 4.
3. See Chap. 2, B, 4, a.

jective correlates of the transcendence of world time intersect; my inner duration is inserted at the same time in world and in social time, and is related to the biological time of the body. If I do not want to drink my coffee bitter, I have to wait until the sugar is dissolved. If I want to ski, I have to wait until it snows or until the fracture is healed again. If I want to know the sum of different partial computations, I must first count the individual items in them. If I want to become a physician, first I have to study medicine. If I am a married man, I cannot at the same time be a bachelor, and if I have once been married, I can be a bachelor only as a widower or divorced person. As citizen of a certain country in the time in which I was born, I cannot keep an entry visa for certain other countries. If Don Quixote is born in the wrong time, only Sancho Panza can establish him in his knighthood.

Therefore, although the situation can also be concretely arranged in its structure through the "incongruence" among world time, biological time, social time, and inner duration, it is absolutely limited by the transcendence of world time. As a consequence the subjective correlates of the transcendence of world time have a special place in the lifeworldly stock of knowledge. As concrete experiences they are not simple, "latent," component contents of the stock of knowledge, which can be applied from case to case according to the situation. They are rather a fundamental element of the stock of knowledge imparted in each situation and each experience. Of course it is only through reflection in the theoretical attitude that I can get them in the grip of consciousness. In the natural attitude, in contrast, they are a necessary component of each experiential horizon, without themselves becoming the core of experience. Thus, the subjective correlates of the transcendence of world time are, as the limit of the situation, a fundamental element of the stock of knowledge, on which orientation in all situations is based.

In a related sense, each situation is also "limited" through the prior givenness of my body. For the body and its routine functionings is presupposed in each situation and experience, without necessarily belonging to the core of experience. The limits of my body vis-à-vis a world whose objects offer it resistance, and the routine functions of the body in the world are the basis of what is first taken as "obvious" in the stock of knowledge. We have good reasons to say "routine" rather than "normal." If I am born blind, colors, for instance, are not a part of the obvious or taken-for-granted realities of my experience of the life-world. I can of course learn from others that there "are" colors. But this is then a specific bit of knowledge formally resembling my knowledge that there "are" the Ural Mountains. Certain irreducible "self-evidencies" concerning my corporeality in the world are always "there." I cannot, to give the most obvious example, be in two places at the same time. Also, without having "acquired" this judgment step by step in concrete experiences, I always "know" about this fundamental reality in every situation. As trivial and self-evident as this example may sound, we only need to consider that it is just *as* "self-evident" and trivial that I can probably *do* two different things at the same time, e.g., drinking and eating. Purely theoretically, a world is quite conceivable in which that would also not be possible—but it is just not true of our life-world. My body is, as Merleau-Ponty has shown,[4] not an object in space, but rather the condition for all my experience of the spatial arrangement of the life-world. In every situation my body acts as a center of coordination in the world, with an above and below, right and left, behind and in front of. First, my body and its routine functioning is a fundamental element of every situation. Principally, it does not form a specific and "latent" component content in the stock of knowledge, but is rather much more a dimension of the stock of knowledge present continually in every experience and every situation. Here, though, a distinction must be maintained between this and the nature of the limitation upon the situation which arises through world time. Corporeality is indeed unalterably imposed on me as such. Thus, for instance, my "knowledge" that I can't be in two places at the same time can never be problematic; no lifeworldly experience can gainsay it. But if I were born blind and through an operation regained my sight, an empirical enrichment of the corporal finitude of my situation would result. The fundamental visual qualities of the life-world become a fundamental element of all further experiences and lose their status as a partial content of the stock of knowledge. Under no circumstances are they "latent" elements of the stock of knowledge, applied or not applied to situations according to their relevance and typicality; nor are they modified by concrete experiences. With this we also come to the transition

4. *Phénoménologie de la perception* (Paris: Gallimard, 1945), p. 119. [English translation by Colin Smith, *Phenomenology of Perception* (London: Routledge & Kegan Paul, 1962), pp. 102, 103.]

from the limited nature of the situation, from the unalterably imposed nature of the ontological world structure, to the structure of the subjective experiences of the life-world.

b. The structure of subjective experiences of the life-world as the second fundamental element of the stock of knowledge

We have seen that the situation is "limited," that this limitation is unalterably imposed on the living subject, and that it is an ever-present, fundamental element of every situation and every experience. We have also already been able to show that experiences within the limitation of the situation have a basic spatial, temporal, and social arrangement. This arrangement is also "imposed" on the living subject—and is derived in a certain sense from the limitedness of the situation. The arrangement of the subjective experiences of the life-world is also "self-evident"; the life-world can only be experienced on the basis of this arrangement. Accordingly, the arrangement is not a partial content of the stock of knowledge (as e.g., the knowledge that a whale is a mammal, or indeed that the president of the United States, but not senators, must be a citizen by birth) but rather forms an ever-present knowledge contained in every horizon of experience.

Since we have already fully described this arrangement,[5] we can confine ourselves here to a short summary. In every situation only a certain segment of the world is given to me. Only part of the world is in actual reach. But around this province, other provinces of restorable or attainable reach are differentiated, their spheres of reach exhibiting a temporal as well as a social structure.[6] Further, I can operate only in one segment of the world. Around the actual zone of operation there are graduated zones that are again restorable or attainable, possessing in any case a temporal and social structure.[7] My experience of the life-world is also temporally arranged: inner duration is a flow of lived experience arising from present, retentive, and protentive phases, as also from memories and expectations. It is intersected by world time, biological time, and social time, and is sedimented in the unique sequence of an articulated biography.[8] And finally,

5. See Chap. 2.
6. See Chap. 2, B, 2, and Chap. 2, B, 4, b.
7. See Chap. 2, B, 3.
8. See Chap. 2, B, 4, esp. B, 4, c, and also B, 6.

my experience is socially arranged. All experiences have a social dimension, just as the temporal and spatial arrangement of my experience is also "socialized." As a consequence, my experience of the social world has a specific structure. The Other is given to me immediately as a fellow-man in the we-relation, while the mediate experiences of the social world are graduated according to degrees of anonymity and are arranged in experiences of the contemporary world, the world of predecessors, and the world of successors.[9]

The above does not concern specific, concrete, and variable experiences, but rather the fundamental structures of experience of the life-world. In contrast to specific experiences, these fundamental structures do not enter into the grip of consciousness in the natural attitude, as a core of experience. But they are a condition of every experience of the life-world and enter into the horizon of experience. They are not conditions in the same sense as when I speak of the circulation of the blood as a "condition" for the perfusion of the brain, and of the perfusion of the brain as a "condition" for thinking. These are component contents of my stock of knowledge, which, arising from a historical phase of a certain science, have entered a certain relative-natural world view, and from which I have acquired knowledge on the basis of my biographical situation. They have in no way entered into the horizon of experience of all my experiences, much less into the horizon of experience of other men who "know" nothing of them. In contrast, each experience "obviously" or "self-evidently" has an unchangeable spatial, temporal, and social arrangement. This arrangement need not arise from theoretical knowledge and enter into the relative-natural world view before everyone "knows" of it. In contrast to specific experiences and typifications of the stock of knowledge built up on them (the whale is a fish), this "knowledge" can never become problematic. And in addition, in the natural attitude it is never articulated as specific knowledge. Concrete experiences and typifications stratified on them, however "abstract" they may be, can always be questioned, modified, or even "exploded" by means of new experiences. This is not the case with the fundamental structures of the subjective experience of the life-world. *Nevertheless*, they belong in a certain sense to the stock of knowledge. I always "know," whether or not an Other is immediately given to me, whether or not an object is

9. See Chap. 2, B, 5.

in reach, whether or not something is in my work zone, etc. In every case each new experience contains such "knowledge" in its horizon of experience. The structure of subjective experience of the life-world is therefore a fundamental element of the stock of knowledge.

Not only the what but also the how of the individual situation in the life-world belongs to the fundamental element of the stock of knowledge. Among its fundamental elements are the complexly stratified limitation of inner duration, the course of the life, within a continuing, fixed, and historical (and thereby social) world time, as well as the limitation of the body (and of its usual functioning) vis-à-vis an objective world which offers resistance. But the fundamental spatial, temporal, and social structures of experience also belong to the fundamental elements of the stock of knowledge. One must stress again that these elements are "on hand" in another way—as specific component elements, of which we can say that they are simply "at hand." [10] They are cogiven in every situation's horizon (i.e., in every horizon of experience), while component elements are thematized as cores of experience in certain circumstances, or play a decisive role in the thematization.

c. Routine in the stock of knowledge: skills, useful knowledge, knowledge of recipes

Between the basic elements of the stock of knowledge and its specific component contents, routine knowledge occupies a middle position. When we differentiate between elements of knowledge on hand in every situation and those simply at hand, routine knowledge seems to be ordered partly according to one and partly according to the other type. Let us look at this curious hybrid position a bit more closely.

Between certain fundamental elements of the stock of knowl-

10. [Here *vorhanden* is translated as "on hand" and *zuhanden* as "at hand," rather than according to the precedent, for example, set by the translators of Heidegger's *Being and Time*, John MacQuarrie and Edward Robinson (New York: Harper & Row, 1962). They chose "present at hand" and "ready to hand," respectively. The choice for our translation was determined by Schutz's own usage. See, for example, *Reflections on the Problem of Relevance*, ed. Richard M. Zaner (New Haven: Yale University Press, 1970), pp. 144 and 145 n. Also, Alfred Schutz, *Collected Papers*, Vol. I: *The Problem of Social Reality*, ed. Maurice Natanson (The Hague: Nijhoff, 1962), pp. 20, 208.]

edge and certain provinces of habitual knowledge, one cannot draw a sharp line. The latter joins with the former. Knowledge about corporeality, its usual functioning and the spatial and temporal arrangement immediately founded on it (the organization of subjective experience of the life-world), a knowledge necessarily given in every situational and experiential horizon, goes over into specific forms of knowledge concerning the usual functioning of the body. Knowledge about corporeality as such (as distinguished from an objective world which offers resistance), as well as knowledge about functioning, which is not really learned but is experienceable and sometimes even "consciously" realized (such as breathing and swallowing), must be considered as part of the ever-present, fundamental elements of the stock of knowledge. Specific expressions of knowledge about the limits of the body, the "body image," although they are based on fundamental elements, are to a certain degree learned and are consequently variable. One can see this from ethnological literature, and from investigations of the effects of the traumatic loss of limbs upon the body image.

But there are also everyday examples of this. Think only of how we get used to the "hole in our mouth" after a tooth has been pulled. First it is completely foreign to us, a motive for continually touching it with the tongue. It is "brought into relief" by its contrast with the "self-evidencies" of the body. In the course of time, we "learn" to come to terms with it; it becomes a completely routine element of our habitual knowledge.

What has been said holds good in much stronger measure for the habitual, functional unities of bodily movement. Although kinetic experience is built up on "nonlearned" basic elements, these are able to be learned. Walking must be learned. Swimming must be learned, eating with cutlery must be learned, even watching a tennis match must in a certain sense (apart from learning the Objective meaning of the rules of the game) be learned. All these are examples of formerly "problematic" experiences (viz., activities) through which the problem was "solved," and indeed "definitively" solved. It is clear that this is only an empirically relative "definitiveness." Such knowledge of mine indeed remains taken for granted as obvious, but the performances can again become "problematic," if only in their execution. After a longer convalescence I have "unlearned" walking; I must learn it again from the beginning. That holds good, even if only in the extreme case, for swimming. If someone wants to ski again after fifteen years, he will notice the discrepancy between his "knowledge" and the performance. Such habitual, functional unities of bodily movement (in the broadest sense) as have built upon the fundamental elements of the usual functioning of the body, we will term *skills*.

There is a province of habitual knowledge which concerns skills, but which no longer really belongs to the usual functioning of the body. We will term this *useful knowledge*. There are in daily life, or more exactly, in the work zone of the everyday world, certain goals of acts *and* "means to the end" that belong to it, and that no longer indicate the slightest problem. They were originally "problematical" but have been "definitively" solved. For the goals of acts there is not a single motivation on hand, and for the "means to the end" there is no known alternative. There are activities that have to a great extent lost the character of acts. I would indeed have to learn them, but the continuing realizability of the goals and the exclusiveness of the "means" that can be used has so often been confirmed, the skills on which they touch are so self-evidently "obvious," that they have won a high degree of trustworthiness (and subjective certainty). It is completely "self-evident" to us that we "can do" this or that. The idealization of the "I can always do it again" cannot miscarry here. We do not need to look at the activities forming this useful knowledge. We do it "automatically," and the activity is "standardized." Let us first introduce examples of this knowledge of usage which are still closely related to skills: smoking, chopping wood, shaving, writing, etc. Obviously, the borderline for these skills is flexible. Further examples: playing the piano, riding, but also adding, talking (especially impressive: speaking a foreign language, whereby we can observe the processes of routinization more or less consciously). Further: heating the oven, frying eggs, etc.

Finally, we can distinguish a form of habitual knowledge, which is not sharply delimited from, has many areas of overlapping with, but is not identical with useful knowledge: *knowledge of recipes*. This knowledge is indeed no longer associated with the basic elements of the stock of knowledge immediately concerning skills. But it is still "automated" and "standardized." This means that it can be on hand as a "self-evident" implication, especially in the horizon of situations, without becoming thematized. For example: a hunter reading tracks, a sailor or mountain climber orienting himself to changes in the weather, an interpreter "automatically" translating phrases, etc. The farther we go from the intersections with this practical knowledge, the more the knowledge of recipes approaches the stock of knowledge in the narrower sense, namely, the "system" of specific component contents.

Habitual knowledge is on hand in situations, not simply at hand from case to case. (This holds true in decreasing measure from skills to knowledge of recipes.) Habitual knowledge in all its forms shares this in common with the basic elements of the stock of knowledge. In any case, it is not necessarily cogiven in the horizon of every situation, viz., experience, rather it is only *continually* "ready to grasp." It is differentiated from the stock of knowledge in the narrower sense, insofar as it is not thematized and is rather automatically included in situations and acts. Habitual knowledge presents "definitive" solutions to problems, which are organized in the flow of lived experience without one having to give them attention. That means that they can be subordinated and coordinated to a core of experience, and above all to a predominant act. I can whistle a song while I walk *and* think about a mathematical problem. I can smoke while I write, write while I look for words, etc. I can play a musical instrument without being careful about the fingering, even without "consciously" reading the notes, and concentrate "completely" on the meaning (the thematic articulation) of the piece being played. Naturally, as many examples of this can be given as one wants. They all concern combinations of skills, useful knowledge, or knowledge of recipes. The possible explications of the horizon of the forms of habitual knowledge under discussion have been discontinued not just "provisionally," for the present problem and until further notice, but "once and for all." Routine knowledge and the "automatized" skills associated with it hold good as absolutely trustworthy, unquestionably realizable. They are applicable and can be included as obvious, taken-for-granted elements, ready to be grasped at any time in the solution of specific "problems." They are unquestionably "means to an end" in the realization of open plans of acts. It is important to stress this unquestionableness vigorously. If I, for example, want to buy a gift for someone, I may consider what may please him, how much I can spend, where it can be bought, etc. But I do not include in my plans the "completely automatized" elements of my habitual knowledge, from skills to knowledge of recipes: e.g., that I must necessarily place one leg in front of the other in order to get to the shop, that I will have to point to the item, that I will have to speak, etc.

Without anticipating the analysis of relevance structures,[11] it can already be maintained that habitual knowledge exhibits a paradoxical relevance structure. It is of the greatest relevance and yet of, so to speak, subordinate relevance. It is a determining characteristic of routine that it can be performed without it coming to one's attention, therefore without it becoming thematic in the cores of experience. Routine is continually ready to be grasped without coming into the distinct grasp of consciousness proper. Habitual knowledge is continually, yet marginally, relevant.

Yet a further point should now be realized. In another sense, habitual knowledge occupies a hybrid position between the basic elements of the stock of knowledge and the stock of knowledge in the narrower sense. The former elements are universal and in principle invariant, with the qualification already mentioned. For example, such basic elements are not absolutely identical for the world of a blind man and the world of the "normal" person. The basic elements of the stock of knowledge are on hand for everyone; they are the same in whatever relative-natural world view he was socialized. The relative-natural world views are differentiated in any case with regard to the degree to which these basic elements are thematized and verbally objectivated. The stock of knowledge in the narrower sense is in contrast different from one relative-natural world view to the next and demonstrates a more or less complex distribution within the society. Habitual knowledge lies in the middle. A certain amount of habitual knowledge (skills and useful knowledge as well as knowledge of recipes) belongs to everyone's stock of knowledge. The "content" of this knowledge is indeed variable, but not in the same sense that the partial contents of the stock of knowledge are variable from one society to the next and within a society.

Even in the border province between the basic elements of the stock of knowledge and routine knowledge, there are forms of knowledge of one's own body which are not the same in all societies and need not be the same within the same society. Thus the limits of the body and even the experience of it as a unity are not in the same way, and always in the same degree, socially objectivated (that is, above all verbally).[12]

This is even more the case with skills. They are different

11. See Chap. 3, B.
12. See, for example, Bruno Snell, *Die Entdeckung des Geistes* (Hamburg: Claassen, 1955).

from society to society as well as within a society. It is difficult but not theoretically impossible to imagine a society of non-walkers. It is a well-documented fact that the style of walking varies from one relative-natural world view to the next. A Roman did not walk like a Hun; an Eskimo does not walk like an American. This example suggests a highly differentiated, intrasocial distribution. A soldier walks differently from a civilian, a sailor differently from a landlubber, a prostitute differently from a matron. But walking must still be considered one of the routines that comes closest to being a basic element of the ordinary functioning of the body. Other functional unities of movement, and the knowledge associated with them, exhibit an increasingly greater intercultural and intrasocial differentiation. Specific work skills and martial, athletic, artistic skills such as archery, riflery, playing the piano (also seen only as "finger skill"), etc., are examples. The transition from skills to useful knowledge and from this to knowledge of recipes is unnoticeable. Think of a particular "recipe"—analogously, proverbs or ways of working in agriculture, riding, finally also in cuisine, etc. Here we are again coming to the stock of knowledge in the narrower sense. A cookbook, for example, is no longer knowledge of recipes in our sense, but is already a thematization and social objectivation of a specific knowledge.

Indeed, a reserve of habitual knowledge belongs to everyone's stock of knowledge. One can even establish an empirical typology of the variability of habitual knowledge. A society of nonwalkers is only theoretically conceivable, but it is an empirical impossibility. The theoretical limiting case of such a typology would be the case in which, contextually, certain forms of routine knowledge would be different for every individual: in this case, what is routine for me would be "problematic" and the reverse for everyone else. Fundamentally, we can say that the farther we go from the basic elements of the stock of knowledge (which above all in this context are to be understood as the knowledge related to the usual functioning of the body), the more differentiated the intercultural expression and intrasocial distribution of habitual knowledge becomes.

With regard to habitual knowledge one must still note that skills and practical knowledge belong to the everyday life-world. This is also the case for an extensive portion of the knowledge of recipes, but not for the knowledge of recipes in general. Routinization can also enter into other provinces of finite meaning-structure. In one (in any case outwardly limited) sense, one can, for example, speak of dream routines. Surely there are forms of habitual knowledge in different fantasy worlds. Some of these forms border on so-called hallucinations. These are "self-evident" with regard to any further explication or variation of discrete elements in the courses of the fantasies. There is habitual knowledge in scientific thinking, even if this cannot be legitimated in terms of scientific theory. Further, there is habitual knowledge in religious-symbolic provinces of reality. There it typically assumes the form of ritual elements. It would, though, be misleading simply to identify ritual as such (it has a socially thematized and objectivated sense) with practically useful knowledge or knowledge of recipes.

d. Biographical character of the stock of knowledge

Situation and the stock of knowledge both have a history. The latter is the "product" of experiences sedimented in it; the former is the "result" of prior situations. We will still have to investigate exhaustively the genesis of the stock of knowledge.[13] But at this juncture let us look at that aspect immediately connected with the situation-relatedness of the stock of knowledge, namely, its biographical character. In general we can begin with the premise that the situation is defined through the insertion of individual existence into the ontological structure of the world. It is "known" not just as an absolute limit (finitude, corporeality, etc.), but is experienced rather as the condition for the sequence of situations during the course of life, and as the reach of action in the situation (zone of operation). It is not only that every actual experience has its prior history. Every present situation is, in addition, biographically articulated within its "known" limits: it is the province of what is open *to me now* to control. In this sense, the biographical character of the present situation forms an element of my stock of knowledge. This must be examined in more detail.

The present situation is biographically articulated. That means that I "know" more or less adequately that it is the "result" of prior situations. And further, I "know" that this, my situation, is in that respect absolutely "unique." Indeed, the stock of knowledge, through which I determine the present situation, has its "unique" biographical articulation. This refers not only to the content, the "meaning" of all the prior experiences sedimented in

13. See Chap. 3, B, 2.

it, in situations. It refers also to the intensity (lived experiential nearness and depth), duration, and sequence of these experiences. This circumstance is of singular importance, since it really constitutes the unique biographical articulation of the individual stock of knowledge (and thereby the actual situation).

Let us assume that two persons have exactly the same stock of knowledge. What would this assumption presuppose? Not only that the two had the same experiences, that is, with regard to their "content," but also that these experiences lasted the same length of time in the two streams of consciousness, had the same experiential depth and nearness, and above all that the sequence of the individual experiences was identical for both. Bergson has shown that in order to grant that the content of consciousness of the two persons is the same, all these presuppositions must be given, and that one then could no longer speak of two persons.[14] This completely ignores the original historicality of the individual situation. Imagine that Aristotle, that is, a child with talents identical with those of the historical Aristotle, was born before Plato. Could he still become "Aristotle"? Or, imagine that Plato and Aristotle were born as identical twins!

Although experiences are in principle "socialized" and inserted in quite anonymous, idealized, and above all verbally objectivated meaning-contexts, and although they enter the stock of knowledge of the individual in this state, they are in principle unique in their biographical articulation. Such Objective, anonymous, and ideal elements of the stock of knowledge indicate their biographically articulated constitution. The stock of knowledge always has a "private" component.

But all experiences are not socialized in the same way. Some provinces of experiences, as we have seen, are only mediately, "weakly," and fragmentarily socialized. But such experiences also enter my stock of knowledge, even if not in the same fashion as the quite socialized experiences of daily life. They enter rather with the subscript "dream experience," "fantasy," etc. Such essentially "private" experiences also have a fundamental meaning for the stock of knowledge and for the use of the stock of knowledge in situations of the everyday life-world, for example in fantasizing projects for possible acts.

Finally, another aspect of the biographical character of the

14. [See Henri Bergson, *Essai sur les données immédiates de la conscience* (Paris: Alcan, 1938), pp. 139–42.]

stock of knowledge must be discussed. My habitual knowledge is in principle biographically articulated. I acquire different skills (walking, talking, etc.), which all others also acquire, even in approximately the same sequence; consequently, individual variations from the socially categorized or even prescribed sequence of acquisition can be of decisive biographical import. Broad provinces of practical knowledge are also more or less similarly socially distributed. This is also the case for broad provinces of knowledge of recipes. There are, however, skills, practical knowledge, and knowledge of recipes which are specifically constituted in "private" experiences. Thus, a highly specific, biographically articulated element enters into the determination of my actually present situation. And, it is obvious that the *combination* of skills, practical knowledge, and knowledge of recipes, completely ignoring the sequence of acquisition, is biographically articulated and "unique."

In short, the sequence, experiential nearness, experiential depth, and duration of experience (even with regard to experiences with "similar content") determine the unique biographical articulation of the stock of knowledge. This even holds good for "highly socialized" experiences, and is especially the case for essentially "private" experiences and various "private" constellations of routine. On the other hand, it must be stressed once again that sequence, experiential depth and nearness, and even the duration of experiences and the acquisition of knowledge, are socially objectivated and determined. In other words, there are social categories of biographical articulation.[15]

e. The determination of the situation

The course of life is a series of situations. It is indeed pertinent that I always find myself (as existential philosophy expresses it) "in situations." But at the same time the situation is "defined," to use a concept which has been adopted by sociology since W. I. Thomas.[16] What does it mean? We have already spoken of [17] the fact that the situation is partly imposed on, partly so to speak "feasible" for, the individual. Let us look more closely

15. See Chap. 2, B, 6.
16. [A pioneer American sociologist (1863–1947). See *Social Organization and Social Personality*, ed. Morris Janowitz (Chicago: University of Chicago Press, 1960).]
17. See Chap. 2, B, 6.

at the relation of these two dimensions of the situation, and how the relation operates in its determination.

In every situation, the ontological structure of the world is imposed on me. The situation is absolutely *limited:* knowledge of this is a basic element of the stock of knowledge.[18] The structure of the subjective experience of the life-world is also imposed on me: the arrangement into provinces of finite meaning-structure with their own experiential style, and further the spatial, temporal, and social structures of every experience. The situation is consequently unalterably prestructured: knowledge of this is a basic element of the stock of knowledge.[19] In this sense, the situation is limited from the very beginning; it is articulated and predetermined.

Further, every situation is biographically imprinted. It has its specific prior history, which I "know." Moreover, I come into the situation with a specific, biographically articulated stock of habitual knowledge of skills, practical knowledge, and knowledge of recipes.[20] My biography is in fact not "imposed" on me in the same sense as the ontological world structure, but it is precisely as unalterable. I could have done this or that differently; then the present situation would be "other." But I did not do it; therefore the present situation is just so and not otherwise.

Here we are at the transition from the imposed to the "open" elements of the situation. I can no longer change the previous history of the situation, but within the present situation there are elements which I can influence, which I can change. In this way I in turn effect a *fait accompli* vis-à-vis future situations. That is a further circumstance which I "know" in the natural attitude.

To be able to act in the situation I must determine it. The situation is, as was said, already predetermined—through knowledge of the limitation of the situation, knowledge of the structuring of subjective experience in it, and knowledge of the biographical articulation of the situation. All this belongs to the basic elements of the stock of knowledge and "automatically" enters into the determination of every situation. The situation is also "open." How are the "open" elements determinable?

Fundamentally, these elements can be *explicated without limit.* Every situation has an infinite inner and outer horizon; it

18. See Chap. 3, A, 1, a.
19. See Chap. 3, A, 1, b.
20. See Chap. 3, A, 1, c and d.

is able to be explicated according to its relations to other situations, experiences, etc., with respect to its prior history and its future. At the same time, with respect to the details constituting it, it is divisible and interpretable without limit. This holds good only in principle. Practically every situation is only *limitedly in need of explication*. The plan-determined interest, which is derived from the hierarchy of plans in the course of life, limits the necessity for the determination of the situation. The situation needs to be determined only insofar as this is necessary for mastering it.[21] The plan-determined interest selects the "open" elements of the situation which are to be determined in greater detail, against the background of the predetermined (i.e., pre-structured) elements of the situation. At the same time the plan-determined interest limits the process of explication through which the situation is determined to that which is "practically necessary," that is, to that which is relevant for mastering the situation.

The determination of "open" elements of the situation occurs as well with the help of the present stock of knowledge, which is brought into the situation. In any case this occurs differently from the way I know "automatically" about the predeterminateness of the situation with the help of the basic elements of the stock of knowledge. We can differentiate various types of determination. First, the situation can be sufficiently determined, with the aid of habitual knowledge, so that the plan-determined interest is satisfied. All "open" elements of the situation can be routinely determined. The situation is then unproblematic, even in those of its elements that are not already predetermined. We will call this kind of situation a *routine situation*. Second, "open" elements of the situation can be on hand, but not routinely determined. If such "new" elements enter into a situation, I must "deliberate." That is, I consciously try to correlate these elements with my stock of knowledge. Let us first assume that completely new elements are also explicated with the help of interpretation schemata and typifications which are on hand, but not sufficiently for my plan-determined interest. My knowledge is not "clear" enough, "sure" enough, not sufficiently free of contradiction, for me to handle the current situation. I must thus further explicate the "open" elements of the situation until they have achieved the level of clarity, familiarity, and freedom from contradiction al-

21. See Chap. 3, A, 1, f.

ready given in the plan-determined interest.[22] We will call such situations *problematic situations*. In contrast to routine situations, I must here either acquire new elements of knowledge or take old ones which are not sufficiently clarified for the present situation, and bring them to higher levels of clarity.

Without entering into a detailed description of the social dimension of the determinations of the situation,[23] we will in anticipation point out that the situation is socially determined in a double sense. First, the categories of *every* determination of the situation have a predominantly social origin, as does general knowledge about the life-world. The categories are to a great extent socially objectivated, above all, in language, as a highly anonymous system of meaning.[24] Second, situations that are in a narrow sense *social* are, however, *reciprocally* determined by the partners in the situation.[25]

f. Mastering the situation

We cannot be satisfied with the previous formal allusions, even though an exact description of the plan-determined interest can be made only in connection with an analysis of relevance structures.[26] What does it 'mean to assert that plan-determined interest enters into the determination of the situation? It means chiefly that the choice to interpret "open" and not routinely determinable elements of the situation is pragmatically motivated. In principle there are in every situation unlimited possibilities for determination which are not followed because they are irrelevant to the mastery of the *current* situation. Let us examine this. If I am busy chopping wood, the situation is routinely determined. Let us assume that the plan-determined interest is "production of firewood" (it could be, for instance, "losing weight," "getting in condition," etc.). Of course, all basic elements of the stock of knowledge "automatically" enter into the situation: I know that I can use only a limited amount of time for chopping wood, that I will get tired; I know that I am avoiding other possibilities for work and experience, that I can injure myself with the ax, even fatally, that I have to carry through movements in

22. See, concerning this, Chap. 3, A, 3.
23. See Chap. 3, A, 1, e, and Chap. 5 [Vol. II].
24. See Chap. 4, B, 2.
25. See Chap. 5 [Vol. II].
26. See Chap. 3, B, 4 and 5.

order to split the logs—objects in the outer world that resist me, etc. I bring certain skills to the situation: I have often chopped wood and am an experienced log splitter. These are all predetermined elements of the situation, partly imposed on me, partly biographically articulated. Through the plan-determined interest, the "duration" of the situation is also predetermined: when I have chopped so-and-so much firewood, I can quit (or correspondingly, if I have spent one hour splitting wood, sweating, losing weight, etc.). This is, thus, a situation belonging completely to the type "routine situation." If I chop at a log that does not split, even with the strongest strokes, a "new" element has emerged. Let us assume that this element is not routinely determinable—e.g., there are knots in the grain, the ax got dull with the last stroke, slipping and falling blade first on a rock. In this case the situation is not yet outside the routine. The situation is now "problematic." I must "remember": what kind of reasons can there be for not being able to split the log? I draw on my stock of knowledge: there are unusually hard kinds of wood; the other logs are indeed ordinary spruce wood, but through an "accident" a different kind of log has gotten mixed in. I look at the problematic log; it does in fact look different. In a way, the problem is solved for me: I put the log to the side and continue splitting the other wood. To which unique variety of wood does this log belong? What kind of "accident" caused it to be mixed in with the other firewood? etc. Such questions do not "interest" me. They are irrelevant for the mastery of the situation; therefore I do not go "to the bottom" of them. The "new" element in the routine situation is consequently determined only to a very low degree of clarity (in contrast, for example, to knowledge: aha! mahogany; the lumber merchant whom I know really made good on his threat in a moment of madness and sawed up his wife's favorite mahogany table, etc.); this degree of clarity is pragmatically sufficient.

Or let us take as an example a problematic social situation. I meet someone whose face I recognize, who speaks to me in a friendly manner, but whose name and other particulars, at the moment I cannot remember. Again, the situation is to a certain degree predetermined in a way analogous to the earlier example, wherein the obvious, taken-for-granted, imposed aspects of a social situation in general, of the specific relative-natural world view, etc., played a special role. The situation is to a great extent "open": I cannot "place" my partner in the situation and must try to determine the situation in greater detail. I use my stock of knowledge in order to interpret further the elements in the situation. He greets me in a friendly fashion, I know the face. He would appear to be a more or less friendly acquaintance. I guess his age, his social status, in order to get a first narrowing of the open possibilities. Then I let him talk; perhaps he will mention a common acquaintance, inquire about some special circumstance in my biography, etc. At some time it will occur to me: that is the brother of my friend X. My wish not to offend the man by having to confess that I cannot remember him, though he obviously knows me well, is satisfied. The situation is sufficiently determined and can be brought into a routine. Again, various aspects of the situation which are in principle determinable remain undetermined, since they are irrelevant to the mastery of *this* situation.

We can concretely see in these examples how the plan-determined interest determines not only the choice of the elements to be determined but also the point at which the exposition can be broken off and can leave the situation sufficiently determined. The plan-determined interest is obviously included in the situation and is also to a certain extent "swept along" by the situation and modified. On the other hand it is incorporated into a hierarchy of plans. That means that it is subjectively experienced as a "task" or a "goal," with a certain level of urgency. This urgency derives from the system of priorities in the course of life, which is ramified in subordinate systems for the course of the day, for work and leisure, for everyday reality, and also for other provinces of meaning (for instance, for specifically religious achievements), etc. We only need remember the example of chopping wood: I split firewood so that I can heat the oven in my study, so that I can, without danger to my health, work on a manuscript that I want to write . . . , etc. If, on the other hand, I engaged in the wood chopping to lose weight, this interest could be similarly placed within the hierarchy of my plans.

A further remark should be added. Naturally, plan-determined interest has had a determining role in all previous situations. It has motivated the routinization of certain elements of knowledge, skills, etc., for situations "typically" of this kind. The plan-determined interest is consequently not only an immediate factor in the determination and exposition of *problematic* situations, but also enters as a matter of course into the formation of *routine situations* and their routine determination.

2. THE ACQUISITION OF KNOWLEDGE

a. Conditions for the acquisition of knowledge

The acquisition of knowledge is the sedimentation of current experiences in meaning-structures, according to relevance and typicality. These in turn have a role in the determination of current situations and the explication of current experiences. That means, among other things, that no element of knowledge can be traced to any sort of "primordial experience." In analyzing the processes of sedimentation which lead to the development of the stock of knowledge, we always encounter prior experiences in which an already determined, albeit minimal, stock of knowledge must be conjoined. Although we especially want to investigate the role of relevance structures and typification in the formation of the stock of knowledge,[27] we can anticipate this analysis to a certain extent and describe the acquisition of knowledge as a process in inner duration. This acquisition, as a sedimentation of experiences, results from situations and is biographically articulated. Let us begin with the description of the conditions of the acquisition of knowledge, since this can be brief. It is concerned fundamentally with the conditions of the situation and the flow of experience in the course of the day and in the course of life, which we have already investigated.[28]

As an event in inner duration, the acquisition of knowledge is articulated in the structures of subjective time.[29] Experiences are constituted by the attentive focusing within "unities of time" which are determined by means of the tension of consciousness and its rhythm—thus in the "flying stretches and resting places" of the stream of consciousness.[30] The actually present phases of the stream of consciousness contain in their horizon retentions and protensions of proximal phases, as well as memories and expectations whose span is determined through the situationally related interest. The experiences are built up polythetically. Their

27. See Chap. 3, B and C.
28. See Chap. 2, B, 4 and 6, and Chap. 3, A, 1.
29. See Chap. 2, B, 4, c.
30. [A phrase taken from William James. See *Principles of Psychology*, 2 vols. (New York: Henry, 1890), I, 243. Also, see Schutz, *Reflections on the Problem of Relevance* (New Haven: Yale University Press, 1970), p. 86.]

meaning, though, can be grasped monothetically by a "motivated" focusing of one's regard. This is of greatest importance for the processes through which experiences are sedimented in the stock of knowledge. In general, the polythetic arrangement of the experiences is "carried off." Only their typically relevant meaning, monothetically grasped, enters the stock of knowledge as "definitively" worthy of notice. The reference back to the polythetical arrangement is indeed necessarily cogiven, but the polythetic steps are only "more or less" empirically reconstructable. Obviously this does not hold good in the same way for experiences with essentially polythetic meaning-structure (for example, a musical theme). In principle we can now say that the degree of clarity and determination of an element of knowledge is decisively influenced by the possibility of reconstructing the polythetical steps in which the experience in question was sedimented in the stock of knowledge. The familiarity of the elements of knowledge also depends in part on this circumstance.

The processes of explication, in which the inner and outer horizon of a problematic experience, or of a problematic situation, is explicated, are naturally processes in inner duration and are articulated in the structures of subjective time.[31] Naturally, this not only holds good for the routine determination of situations and the routine flow of experiences and processes, which are, so to speak, "automatic" and which presuppose a relatively slight tension of consciousness. But this also holds good for explications in a narrow sense, that is, for assumptions, judgments, inferences, etc., thus for thinking that is, at least in principle, executed through the categories of formal logic. Every predication is an event in inner duration. The execution of the judgment "S is p," is a polythetical dissection of a unitary "natural" experience—"The-package-of-cards-on-the-table," as William James clearly described such an experience.[32] In executing the judgment, this experience is a step-by-step breaking up into individual elements, and these are then placed in relation to one another. "S is p" is the result of a process of explication, in which, among other things, it was considered that S is not only p but also q and r, etc. In virtue of the situationally related interest in the previous problem, the p-quality of S was selected out as noteworthy (and re-markable). After this process of explication, I

31. See again Chap. 2, B, 4, and also Chap. 1, B.
32. [James, *Principles*, I, 278–79.]

can thus monothetically grasp the relation "S is p" so that the q-, r-, s-, etc., qualities of S are no longer in my grasp. The polythetic-monothetic structure of the acquisition of knowledge is illustrated even more strikingly by an example taken from secondary education. In school we derived the Pythagorean theorem from the Euclidean axioms and theorems, until we got the formula, $a^2 + b^2 = c^2$. We understand the sense of the theorem without having to repeat the individual steps of the derivation again and again: in a right triangle, the sum of the squares of the sides is the same as the square of the hypotenuse. In principle, the derivation is always reconstructable, even if we have "forgotten" it. But it is clear that the degree of clarity, and in a certain sense even the degree of familiarity, in my knowledge of the Pythagorean theorem is essentially influenced by whether I can "more or less" repeat the polythetic steps of the derivation or not. In this sense, we can establish the temporal articulation of the sedimentation of experience as a condition for the acquisition of knowledge. We can say further that all conditions for the constitution of experiences in situations are mediately the conditions for the acquisition of knowledge. But even the *sedimentation* of experiences, thus the actual acquisition of knowledge, obviously takes place in situations where the conditions of the situation are at the same time also immediately the conditions for the acquisition of knowledge. So the limits of the situation are at the same time also the limits for the acquisition of knowledge. We have already noticed that knowledge concerning this circumstance is one of the basic elements of the stock of knowledge on hand.[33] The acquisition of knowledge as such falls under the principle of "first things first," in its employment both in the course of the day as well as in the course of life. It is interrupted by exhaustion, requires waiting for the "right" time, etc. If I look up an article in a lexicon, I can be "misled" by interest in the subject to look up a cross-reference to another. But then I have to "sacrifice" time I had previously, in my daily plan (and my life-plan), assigned to work on an essay.

Along with all the other elements imposed in the situation, the structures of subjective experiences of the life-world are also conditions for the acquisition of knowledge. The temporal, spatial, and social arrangements determining the form of actually present experience remain, in principle, contained in the sedi-

33. See Chap. 3, A, 1, a.

mentation of experience in the stock of knowledge. One aspect of this is in a way analogous to the preservation of polythetic elements of monothetic meaning: the experiences are modified, that is, idealized, anonymized, typified, if they enter into the stock of knowledge. Thus, the structural "predelineations" of the actual experience are "neutralized," that is, reshaped. They thus do not remain in grasp and normally do not become a component of the elements of knowledge. They can, however, in principle be reconstructed (even if only "more or less" exactly) in memory and in this way can "sustain" the degree of familiarity in the idealized and anonymized elements of the knowledge concerned.

Further, the arrangement of the life-world into various provinces with finite meaning-structure is a factor in the sedimentation of experiences, if not a "condition." The respective "predelineations" of the actual experiences undergoing sedimentation are preserved. They go into the stock of knowledge, entering the respective provinces of it as everyday experiences, as fantasies, as dream experiences.

And finally, the acquisition of knowledge is, as is every situation, biographically molded in the situation in which it occurs. The acquisition of knowledge as such has its history: in a strict sense, the history of the successive acquisition of elements of knowledge. In an individual course of life, this history can at the same time be grasped more broadly as the "history of ideas." In any case, the acquisition of knowledge is irrevocably inserted into the whole biography.

b. *The structuring of the stock of knowledge through the forms of the acquisition of knowledge*

We must proceed from the fact that the lifeworldly stock of knowledge is not the result of rational cognitive events in the theoretical attitude. The elements of the lifeworldly stock of knowledge are not clear and contradictionless propositions which are systematically ordered into a hierarchy of universality. The structure of the lifeworldly stock of knowledge resembles neither the logical systematic of a nonempirical science, as for instance algebra, nor the fabric of the interpretational schemata, taxonomies, laws, and hypotheses found within the empirical sciences. Insofar as there are similarities at all, they are to be traced back to the fact that the theoretic-scientific attitude is founded on the natural attitude. It would be misleading if we proceeded with the description of the lifeworldly stock of knowledge with an ideal of knowledge that was historically, socially, and culturally limited —no matter how decisively such an ideal may determine our own interest in an exact analysis of the life-world.

Rather, we must proceed from the fact that the lifeworldly stock of knowledge is the result of the sedimentation of subjective experiences of the life-world. If the structure of the stock of knowledge contains heterogeneous elements, then it can in principle be traced back to the heterogeneity of the events in which lifeworldly knowledge is acquired. We can first grasp such a concept in a broad sense, and assume that the stock of knowledge contains provinces of knowledge which refer back to experiences in various provinces of reality with finite meaning-structure. Thus we can speak of knowledge of dreams and fantasy, of religious knowledge, and of everyday knowledge. Since the everyday life-world is the paramount reality—above all, because the most important means for the objectivation of knowledge, language, finds its home in it—we can grasp the knowledge based on it as the core area of the lifeworldly stock of knowledge. We want to devote an in-depth analysis to this province. Thus from time to time we will merely refer to the elements of knowledge that are based on other provinces.

Apart from the arrangement of the life-world in different provinces of reality, the most important factor in the structuring of the stock of knowledge is the difference between experiences entering into it as unquestioned, as already-constituted "unities" of the natural attitude, and experiences requiring explication in problematic situations before they are sedimented as elements of knowledge. Although we want to devote detailed investigation to the structure of the stock of knowledge, we can already indicate that this difference has a decisive place in the sedimentation of elements and thus in the structure of the stock of knowledge. It is connected with the ordering of elements of knowledge according to various degrees of credibility. In conjunction with the set of types found in the stock of knowledge, it conditions the degree of certainty of the elements of knowledge. And in addition it is the basis for the lack of contradiction between the elements of knowledge. For this reason, before we can turn to the analysis of the structure of the stock of knowledge we must first investigate the forms of its acquisition.

Now we have to differentiate between the acquisition of knowledge in the broader and in the narrower sense. In itself, the acquisition of knowledge is identical with the sedimentation of all actual experience in meaning-structures "connected with it," that is, united according to relevance and typicality. Experiences that elapse "unquestionably" and are not interpreted bring "nothing new" into the stock of knowledge. They fit into the types that have already been sketched out and confirm only existing elements of knowledge. Thus in many contexts it can be useful to speak of the acquisition of knowledge in the narrower sense, the knowledge that arises from the sedimentation of "new" explications. In that regard one should not forget that experiences which elapse without being questioned also make a certain contribution to the content of the stock of knowledge, i.e., to the solidification of the elements of knowledge. And in addition, the unquestioned character of actual experiences can be traced back in a natural fashion to the prior explications. Yet in every actual situation one can delineate a difference between unquestioned and problematic experiences, and this can serve to define the acquisition of knowledge in the narrower sense.

Continuation of the acquisition of knowledge is thus identical with the flow of experience. Whatever determines the *continuation* of the flow of experience determines at the same time the continuous sedimentation of the elements of knowledge. Whatever determines the *interruption* of the flow of experience determines at the same time the interruptions in the acquisition of knowledge. These statements must be made precise, especially with respect to the acquisition of knowledge in the narrower sense.

c. *Concerning continuation of the acquisition of knowledge*

The analyses of the structure of experience and the processes of explication have already yielded all the essential points for solving the problem at hand,[34] as far as this was possible without an exact investigation of the role of relevance structures and typicality. We will limit ourselves to summarizing these points briefly.

The "taken-for-granted" flow of experience as well as the processes of explication take place within the structures of subjective time. On the one hand they are subjugated to the rhythm of inner time, its accelerations and retardations, the changes in the tension of consciousness, etc. On the other hand, the mean-

34. See esp. Chap. 3, A, 2, a and b; also Chap. 3, A, 1, a and b.

ing of the experiences is inserted into the superimposed, biographically articulated meaning-structures. Because of this, the polythetic construction of experiences, and the possibility of grasping their meaning monothetically in hindsight, is of special importance.

"Taken-for-granted" experiences as well as explications happen in situations. Whether an experience elapses unquestioned or whether an explication is necessary depends on the situationally related concretization of the pragmatic motive, of the biographically expressed hierarchy of interest. The situation is variously limited, and the subjective knowledge of this limitation becomes a basic element of the lifeworldly stock of knowledge. Within these limits routine situations are developed: they are routinely determined and routinely mastered. In routine situations, experiences elapse "unquestioned," explications are "unnecessary," and no "new" elements of knowledge accrue to the stock of knowledge. In situations in which habitual knowledge appears to be unavailable, i.e., in situations whose "novelty" is imposed by the world, experiences become problematic. The explications begun there are determined from a pragmatic motive and are continued until the requisites of the situation are satisfied, or until an interruption of explication is "imposed." This point will be examined in greater detail in the analysis of interruptions in the acquisition of knowledge.

Further, as was already noted, the arrangement of the lifeworld into various provinces of reality with finite meaning-structure is of decisive importance for the continuation (and correlatively for the interruptions) of the acquisition of knowledge. The style of lived experience (or the style of understanding) of the province which receives the accent of reality in the actual experience (or explication) determines both what is taken for granted and what is problematic in the processes of experience and explication within that province. As will be shown, interruptions in the thematically connected flows of experience and processes of explication are determined by both "motivated" as well as "imposed" transitions (or "leaps") from one province of reality to the other. Consequently, such transitions also condition interruptions in the continuation of the acquisition of knowledge.

We can also turn the question around and ask ourselves how interruptions in thematically uniform flows of experience and processes of explication come about. What consequences do such interruptions have for the sedimentation of elements of knowl-

edge in the stock of knowledge? Here we can in part reach back
to prior analyses in which we systematically expanded our observations concerning the levels of the processes of explication.[35]
Only one more evaluation of the results of these analyses, expressly related to the problems of the acquisition of knowledge,
is required. Thus, the question is how it comes about that the explication begun in a problematic situation is interrupted, even if
the problem is not yet "solved." Under what circumstances are
the analyses only interrupted "for the time being"? Under what
circumstances does a problem that was almost "solved" once
again appear to require a new analysis?

d. Interruption of the stock of knowledge

i. "Definitive" interruptions (discontinuance of the flow of experience and the overlapping of the theme)

The theme of a flow of experience, or the problem of a process of explication, can completely "disappear." This interruption
is really a discontinuance; it is not compatible with the intention
of bringing up the theme or the problem again. One of the most
important and most frequent causes of discontinuance is connected with change (perceived subjectively as a "leap") from one
province of reality with finite meaning-structure to the other.
With the change to another style of lived experience or understanding, the relevance structures which were unique to the
former are "left behind."

If we, for example, dream of a problematic situation, the solution of the problem is motivated and determined by the relevance
structures of the dreamworld. (If I, for instance, cannot solve a
dream problem having a high level of urgency, the dream becomes a nightmare.) If I wake up without having solved the
problem in my dream, the problem (that may still be "understandable" to me in a wakeful state) has completely lost its
urgency. If we think back to the dream, the dream interests are
neutralized. The theme of the dream with the relevance structures belonging to it, which are manifested in the dream as levels
of urgency, possibilities of solution, etc., appears in the perspective of daily life. If I refer to the dream, the processes of explication are motivated and limited by the relevance structures and
the style of understanding in daily life, not by the situationally
related dream interest. Let us assume that I dreamed that some-

35. See, above all, Chap. 3, A, 2, b; also Chap. 3, A, 2, a.

one stole an expensive object of extreme importance to me. I try to run after him, but I cannot, since in the dream (as I find to my horror) I no longer possess the skill of running. If I remember the dream the next morning, it is obvious to me that I can run, that no specific problem exists any more for me, as it did in the dream when I couldn't use this skill. If in the dream I lack a less strongly routinized element of my knowledge, it may also be not *so* obvious in my waking state that I possess it; thus I may want to assure myself that I do have it.

The problem of one province of reality "disappears" as a *problem* after the "leap" into the other province. But it has in a certain sense left a "gap" behind. I can still "remember" the problem, though it is no longer a problem and no longer requires an explication to lead to its solution. The explications related to this "gap," the neutralized problem, are interpretations of the "meaning" of the dream which are carried out in agreement with the meaning-structures of the daily life-style. The "gap" left behind by the dream problem thus became, so to speak, an enclave in a province of reality with a completely different meaning-structure, in that it was filled up by a new problem: what does the dream mean? Such enclaves belong, in a certain sense, to both provinces of reality. They "find" themselves in one and "relate" to the other. A theme that spans two provinces of reality in this way will be called a *symbol*. At this point the symbol cannot be sufficiently understood, but we have uncovered an important factor in its genesis.[36]

We have chosen an example that presents the discontinuance very intuitively. But the same holds good in general for all interruptions in the flow of experience, or the acquisition of knowledge, which are connected with the leap from one province of reality, from one style of lived experience or understanding, into another. "Gaps" are left behind that can in principle be explicated in the relevance structures of the other province of reality. The theme of a play, the theme of a religious experience, leave enclaves behind in the everyday world, which are only "symbolically" represented in the style in which one understands daily life. The "inadequacy" of the relevance structures of everyday life for the explication of the enclaves left behind by other provinces of reality may, moreover, find its subjective correlate in feelings of reverence, of alienness, or even of a deprecating lack

36. See Chap. 6 [Vol. II].

of understanding. On the other hand, themes of everyday reality leave behind "gaps" in other provinces of reality, yet with a difference. Unsolved problems of everyday life, for example, are irrelevant in the province of a fantasy world; but in principle they do not "definitively disappear." For instance, they are not like the unsolved problem of a play, after I turn my back on it. The everyday life-world is distinctive in this fashion: the basic elements of my situation are unchangeable in it, and the problems associated with this must be solved "sooner or later." We are thus only concerned here with provisional interruptions in the acquisition of knowledge.

The interruptions in the flow of experience, as we now note, are either imposed or motivated. That is, they are either immediately derived from my situation in the world, or they are determined by the spontaneity of inner duration and, mediately, by the biographically imposed meaning-structures. Thus, for example, the waking reality is imposed after the dream. The jump into the world of tragedy, of a book, is motivated just as the return into the daily world can also be motivated. The difference between imposed and motivated interruptions is not just restricted to interruptions connected with leaving a province of reality with finite meaning-structure. As we will show, it holds good also for interruptions that happen within the same province of reality.

Let us illustrate the interruption of a process of explication, by which the problem "disappears" without my leaving the province of reality. I sit in my room and write a letter. Suddenly there is a bang in the street. Was it a shot? An explosion? I go to the window, look out, notice nothing out of the ordinary, and sit down again in order to finish the letter. I have not solved the "problem." I have simply determined with some assuredness that among the possible actions relevant for me (hurry to help someone, go to safety, etc.) none probably applies. The situation was problematic for me only so long as such possibilities were under consideration. After discarding these alternatives I interrupt further explication, since it doesn't "interest" me which among the other possibilities was actually the cause of the report (for instance, an especially loud backfiring, a metal sheet that fell down in the cellar of the neighboring house, etc.). In this case the problematic theme to be explicated left behind no "gap." For the problem was, strictly speaking, only *hypothetically relevant*. In my stock of knowledge, perhaps even in the province of my habitual knowledge, explosions and shots are "important" events requiring precautions, though backfirings are not included. I only need to explicate an imposed interruption of my activities insofar as it is necessary to the distinguishing of relevant and irrelevant possibilities of interpretation. If in the process I solve the problem, fine (if the only possibilities are an explosion, a shot, or a backfire, then I only have to explicate until an explosion and shot are eliminated; though I also know that it may have been a backfire, this knowledge does not "interest" me). If I don't solve it, that's good too, for it was, as I know, a problem not relevant for me. We will have to deal with the problem of hypothetical relevances again when we come to the analysis of the relevance structures of the stock of knowledge.[37] Here it need only be noted that hypothetical relevances of this sort, and the levels of explication conditioned by them, enter into a great deal of the more or less routinized acts of daily life, acts characterized by a typical "if . . . , then . . ." style.

Another form of "definitive" interruption in the flow of experience or the acquisition of knowledge is characterized by one problem being *overlaid* by a new problem. An especially typical case is the overlaying of a goal of acts by new goals which were formed during the course of the act.[38] If I have a goal in mind (I thus anticipate a result of my act), then I must outline the steps which should lead to its realization. While I run through these steps one after the other, the original goal can lose its relevance for me. The reasons for that are several.

First, an individual "step" that I am just then going through can have horizons of experience which include unseen consequences in the flow of lived experience. They can, for instance, invest the individual "step," which was previously subordinated to the original goal, with an importance that obscures the original goal. The "means" can become "end."

Second, in the course of an act it may have appeared that the original goal—in my daily plan, in my life-plan—only has meaning if it is subordinated to new goals. I can then discontinue the act or proceed with relation to the new goal, whereby the "end" is thus degraded to a "means." The original goal thus has not vanished, but it will be radically modified and is relevant only in the new context of acts.

Third, in the course of an action it may turn out that the

37. See Chap. 3, B, 2, c.
38. See the analysis of the action in Chap. 4.

necessary steps toward my original project are not feasible. The means to the end are not within the province of what is feasible for me. Then, either the act is discontinued or new means are projected, concealing the old ones. To a certain extent the original goal is thus also changed.

Finally, in the course of an action it may turn out that the steps are indeed feasible, but, as soon as they are accomplished, they lead to results I had not anticipated. Since the result of the act is necessarily different from the projected goal (with routinized skills this is the case to a very slight, irrelevant extent, but in other cases it is often so to an important extent), this possibility is of special importance empirically. It is worth noting that there is often an associated reversal of meaning. Looking back at the act, I read the result of the act into the original act's project. I say that it was implied or hidden in the original goal of the act. In hindsight I then grasp the event not as overlaying the original goal, but rather as a discovery. This is very often the case if unforeseen elements of the situation, imposed on me, are inserted into the course of the act. The history of discoveries and inventions offers numerous examples: the discoveries by alchemists, who were looking for a way to make gold; the discovery of America by Columbus, who was seeking a new passage to India, etc. But even daily life does not lack examples: if I write a letter, new ideas, new nuances so to speak, come to me out of my pen while I am writing down ideas which have already been clearly planned. The result seems other than what was projected. No matter how routinely I groom a dog, the "result" is determined by the unforeseen properties of the dog. Other provinces of reality are also characterized by this factor: artistic design ("resistance of the material"), play (the continuing modification of my plan in a chess game due to the characteristics of my opponent), etc.

The last examples bring us to a further point. In social interaction the goals of my fellow-man are in a certain sense [39] imposed on me. The overlaying of my original goals by projects that necessarily bring his goals into consideration, and vice versa, constitute the reciprocity of social interaction. One need think only of the planning and replanning by a troop commander (and the "war games" of the general staff, maneuvers, etc., which try to anticipate these circumstances), the conduct

39. See Chap. 5 [Vol. II].

of a businessman under the influence of the acts of his opposition, etc. Astonishment, as a subjective correlate accompanying such an overlaying of goals, is very strongly expressed in the province of social action and is not completely absent even in very routinized acts.

ii. "Temporary" interruptions

The sedimentation of experience can be interrupted with the intention of again taking up the flux of experience at the points of interruption, or continuing the processes of explication. The theme of experience or the kernel of the problem has in this case neither disappeared nor been completely overlaid. Rather, the continuation of experience, the explication of the problem is put off; the relevance is only temporarily neutralized: "postponed, but not suspended." It awaits the problem of resumption, the relevance of reactivization. The causes of such interruptions, as we have already pointed out, can be either imposed or motivated, just as "definitive" interruptions are. Let us begin by considering the former.

The data of the world imposed in the situation do not allow certain activities, as for instance some explications of problematic situations and experiences, to be carried out in one thrust. Continuation of the acquisition of knowledge is above all conditioned and limited by the changes in the tension of consciousness and the rhythm of inner duration, which show themselves subjectively to be the limited aspects of corporeality, attentiveness, and "will power." Acts whose scope exceeds the duration of individual phases of this rhythm must be interrupted in order to be picked up again later. Certain acts which are inserted into world time (the seasons, social time, etc.) demand periods of waiting until the "right" time has come, and must be interrupted when the time is "over" in order to be taken up again later. (Think about the sadness of the child when it gets dark and he must interrupt his play, or the waiting of the skier for winter, the rhythm of working the land, etc.) The scope of acts in its turn refers to elements in the situation which are imposed above all on the spatial, temporal, and social structures of experiences (I have to undertake a sequence of steps to get from New York to London—in between I can read, eat, sleep, etc.; if I want to become a lecturer in mathematics, I must, among other things, learn step-by-step, systematically organized areas of knowledge,

I have to routinize certain forms of knowledge, etc.—in between I have to eat and sleep; I can become a father, go to the movies fifty times, join a singing society, break a bone and have it heal again, etc.).

The elements imposed in the situation are, as we have already shown, bound up with one another.[40] I experience them subjectively as hindrances for continuation of the present flux of experience, as barriers to my action, which must be overcome, like the necessity of waiting until I can again take up any interrupted activity. But interruptions of the flux of experience are not just directly imposed. They can also be motivated. I could keep on working, but I decide to take a break. I could indeed solve the problem in one thrust, but I decide to postpone continuing the explication. Finally, the motivated interruptions are determined by elements of the world-structure that are imposed on the situation, above all by the concrete expressions of the principle of "first things first" in the course of the day and of life. The hierarchies of plans motivated by my finitude determined the motivations for the interruption. In both cases, directly imposed as well as motivated interruptions, the question to be answered is what happens to the theme of the interrupted flux of experience during the duration of the interruption, or to the postponed problem? In what sense can I pick up again tomorrow where I stopped today?

Let's begin with a simple example. If I am reading a voluminous book, I cannot read it all at one sitting. If this evening I have read to page 151, I can note the page or put in a bookmark and close the book: I know that I will find the continuation of the story on page 151 tomorrow, day after tomorrow, next month. In between, I can sleep; after waking up I have to go to the office; I can read the newspaper or even another novel. With all the other activities, other themes are in the foreground of my attention. I meet new situations, my experiences go along routinely or become problematic and need explication. These situations have their own relevance structures; their plan-determined interest is derived from my daily plans and life-plans, which in turn are subclassified into work programs, leisure programs, etc. The appropriate relevance structures motivate my work, my leisure activities, etc. The relevance structures in literature and the

40. See Chap. 2, B, 4, c, ii, and B, 6.

horizons of explication dependent on them naturally do not "fit" in at work. But neither do they disappear; they are rather only neutralized. The theme, for example the adventures of Don Quixote which I interrupted after the episode with the windmills, is accessible at any time; in principle I could also reactivate it during work, if the plan-determined interest of the work situation did not "hinder" me from it; vice versa, the themes connected with my work are neutralized while the reading of Don Quixote continues.

This example is quite obvious because the interruption, in one "leap," collapses into another province of reality. There are in fact not only many "definitive" but also many "temporary" interruptions in the acquisition of knowledge that are on hand after such a leap. But in situations that belong within the same province of reality with finite meaning-structure, there are temporary interruptions with pauses, postponements, periods of waiting, etc. If we interrupt activity a_1, and pick up activity a_2 with the view of continuing a_1 after finishing a_2, the theme a_1 with its thematic relevances has been replaced by the thematic relevances belonging to a_2.[41] But a_1 has not disappeared; this theme with its thematic relevances enters in a neutralized form into the horizon of the course of a_2. The difference from the other kinds of interruptions is obvious. The theme has not "disappeared" nor is it "definitively" overlaid; rather it is only temporarily replaced by another theme and awaits "unchanged" for its resumption. If in the "disappearance" of a theme a gap remains, this is incorporated into the relevance structures of the following situation. In being overlaid, the original theme is, so to speak, changed beyond recognition. In "temporary" interruption the original theme remains preserved, together with its thematic relevance structures. It is independent of the new theme and bound to it only through the unity of the flow of lived experience.

The observation that a_1 remains unchanged during the interruption is, strictly speaking, not correct. It involves the life-worldly idealizations of "I can do it again and again" and of "and

41. For the distinction between thematic, interpretational, and motivational relevances, see Chap. 3, B; in this passage, we anticipate this material only insofar as it is absolutely necessary for the problem at hand. [See also Schutz, *Reflections on the Problem of Relevance.*]

so forth." I cannot pick up the activity a_1 again exactly "there" where I interrupted it. For during the duration of the interruption it was in the horizon of a_2 and automatically obtained a coloring, if ever so minimal. The activity a_1 was not explicated from a perspective determined through the relevance structure of a_2, and it was not consciously modified; it was carried along during the flux of experience that was determined by the relevance structures of a_2. If I continue a_1 again, the activity has at least obtained a new biographical cast: a_1 after a_2. Subjectively, I experience this as an exertion either great or small, which is required in order to "accustom" me again to a_1. For the *meaning* of a_1 it is decisive that the idealizations "I can do it again and again" and "and so forth" have entered both into the interruption and the resumption. With this restriction we can then correctly say that we resume a theme "there" where it was left at the interruption. The role of objectivated meaning-structures, above all that of language (and especially of writing, of significant marks, etc.), is of great empirical importance here. This was especially clear in the example from literature.

Motivated "temporary" interruptions are for the most part inserted into the day's plan and the life-plan. As already shown, the superimposed relevance structures, which determine the plan-determined interest in individual situations and activities, are also the "motivation" for interruptions and for the resumption of activities, the processes of explication, and the flows of experience. In other words, they are articulated as a system of the continuation of experience and the interruption of experience. This system is for its part extensively routinized, so that I know more or less "automatically" when it is "time to stop and to start."

Although the system of motivated interruptions tends through its regularity to become habitual knowledge, interruptions, chiefly imposed interruptions, can in general have different qualities of lived experience. They can be startling, pleasant, but above all disturbing. Deficient routinization or even the destruction of routinized chains in the continuation of experience and its interruptions, can lead to psychopathological phenomena. These can manifest themselves as an "inability" to interrupt an activity, whatever the exigencies of the situation may be, as enforced sequences of action and imagination, whose interruption is reacted to with shock, or conversely as an "inability" to "concentrate" on an activity which cannot be "diverted."

3. THE STRUCTURE OF THE STOCK OF KNOWLEDGE

a. Knowledge about the basic elements of the situation and habitual knowledge in the stock of knowledge

We saw that the structure of the stock of knowledge is in essence derivable from the forms of the acquisition of knowledge and thus from the processes of the sedimentation of experience. This is the case for the levels of familiarity in knowledge as well as for the arrangement of the elements of knowledge according to their clarity, or their determinateness and lack of contradiction. It is also the case with the degree of credibility accompanying the elements of knowledge. Before we pursue this in its particulars, it should be observed that two provinces of the stock of knowledge, namely, their basic elements and habitual knowledge, do not fit straightforwardly in these dimensions.

The basic elements of the stock of knowledge [42] are not the result of the sedimentations of specific experiences. They consist of knowledge concerning the limiting conditions of *all* such experiences, a knowledge that is more or less automatically given along with every experience. The basic elements of the stock of knowledge are still confirmed, modified, or refuted by means of individual experiences, just as my knowledge of the weather conditions in the mountains, of the character of a friend, etc., that has arisen through specific experiences, is later modified and confirmed in such experiences. The knowledge of the what and how of the human situation in the world is given along with every experience, even if in a peculiar way, namely, as a datum in the horizon of the situation or experience. Knowledge about the limit of inner duration, about the historicality and finitude of the individual situation within world time, about the limits of corporeality and about the spatial, temporal, and social structures of experience, is the substratum of the determination of every concrete situation. Specific elements of the stock of knowledge, in contrast, sedimented out of specific experiences, are thematized as the core of an experience. Or, in any case, they play a direct role in the thematizations. In this respect, the "familiarity" of the basic elements of the stock of knowledge is essentially of a different kind than the levels of familiarity in specific and acquired contents of the stock of knowledge.

42. See Chap. 3, A, 1, a and b.

Also, habitual knowledge [43] cannot, without further ado, be coordinated with the levels of familiarity in which the partial contents of the stock of knowledge are ordered. It must be remembered that no sharp line can be drawn between certain basic elements of the stock of knowledge and certain provinces of habitual knowledge. Above all, the skills can be viewed as concrete expressions or "dimensions" of knowledge about lived corporeality. Such knowledge is a basic element of the stock of knowledge. As was mentioned, habitual knowledge occupies a middle ground between basic elements and the contents of the stock of knowledge. The basic elements are universal, and they do not arise out of sedimentations of experience. In contrast the more or less variable habitual knowledge, from skills concerning practical knowledge to knowledge of recipes, is obviously the result of the sedimentation of experience. But it is differentiated from explicit, partial elements of the stock of knowledge by the fact that, similar to the basic elements, it is always on hand. One can automatically reach back to habitual knowledge. Its elements are *no longer* grasped as elements of knowledge, as independent themes of experience, but rather are given in the horizon of the flow of experience. We want to make this a bit clearer. If I learn a foreign language, the words, grammar, accent, etc., are specific partial contents of my stock of knowledge, which I learn individually. I can then present them in specific experiences as special themes in the flow of experience. In this regard, it would be meaningful to speak of levels of familiarity. Many words are more familiar to me than others. Or again: French is more familiar to me than Russian. There comes a point in time when I begin to "think" in the language. My knowledge of the language becomes habitual knowledge. It is questionable, then, whether there is any sense still in speaking of levels of familiarity. I *make use* of the language and indeed automatically for the most varying reasons. If we turn to the example of the mother tongue instead of a foreign language, the state of affairs becomes completely clear. Surely I also had to learn my mother tongue. It was a lengthy process of sedimentation, which was variously routinized and finally consists of skills as much as of practical knowledge or knowledge or recipes. Familiarity here went over a threshold, so to speak, after which it is hardly still meaningful to speak of levels of familiarity.

43. See Chap. 3, A, 1, c.

The basic elements of the stock of knowledge as well as of habitual knowledge have a special place in the structure of the stock of knowledge. They are always on hand, not simply at hand from case to case, like the contents of the stock of knowledge. They are "automatically" given, not articulated as themes of experience. They are, thus, so self-evidently "familiar," that one no longer would like to order them in the arrangement of the stock of knowledge according to levels of familiarity. The same obviously holds good for the gradations of clarity and credibility in the stock of knowledge. These also are derived, in essence, from the forms of the acquisition of knowledge. It would be senseless to speak of the credibility, let us say, of finitude or of the clarity and distinctness of walking.

Finally, it should again be stressed that the basic elements of the stock of knowledge and of habitual knowledge are different in origin. The latter arose from acquired, specific elements of knowledge, in contrast to the universal and "autonomous" basic elements of the former, despite the points of contact between them that have been mentioned. Habitual knowledge arises from elements that were originally ordered in levels of familiarity (and fundamentally also, according to the degrees of clarity and credibility) in the stock of knowledge. In the *present* structure of the stock of knowledge they have a place—as soon as they are routinized—similar to the basic elements of knowledge.

b. The familiarity of elements of knowledge

i. Levels of familiarity

The word "familiarity" can characterize various heterogeneous states of affairs. Therefore we want to pin it down for our use. In his *Principles of Psychology*, William James distinguishes between two kinds of knowledge, which he calls *knowledge about* and *knowledge of acquaintance*.[44] This distinction rests on the view that there are many things we know: we know that there is "such a thing," we have "heard of it," and we have more or less unclarified ideas about it. On the other hand, there are also a few things with which we are really familiar. We have insight into the nature of these matters and into their connection with other objects and circumstances. Certainly, the Jamesian distinction has a role with regard to clarity in knowledge, even

44. [James, *Principles*, I, 221 ff.]

though it does not lead to the determination of fine gradations of familiarity. Yet it is useful for a first distinction between quite familiar and unfamiliar knowledge. It is misleading if one speaks, as do many psychologists, of "qualities of acquaintance," as if these cling to objects and events, so to speak, as tertiary qualities. Certainly, we experience objects and events as more or less familiar. The processes of consciousness, which are the basis of such familiarity, must now be investigated in detail. Let us first illustrate this matter with a few examples.

Everyone who cooks eggs knows that eggs are "soft-boiled" in boiling water after approximately three minutes, and that they are "hard-boiled" after a few more minutes. In spite of a high degree of familiarity with this piece of knowledge, most people have no clear idea how such a result "really" comes about. I know "self-evidently" that the trees now bare of leaves in the winter will again foliate in the spring, without being familiar with the processes leading to this. We press buttons and turn switches and know what the consequences will be: the light goes on, the elevator remains on the third floor, etc. I mail a letter and know that it will reach the addressee in a few days. The same degrees of credibility do not indeed belong to all the elements of knowledge in these examples. For example, I know "for sure" that the trees will be green. But I only know with "greatest probability" that the letter will reach the addressee. The degree of clarity or determinateness and the uncontradictability of the elements of knowledge are still necessarily identical. All examples are so chosen that in principle further knowledge would be possible: I could become informed about the chemical processes that happen at certain temperatures to the egg white and egg yolk; I could trace out biological, religious, or magical explanations for the foliation of trees and seek physical explanations for technological processes. I could inquire very precisely about post offices, the conveyance of mail, postal personnel, etc. The examples in general are so chosen that I know that there are "more precise" explanations for the events familiar to me and even that there are certain "people" who can transmit this knowledge to me: scientists, post-office officials, electricians, shamans, etc. Although I know that, I am really not interested in acquiring further knowledge about it. I am sufficiently familiar for "my own purposes." The interest involved here is in the broadest sense a pragmatic one that determines the acquisition and the interruption of knowledge. I would, perhaps, in principle be "interested" to know more about these things, but under the principle of "first things first" I have "no time," since I must "first" acquire knowledge more relevant for me. I want to keep a "place" open for more important or more urgent experience. When we describe the opacity of the life-world,[45] we will examine the other case, in which I know that certain elements of knowledge cannot in principle be acquired.

In general, we are not interested to the same extent in all provinces of the life-world and in all the objects and events taking place therein. Plan-determined and situationally related interest (in the biographical molding of the acquisition of knowledge) organizes the world in strata of greater and lesser relevance. Above all, those objects and processes are selected from the world in my actual and potential reach which are involved in the execution of my plans as ends and means, as hindrances and preconditions, or which could come into question during the execution of plans merely proposed. This is naturally the case with both plans of biographical articulation, that of the daily plan as well as that of the life-plan. I familiarize myself with the "relevant" elements and aspects of the world only insofar as it is necessary to master the situation. This statement is not to be understood in a radically pragmatic or even behavioristic sense. It is concerned not only with situations in the everyday life-world but also with situations which occur in other provinces of reality. It is not simply concerned with the satisfaction of some "biological necessities."

Daily life is, above all, although not exclusively, concerned with the mastery of typical, recurrent situations. A broad range of goals, means, conditions, hindrances confronts us again and again. The most important reason for this is that we meet in all situations the universal, unchangeable, imposed elements of a situation. Our plans are naturally also biographically articulated and enter into the biographical molding of relevance structures and interests. The explications of certain goals, means, conditions, and hindrances for the carrying out of our plans are correspondingly routinized and enter into the province of habitual knowledge. Other acts, even if they are not completely routinized, are based on goals which are recurringly familiar and have proven sufficiently familiar; these acts use just such means and master just such hindrances. The absence of any necessity to

45. See Chap. 3, A, 3, f.

engage in further explications is confirmed again and again. As a whole, the elements of knowledge involved in such acts make up the degree of familiarity of the act complex and of the knowledge complex. This is the case (to stress it once more) with elements of knowledge that have the most varied levels of clarity, as has been shown by the examples of the soft-boiled eggs, mailing a letter, etc.

If we start by determining levels of familiarity within the actual experience, we can establish certain general differences. First, one recognizes objects and events as similar to those one has met in previous experiences. Second, one grasps objects and events as similar in essential characteristics to those experienced earlier. Third, they can only be similar to previously experienced objects and events in some of their characteristics; in other respects they are dissimilar. Finally, there are objects and events which appear in the set of types stored in the stock of knowledge. Further, it could also have been seen that a determination of familiarity is based on the subjective acquisition of knowledge from an actually present Object of experience. Objects are more or less familiar according to whether they more or less agree with previous experiences.

Thus we return to the origin of the gradation of familiarity, the forms of the acquisition of knowledge. The degree of familiarity of an element of knowledge depends on the extent to which the inner and outer horizons of the experiences which enter into the stock of knowledge have been explicated. Indeed, the degree of familiarity is constituted in the circumstances of the acquisition of knowledge. We have seen that in the latter the plan-determined interest motivates the determination of the situation and the explication of experiences, prescribes the level of explication, and in that way establishes when the explication should be interrupted, that is, discontinued. In other words, the explication of a situation or experience is in general broken off when the knowledge constituted by the explication is sufficient for the mastery of the situation. Many possibilities of explication remain irrelevant; many possible continuations of the explication prove to be unnecessary. That means that the explication can be broken off or terminated on the most varied levels of clarity and credibility and still be "sufficient" for the plan-determined and situationally related interest. Every explication legitimated in general by a situation also establishes a degree of familiarity sufficient for this situation. The element of knowledge so constituted is sufficiently familiar for all situations which are the same or similar. This applies to all routine situations (or experiences) perceived "beyond question" as being similar, as well as to situations or experiences not thoroughly routinized but typically recurring. The elements of knowledge involved in this are highly familiar on the basis of their prior history, whatever their degree of clarity may be; the familiarity of the actual experience or situation is then also judged according to that. This point anticipates the analysis of the relations of the set of types and degree of familiarity.[46]

Even if the degree of familiarity of the elements of knowledge can be derived from the circumstances of the acquisition of knowledge, that is, from the situationally legitimated explications, the question remains why all elements of knowledge are not highly familiar. There are three reasons for this. *First,* we continually meet new situations. They "resist" our attempt to determine them by means of familiar elements of knowledge. Our plans do not lead to the desired result; the situation cannot be mastered if they are determined exclusively with the stock of knowledge at hand. That causes us again to take up the explications, originally seen as closed, until the actually present situation can be determined and the problem as a consequence is mastered. The situation which showed itself to be unfamiliar is made familiar. The relevant elements of knowledge, formerly highly familiar, were proved to be insufficiently familiar in their use and were carried over into new familiarity. It becomes clear here that at this juncture the dimensions of familiarity and clarity (i.e., determinateness and uncontradictability) are in harmony, however different they are in essence.

We try to determine new situations as familiar. Only when they resist such a determination do we consider them "problematic." The resistance of the situation is to be traced back to the elements imposed on us by it. With this, we also touch on the *second* cause for the unfamiliarity of elements of knowledge. We will mention it here and only later take it up separately: the fundamental opacity of the life-world that is imposed on me in a certain sense as an element of my situation.[47]

Third, certain elements of knowledge are unfamiliar to me because I had indeed broken off their original explication before

46. See Chap. 3, A, 3, b, ii.
47. See Chap. 3, A, 3, f.

the plan-determined interest was sufficient for this situation. New situations intruded before I could master the original one; the explication *had* to be interrupted because I, in terms of the principle of "first things first," had to turn to new problems, etc. The connection between interruptions in the acquisition of knowledge and the elements imposed in the situation of the acquisition of knowledge along with the biographical molding of life-plans and daily plans has already been described.[48]

Further, not only are interruptions of the acquisition of knowledge imposed as well as motivated, but so also in a certain sense is their continuance. We come to situations in which we, *malgré nous,* cannot interrupt the acquisition and become more familiar with certain elements of knowledge. The continuance of the acquisition of knowledge and the increase in its degree of familiarity is, considered in itself, primarily unmotivated. But then, the *omission* of the interruption is motivated. In social situations we meet the most important examples of such mediately, so to speak secondarily, motivated continuations of the acquisition of knowledge. It happens that I become a "prisoner" of a social situation and listen "uninterestedly" to the endless speeches of an enthusiastic football fan about the achievements of the "Liga Club" in the last season. Thus I become familiar with provinces with which I did not at all "want" to become familiar. The knowledge, however, remains "stuck." Such an acquisition is thus not motivated by the actual or potential situationally related interests. But the situation *in* which the acquisition of knowledge occurs can only be mastered when I do not interrupt the acquisition—as happens if, in the example used, the football fan is my boss. In any case, the distinction between an imposed and a motivated continuance of the acquisition of knowledge, as well as between an imposed and a motivated interruption, is not to be thought of as if these were independent of one another. Their reciprocal relatedness is especially clear in social situations and most particularly in reciprocal social action: the motives of the fellow-man are imposed on one partner in the situation and vice versa.[49]

ii. Familiarity and typicality

Between familiarity and typicality there is, as we have already seen, a close connection. The problem of types stored in

48. See Chap. 3, A, 2, d.
49. See Chap. 5 [Vol. II].

the stock of knowledge must be examined in yet more detail. We can now describe this connection more carefully here: how does it happen that actual experiences are more or less familiar?

One can be familiar with an object in a certain sense, as well as with object relations, and with persons, in such a way that one knows their "identity." The actual experience of an object or a person refers to a prior experience of the same object or the same person. The object or person is recognized again. This recognition is not necessarily restricted to high levels of clarity and determinancy of prior experience. I can recognize a stretch of road I traveled once years ago, just as I can recognize the street I take daily. I can recognize the beggar on the street corner where I only seldom pass, and the friend with whom I have been together often and for a long time. The levels of clarity and determinancy in the Object of experience, its lived experiential nearness, its embedding in my biography, etc., are naturally radically different. And even if the degrees of familiarity bound to these dimensions of experiences can be different, they have something in common: they are adequate for the situations under consideration, and they are related to an Object of experience recognized as identical. Such quite specific elements form an important sector of the stock of knowledge, perhaps best described as the province of memory.

Above all, another sector is more important for the mastery of new situations, namely, the province of typifications stored in the stock of knowledge. This sector contains elements of knowledge related not to specific objects and persons but rather to typical aspects and attributes of objects, persons, and events. Moreover, we have, with reason, not spoken of events as elements of the province of memory. They are experienceable even in the natural attitude of daily life, prior to any philosophical observation, as typically repeatable, as analogous, but not "really" as identical. In contrast, objects and persons are experienced as the same even if, due to circumstances, they are changed. We need not consider here that a philosophical problem of identity may also exist with regard to objects and persons, since the identity is taken for granted in the natural attitude.

If I meet with objects, persons, or events which were not given in actual presence to me in prior experiences, which I thus cannot recognize, then the present experience of them is "new" but not necessarily "novel." In order to investigate what this statement involves, we will begin with a simple, graphic example.

We cannot avoid anticipating the analysis of the set of types, which is to follow.[50] We will anticipate it only insofar as it is absolutely necessary for an understanding.

Let us assume that I encounter a dog on the street. This particular dog is unfamiliar to me. I cannot identify its breed, who its owner is, how old it is, or whether it bites, etc. I notice at a glance its bodily form, size, style of movement, in broad outline its "attitude." All these possibilities for determination join in a familiar unity of experience: dog. I have indeed never seen this particular dog, but innumerable other animals which had the same possibilities for determination as this animal are in my actual experience. In the continuation of the acquisition of knowledge, the type "bowwow," which included everything moveable from which sounds issued, is narrowed to a single type containing only animals of a certain order of magnitude. With further narrowing, I then succeed to a type containing only dogs as opposed to cats, foxes, wolves, etc. The actually present and perceived animal encompasses every possibility of determination (bodily form, style of moving, etc.), consistent with the type "dog," sedimented in prior experiences. At the same time it encompasses in a "negative" contrast what in a *relevant fashion* it is not. It is irrelevant for me in my actual state of knowledge that the Object of experience is not a snow crystal, a tree, an elephant, etc. Yet it is relevant that it tamely runs around on the street and therefore most probably is not a wolf; that it does not move like a cat, and therefore is not a cat. In short, within a situation familiar to me and in reference to typical possibilities of determination familiar to me, the actually present Object of experience is familiar to me.

Although the animal is familiar to me as "dog," even quite familiar, it is in another respect unfamiliar to me. With this example let us clarify the relation of levels of familiarity to the set of types in the stock of knowledge. The animal is unfamiliar to me in respect of the breed to which it belongs. That is, there is in my stock of knowledge no type with which the determining characteristics of this dog are unquestionably compatible. This may (according to the situation) also not interest me. In that case, I go on, and the dog "disappears" as "dog" from my situation. But if I am interested in a closer determination, an explicatory process takes place. The animal does not fit into a subtype

50. See Chap. 3, C.

of dog breeds on hand in my stock of knowledge. If I compare the perceived determining characteristics with the determinations of these subtypes, I recognize only fragmentary agreements. The dog has size and fur like a wolfhound, but muzzle and floppy ears like a setter. I may assume that the animal represents a cross of these breeds, or belongs to a breed unfamiliar to me. If I am an expert on dog breeds, this last possibility is excluded, and the problem is unequivocally solved: a mixture. Thus, on the basis of these processes of explication I have converted the experience into a new familiarity and at the same time to a more specific level of determination. I can, if it is asked of me, press on still farther and put other possibilities of determination in relation with the elements of knowledge of the type. Finally, I reach a point where this dog is unfamiliar to me in its particularity and where I no longer can find any typical elements of knowledge relevant for the perception and congruent with it.

Having reached this point, I can be satisfied according to the situation with the newly acquired level of familiarity with the experienced Object. If I am motivated by the situation (e.g., as a mailman who wants to learn to know all the dogs of the neighborhood from the point of view of their "biting or not"), I can become familiar with the dog in its "individuality." I have to observe its conduct under various circumstances for a considerable time. I look up its owner, question him, etc. Then, as must be stressed, I also grasp the dog according to ever-new typifications (its biting, white spot on its neck) whose individual constellation finally allows me to recognize this dog again as this particular dog, which has now become familiar to me.

With this example we have illustrated the relation between levels of familiarity and typicality, as well as the levels of clarity or determination in the stock of knowledge. In anticipation of the analysis of typicality, we can generalize. The set of types is more or less anonymous. The more anonymous and (correspondingly) the further away the type is from the sector of memory, the more aspects of experience can be grasped under it (i.e., are compatible with it). A type on a given level of anonymity is sufficiently familiar for the mastery of situations in which objects, persons, events, on the *same* level of anonymity must be determined. More exactly stated, the actually present, perceived objects, persons, and events appear in this case sufficiently familiar. The more anonymous the type, the more type-irrelevant (and under the circumstances also the more atypical) characteristics the Object of experience manifests. But when the determination of these characteristics is necessary for mastery of the situation, if, for example, I must grasp the objects, persons, and events in "complete" concreteness though no correspondingly quite specific types are on hand in my stock of knowledge, they then appear to me as unfamiliar. The situation remains problematic until I can convert it into a new state of familiarity. A dog running past on the street can remain a "dog." But if I am a mailman, I must at least notice the ones who bite. And if I own a dog, I want to pick him out again from all the other dogs. In short, to be sufficiently familiar with something means that it can be "concretely" determined with the aid of typifications at hand in the stock of knowledge, in order to deal with the plan-determined necessities of the situation.

Familiarity is thus characterized by the fact that new experiences can be determined with the help of a type constituted in prior experiences, and this determination holds good in the mastery of the situation. The relative unquestionableness corresponds to the levels of familiarity with which the determining (indeed already "selectively perceived") characteristics of the situation or experience occur in the typical unity of a type of situation or experience. In the application of habitual knowledge this happens in completely passive syntheses of recognition; the grasp of the type is "automatic." The Object of experience without a process of explication is proven to be typical: similar, the same as, resembling typical aspects of the prior experience. The more questionable the agreement between the type and the determining characteristics of the current experience, the less familiar it appears to me. If the current experience finally appears not "sufficiently typical" for determination and mastery of the situation, processes of explication are induced in which new typifications on other levels of determination are rendered familiar.

c. The determination of elements of knowledge

With the description of the connection between familiarity and typicality we established that there are several relations between the various dimensions of the stock of knowledge. The reason for this can be found in their common origin in the situations of the acquisition of knowledge. Nevertheless, in the prevailing structure of a subjective stock of knowledge, familiarity, clarity, determinateness, and credibility are in no way identical; neither do they only involve different aspects of the same content. A quite familiar element of knowledge can at the same time also be, to a high degree, unclear, an unequivocally clear element of knowledge less credible—according to how far the explication was developed, what the interests were that determined the originary situations of the acquisition of knowledge, under what circumstances the acquisition of knowledge was interrupted, etc.

With the analysis of the acquisition of knowledge, as well as with the description of the levels of familiarity, we have already encountered the dimension of clarity in elements of knowledge. But we have not yet investigated these that carefully. We want now to make up for that. First, we must differentiate between clarity and determinateness, of which we have up until now spoken in one breath. Probably clarity and determinateness are most especially bound up with one another as features of the lifeworldly stock of knowledge. It is, nevertheless, the determinateness of the elements of knowledge that forms an independent dimension of the stock of knowledge. Clarity is, on the other hand, a "composite" aspect of these elements; it is immediately founded on their degree of determinateness, but it is based on their mutual lack of contradiction. Freedom from contradiction is, furthermore, not an attribute of the elements of knowledge but rather involves their reciprocal relations and must be investigated separately. After analyzing the degree of determinateness and the freedom from contradiction, we will not need to describe separately the clarity of the stock of knowledge. We can already grant the premise that elements of knowledge, which possess a given degree of determinateness and stand in a given relation more or less free from contradiction with other elements of knowledge, can be ordered in appropriate levels of clarity.

If we ask ourselves what degrees of determinateness are, we can refer to certain analogies with the levels of familiarity. As there is no absolute familiarity, so there is no absolute determinateness. It is possible to be so highly familiar with an Object of experience that it can offer "no more surprises" in rather similar experiences in similar situations. But it is fundamentally impossible to be so completely familiar with it that there would be nothing more unfamiliar to discover. Apart from the role of new situations in making the apparently familiar something alien, this state of affairs is associated with the relativity of the degree of determinateness. What does that mean?

Every Object of experience necessarily has a horizon of experience. It contains imposed, determined elements to which I can unhesitatingly turn in the next phase of the flow of experience. The horizon is open; it contains elements which are still undetermined. We will entirely disregard the problem of the fundamentally undeterminable, to which we will later turn our attention. Here, we will only inquire into what is indeed undetermined but potentially determinable.

Every Object of experience has an inner horizon; its details are either not at all, imprecisely, or precisely determined. Thus an Object of perception can be split up into details: the design of the tablecloth into its ornamental particulars, the forest into trees, etc. The inner horizon of an experienced Object may already have been polythetically experienced in respect to some or many of its elements. Correspondingly, the inner horizon of an actually present Object which is monothetically grasped is more or less determined. We have already stressed the significance of the polythetic construction of the acquisition of knowledge for the structure of the stock of knowledge: [51] the possibility of tracing a monothetically grasped element of knowledge back to the polythetic constitution of its meaning quite decisively coconditions the degree of determinateness of the element.

The Object of experience also has an outer horizon which contains already determined and undetermined, but determinable, elements. The possibilities for determination are related on the one hand to things essentially connected with the theme of experience, on the other hand to "accidental" situational features of the experienced Object. With regard to this Object, the present insertion of experience into inner duration and its place in the biography are singularly "accidental." For the experienced Object, it is an "accidentally associated factor" that I read Andersen's fairy tales when I was seven years old while in bed with diphtheria, that the Pythagorean theorem was explained to me by a doddering mathematics teacher, etc. As regards this Object, it is essential that it is imbedded in the structure of the world and that it is thematically explicated in the context of experience. The possibilities for determination here include explications of the relation of the experienced Object to other Objects and events as well as to the qualities of lived experience "necessarily" associated with it. They refer to the spatial, temporal, and causal struc-

51. See Chap. 3, A, 2, a.

tures, in which the Object typically appears and has appeared. For example, the genus, geographical distribution, ecological niche, color, growth, mode of reproduction, etc., of tree may all belong to the theme "tree." [52] The outer, like the inner, horizon contains elements in part already determined, in part still undetermined. The possibilities for determining the outer horizon are, as is immediately obvious, in principle unlimited. Just the explication of "causal connections" alone could be carried on to infinity. Various practical degrees of determinateness can, however, be distinguished, ranging from an otherwise unspecific ordering in a province of reality to a precise determination of relations relevant to the Object of experience. In a borderline case the latter can be determined simply as a dream Object, or an object in the outer world, etc. It can be determined to be a tree, rather large and apparently equipped with needles, and certainly belonging to the plant kingdom, probably propagating itself somehow, most likely presupposing a certain type of soil, etc.— or as *picea excelsa,* growing primarily in sandy and dry earth, producing cones and seeds within one season, etc., etc. Our example, at any rate, should not mislead us into believing that only scientific systems have a high degree of determinateness. Our observations apply as well, often to a still stronger degree, to the classification systems used by "primitive" societies. But global differences in the degree of determinateness of experiences are subjectively noticed. To take an example, for a hypochondriac various bodily symptoms are highly determined and are interpreted according to various disease syndromes, while he has only a vague idea of the topography of the city in which he lives; another person knows only that he feels "good" or "bad," but knows every little alley in his home town.

Up to now we have spoken of the determinateness and determinability of the *Object* of experience. Now, the *experience* of the Object in its relative determinateness as an element of knowledge enters into the stock of knowledge. Determinacy of the "accidental" kind is indeed in principle unimportant for the sedimentation of experiences in the stock of knowledge. Only that which appears essential for the theme of the experience is a possible determination relevant for the stock of knowledge. The

52. For an exact analysis of the problems only touched on here, see Aron Gurwitsch, *Théorie du champ de la conscience* (Paris: Desclée de Brouwer, 1957). English translation, *The Field of Consciousness* (Pittsburgh, Pa.: Duquesne University Press, 1964).

explications necessary in the situation *and* those foreseen as necessary for a subsequent, typically similar situation are based on this. Even here, the relativity of the degree of determinateness is not overcome. What is "essential" and what is "accidental" are functions of the prevailing state of knowledge: changeable from childhood to the state of knowledge of the adult, differing among the relative-natural world views, and socially distributed within a society.

Although there is thus no absolute basis for the definition of the degrees of determinateness, one can establish that there are empirical differences in the degree of determinateness in the elements of knowledge. This holds good in a certain sense for the structure of the subjective, lifeworldly stock of knowledge. At any rate, the question remains open how, for instance, the determinateness of the elements of knowledge concerning the animal kingdom is comparable to that of similar elements which pertain to religious notions. Although familiarity is above all meaningfully definable in a subjective way, what suffices for the mastery of a situation is familiar to me—degrees of determinateness also have a social component. In the intersubjective life-world, I know from the beginning that there are determinations "suitable to a subject" that have already been encountered by "Others" (ancestors, "experts," etc.) and which are in principle learnable by me. An empirical definition of degrees of determinateness must consider first the relatedness of the degrees of determinateness in an element of knowledge and in a province of knowledge, as well as the possibilities of determination within a relative-natural world view, and then also take into consideration the social distribution of knowledge.[53]

On the other hand, it can be formally demonstrated that the degree of determinateness in an element of knowledge is greater, the further the explication of the inner and outer horizon of the experience concerned is carried, while an experience which is only vaguely prominent as a unity in the flow of experience has a correspondingly small degree of determinateness. We have seen that such degrees of determinateness, just as those of familiarity, are constituted in the processes of explication in the acquisition of knowledge. The question still remains to be answered whether in the acquisition of knowledge there already exists a difference between the constitution of the degrees of determinateness and

53. See Chap. 4, B, 3, and C, 2.

levels of familiarity. With a certain simplification, the question can be answered in the affirmative. Levels of familiarity are constituted with relation to the subjective mastery of typical situations through explications typically "sufficient" for the task. They are thus conditioned by means of the pragmatic motive, even in a narrow sense. Degrees of determinateness are indeed related to the "Objective" possibilities of determination. But these possibilities are *fundamentally* "historical" and relative. Empirically, they are thus to be defined on the basis of the state of knowledge in the relative-natural world view—depending on the question—or even according to the "typical chances of access" by the individual to a given state of knowledge.

The difference between levels of familiarity and degrees of determinateness, then, has its origin in the acquisition of knowledge. The *situation* of the acquisition of knowledge—the "occasion" for familiarity as well as for determinateness—is obviously the same. What was said about the imposed and motivated moments of the acquisition of knowledge holds good for the origin of all dimensions of the structure of the stock of knowledge. The situation may have required an exhaustive determination of the horizon of an experienced Object, or may have "demanded" such an explication. A professional winetaster, for example, sees himself as having to acquire a highly determined knowledge set down in all its particulars concerning the varieties of grapes, composition of soil, localities, fermentation, storage, etc., while an ordinary wine drinker is probably satisfied with determinations like red wine (Chianti), white wine (Moselle), etc. These elements of knowledge with such variation in degrees of determinateness can have high levels of familiarity with wine, though just on the level of determinateness at which wine is differentiated from beer, red wine from white wine, etc.

Degrees of determinateness are also constituted (as are levels of familiarity) in an interplay of imposed and motivated elements of acts which effect the continuation or interruption of the acquisition of knowledge. I can, for instance, acquire a quite determined knowledge of Mozart's string quartets, not because I am specifically motivated to do so as a musician or critic is, but rather because I have received the records of the quartets as a gift and I play them over and over because I have only a few records.

We have already indicated that the determinations of the Objects of experience are precipitated in the set of types in the stock of knowledge. On the other hand, every determination of an Object of experience depends on the set of types found in the stock of knowledge. The connection between degrees of determinateness and levels of familiarity rests on this. An animal which I encounter is determined as a "dog" and is familiar to me as "dog." That means, first: the determining characteristics which I perceive and consider on the basis of the relevant typifications on hand in the stock of knowledge are compatible with the type "dog." And, second: the situation does not require any determination transcending this type. The animal, as I also always know, can be determined in greater detail. Only if I am induced to seek a further determination, and if the perceptible characteristics cannot be brought into coincidence with a type already on hand, does the animal appear to me as inadequately determined, and at the same time unfamiliar. In such a situation, I then have a motive for acquiring further knowledge conducive to a closer determination of the type, to its modification, or to the formation of subtypes. By means of a further determination, the higher degrees of the determinateness of the element of knowledge (the type), together with the actual experience, are converted into a higher degree of familiarity.

The type conditions the unity of experience or the prominency of the present Object in the flow of experience. The type itself is constituted in explications of the horizons of experience. In a certain sense, it draws the line between the determined and the undetermined, the familiar and the unfamiliar.[54] The determinateness of the type is grounded in the determinateness of the experiences sedimented in it. The determinateness of the type in turn conditions the degree of determinateness in the current experience which it is at that time entering. This state of affairs is evident, insofar as we consider the possibilities of determination given in the inner horizon of experience, the limit of which is established first of all by the type presently brought into experience.

The degree of determinateness of an experience is also conditioned by the explication of the outer horizon of such an experience sedimented in the stock of knowledge. It thus depends on the determination of the Object of experience in its relations to other Objects; more exactly, to the types of Objects of expe-

54. See Chap. 3, A, 3, b, ii; also Chap. 3, C.

rience; and indeed above all to such types on the same or on a higher level of determinateness. Let us take as an example an Object having some complexity, one whose inner horizon can be determined in multiple, polythetic "partial experiences." I know a lot, and in fact with a high degree of determinateness, about the melodies, instrumentation, arrangement, etc., of Mozart's string quartets. I also know a lot, and in fact again in a highly determined fashion, about the relation of these quartets to the other chamber-music compositions of Mozart, his symphonies, operas, etc., as well as about their relation to the string quartets of the contemporary Italians, the string quartets of Haydn, their place in Mozart's biography, etc. But I can also know a lot about the first group of possibilities of determination and little about the second, or vice versa, I can know a lot or little about both, etc. The matter is vastly simpler with Objects of experience which do not have such a complex structure and do not involve historical states of affairs and aspects of experience from various provinces of reality. But in principle it must be maintained that the degree of determinateness of an element of knowledge depends as much on that of the inner as of the outer horizon.

That the explication of the outer horizons of an Object of experience is also necessarily in relation to the set of types found in the stock of knowledge derives from the above. First, the unity of experience and thus also the border between that which is currently outer and that which is inner horizon, is conditioned by the current relevant type. Instead of "all Mozart's string quartets" (a complex, polythetically built up "far-reaching" unity of the meaning of the experience) we could just as well take one of its members as the actually occurring Object of experience; for example, the Adagio from the Adagio and Fugue in C Major for String Quartet (K. 546), to whose "outer horizon" the fugue would already belong. But more important is the fact that there are not only typical Objects of experience but also typical Object relations which are likewise sedimented in the set of types in the stock of knowledge. Here we are touching on a new dimension of the stock of knowledge, the freedom from contradiction among elements of knowledge. This is indeed a different dimension, since it concerns the relation between elements of knowledge, not the attributes of an element. It must thus be *formally* distinguished from the typical Object relations sedimented in the stock of knowledge. Factually, the relation between elements of knowledge is immediately founded on knowledge concerning the relations between the Objects of experience to which these elements refer.

d. The compatibility between elements of knowledge

As was said, freedom from contradiction is a dimension of the stock of knowledge of a different sort than familiarity and determinateness. While elements of knowledge are individually graduated according to familiarity and determinateness, freedom from contradiction concerns the relation between elements of knowledge. The lifeworldly stock of knowledge contains determinations of experiences of Objects of experience, as well as of relations between Objects of experience which do not agree with one another. The general formal reason for deficient agreement between elements of knowledge is known to us from the analysis of the acquisition of knowledge. Elements of knowledge are sedimented in various situations and are related to the mastery of heterogeneous situations. Specific elements are not "always on hand," like knowledge of the basic elements of the situation and habitual knowledge in the narrow sense. Rather, they are simply "at hand"; they come into use from case to case according to their relevance for the mastery of a current situation. In the natural attitude, there is no motivation to keep *all* the elements of knowledge in fundamental agreement. Even if elements of knowledge are "theoretically" in contradiction with one another, that is, if they contradicted one another within a closed, formal, logically ordered system of knowledge, they do not need to conflict in the natural attitude. A conflict only occurs if it turns out that those elements in a situation that have been taken to be relevant in a taken-for-granted way up to now do not suffice for mastery of the situation, thus making it necessary for such elements as until now appeared as "less" relevant to be drawn on. If these elements that are now drawn on are inconsistent with the element originally employed, with regard to their meaning, then both elements of knowledge become problematic. Both are then tested in conjunction with a provisional level of credibility. After weighing the relative credibility and, if necessary, after further explication and determination of the Objects and relations of experience involved in the situation, a decision is reached. The decision confirms the credibility of one element and annuls the other, or develops a new element of knowledge subordinated, in respect to meaning, to the earlier element and having a sufficient level of credibility for coming to terms with the situation. In this way the contradiction which had come to light between elements of knowledge in the situation is converted into a state free of contradiction. It is possible that in a situation the contradiction between elements of knowledge would come into the grasp of consciousness, although the mastery of the situation would yield no solution to the contradiction. In this case, even contradictions which had become conscious could remain as such within the structure of the stock of knowledge.

Thus it is asserted that, fundamentally, elements of knowledge which are "theoretically" self-contradictory need not necessarily conflict in the natural attitude. The *origin* of the "theoretical" contradiction is derived from the heterogeneity of the situations in which knowledge is acquired. The *continuation* of the "theoretical" contradictoriness into the lifeworldly stock of knowledge, on the other hand, is derived from the heterogeneity of the situations in which the elements of knowledge are used. If the elements of knowledge "have nothing to do with one another," if they are mutually irrelevant, their value (present determinateness, present credibility) remains unrevoked even if they are "theoretically" incompatible with one another. This must be more closely examined.

Let it be stressed once again: we are dealing with the lifeworldly stock of knowledge, not with the structure of a science or a logical system. It falls to us to describe the acquisition of knowledge as it emerges from the prepredicative experience of the life-world and from the "thinking" founded on it. This thinking consists of the processes of explication, unique to the style of knowledge in daily life. It does not consist of the predications, judgments, conclusions, etc., of formal logic. Husserl dealt with this in order to show that the categories of formal logic are founded on the structures of prepredicative experience. For the purposes of the present investigation, it is sufficient to show that the categories of formal logic belong to special levels of knowledge and that the formalizations lying at the basis of these levels of knowledge find divergent expressions in various relative-natural world views. They are not identically objectivated in different languages. We are occupied here with the subjective forms of the acquisition of knowledge and the subjective structure of the lifeworldly stock of knowledge in general, and we will now leave the various cultural or linguistic superstructures until later.

The simplification which lies at the basis of this method of inspection is expressly acknowledged: all knowledge is in fact subjectively acquired. The acquisition of knowledge, though, does not necessarily occur through subjective processes of explication. As will be shown later, knowledge is, to an empirically most significant extent, not only socially distributed, but also already *presupposed* in the relative-natural world view, and above all in the set of types of the language.[55] This involves neither a genealogy of logic, nor an empirical sociology of knowledge, nor a historical semantics. The findings about the basic forms of the acquisition of knowledge and the basic structure of the life-worldly stock of knowledge should hold good for the natural attitude in general, whether a "scientific" or "magical" world picture is socially built up on it.

What are the most important of the structural conditions which cause the elements of knowledge to "have nothing to do with one another"? Particularly elements which have been formed out of experiences in different provinces of reality with finite meaning-structure are fundamentally characterized by a reciprocal irrelevance.[56] The styles of lived experience or knowledge on which experiences are based radically differ from one another. The experiences are sedimented in the stock of knowledge with their corresponding "prior indications" and are consequently imbedded in meaning-structures which do not intersect —leaving the special case of "enclaves" out of consideration. In general, it is the case that elements of knowledge referring to different provinces of reality do not have a meaning-relation with one another. Consequently, the discussion of these elements involves neither a genuine contradiction nor freedom from contradiction in the proper sense of the word. Let us take an example to illustrate. I have repeatedly dreamed that I am flying. It belongs to the store of my knowledge about my dream reality that I can (sometimes, often, always) fly. In the everyday life-world I cannot do it, a fact that I know very well after an ill-fated attempt in my childhood. These two elements of knowledge are not in a genuine contradiction with one another; they are mutually irrelevant.

Although elements of knowledge originating from different provinces of reality are not in principle related to one another,

55. See Chap. 4, A, and 4, B, 3, b.
56. See Chap. 2, A.

elements of knowledge which have the "prior indications" of the same style of knowledge are in principle related to one another, but they *need* not be so related. We have already brought out the reason for this: since they are acquired in different situations, and employed in different situations, potentially contradictory elements of knowledge do not come in contact with one another. Only in changed or novel situations do heterogeneous elements of knowledge meet one another, and only then is the potential contradiction actualized. The relation between the elements then comes itself into the grasp of consciousness. These elements and their mutual relations become *problematic*. Thus an occasion arises for continuing the acquisition of knowledge, for further explication and change, or for annulling the elements of knowledge until now accepted as unquestioned. What was said about the acquisition of knowledge in general holds good here, although it does not actually concern the explication of the experience or situation as such. It rather concerns the explication of the elements of knowledge relevant for it and their reciprocal relations. Naturally, this is also the case where the elements of knowledge in question are looked on as relevant within a situation and for accomplishing the mastery of typical situations. It holds good as well for elements of knowledge referring to Objects of experience ("this is a fir; this is a pine; but wait, they both have the same cones, arrangement of needles, etc.—perhaps this is also a fir." And then the motivation toward a resolution: "well, it is all the same to me," or, "I will soon take a forestry examination; I must absolutely be able to differentiate, etc."), as well as for relations between Objects of experience and events ("barking dogs do not bite; this dog yelps without pause, now he has bitten me").

With respect to the elements of knowledge constituted within the same province of reality, there are greater and lesser probabilities of relation, which depend immediately on the degree of determinateness of the types involved. On the one hand, an element of knowledge having a lesser degree of generality can modify an element of knowledge with a higher degree, if it is related to the same experiences; or it can reduce its credibility. It can, on the other hand, be bracketed as an "exception" ("barking dogs don't bite" isn't true, or "in general it is true, but in any particular case one can never know"). It is obvious that the concern here is with processes of explication on which the formal induction is based. There is an essential difference here. Processes of explication are pragmatically motivated, while the degrees of credibility under discussion refer to subjective hierarchies of interest and not to a scientific canon.

Elements of knowledge having the same degree of generality can enter "into competition" with one another during the explication of an actually present, problematic experience. ("Is the object there in the fog a tree on the side of the street or a pedestrian in the middle of the street?") In this case it does not really involve a contradiction between elements of knowledge as such. It is not the relation between the elements that is problematic. Rather two different, "hypothetically" relevant elements with regard to the further determination of the actually present experience are momentarily equally credible. This is thus not a case of dealing with the lack of contradiction in the stock of knowledge, but rather a case of the question of credibility [57] and of relevance structures.[58]

Let us summarize. The already-given structure of the world and the subjective structure of experience, especially the forms of the acquisition of knowledge in their biographical expression, cause the formation of closer and more distant relations between elements of knowledge and at the same time condition the mutual irrelevance of certain elements. The closer the relation, the greater the probability that potential contradictions in current situations will be grasped by consciousness and (with given motivation) converted into a state free of contradiction. In the latter case, element of knowledge A is grasped according to its "meaning" (determinateness, type, credibility, etc.) as related to element B, and vice versa. According to the necessities of the situation, the contradiction is then bracketed (the contradiction is "unimportant") or solved, in which case either A and B (or, A or B) changes, or in the most extreme case is annulled (for example, "I must have been mistaken," "I perceived it incorrectly," "in the school of life I had to revise much schoolboy wisdom," or even, "there are two opinions about that," "it is either thus or thus," etc.).

e. The credibility of the elements of knowledge

Familiarity, determinateness, and freedom from contradiction among elements of knowledge are essential dimensions of the structure of the stock of knowledge. The credibility of the

57. See Chap. 3, A, 3, e.
58. See Chap. 3, B.

elements in a certain sense is the most important dimension. It is more immediately interwoven with action in the life-world than the others, since it determines the considerations about the feasibility of projects for acts.[59] It is, further, subjectively more easily graspable as a component of lifeworldly knowledge than the other dimensions. Familiarity is usually graspable only in the negative, through "effects of alienation," which occur when something hitherto familiar suddenly "explodes." Determinateness is so finely graduated, so variable from experience to experience and taken for granted in the types embedded in language, that it rarely comes into grasp or only in the relatively infrequent cases of conscious explication of predicates. On the other hand, credibility also appears to us in the natural attitude as a characteristic of elements of knowledge. We can usually without difficulty say what weight is assigned to an element in our stock of knowledge. Language offers many turns of phrase which characterize the gradations of this dimension, from highest credibility ("I know that most certainly") to different, in-between levels ("most probably," "possibly," "if I am not mistaken") to the least credibility ("appear thus to me," "it may be so . . . but yet again . . . ," etc.). It is significant that, in many languages, references to the credibility of assertions are even brought into the formal determination of predication.

In the analyses of the familiarity and determinateness of elements of knowledge, and also in the description of freedom from contradiction among them, we have had occasion to allude to the connection of these dimensions with the credibility of the elements. We have seen that this has been traced back to their common origin. Now the task still remains to make this general assertion precise with regard to the origin of the degrees of credibility.

Many elements in the stock of knowledge are sedimented from more or less unexplicated experiences as taken for granted. Their credibility is based on the straightforward givenness of these experiences and on the circumstance that they have remained uncontradicted in the further flow of experience. We can assume as a hypothetical, borderline case that an experience enters into the stock of knowledge without any explication; its degree of credibility would be similar to the "animal faith" of which Santayana speaks. Further, in every stock of knowledge there are many

59. See Chap. 5 [Vol. II].

elements whose explication was broken off so early (usually this means: at a very low level of determinateness) that there could be no (potential) contradiction with other elements of knowledge already established. In the situation the least explicated experience in any case appeared sufficiently familiar; there was no interest in having greater familiarity on hand, or the interest was so weak that it was "immediately" eclipsed by other interests. A somewhat higher degree of credibility attends such elements of knowledge as were sedimented from experiences where an, at least, provisional agreement appeared plausible with other elements of knowledge that were relevant in the situation and already established. All these nuances in degrees of credibility are characterized by the originary sedimentation of the element of knowledge not being brought into question by further similar experiences. We can best characterize the total province of these degrees of credibility with the expression "credible until further notice." With such elements of knowledge the credibility, even with relatively high degrees of familiarity, remains provisional and low. If, for instance, I hear thunder far off in a sunny sky, I may be so busy with other things that it does not make much difference to me whether I determine the event more carefully. Without actually contemplating the horizon of other, actually present themes of experience, I "assume" that it does not involve a meteorological event; perhaps it is an explosion, target practice, etc. I do not consider these possibilities closely and do not compare them with one another. The event may be repeated quite often. I still do not have any "explanation" for it, nor do I look for one. But I have to a certain extent become familiar with the event. If it is repeated and I register this also only half-attentively, I can still in a dim way expect that it will be repeated again. I can surely not predict the repetition, since I do not have an "explanation" for the event as such; I am interested neither in an explanation nor in a prediction. Nothing has contradicted the possible causes, which were not really clearly set out and which I only took vague notice of. With a certain, albeit low, credibility, an element of knowledge has thus been sedimented— which is expressed in my vague and uninterested "assumption" that the event will be repeated.

Further, there are elements in the stock of knowledge that are sedimented from experiences which were originally brought into question and with which the explication has proceeded up to a certain point. The differences in the "totality" of the explication determine the differences in the degree of credibility of the element of knowledge in question. Thus the case in which the explication was interrupted before genuine alternatives had been formed is included in the already-mentioned province of degrees of credibility. (I see something rustle past me in the forest; under the circumstances it may be not unimportant for me to find out what it was, but there are many possibilities: I only imagine the wind blew something past; it was an animal, perhaps a deer, a dog, a fox, etc.) The cause for the explication being interrupted, although I was interested in the original situation, can lie in the "disappearance" of the problem, i.e., the objects of experience to which the problem refers (just as with the above example). The explication may, however, also have been broken off because new, situationally conditioned interest overlaid the original interest. (I want, for example, to look up Timbuktu in the lexicon, knowing from the original context only that it presumably had "something to do with Africa." But in paging through, I find the heading for Tibet. As I was only interested in Timbuktu because the word could perhaps someday be of use to me in solving a crossword puzzle, or for the purpose of "general education," etc., and since the same holds good for Tibet, I first read through the entry on Tibet. Subsequently, I have to hurry to an appointment, and the problem "Timbuktu" remains unexplicated. That it has "something to do with Africa" may have a high degree of credibility. But since this determination is not sufficient for me, closer and probably already envisaged possibilities of determination, "city, river, mountains," etc., have no high degree of credibility either.) Explications broken off "all too soon" have (with respect to the prevailing degree of determinateness of the element of knowledge) a correspondingly low degree of credibility ("it could have been this or that, but perhaps also something else," "nothing can be said about that with certainty . . .").

The explication can furthermore have served up to the point where genuine alternatives have been formed, but the indicated value of the Object of experience does not suffice for reaching a decision by means of the typifications stored in the stock of knowledge. (This is in any case a mushroom, but I am not sure whether it is edible or poisonous.) This case again includes the previously discussed one. Even if already genuine alternatives have been formed, the problem can "disappear" (the mushroom I took along was rubbed to bits in the knapsack, and I can't find any more mushrooms of the same kind), or it can be overlaid by new interests (there is an important message waiting for me at home, and I "forget" to look the mushroom up in the mushroom book). Elements of knowledge of this kind have a unique degree of credibility. The alternatives are very credible in conjunction with one another, since all other possibilities have already been excluded through the previous process of explication (either an edible or poisonous mushroom; Timbuktu: a city in either south Sudan or west Sudan; spruces: either pines or firs—and I would be ready to bet a month's salary if someone maintains that they are something else; I had found a potato; Timbuktu is a mountain in Tibet; spruces are called "Scotch pines" in northern Germany). The degree of credibility of each alternative is by itself relatively low and in any case subjectively perceived as provisional. Since no substantiated decision between the alternatives was made, although one assumes that such is possible, one leans toward abstaining from judgment about the credibility of the individual alternatives. If one now actually already had something to say about the credibility of the alternatives, one could decide, according to the circumstances, in favor of one or the other of the alternatives.

If a decision is reached after considering the indicated worth of the individual alternatives in relation to other elements of knowledge already established, then an alternative enters into the stock of knowledge as a highly credible element. Originally, both alternatives were more or less credible, and one found oneself in doubt as to which would have priority. After the decision is reached according to one's "best knowledge and in good conscience," the credibility of the one alternative is revalued upward, until it is identical with the combined credibility of both alternatives. At the same time, the credibility of the other alternative is annulled. In the natural attitude, we are hardly conscious that these levels of credibility ("I am quite sure," "nothing can be changed about that") also hold good only "until contradicted." As improbable as it may seem to me, such an element of knowledge can also be changed by means of new experiences, and further explications in the extreme case can even be annulled. This level of credibility corresponds to the case of "empirical certainty" [60] which Husserl described in detail. The certainty has

60. See Edmund Husserl, *Erfahrung und Urteil* (Prague: Academia, 1939; 2d ed., Hamburg: Claassen & Goverts, 1948), pp. 368–71. [English translation by James S. Churchill and Karl Ameriks, *Experience and Judgment: Investigations in a Genealogy of Logic* (Ev-

arisen empirically, has been empirically ascertained, but can also in principle be empirically contradicted.

Thus we have traced the main differences in degrees of credibility back to the processes of the acquisition of knowledge. The procedures of consideration and decision are completely understandable only after analysis of the relevance structures determining them.[61] What has been said suffices in order that credibility can be arranged in typical levels. These are related only to the acquisition of knowledge through subjective procedures of explication. We have, again, disregarded a circumstance of decisive importance for the constitution of levels of credibility. Only a fraction of the subjective stock of knowledge is acquired through subjective procedures of explication. A larger province of the elements of knowledge is socially distributed, and this is only to a small extent subjectively "retested" through procedures of explication. To a great extent, such knowledge comes from monothetic meaning-structures, whose polythetic construction one takes for granted, in "recipes," methods of thought and act, etc., which one has "learned." Such elements of knowledge can have a high degree of credibility even if no genuine alternatives through which one could reach a decision "established" through subjective processes of explication are available. The degree of credibility of socially distributed knowledge is rather far more essentially codetermined by the "authority" of the source. The problems affecting the relation of the stock of knowledge, the acquisition of knowledge, and society, will be taken up separately later.[62]

f. Concerning the structure of negative knowledge [63]

i. The limitations of the stock of knowledge and the relative intransparency of the life-world

Although broad provinces of the stock of knowledge are routinized (whereby large areas of the life-world become familiar and taken for granted), in principle the acquisition of knowledge

---

anston, Ill.: Northwestern University Press, 1973). A new German edition is soon to be published by Felix Meiner, Hamburg.]

61. See Chap. 3, B.

62. See Chap. 4.

63. [As noted by Professor Luckmann, this section was developed "by reference to the suggestion" in Schutz's earlier, incomplete manuscript, now published as *Reflections on the Problem of Relevance*. See esp. Chap. 6.]

is never concluded. The lifeworldly stock of knowledge can never be "complete;" although it may suffice for the mastery of many, and even of most, subjectively predictable situations. There are surely empirical differences: in being able to explicate prior events anew, and in openness vis-à-vis new things; in individual "talents," between different age levels, etc. Certain elements, especially the mythical and religious ones of many relative-natural world views, are also relatively closed in comparison with the modern outlook on the world. A completely torpid world, a definitive conclusion to the acquisition of knowledge, is on the other hand impossible for the normal person on the basis of the individual's situation in the life-world: the relative opacity as well as the absolute intransparency of the life-world is imposed on the individual situation in the life-world. That this is the case must be shown in greater detail.

While the acquisition of knowledge as such can never in principle be concluded, it is possible to incorporate into the stock of knowledge specific elements of knowledge as sufficiently familiar, and to look at the explication of the Objects of experience and situations concerned as "definitively" concluded. It is of the essence of an explication that it is selectively directed to a situationally conditioned problem, and all explications in the natural attitude are essentially determined by a pragmatic motive. What one knows, one knows because one wants to or has to know it. The stock of knowledge is the sedimentation of all this: whatever one has to be "concerned" with, and that with which one has had to come to terms. But the opposite is also the case, as we want to show: all that one does not know is also derivable from the history of the acquisition of knowledge.

The relation of negative knowledge to this history is clear in the case of that element of knowledge which one sought to incorporate into the stock of knowledge, but whose explication one "had to" interrupt before it was sufficiently determined and familiar. If one interrupts an explication, one is also conscious of the fact in the natural attitude of daily life that the problem is "unsolved," that something still unrecognized is hidden behind the situation or the Object of experience. The insufficiently familiar indicates something unfamiliar; the inadequately determined, something undetermined. As long as the unfamiliar and undetermined are taken to be, in principle, capable of being rendered familiar and determinable, interrupted explications adjoining provinces of the life-world with merely relative opacity have an opacity consisting of an "accidental" and "provisional" intransparency.

The same holds good in principle for explications that were seen by the subject as "definitively" terminated. At all times, the lifeworldly stock of knowledge also contains some elements of knowledge which indeed appeared sufficiently explicated in the original situation of the acquisition of knowledge, where the explication was then "definitively" concluded, but which were determined in subsequent situations to need further explication. The "definitive character" of the original explication may be withdrawn from such elements. Even there, the relative opacity of the life-world is able to be subjectively grasped. Yet in the natural attitude the suspicion that "definitively" concluded explications could in principle be similar to concluded explications is not generalized. It is probably transferred to specific results of explications, where there are already other motives present to weaken the degree of credibility, but without this leading to an insight into the fundamental limitation of the stock of knowledge and the absolute intransparency of the life-world.

We can, though, state that the explication through which specific elements of knowledge are constituted is fundamentally incomplete. The inner and outer horizon of experiences to which the explications refer is in principle unlimited, but the explications themselves are fundamentally limited. This is the case with interrupted explications, where the intransparent residuum appears as relevant or potentially relevant, so that the relative opacity of the life-world enters into consciousness. But it is also the case with "definitively" concluded explications, where the intransparent residuum appears as irrelevant—so that the opacity of the life-world is given only in the far horizon of the explication. In the first case, the unrecognized residuum "threatens" the degree of familiarity of the Object of experience or element of knowledge; in the second case it does not impair its familiarity.

Yet a further circumstance in the history of the acquisition of knowledge refers the subjective experience to the relative or provisional opacity of the life-world. Everyone who has acquired a relatively complete knowledge of *A, B,* and *C* knows that this was only possible in that he at the same time "gave up" a more complete knowledge of X, Y, and Z. Under the force of the lifeworldly situation, in terms of the principle of "first things first" and on the basis of the subjective, biographically expressed hierarchy of interests, *A, B,* and *C* were more important or more urgent to him. Even if X, Y, and Z were not unimportant, he had to decide whether he should use the time "at his disposal" for completing his knowledge about A, B, and C, or X, Y, and Z. In the natural attitude this circumstance also indicates only an "accidental" (one could have decided also on X, Y, and Z) limitation of the stock of knowledge; thus the relative opacity of the life-world ("I had no time to go into that further," "That wasn't sufficiently interesting," "Originally I vacillated between the study of biology and theology," etc.).

But it is not only discontinued and "definitively" concluded explications that refer to the relative opacity of the life-world and let it come into consciousness. The refutation of past explications also does the same thing. In the various situations in which earlier explications become problematical and new explications are produced, it can happen that the original explication is expressly confirmed. In this fashion its degree of credibility is strengthened. But if the original determination comes into contradiction with the actual new determination founded on observation of the Object of experience and by means of other elements of knowledge, the degree of credibility of the first can be completely annulled. The validity of the element of knowledge in question is annulled and overlaid by a new element of knowledge. Let us assume that I had formerly assumed that a whale is a fish because it lives in water. In the meantime, I have learned a bit about the structure of the animal body and the classification of the animal kingdom based on this. I know that all fish live in water, but that not everything that lives in water is a fish. The whale must be determined as belonging to the newly established type "mammal." Thus the degree of credibility of the original element of knowledge is annulled; the determination is negated and overlaid by a new determination. The Object of experience, which was originally determined as fish and was familiar as such, is now determined as mammal and is familiar as such. Yet the formerly familiar determination "fish" remains provisionally retained in the horizon, so to speak with a negative sign. The whale is then experienced as "non-fish: mammal," then as "mammal: non-fish-how-stupid-can-a-person-be," until finally the determination "non-fish" is "completely" overlaid. Thereafter a careful explication of the acquisition of this element of knowledge is needed in order to "discover" the annulled determination "fish" in the horizon of the actual experience. We will have to look more closely at this circumstance, which is relevant for the structure of negative knowledge. We will provisionally maintain that the relative opacity of the life-world is read off not only from the "positive" aspects of the stock of knowledge, the credibly determined elements of knowledge, but also from the "negative" determinations contained in the horizon of these elements of knowledge. In both, the limitation of the stock of knowledge is subjectively graspable.

Until now we have stayed with the acquisition of knowledge in the narrower sense of the word: the history of specific explications. But one can also grasp the acquisition of knowledge more broadly, as the sedimentation of experiences in general. Thus we come to the opacity of the life-world for the individual. His experiences of the life-world are temporally, spatially, and socially ordered, in other words temporally, spatially, and socially limited.[64] From the current phases of consciousness with their retentions and protensions, memories and explications flow out. Restorable, attainable, and nonattainable provinces are arranged around the sector of the world in reach. The contemporary social world, the preceding world, and the succeeding world are stratified around the immediately given, social environment. The temporally, spatially, and socially arranged horizons of every actual experience or situation in general extend in the direction of decreasing familiarity, determinateness, and credibility. They point to distant horizons of relative opacity: to temporally, spatially, and socially arranged provinces of the life-world, which are unfamiliar and undetermined on the basis of the prior acquisition of knowledge. This holds in principle for the inner and outer horizons of all experiences. Consequently, "self-evident" experiences, which unproblematically run their course as "natural unities," contain in their horizon a reference to the opacity of the life-world. In this sense, "self-evidently" limited experiences are also "open."

Such "self-evident" or taken-for-granted unities of experience are the result of past processes of explication, although the memory of the specific explications has been obscured. What was said about the relation between the processes of explication and the opacity of the life-world holds good in principle for "naïve" unities of experience, with the difference that the opacity of the life-world cannot be subjectively grasped in them. Only if the unities "explode" in problematical situations and reveal "new

64. See Chap. 2, B.

connections," that is, only if specific processes of explication occur, does the limited nature of the stock of knowledge come into conscious awareness in the natural attitude. Then, what in general takes place in novel situations holds good here. On the basis of the history of the prior acquisition of knowledge, one knows that objects and events which were originally unfamiliar and undetermined can be rendered familiar and more closely determined. Consequently, the current, "still" intransparent aspects of the situation are experienced as in principle capable of being rendered transparent and inspected by means of the types stored in the stock of knowledge. The relative opacity of the life-world is thus already formed through the arrangement of subjective experience of the life-world. It can be read off from the decreasing degrees of familiarity and determinateness in the horizon of experience; it forces itself on subjective insight, whenever the naïvely delineated unity of experience becomes problematic and its inner and outer horizon must be explicated anew.

The opacity of the life-world and the limited nature of the stock of knowledge is presented most forcefully whenever one must predict the future, whenever one projects acts, ponders their feasibility, and estimates their consequences.[65] Situations and the flows of experience, events in the natural world and social world, are sketched out in advance and one's own actions adjusted on the basis of the stock of knowledge at hand, and above all with the help of the set of types stored in it. Again and again the stock of knowledge proves to suffice only in very limited fashion for the determination of the future. Unforeseen situations intrude on us and relatively new elements of situations arise again and again. In fact, even completely novel situations, or in any case elements of situations, surprise us. The history of the acquisition of knowledge is the history of such surprises. The intransparency of the future is similar, in a certain sense, to the relative opacity of the present and past life-world. Many surprises are quite mild, since they come within the scope of a "wide-meshed" typicality. In addition, it must be added that the future must be grasped not as "absolutely" intransparent but only as "temporarily" opaque. In a certain sense, past, present, and future thus appear in the life-world as opaque due only to "technical," "accidental" reasons. If one had taken the trouble to get to

65. For a more exact analysis of the problems involved here, see Chaps. 3, C, 4, and Chap. 5 [Vol. II].

know X better, one would know more about X. In principle, one could still repeat that. If X lies in the future, one need only "wait" until it comes up, and inform oneself about it then. In any case, we have referred here to a new dimension of opacity, which cannot even subjectively be traced back to a purely "accidental" limitation of the stock of knowledge. The "technical difficulties" are of another kind. Since the past presents a chain of actualities among many congruent possibilities, the future is thus a province of pure possibilities. These have indeed different "weights," insofar as they, as such, can be ordered in the set of types stored in the stock of knowledge. The possibility of action, the confirmation of predictions, and the restriction of surprises are based on this. Still, radical surprises come up again and again. Knowledge of this fact indicates the limited nature of the lifeworldly situation in general, not simply the biographically "accidental" limitation of the stock of knowledge. The lived experience of radical surprises refers forcibly to the fundamental intransparency of the life-world.

ii. *The fundamental intransparency of the life-world*

We have seen that every experience entering into the stock of knowledge is limited by the situation of the acquisition of knowledge. Every explication points to other, similarly possible explications. Even "definitively" concluded explications contain the possibility of further explication. Even credible elements of knowledge can be refuted. In every situation novel elements can appear. Since every experience has an in-principle-unlimited, explicable inner and outer horizon, there is always something unfamiliar sketched behind the familiar, something undetermined behind the determined, although the processes of explication themselves are necessarily articulated biographically and thus limited. These "residua" of opacity, which can be demonstrated in every element of knowledge, announce the intransparency of the life-world. Also, in the natural attitude this intransparency appears to be only relative, since it is derived from a limitation of the stock of knowledge, which indicates the "accidental" biographical articulations of the acquisition of knowledge. The life-world is experienced as only relatively (with respect to the prevailing state of knowledge) intransparent, but in principle transparent. The "accidental" limitation on the lifeworldly stock of knowledge is determined by the essential limitation of the acquisition of knowledge by the lifeworldly situation. It will be shown that it must be traced back to the fundamental intransparency of the life-world. Even in the natural attitude, the relative intransparency of the life-world can be grasped subjectively at any time. Any specific process of explication can serve as an occasion for this. But in theoretical reflection, the lived experience of the inadequacy of specific explications leads to an insight into the essential nature of the limitation of the lifeworldly stock of knowledge in general. While in the natural attitude there is no motive at hand for generalizing the suspicion of inadequacy which arises in specific explications, there is on the other hand no reason theoretically to exclude any specific explication from this "suspicion." This fact affects every element of knowledge and thus also the stock of knowledge in its entirety. Theoretically, one knows that he knows only "partial contents" of the life-world, and even these only "in part," and that this is not a biographical "accident" ("I am a chess expert, but I know nothing of agriculture"), but rather a condition of lifeworldly knowledge in general, given through the lifeworldly situation ("one can't know everything").

The finitude and the historicality of the lifeworldly situation condition and limit the biographical expression of the acquisition of knowledge. Every actual situation, every phase of the acquisition of knowledge is biographically articulated. Every situation is the result of a chain of past matters of fact, which has been taken out of countless mere possibilities. The course of life (and with it the acquisition of knowledge) stands out against situations and experiences which are considered, feared, desired, but not engaged. Without further ado, this takes care of the natural attitude. But in the theoretical attitude we can also grasp the course of life in contrast to a background of feared possibilities. We have not had to consider, have not desired or feared, possibilities which have subjectively not even appeared as such ("what would my course of life have been as a Sumerian?" "what experience could I have if I could travel in another solar system?"). Where subjective experience comes to the limits of the lifeworldly situation in general, the provinces of relative opacity flow into a province of fundamental intransparency ("that goes beyond my capabilities of grasping it"). We can say that the limitation on the situation, which is imposed on the subject, finds its knowledge correlate in the fundamental intransparency of the life-world. Even the "accidental" biographical limitation of the stock of knowledge is an essential element of the limitation of the situation. *Thus* understood, the relative opacity for the individual subject is derived from the fundamental intransparency of the life-world for everyone.

From the theoretical viewpoint, knowledge of the life-world is thus *necessarily* fragmentary, even if the limitation of knowledge appears subjectively as the result of biographical "accidents." In the natural attitude the fundamental intransparency of the life-world does not become a "problem." The lifeworldly stock of knowledge is confirmed in the mastery of situations, and the relatively opaque provinces of the life-world can, insofar as they are relevant, be elucidated step by step. But this is so only step by step, and only so far as the pragmatically motivated interest suffices, and through a choice which is made by the principle of "first things first." Otherwise put, the "suspicion" of a fundamental inadequacy of the lifeworldly stock of knowledge cannot arise in the natural attitude, or is not confirmed in it. What is taken for granted in daily life can routinely be mastered, new situations determined and ordered. Practically, the stock of knowledge holds good in its *entirety*, even if not often enough in specific elements of knowledge.

The "suspicion," if it affects the various moments of the relative opacity of the life-world in general (mostly through the shock of "crises" not easily mastered), can motivate a "leap" into noneveryday provinces of reality. From these provinces the lifeworldly stock of knowledge can appear as completely insufficient. The world can become a mystery that becomes transparent only by means of knowledge superordinated to everyday reality—knowledge of a religious, philosophical, or scientific kind. If the fundamental intransparency of the life-world in general comes to be grasped by consciousness, a need appears to arise to elucidate it again by means of "higher, metaphysical" insights.

iii. The gaps in the stock of knowledge

We have described the conditions of the limitation of the stock of knowledge, and have shown that the relative opacity as well as the fundamental intransparency of the life-world must be traced back to the limits of the individual situation pertaining to the arrangement of subjective experiences and to the unchangeable limitation of explications. It must now be shown how knowledge and negative knowledge are fitted together in the structure of the stock of knowledge.

We have seen that all elements of knowledge contain negative determinations alongside positive ones. To be familiar with an Object of experience also means to be familiar with what it is not. Even familiarity with negative determinations is to be traced back to processes of explication, thus to the situation of the acquisition of knowledge. It is accordingly relevance-conditioned. (The familiar horizon of the element of knowledge "whale" typically contains, for instance, the negative determination "not fish" but not "not tree," although formally both are correct and in principle possible.) Only that which under certain circumstances could perhaps be an Object of experience on the basis of the prevailing set of types stored in the stock of knowledge reaches the grasp of consciousness, first in explication and then in the use of the element of knowledge. Here, two closely related possibilities should be distinguished. In the original explication, determinations possessing a hypothetical credibility can be weighed against one another. A decision is reached, "according to one's best knowledge and in good faith." One alternative enters into the stock of knowledge as a positive determination (a determination with a positive degree of credibility), the other enters as a negative determination. But even determinations which are originally taken into the stock of knowledge with a positive degree of credibility can in later use become problematic. If they lose the degree of credibility in later usage and are replaced by new positive determinations, they remain fixed in the element of knowledge as negative determinations.

The positive determinations constitute the core of the element of knowledge. They are related to other determinations having higher or lower levels of generality, but they exclude other positive determinations on the same level of generality. This does not hold good for negative determinations, of which one can say in general that they run in the direction of decreasing relevance. Negative determinations can only be differentiated as they were acquired, above all in relation to the positive determinations. Thus they can originally have been credible, positive determinations, which were later annulled in a specific act of explication. They may originally have been simply hypothetical possibilities of explication, which were already negated in the original act of explication in favor of other determinations. Finally, they can involve possibilities of determination, which only vaguely came up on the horizon of the original explication, without having become genuine alternatives, in contrast to the actually valid determinations. It should also be remarked that positive determinations can typically be "confirmed" in later use and strengthened, possibly becoming completely routinized. But in the normal case, negative determinations (as expressly negative determinations) do not experience such "confirmations" and are again and again thrust into the undetermined horizon of the element of knowledge, or the Object of experience.

The stock of knowledge thus consists of elements of knowledge which contain not only positive, but also negative determinations. Both come from the situations inherent in the acquisition of knowledge and are (with the just mentioned differences) brought into the structure of the stock of knowledge. The life-world is grasped not only as that which it is, but rather also as that which it is not. What was said about the limitations of the stock of knowledge and the sources of these limitations naturally holds good for both these forms of grasping. Thus the negative aspects of the stock of knowledge cannot really be perceived as gaps in the stock of knowledge, although they refer to the relative opacity of the life-world. However, it becomes clearer in them than in the positive determinations that the stock of knowledge is *potentially* full of gaps. In grasping specific determinations one can, as was brought up earlier, encounter the fact that "residua" that have not become transparent are hidden behind every determination. In specific negative determinations, something further is added. One is conscious that positive determinations can be annulled, that is, that positive determinations can hide a bit of ignorance. Current, negative determinations thus refer to gaps which are hidden by false knowledge; vice versa, negative determinations are knowledge of earlier ignorance. For them, there is in principle the possibility of "rehabilitation." This possibility is shown in the case of specific experiences by which determinations with a negative degree of credibility had to be acknowledged on the basis of new explications as having a positive degree of credibility. In this sense, negative determinations : ent knowledge that is overlaid by positive determinations, but can be again uncovered. We will come to this point in a moment.

With the aid of negative determinations one can thus achieve a general insight into the potentially fragmentary nature of the stock of knowledge. Subjective knowledge about *specific* gaps has another origin. The analysis of the structure of the stock of knowledge has shown that the inner and the outer horizons of the elements of knowledge, or the experiences to which these are related, develop in the direction of decreasing familiarity, determinateness, and credibility. The arrangement of the elements of knowledge themselves and thus of their meaning-cores, is based on this, according to degrees of familiarity, determinateness, and credibility. We have also investigated how specific elements of knowledge are modified, completed, and amplified, and how their degree of credibility is confirmed, increased, narrowed, or annulled. Much that appears adequately determined must be more closely determined; much with which one had been satisfied with a relatively low degree of credibility must be converted into a higher degree of credibility. We have further shown that these moments of the structure of the stock of knowledge are the source of the subjective insight into the relative opacity of the life-world, that through them the limitations of the stock of knowledge can be grasped by consciousness. Even without theoretical reflection one knows that one does not know everything. Similar moments in the structure of the stock of knowledge also bring specific gaps in the stock of knowledge into consciousness. This happens in the form of "comparisons."

In the natural attitude one is also motivated at times to compare elements of knowledge or provinces of elements of knowledge in one's *own* stock of knowledge with one another as to their familiarity, determinateness, and credibility. Thus one says to himself, for example, that one understands more of plants than of animals, but also that one does not know everything in the plant kingdom in the same depth, knowing more about trees, less about flowers. Or one says to himself that one can cook good puddings but does not really do well with soups, etc. Now, such comparisons are conditioned in the natural attitude by the situational relevance. One can compare some provinces of knowledge with each other, others not. Yet in this way, a kind of knowledge about the structure of the stock of knowledge originates in the natural attitude. One can say what one knows a lot about, a little, or nothing.

The comparison of elements of knowledge and provinces in one's own stock of knowledge with the corresponding knowledge of certain fellow-men is of still greater importance than simply "internal" comparisons for the origination of such "structural knowledge." Such comparisons take place in the most dissimilar social situations and are often motivated by the requirements of common action or through conflicts. Still more important as a motive is the necessity of asking "experts" in order to take advantage of their knowledge or in order to "use" their knowledge, without acquiring it oneself. Thus one attains, for instance, the insight that one's father knows more in money matters, about football, etc., than oneself. One goes to school and the teacher transmits knowledge about completely new provinces. One consults a shaman, a wise old man, a physician, etc. It is on the basis of such comparisons that specific, new gaps in one's own stock of knowledge appear in consciousness. It is clear that such comparisons have a direct relation to the social distribution of knowledge.[66]

Finally, one compares one's own stock of knowledge with "Objective" knowledge. In the natural attitude it is observed as previously fixed in the life-world, as a datum, which one can to a certain degree acquire through "discovery," learning, etc. Others can also acquire it or have already done so; it was known to earlier generations and in the meantime has been lost; perhaps there are discoveries which are kept in reserve for later generations. Without going into the origin of "Objective" knowledge here,[67] we want to maintain that it is intersubjectively valid in the natural attitude and is perceived, for the most part, as freed from the subjective organization of experience and the "accidental," biographical articulation of the acquisition of knowledge.

Thus "inner" comparisons of elements of knowledge, comparisons of one's own knowledge with the knowledge of Others, and comparisons with "Objective" knowledge lead to insights into the fragmentary nature of one's own stock of knowledge. They fix specific gaps and effect the development of a "structural" knowledge about one's own stock of knowledge. According to the state of one's interest and actually present, motivational contexts, specific gaps can be irrelevant; that is, no situation is predicted in which the missing knowledge would be urgently needed. Or the missing knowledge is looked on as relevant, but able to be left to the "experts." And finally, gaps of knowledge can be seen as threatening. In this case one is, so to speak, "structurally" motivated to the acquisition of knowledge, not by the *actual* situation, but rather by the typically anticipated requirements of knowledge. The gaps in the stock of knowledge, as well as the processes by which they are "filled," thus stand in immediate connection with the subjective relevance structures.[68]

66. See Chap. 4, C.
67. See Chap. 4, B.
68. See Chap. 3, B.

iv. Negative knowledge as potential knowledge

The relation of negative knowledge to knowledge can be described by analogy to the spatial arrangement of the lifeworldly experience. The sector of the world in actual reach is surrounded by sectors in potential reach, and indeed by a sector in restorable reach and a sector in attainable reach.[69] Negative knowledge can, as far as it is not related to the fundamental intransparency of the life-world, be correspondingly viewed as potential knowledge. Potential knowledge consists of restorable and attainable knowledge.

Restorable knowledge is prior knowledge that has either been lost or hidden by other knowledge. When we speak of *loss of knowledge*, two different states of affairs are involved. It can mean that certain aspects of an element of knowledge have been "forgotten," although its "kernel" remains. The most important example of this is the forgetting of the polythetic constitution of an element of knowledge while its monothetic meaning remains (for instance, the formula for the Pythagorean theorem). There are many everyday examples of this: one "commands" some information without being able to explain how; one knows something without being able to remember "all the particulars." First, this holds good for the subjective stock of knowledge. But also in the social distribution of knowledge, "particulars" get lost, while the meaning, for instance, of a certain tradition (the man walks to the left of the woman) remains. On the other hand, the meaning-context in which an element of knowledge exists can get lost, although individual determinations of the Object of experience remain. Further "logical" connections between elements of knowledge that were once established, especially contradictory relations and their typical connections, fail to be on hand. Although there are everyday examples of this, this case is most forcefully illustrated by the (mostly pathologic) collapse of the functional unity of meaningful action, as in certain forms of aphasia.

Negative knowledge as *hidden knowledge* arises out of formerly positive determinations, which have been annulled and replaced by new positive determinations and hidden, so that they are no longer given in the familiar horizon of the element of knowledge.[70]

69. See Chap. 2, B, 2.
70. See Chap. 3, A, 3, f, iii.

Negative knowledge as *attainable knowledge,* in contrast, has never been on hand in the stock of knowledge. There are provinces of the life-world about which one knows nothing, almost nothing, or but little. One has not been motivated to acquire further instruction, one has deferred the acquisition of knowledge, or it was interrupted. On the basis of the set of types stored in the stock of knowledge, this negative knowledge appears capable of being converted into knowledge. That is, it refers to the province of the relatively opaque, not the absolutely intransparent.

Attainable knowledge is graduated according to its degree of attainability, which is established first according to the distance of the potential knowledge from the province of the fundamentally intransparent. In other words, it is established according to whether one can trace back specific gaps in one's own stock of knowledge, more or less immediately, to the biographical accidents of one's own acquisition of knowledge (absence of "interest," time, etc.), or whether one looks upon them as referable to the "Objective" difficulties of the case. Second, the attainable knowledge is graduated according to its typical attainability by the completely determined individual. One knows that knowledge about this or that is indeed attainable, but that on the basis of typical prior experiences it is harder to acquire for one person than for another. According to "talent," "education," etc., knowledge, is individually more or less "easily" attainable. And third, attainable knowledge is classified according to one's present state of interest, urgency, etc., in short, according to its current subjective relevance. Let us illustrate these arrangements with a few examples.

I have heard that there are people who play chess blindfolded at twenty tables at once. I am not at all sure that this is really possible, but I am quite sure that I could not do it, no matter how hard I tried. I know that some people are excellent mountain climbers and am sure that I could learn to climb the high Alps. I possess the necessary skills and talents, such as freedom from dizziness, finger dexterity, etc. But such things do not interest me. I accept less surely that I could have learned to play the piano, and that it is probably now "too late." I would indeed be interested in trying it anyway, but because of my other areas of interest cannot spend sufficient time on it. I know that I could never learn to cook well, although there are many good cooks, because I possess defective nerves of taste and smell. But I am sure that I will learn Arabic in the course of the next few years. Not only is it in principle possible, but I am also sure because of earlier experiences in learning foreign languages. Since I will subsequently accept a position in a country where Arabic is the spoken language, filling in this gap has the highest level of urgency for me.

g. The contours of the obvious

We can ask the question toward which the preceding analyses headed: how is the life-world presented in the stock of knowledge? To answer this question we need a clear picture of the structure of the stock of knowledge. Since in the description of the individual dimensions of this, their reciprocal interdependence was already clear, we can be satisfied with summarizing the results of this description.

The presuppositions for the development of specific elements of knowledge are given in the limitedness of the lifeworldly situation and in the arrangement of the subjective experiences of the life-world. These presuppositions are at the same time also the cause of the limitations of the lifeworldly stock of knowledge. "Knowledge" about these presuppositions or limitations is co-given in the horizon of every experience and explication and enters into the stock of knowledge as a basic element. In contrast, specific elements of knowledge are formed in specific, biographically molded processes of explication. Their sedimentation in the stock of knowledge and their use in specific situations is in any case biographically articulated. On the basis of the biographical situation, certain elements of knowledge are routinized. Such knowledge, which includes skills, practical knowledge, and knowledge of recipes, has a mediate place between the "always-on-hand" basic elements of the stock of knowledge and the specific elements of knowledge.

The latter form a "system," containing the dimensions of familiarity, determinateness, and credibility. The ("syntactic") connection between the elements of knowledge is expressed in the dimension of freedom from contradiction. The ("semantic") meaning-context between the "contents" of the elements of knowledge is based on the set of types, which "offers" itself for the explications as relevant for the Objects of experience. The structure of the lifeworldly stock of knowledge thus consists of relevance-conditioned meaning-contexts between more or less familiar and more or less credible typical determinations, which are in more or less noncontradictory relations with one another.

The specific elements of knowledge refer to the originary situation of the acquisition of knowledge and the biographical molding of the sedimentations of experience. On the one hand, the specific elements of knowledge—insofar as they are completely routinized—border on the basic elements of the stock of knowledge. On the other hand, specific knowledge goes over into negative knowledge. The structure of the latter in any case indicates the limits of the lifeworldly situation, the arrangement of subjective experiences of the life-world, and the biographical articulation of the acquisition of knowledge.

Thus, to the question concerning how the life-world is delineated in the stock of knowledge, we can first give a formal answer. A core area of the life-world appears relatively determined and sufficiently familiar and credible for mastery of typical situations. This is a province of biographically achieved, relative transparency. A province of biographically conditioned, relative intransparency, a province that could in principle be elucidated by specific knowledge, adjoins this. A province which is in principle opaque adjoins this where subjective experience impinges on the limits of the lifeworldly situation in general.

With this formal answer we have not yet satisfactorily solved the question raised at the beginning. The organization of the life-world into relatively clear, relatively opaque, and fundamentally intransparent provinces is derived from the *structure* of the stock of knowledge. In the natural attitude, however, "structural" knowledge—that is, knowledge about the stock of knowledge—is developed only in small amounts. We therefore have next to ask how the life-world is concretely presented in the natural attitude by means of the stock of knowledge.

Certainly the life-world in the natural attitude is now grasped in the form of a structured *stock of knowledge*. It is *not* presented as a well-circumscribed, free-from-contradiction system of the familiar, the credible, the determined, which is inserted into an equally well-circumscribed province of the relatively opaque, which is itself surrounded by an area of the (in principle) intransparent. Rather, the relation between the stratified structure of the relatively clear and the relatively opaque determines every individual experience of lifeworldly Objects and the understanding of the connection between them without *as such* coming into the grasp of consciousness. We can graphically imagine this in the following manner: Hatched contours are sketched on the Objects of experience and in situations which have been formed as elements of knowledge through processes of explication. The density of hatching is dependent on the levels of familiarity, determinateness, and credibility. Around these hatchings are the "empty places" of the relatively opaque—but one knows that one needed only to survey these places in order to be able to fill them in similarly with hatchings. The life-world is sketched in the stock of knowledge as a contoured "whole" of affairs taken as obvious or "self-evident." According to the relation of hatching and empty stretches, the contours are sharper or hazier. Only that which is intransparent in principle forms a genuine *terra incognita*.

Of what kind is this "whole"? The stock of knowledge originates in sedimentations of unities of experience, whose constitution is determined as much by the resistance of the world (transcending inner duration) as from the processes of explication (following the "logic" of the natural attitude). But this "logic" is objectivated in a relative-natural world view and in the corresponding forms of language, and thus forms a basic element of the social a priori. It is imposed on the individual and plays an important role in the formation of the taken-for-granted unities of subjective experience and explication. The course of sedimentation itself is biographically molded "accidentally." But it has a total systematic character insofar as the unities of experience are brought into broad, encompassing meaning-contexts within the perspective of the course of life. To this it must be added that the molding of the course of life is socially superstructured by the objectivated categories of typical "meaningful courses of life." Thus we can say that the life-world is sketched as a "whole" in the stock of knowledge in a double sense. On the one hand, it appears as a whole from "the inside out," illuminated by the subjective biography. On the other hand, it is presented in systematic meaning-contexts, which follow the socially objectivated "natural logic" (agriculture, alchemy, cooking, reindeer hunting, art of war, etc.). Thus the life-world is not marked out in the stock of knowledge as a simple aggregation of sedimented individual experiences or Objects of experience; it is furthermore not presented as a copy of the structure of the stock of knowledge.

And most surely it does not possess the systematic character of a science—an "Objective" meaning-structure freed for the most part from the subjective organization of experience and biographical articulation.

The life-world is thus grasped with the help of the stock of knowledge, much in the way one locates himself in a countryside with the aid of maps. The explanations of signs, descriptions of places, etc., are taken from the now prevailing "Objective" geography. The choice of maps, and above all the choice of the scale to be used, is motivated subjectively. There are special maps for traveling on which the outlines of regions which are traversed daily are most exactly noted. In part, these outlines are already so familiar that one hardly need refer to the map on his way. Then there are also maps, still in relatively small scale, for areas through which one goes not too infrequently. In rough outline the contours of these areas are also familiar, but one comes again and again into situations in which one has to refer to the map. One may also possess a few self-prepared maps, where the scales are confused with one another. On them there are regions through which one had once traveled. One has recorded several rough outlines and perhaps also various details, but for proper orientation such a map would hardly still suffice after any long period of time. Finally, there are maps having a large scale. They suffice to place the "rest" of the world in relation to the regions for which one has special maps. The entries on such maps are limited to the roughest outlines and contain many empty areas.

Where do these maps come from? Many had to be painstakingly drawn by someone. They contain many details and many purely "private" notes which would be incomprehensible to others. Other maps have indeed been taken over from Others, but they could have had their reliability examined in the meantime. Again, one has taken over others simply on faith and belief. In general, one knows that one's own special maps for hiking present parts of areas for which Others have only maps on a larger scale. And vice versa, one knows with great probability that one could draw special maps of areas for which one has all too inexact maps, in the event there are none already in other hands. Scale and exactness of the self-prepared maps are in relation to the attentiveness with which one has noticed the areas traveled through. The conversion of one's own preceptions into contour lines, demarcations, hatchings, etc., in the map presupposes (as may not be forgotten) the lifeworldly idealizations and anonymizations.

[B] RELEVANCE

1. KNOWLEDGE, RELEVANCE, AND THE EXAMPLE OF CARNEADES

IN THE ANALYSIS of the acquisition of knowledge and the description of the structure of the stock of knowledge, we have repeatedly come to a point at which we were forced to break off the analysis, and we had to be satisfied with indicating that this or that event was "conditioned by relevance." It was the same with the constitution of a circumscribed theme in the flow of experience and with the determination of the situation. It is also the case with the way certain experiences become problematic and with the explications related to problematic experiences—especially with their discontinuance at a certain level of explication, and finally, with the sedimentation of the results of explication in the stock of knowledge. What does it mean when we say that all these processes are conditioned by the current subject-relevance system?

A distinction can be made in the life-world between what were characterized by Husserl in another connection as the attitudes of "living-in-the-relevances" (whereby the relevances themselves do not come into grasp of the consciousness) and the reflecting (although not necessarily "theoretical") "looking-to-the-relevances." [71] Even in the natural attitude we ask ourselves whether we see "things in the right light," whether we should restrict our "interest" to a given problem, whether something "really matters" to us, etc. In so doing, we consciously inquire into our own relevance systems, which we observe as obvious subjective givens. In this fashion, the relevance structures, which

71. [This distinction is between the lived experience of the relevances and reflection on the relevances. Husserl's contention was that such reflection did not distort that which was reflected on. See *Cartesianische Meditationen und Pariser Vorträge* (The Hague: Nijhoff, 1950), §§ 34 and 46. English translation by Dorion Cairns, *Cartesian Meditations* (The Hague: Nijhoff, 1960).]

determine the acquisition of knowledge and thereby the structure of the stock of knowledge, are themselves also a component of the latter. Thus someone can say of himself: "I know that such things don't interest me," or of an acquaintance: "under such circumstances he will always do things, as if matters of this sort were of no consequence to him."

All experiences and all acts are grounded on relevance structures. Every decision more or less explicitly introduces, besides the actor, a series of relevances. The relevance problem is perhaps the most important and at the same time the most difficult problem that the description of the life-world has to solve. What is the role played by relevance structures in the constitution of lifeworldly situations? How do they determine the course of explications, and how do they establish a relation between the prevailing stock of knowledge and the actual experiences and acts?

The Greek skeptic Carneades has already provided an extremely careful investigation of questions which immediately concern the problem of relevance. It is contained in a report by Sextus Empiricus (*Adversus logicos VII*). We will start our own investigation with the analyses by Carneades and in particular will develop them with the aid of the famous "third example." [72]

Carneades begins his investigation of the plausible (πιθανόν; *probabile*) with a critique of the Stoic use of this concept, especially that of Chrysippus. Chrysippus divides representations into those that are plausible and those that are not, and maintains that both kinds are either true, false, or neither true nor false. Carneades decisively rejects this division, denying the possibility that one could ever grasp "the true." He distinguishes instead between what is unknown to us (ἀκατάληπτον; *incomprehensible*) and what is uncertain (ἄδηλον; *incertum*). "The true" as such does not exist; there are only truths for us, thus necessarily problematic truths. Although human representations cannot grasp "the true," they can be more or less plausible. The plausibility of a representation is conditioned by the state in which one finds himself at that time. Whether a representation is plausible or not depends on whether it is in contradiction with other representations or agrees with them. Carneades' basic conception naturally contrasts sharply with the Stoic theory of φαντασία καταληπτικά

72. In presenting the theory of Carneades, we will rely on the excellent account by Léon Robin, *Pyrrhon et le scepticisme grecque* (Paris: Presses Universitaires de France, 1944). [See also the analysis by Schutz in his *Reflections on the Problem of Relevance*.]

(comprehensible representation), the representation which grasps things as they are and which governs the behavior of the sage. For the skeptic, the sage can only be a man, too, and the truth he grasps only a human truth. The sage is not cut from stone, but rather moves about in a body and a soul. His impressions, perceptions, knowledge are conditioned by his human nature. The truly wise man will consequently suspend judgment concerning the true nature of things. Similarly, in his practical conduct and action he will not wait for a knowledge that must remain denied to him. If he, for example, undertakes a sea voyage he does not strictly speaking know how it will end. But although the conclusion of the trip is unknown ($\dot{\alpha}\kappa\alpha\tau\dot{\alpha}\lambda\eta\pi\tau\sigma\nu$) he need by no means be uncertain ($\ddot{\alpha}\delta\eta\lambda\sigma\nu$) about it. If he has chosen a good vessel, commanded by a reliable captain, and if the weather is favorable, he believes that he is sure to reach the final port safe and sound. If he had to wait for true knowledge, he would be condemned to inactivity. He acts on the basis of such more or less probable representations, which serve as his *"consilia agendi ut non agendi,"* as Cicero formulated the principle. Although the sage is epistemologically a skeptic, he will not omit testing the degrees of credibility of representations or motives, which motivate his practical conduct. He does indeed realize that "certitude" is only a form of belief. But he knows at the same time that definite motives and causes are the basis for it, and that these can be assessed. Motives are understandable, determinable bases for holding an opinion. Causes in contrast do not have the understandability of reasons. Causes involve passions, prejudices, habits, as well as the constraint of social circumstances. The opposite of certitude is uncertitude. But between the two extremes, well-founded certitude and complete uncertitude, there are many intermediate levels for which Carneades offered a typology.

Two contrary possibilities can have the same simple probability. Sextus Empiricus offers the following examples: I am pursued by enemies and see a ditch. The ditch could serve as a hiding place for me. On the basis of my prior knowledge, however, the possibility also exists that other enemies are hidden in this ditch. Since I cannot afford to test whether my first hope or the fear that followed it is well founded, both possibilities remain open for me. So far as my practical conduct is concerned, it will probably be safest under the given circumstances for me to look for another hiding place.

A representation can also transcend "simple" probability. It can be "twisted" or "bent" (περίσπαστος) or, as we can perhaps state it better, annulled. Let us consider how Alcestis was led back from the underworld by Hercules. He brings her before Admetus, who doesn't believe what his eyes tell him. The idea of a "living Alcestis" is annulled by his prior knowledge that Alcestis is dead. Without this prior knowledge the idea would not have been annulled and would have a relatively high degree of probability.

Finally, a confirmed representation has the highest credibility. It presupposes "simple" probability. It in any case presupposes that it was not annulled. If it is confirmed, then there is a further basis on hand for one's "certitude." The relation between the individual levels of plausibility is clear in Carneades' third example. A man enters a poorly lighted room and thinks he sees a coiled rope in the corner of the room. But he sees the object only dimly. Thus he asks himself whether it is then really a coiled rope. Couldn't it also be a tightly coiled snake? That is also possible. (This is the first level, comparable to the "simple" probability of the first example and corresponding to problematic alternatives, as Husserl defined them.) [73] Since the second possibility is similarly probable, the man will mistrust his first impression. He becomes unsure and oscillates between the two possibilities. He goes closer to the object. It does not move. Coiled ropes do not move; perhaps the object is indeed a coiled rope. Now the man remembers the fact that snakes have a color similar to the object in the corner, and in addition to this he recalls the fact that snakes become torpid in the cold of winter and do not move. Since it is now winter, lack of movement cannot count as a sufficient reason to consider the object a coiled rope. Therefore the man makes an inspection tour (περιόδευσις), so to speak, around his representation. He finds in the process that every alternative has its own weight that balances the weight of the other alternatives. Therefore he has no basis for deciding to give assent (συγκατάθεσις) to one or the other alternative. In this state of affairs, which of the alternatives he will give more credence to, or which alternative he will be inclined to annul, will depend only on whether he is fearful or not. If he wants to achieve a higher measure of certitude, he will have to look for further bases for a decision. Consequently, as Sextus put it, he will have to make use of the method of the Athenian courts, which had to examine the claims of candidates to public office, or the method of physicians

73. [*Erfahrung und Urteil,* § 21.]

when they have to make a diagnosis. That means that the man may not rely on individual "symptoms," but rather must take into consideration the connection of all the symptoms, the "syndrome." If the syndrome contains no counterindication, he will be able to say that the representation is "true." If the man takes a stick, touches the object, and it still does not move, he will have acquired the conviction that it indeed cannot be a snake. With this last proof he has completed the tour of inspection in all its necessary details (διέξοδος). Now he can assent to the conviction that he must have been in error to have taken the object for a snake. Consequently, the uniquely valid criterion of all convictions is to be sought in a well-founded, methodical command (διέξοδος) of the probabilities and degrees of probability (πιθανόν).

It is worth noting that there are great similarities between Carneades' theory of degrees of probability or plausibility (πιθανόν) and Husserl's analysis of problematic possibilities in *Erfahrung und Urteil*.[74] One has in general assumed that Carneades' theory refers only to the province of practical action. But Robin,[75] after a very careful examination, comes to the conclusion that it is related to all forms of thinking, judging, and perceiving. This also is in accord with Husserl's conception. It appears, in any case, that in his theory Carneades had only thinking acts in mind, while for Husserl the constitution of problematic possibilities originates from the prepredicative sphere and is founded on the passive syntheses of identity, similarity, etc. In any case, we can begin with Carneades' considerations and use his third example as a point of departure for an analysis of the various forms of relevance.

2. THEMATIC RELEVANCE

a. Forced attentiveness ("imposed" thematic relevance)

If we look at Carneades' example more closely, various questions arise. We could ask ourselves how the man comes to vacillate between just these two possibilities: the snake and the coiled rope. Couldn't the object in the corner also be something else? If we answer that other possibilities are not "relevant" to him, we then introduce a problem which we will treat in detail in the

74. [Ibid.]
75. Robin, *Pyrrhon et le scepticisme grecque.*

analysis of interpretative relevance.[76] And, if we say that it is especially important for an apprehensive person in such a position to be able to decide whether the object is one which could threaten danger, so that he could then take appropriate measures, we touch on a problem that will be more closely investigated in the analysis of motivational relevance.[77]

But as a preliminary, we will turn to the question immediately introduced by starting with the example. How does it come about that just this object in the corner, whatever it may be, "interests" the man? There are surely other objects in this corner, as there are also other corners with objects, which can be seen equally as dimly. But these objects do not "interest" him. Although they are in his field of perception, "they aren't conspicuous," "they aren't brought into relief." They "don't draw his attention to themselves." How does this happen?

There are four main forms of "imposed" thematic relevance: the unfamiliar draws attention to itself within the surroundings of the familiar; one meets new themes in the "leap" from one province of reality with finite meaning-structure to another; changes in the tension of consciousness within the same province of reality can lead to "unmotivated" changes of theme; or, attention can be forced socially.

The first form is in a certain sense the most important. It is at the basis of other forms, if one grasps them according to their general characteristics. Taking the example of Carneades, let us illustrate how the unfamiliar is conspicuous within the surrounding of the familiar and is brought into relief by it. In this context, we can refer back to the results of the previous analysis of familiarity as a dimension of the stock of knowledge.[78]

Let us assume that the man in the example returns to his own room. He is completely familiar with the room from long usage. That is, the outer horizon (the location of the rooms in the house, etc.), as well as the inner horizon (the various objects in the room, their order, etc.) of the room, is sufficiently determined, and the determinations have become a component of the habitual knowledge of this man through continuous use and activity. He can routinely orient himself in the room. From this it

76. See Chap. 3, B, 3. [Also, *Reflections on the Problem of Relevance*, pp. 35–45, 53–74.]
77. See Chap. 3, B, 4. [Also, *Reflections on the Problem of Relevance*, pp. 45–52, 53–74.]
78. See Chap. 3, A, 3, b.

follows that the returning to this room in itself contains nothing problematic for the man. Thus when entering the room, he is immersed in other thoughts; he remembers, for instance, a conversation that he had shortly before with an acquaintance. But with these memories, which form the theme of his actually present flow of experience, he routinely places one foot before the other and routinely opens the door to his room. Thus he automatically expects, without thematizing this expectation, to find the room again as he had left it a few hours before. The automaticity of this expectation is based on the idealizations that have already been discussed in various connections: the "and-so-forth" and the "I-can-always-do-it-again."

In order to clear up misunderstandings, we must describe the state of affairs quite exactly. The memories of the conversation form, as we said, the theme of the flow of experience. In a moment he may, for example, think of a certain phase of the conversation: this forms the actually present, thematic kernel. The other phases of the conversation, the man's representations, what he really should have said, how he could have formulated it better, etc., do not indeed belong to the actually present kernel but to the thematic field, to use an important distinction introduced by Aron Gurwitsch.[79] The consciousness of the motor process of his walking, the accompanying feeling of fatigue, the consciousness of noise on the street, as well as the automatic expectations involving the room, are obviously in contrast not in the thematic kernel, nor in the thematic field, but rather simply in the horizon of the actually present flow of experience. (We will here neglect the difference between noetic and noematic analysis.)

If the man should find his room in fact unchanged, then the accompanying actual perceptions of the room could remain in the horizon of the flow of experience. Nothing could disturb his being further immersed in the thoughts of the conversation. This is not the case. An unfamiliar object is there. The actual perceptions of the room do not "confirm" the automatic expectations. The unity of the field of vision "collapses," since an unexpected element is on hand in the field of vision. Since the man routinely expects only the familiar in his room, the perceived unexpected element becomes "problematic": that is, the object must be the-

79. [Gurwitsch, Théorie du champ de la conscience (The Field of Consciousness).]

matized. It jumps out of the horizon of the flow of experience, in which it would have remained had it been inserted into the automatic expectations, into the core of the flow of experience. At the same time the former theme, the memory of the conversation, is abandoned. As we brought out in the investigation of the continuation and the interruptions of the acquisition of knowledge, there are two possibilities here. Either the theme is given up "definitively" or it is only "provisionally" shoved to the side.[80] If, for instance, before entering the room the man had been occupied with thinking through an important problem, he would now have to turn to the principle of "first things first," indeed to the object in the corner as a new problem. This would introduce, so to speak, a gap to be filled in later. In contrast, in our example the man had nothing better to do at that moment and had remembered the conversation without it being problematic for him. He now definitively lets the theme drop.

With this we have established the most important case of "imposed" thematic relevance: it arises from an enforced change of theme, which happens as a result of a break in automatic expectations (more generally: as a result of a cessation in lifeworldly idealizations). The new theme intrudes in the form of something conspicuous and unfamiliar.

A nonmotivated, and thus, strictly speaking, also an imposed change in the theme, can be caused, furthermore, by a "leap" from one province of reality with finite meaning-structure to another. Through the radical change in the tension of consciousness and the style of lived experience or knowledge, a flow of experience is discontinued with its theme, and a new theme is confronted. This case of "imposed" thematic relevance can in general, as was already discussed, be grasped as a special case of the cessation of lifeworldly idealizations. Since we have investigated in another connection [81] the processes by which one "leaps" from one province of reality to another, we need only allude to them here.

Further theme changes can enter as a result of changes in the tension of consciousness and in certain dimensions of the style of lived experience or knowledge—above all in the time dimension and in the depth of lived experience, even if these occur in the flows of experience within the same province of real-

80. See Chap. 3, A, 2, c and d.
81. See above all Chap. 2, A.

ity.[82] It must be clearly understood with regard to the two last-mentioned cases of theme change that we can take notice of only those "leaps" between provinces of reality and those changes in the tension of consciousness within the same spheres of reality which are not, *sensu strictu*, "motivated." Otherwise, the same processes, in the event they are motivated, belong much more properly in the category of thematic relevance, which is to be discussed in the next section: the category of voluntary advertence.

Finally, a further form of "imposed" thematic relevance should be mentioned, namely, the socially "imposed." In daily life it is of the greatest importance. The actions of fellow-men (indeed, the courses of acts as well as their results) place themes before the individual to which he must turn himself.[83] This form of "imposed" thematic relevance surely intersects with other forms. Courses and results of acts can, for example, be completely unexpected; they are not brought into the routinized expectations which refer to fellow-men. Obviously in this case this form of "imposed" thematic relevance involves the conspicuousness or outstandingness of the unfamiliar in contrast to the familiar background. But fellow-men can also reach into a flow of experience, force new themes on the individual, without their action appearing as atypical or unfamiliar in the resulting interpretation.

b. Voluntary advertence ("motivated" thematic relevance)

i. Theme change

Not all thematic relevance is "imposed" in the sense just investigated. Another relevance structure is manifested in voluntary advertence to a theme. The man in the example was busy with other thoughts as he entered the room. It would be senseless to assume that the man's flow of lived experience was previously unstructured, "without a theme." Thus it was already necessary to speak there of a theme change. It was there that a new theme intruded "on its own" as a consequence of its unfamiliarity, which was brought into relief opposite the familiar field. We need only vary the example somewhat to acquire another form of theme change, namely, the "motivated" one.

82. See Chap. 2, B, 1; also Chap. 3, A, 2, c and d.
83. See here esp. Chap. 5 [Vol. II].

Let us assume that the man in Carneades' example is not very familiar with the room. It is not his room, but he has occasionally entered it before. From this it follows that he has automatic expectations which are not completely empty of content but rather, on the basis of his previous experiences of the room, demonstrate a certain contextual determinateness. Only the object in the corner is completely unknown to him; the rest of the objects in the room enter without further ado into his automatic expectations. Thus the break in his automatic expectations and the conspicuousness of the unfamiliar also force a new theme on him.

But now we want to vary the example still further. Let us assume that the man has never yet been in this room and that furthermore this room has not been described to him by its occupant. Even then, his expectations will not be completely empty of content. They concern rooms in general; they are derived from the set of types stored in his stock of knowledge. He knows approximately what latitude in variations exists for typical rooms; he knows within what latitude typical objects in typical rooms exist, and in what typical arrangements they may be. If he enters the room, the object in the corner will "leap to his attention" again because it is not included in this set of types. We need not belabor this point further, because it has already been discussed in some depth in another place.[84]

We have here, however, come upon an important aspect. We still spoke of typical expectations. But it is no longer obvious that these expectations are automatic. We can state generally that the less familiar a total situation is the greater the attentiveness will be with which one turns to it, so to speak, "on one's own." The unfamiliar total situation which one approaches is already thematized from the beginning. Whereupon the different elements of this situation are subthematized according to sequence until they can be ordered and arranged as more or less typical and familiar. In other words, if one cannot be routinely oriented in a situation, one must explicate it. And if one knows that in advance, then he also in advance turns to it "voluntarily." That means as well that one cannot be unlimitedly immersed in "other thoughts," but rather is motivated to turn "promptly" to the situation or to certain aspects of it. It speaks for itself that "promptly"

84. See the expositions of familiarity and typicality, Chap. 3, A, 3, b, ii.

is closely connected with the principle of "first things first" and with the typical levels of urgency sedimented in the stock of knowledge for mastery of typical situations and problems. Applying this to the last variation of the example, it means that the man had already "voluntarily" let his memories of the conversation with his acquaintance go as soon as he entered the room and had thematized the impending situation: the room unfamiliar to him or his orientation in it. He would accordingly be "motivated" to change the theme. After a more or less attentive explication of the total situation, the object in the corner, as already pointed out, would strike him as especially atypical.

Here is a further consideration. The different variations of the example show that it is difficult to draw a sharp line between "imposed" and "motivated" changes of theme. Between forced attentiveness and voluntary advertence there are gradual differences. Every flow of experience in its different dimensions and every situation in its different aspects demonstrates an intertwining and an interplay of imposed and motivated moments. This is the case in general not only for thematic relevance, but for relevance structures as such.[85]

What is meant in this connection by "prompt" advertence has already been mentioned. Naturally, this factor also plays a role in the distinction between "imposed" and "motivated" advertence. The man in the example could have been so busy with recollecting the previous conversation (if it had, for example, posed decisions vitally important to him), that he "forgot" to reorient himself "promptly" to the new situation. In this case the theme change would then occur only later, and would not be "motivated," but rather "imposed." Whether a thematic relevance should be considered as chiefly "imposed" or "motivated" also depends on what "weight" the actual theme has in a given situation, on how important is its mastery in relation to the impending situation, as well as on the "personality" of the actor (for example, his biographically conditioned insecurity in relation to new situations in general, his insecurity in relation to situations of this specific type, etc.). In general, thematic relevance is interwoven with the structure of motivational relevance as such, through the distinction between "imposed" and "motivated."

As has already been shown in the analysis of "imposed"

85. In the analysis of the forms of knowledge and the continued acquisition of knowledge, see Chap. 3, A, 2.

thematic relevance, theme change can be linked not only with "leaps" from one province of reality to another but also with less decisive alterations in this style of lived experience of knowledge, in the dominant time dimension, in the depth of the lived experience, etc. This is in general also the case for non-"imposed" thematic relevances. Only, in this case the "leaps," the alterations, and the theme changes linked to them, are "motivated."

ii. Theme development

Besides "voluntary" thematic relevance, which we have described as "motivated" theme change, there is still another form of this relevance. The current theme can remain in the grasp of consciousness; therefore no theme change takes place. Nevertheless, "motivated" thematic changes ensue: one turns to the explication of the implications of the current theme. Since we have already, in another connection, described the most important aspects of this process, we can limit ourselves here to applying the results of this description to the present problem.

As Husserl has shown, every theme has an, in principle, unlimited inner and outer horizon.[86] The outer horizon contains everything that is given contemporaneously with the theme in consciousness. It therefore contains the retentions and memories which refer back to the original constitution of the current theme, and the protentions and expectations which refer forward to possible further developments of the theme. Furthermore, everything that is linked with the theme in passive syntheses of identity, similarity, etc., belongs to the outer horizon. The inner horizon, on the other hand, contains everything that is contained "in the theme" itself, therefore the various elements into which the theme can be "resolved," the partial structures of these elements and their total context, through which they become a homogeneous theme. We want here to appropriate the result of Gurwitsch's further development of Husserl's train of thought.[87] With him, we distinguish between those components of the horizon which belong "essentially" to the theme and those which "really" have nothing to do with the theme. To the latter belong, for example, the continuing, mostly passive adumbrations of the

86. [See Edmund Husserl, *Ideen*, Vol. I: *Allgemeine Einführung in die reine Phänomenologie* (The Hague: Nijhoff, 1950), §§ 82, 113, 114; *Erfahrung und Urteil*, §§ 8–10.]

87. See Gurwitsch, *Théorie du champ de la conscience* (*The Field of Consciousness*).

consciousness of one's own body, perceptions which are "forced on it" but which do not reach thematization—as for instance a not very loud noise on the street occurring while one reads a book in his room, etc. These components of the horizon are, as Gurwitsch maintained, in purely temporal relations with the theme. In the horizon of the theme, there are also aspects which are in perceptual connection (perspectives of explanation) or meaning-context (contextual relations) with the theme given in the actually present flow of experience. We want to follow Gurwitsch and term these the thematic field. Being unable to go into the details of Gurwitsch's analysis of the noetic and noematic, we will be satisfied with the statement that the thematic field consists of thematic relevances which implicitly belong to the theme and were originally stored in prior experiences or are given in the actual experience.

One can "voluntarily" advert to the thematic field. One is "motivated" not to be satisfied with the theme, as it would be grasped simply in its core. Attention shifts rather to the "details" (the inner horizon) or the relations of the theme to other themes (the outer horizon). One still keeps the main theme in the grasp of consciousness. But what was only implicitly pregiven in the thematic field is made explicit in advertence. In other words, the main theme is further developed in various subthematizations.

In general, the differentiation between theme change and theme development is also of the nature of an ideal type. We can only speak of theme development so long as the main theme is not let out of the grasp of consciousness. But there is obviously the possibility that the theme development more or less noticeably flows into the theme change, if the main theme is given up in favor of a subthematization. The topics in a lexicon offer enlightening examples. One begins with one topic which appears most relevant for answering a question under discussion. One then follows the implications of the original problem, by looking up the cross references which were given under the first topic. Then, while reading through a new topic, one "discovers" a new fascinating problem. It then often happens that one forgets the original problem, together with its implications, and remains with the topics which have nothing more to do with that problem. Nevertheless, one has followed a chain of thematic connections; one has in this sense "further developed" the original theme until at a certain point one "gave up" the theme.

Since we treated as a category of "voluntary" thematic relevance the development of a theme through the advertence of attention within the thematic field, we must now accept a certain limitation. It is surely the case that advertence to the thematic field and its further development is "motivated." It requires a "voluntary" act. The thematic field is, on the other hand, implicitly contained "in the theme"—as, vice versa, there is no isolated theme, but rather, it is already brought into relief by a thematic field. In this sense the thematic field has an unalterable, so to speak, "imposed" prior history. That means that the direction for further development of the theme and for the possibilities of the subthematizations are to a certain extent previously given. While the total horizon of the theme is, as has already been said, in principle unlimited, the thematic field is "practically" more or less clearly circumscribed, that is, in view of the actually present, prior history of the experience.

Finally, it should be noted that theme development can be grasped as a process of explication. It thus plays into the province of interpretative relevance structures.

c. Hypothetical relevance

The previously discussed thematic relevances concern only the simpler time structure of the flow of experience, that which is actually brought into present relief, as well as actually motivated theme changes, etc. Only in the one variation of the example, where it was a matter of the man "promptly" dropping the old theme and turning to a new one, did we touch on a less simple time structure. There is a form of relevance, though, which points to a far more complicated time structure; we will term it *hypothetical relevance*. Let us say beforehand that in hypothetical relevance all the chief forms of relevance structures (not only thematic but also interpretational and motivational relevances) are most closely interwoven with one another. It is only because hypothetical relevance, in any case, necessarily involves thematic relevance structure that we will discuss it here.

Furthermore, we have already encountered the problem of hypothetical relevance, in fact, while describing the forms of interruption in the acquisition of knowledge.[88] We developed the problem there with the aid of an example: I am sitting in my room and am busy writing a letter. Suddenly I hear a loud report in the street. This report intrudes on my attention. I interrupt my

88. See Chap. 3, A, 2, d, i.

writing. A report of such intensity, on the basis of the experiences sedimented in my stock of knowledge, is not a part of the typically "familiar" events which take place on the street—as for instance the noise of automobile motors, men's voices, etc. So far it concerns a thematic relevance of a sort which was already described: something unfamiliar stands out from a background of the familiar. I know, if I advert to the event, that it probably was a shot or a backfire. If it was a shot, I am motivated toward certain rules of conduct. I go to the window, notice nothing out of the ordinary, and on this basis write off this possibility as improbable. The case is obviously parallel with Carneades' third example: snake or coiled rope? In both cases, I am motivated to a "tour of inspection" of the theme. To what extent is this kind of relevance "hypothetical"?

Shots are ordered in my stock of knowledge as typically important events which usually require certain modes of conduct. This element of knowledge is thus coupled with certain motivational relevances. The coupling is of a special kind: if event X, then modes of conduct Y and Z. That is, Y and Z are "neutralized," but so that they can be "activated" again at any time by X. But it was the case that I cannot say with subjective certainty whether X has taken place. I only know that the event *could* be of type X. Strictly speaking, therefore, a hypothetical relevance was "imposed" on me by the event. If the event was a shot, then it was thematically relevant (i.e., then my forced advertence was not "superfluous"), and then it is motivationally relevant. But if, after the necessary steps of explication, it proves to be the case that the event was not a shot, then the motivational-like thematic relevance of the event is annulled in retrospect.

Our conduct in the life-world of everyday life is to a great extent coguided by hypothetical relevances. Our action is frequently adjusted so as to give rise to situations in which it is possible to determine whether a hypothetical relevance should be converted into a "valid" relevance or be considered as void. If such confirmations or annulments are independent of our action, one must often simply "wait." Then the expectations of future events, ignoring all the other meaning-structures characterizing them, are also adjusted to find out whether a past, hypothetically relevant event was "really" relevant or not. Finally, many routine "safety precautions" have originated from hypothetical relevances. One can "often not afford" to suspend rules of conduct until the facts of the case are definitively settled. Hypothetical relevance structures are naturally also of great importance in social action —above all in institutionalized action.

Yet a word about the temporal structure of experiences, and its relation to hypothetical relevances, is in order. The hypothetical relevance is actually now "really" relevant, since one cannot for certain say whether the "hypothesis" will be confirmed in the future or not. The difference from nonhypothetical relevances consists in the fact that the actually present grasping of the theme is, so to speak, transposed into the future, thus to a future where the actually present, hypothetical relevance will be "past," whereby it will have been proved to be "really" relevant or irrelevant. The time-structure of such experiences we will characterize with the expression, *modo futuri exacti*. It will play an important role in the description of action in general.[89]

Hypothetical relevance is interwoven in many ways with the structures of motivational relevance. It has already been said that a hypothetically relevant theme motivated certain modes of conduct. But it also should be noticed that the possibilities of (future) confirmation or annulment of a hypothetically relevant theme must not have the same subjective weight. This depends in part on the set of types stored in the stock of knowledge: experience has shown that some hypothetical relevances are more often, others less often, presented as "really" relevant. Yet one may fear a confirmation of the hypothetical relevance; he may hope for or remain neutral to it. One may, according to his biography and "character," "be on his guard against everything possible," or usually be "too lazy," or "chance it" because of the fun of the risk, etc.

3. INTERPRETATIONAL RELEVANCE

a. Routine coincidence between the theme and the elements of knowledge ("imposed" interpretational relevance)

The description of "imposed" and "voluntary" thematic relevance revolved around processes by which a theme is forced upon consciousness or is taken up in motivated acts of consciousness. But what happens once a theme is "there"?

In adverting to a theme, one does not grasp it as unique and without relation to other experiences. Just as the theme is constituted for consciousness, it is brought into coincidence with "relevant" elements of knowledge. Here we are obviously treating something other than thematic relevance. We shall call this "interpretational relevance."

The concept of "interpretation" should not be understood too narrowly. We can distinguish two principal forms of interpretational relevance, of which only one involves explications in the strict sense. A theme may still be routinely coincident with elements of the stock of knowledge which are sufficiently familiar and certain. Here, "sufficiently" means: sufficiently for a mastery of the given situation. In such a case, there are no problems and the experiences go along as before. Only if an adequate coincidence, in this sense, does not occur between the theme and the element of knowledge does the routine flow of experience falter and the theme become a problem. The problem must be solved, the theme explicated. With routine coincidence, "interpretation" is automatic. No explicitly judging explication occurs in which, on the one hand, the theme, and on the other hand, the relevant elements of knowledge, come separately into the grasp of the consciousness to be "compared" with one another. This form of interpretational relevance belongs to the category of "imposed" relevances. Should the theme become a problem, a motive then arises for more or less explicit, step-by-step "judging" explication. In this case, a "motivated" interpretational relevance is involved. It hardly need be stressed that this distinction also has an ideal-type character. Various transitions go from completely automatic coincidence to clear and explicit explication, in which the theme and the elements of knowledge are compared, until a founded judgment of similarity, sameness, etc., can be passed.

Although interpretational relevance is therefore not identical with thematic relevance, it is nevertheless closely and systematically associated with it. This is generally in keeping with the meaning of interpretational relevance; every interpretation presupposes thematic relevance structures. The interweaving of these structures is, however, most especially clear in the routine coincidence between the theme and the elements of knowledge. In this case, interpretational relevance does not enter separately into conscious awareness, but rather already appears to be taking part in the constitution of the theme. For a closer investigation of this form we turn again to the example of Carneades.

When the man entered the room, an unfamiliar object caught his eye. That which was brought into relief as something unfamiliar in a familiar surrounding was offered in different visual adumbrations as a more or less discrete form. But it was from the beginning experienced not simply as a visually grasped, unfamiliar something, which, as it were, "accidentally" had this particular form. It is rather experienced as an "object-in-the-corner-perhaps-a-coiled-rope," or as an "object-in-the-corner-perhaps-a-snake." The theme is automatically coincident with certain elements of knowledge, as it is constituted in its visual adumbrations as a perceptual Object. It is experienced as a *typical* something. But in Carneades' example, two possible typifications are in conflict with one another, so that it is of no importance which of the two was "first" offered. The theme becomes problematic and requires a step-by-step explication. Therefore, as it stands, the example belongs to the second level of interpretational relevance. We could naturally ignore the fact that no adequate coincidence occurs. But it is perhaps less confusing if we take another example. Let us assume that the man enters a dark room and stumbles over a hard object. The thematic relevance is once again "imposed," here even in a palpable sense. As the theme is constituted, a coincidence automatically occurs with a type which is on hand and which is exclusively free of contradiction and stored in the stock of knowledge: a piece of furniture.

On both levels of interpretational relevance, that of the automatic coincidence and that of the explication of the problem, only certain elements of knowledge are taken up—that is, most elements on hand in the stock of knowledge remain irrelevant. The man knows, for instance, that the sun rises in the east, two times two is four, butchers sell sausages, ducks are birds, sweet wine doesn't suit him—to take but a few elements from his stock of knowledge. None of these is actualized in the given situation. Other elements present themselves "on their own." Sometimes past experiences of similar objects are actualized in their individuality. Above all, however, *typifications* of objects of similar or, in borderline cases, the same dimension, form, color, etc., present themselves. Obviously, these typifications are the result of sedimented individual experiences. These do not need to be awakened separately any longer.

Interpretational relevance, therefore, has a strikingly double character. On the one hand, there are certain aspects of the perceived object; more generally, certain thematic elements are brought into relief, are "offered," and are relevant for interpretation. On the other hand, there are certain elements of the stock of knowledge, and indeed right now just these and not others, which are within the grasp of the actual theme and are relevant for interpretation. Neither all aspects of the theme nor all elements of knowledge are relevant for interpretation, or are relevant in a similar manner.

It is not at all the case that all elements of knowledge "pass by" the theme in some order of sequence, until the "pertinent" element of knowledge is reached. Experiences are sedimented in the stock of knowledge according to their typicality. A given theme, with its determinations, awakens only typically similar elements of knowledge. These are brought into coincidence with the theme and its determinations in an event.

What is meant by routine coincidence must be still more exhaustively investigated. To illustrate the process, one could say that certain elements of knowledge are "chosen" and "held in front of" the theme, as, on the other hand, certain thematic elements which are brought into relief are brought "into agreement" with the elements of knowledge. In doing this one must guard against assuming that acts of consciousness (in the strict sense of ego acts) are necessarily involved in the processes through which the theme is brought into correlation with elements of knowledge. As Husserl has shown in *Erfahrung und Urteil*, processes of this kind belong to prepredicative spheres; they form the basis for a judging explication.[90] The actually present perception (the theme on hand) awakens themes of the same type sedimented in the stock of knowledge. Coincidence takes place in passive synthesis.

It should be stressed once more that the coincidence between theme and elements of knowledge does not have to be "complete." "Complete" coincidence would imply that the object is again recognized as being itself, and thus would involve a synthesis of identity. This is a borderline case that indeed is not without importance, but it need not concern us further here. Furthermore, the theme, as was already said, can be brought into coincidence with remembered objects of the same type, whereby the individuality of these objects becomes an individual future. The coincidence then concerns only typical similarities. For us the most important case is the one with the greatest frequency in the orientation of daily life: the coincidence between the theme and

90. [Husserl, *Erfahrung und Urteil*, §§ 8, 22, 24, 25, 26, 80, and esp. 83 a and b.]

the type stored in the stock of knowledge. The relation to specific prior experiences is in this case "indirect," insofar as the type is sedimented in just these prior experiences. In all these cases, there are gradual transitions from coincidence to partial coincidence to lack of coincidence. The "extent" of the coincidence must suffice for mastery of the actual situation, a fact clearly indicated by the way in which interpretational and motivational relevances are interwoven. If coincidence is in this sense sufficient, then the adequacy of the coincidence never comes to be grasped as such by consciousness. The experience proceeds routinely. Only in the negative case, when the coincidence is insufficient and thus when a problem arises, does this circumstance come to consciousness. As will be shown later, the extent and adequacy of the coincidence are constituted as more or less explicit dimensions of the processes of explication which are instituted on their basis.

It follows from what has been said that in the structure of interpretational relevance, unequivocal relevance and unequivocal irrelevance represent only borderline cases. In routine coincidence, it appears to be senseless to speak of more or less relevant elements of knowledge. A tree is experienced as a tree, if the flow of experience proceeds routinely and without interruption. In fact, it will be easier in the analysis of explicit processes of explication to develop the thesis that interpretational relevance has a "more or less" character.

b. Explication of a problem ("motivated" interpretational relevance)

In the analysis of the explication of a problem we can go back to the results of various prior investigations. This is the case above all with the description of the routine coincidence between the theme and the elements of knowledge. As had already been shown, explicit explications of problems are founded on automatic processes in the predicative spheres. Furthermore, we have already encountered the question concerning how the routine flow of experience is interrupted and how this constitutes a problem. This happened when we were occupied the first time with the relation between what is taken for granted and the problematic,[91] and then as we analyzed the acquisition of knowl-

91. See Chap. 1, B.

edge and especially the interruptions in this acquisition.[92] We have already tried in these places to describe the processes at the basis of the solution to the problem—after it has been brought into prominence. This was possible only to a limited degree without a definition of the relevance structures at the basis of those processes. Before we turn now to this definition, we want to summarize briefly the results of these analyses.

A problem arises if an actual experience does not readily "fit" into a type on hand in the stock of knowledge (and indeed on the level of type-determined, situational relevance). That is, a problem can arise when no routine coincidence is achieved between the theme and the element of knowledge. A problem can also arise, though, when the experience fits into a type on hand in the stock of knowledge, but the determinateness of the type does not suffice for mastery of the situation—that is, if it turns out that the processes of explication sedimented in the type were interrupted "too early." Finally, there can also be a problem if, on the basis of an actual experience, one becomes cognizant of the incompatibility ("contradiction") between two elements of knowledge which until now coexisted in a taken-for-granted way in the stock of knowledge. That is, this occurs when an actually present theme must be brought into coincidence with two elements of knowledge which present themselves as relevant, while these elements are, however, reciprocally incompatible. With the aid of the example of Carneades, we can now pursue further the processes of problem explication.

How does a coincidence between the theme "object-in-the-corner" and the element of knowledge "typical-coiled-rope" come about? In this example, it is above all the perceived form of the object which agrees with the form type "coiled rope." Consequently, the dimension as well as the order of the elements in the perceived whole coincides with the type. Thus, for example, the "same" ordering of elements, with a tenfold increase in size would no longer be compatible with the type "coiled rope." The interplay of different prior experiences sedimented in the type already becomes clear. The man in the example may by accident have never seen a rope rolled up, but he has probably seen ropes in other arrangements: in knots, loose, lying flat, etc. On the other hand, he may have seen coils, not out of rope, but only out of wool. Both typifications are compatible with one another and

92. See Chap. 3, A, 2; esp. A, 2, d.

interpretationally relevant in their combined use ("coiled rope") for the current perception. In contrast, other similarly perceived characteristics of this object, for instance its color, are irrelevant in relation to the type "coiled rope." The man may have seen coiled ropes in different colors, so to be sure certain colors may have occurred in his experience more often than others. But since all colors are compatible with the type "coiled rope," the color of the perceived object is not immediately interpretationally relevant. The object in the corner could therefore exhibit a color which the man in the example has never yet seen in a rope, without this circumstance being incompatible with the interpretation "coiled rope." On the other hand, it should be noted that, if the object in the corner had a color which the man had experienced as "very frequently appearing with ropes," this circumstance would support the interpretation "coiled rope." And further, to be more exact, if two typifications, "coiled rope" and "snake," were "equally probable" on the basis of the "more important" interpretational relevances, a "second-order" interpretation such as color could assist the decision. Finally, if the man in the example had *always* seen only yellow coiled ropes, we may assume that color would also be of the first order of interpretational relevance for him. It would belong essentially to the type determination "rope."

In general, we can say, therefore, that "imposed," as well as "motivated," interpretational relevance leads to coincidence between reciprocally "awakening" aspects of a theme and the determinations of elements of knowledge. Not all thematically relevant moments are interpretationally relevant; in any case they do not have to be. And not all experiences sedimented in the stock of knowledge are relevant, but only those whose typical determinations are compatible with the theme. We can therefore already say on the basis of these considerations that interpretational relevance is a function of the prevailing stock of knowledge, consequently of the biography of the individual.

Interpretational relevance is in a certain sense also situationally conditioned. Let us assume first that a coincidence took place between the theme and the type "coiled rope." What credibility does this interpretation have? This is connected with the various, so to speak, "second-order" interpretational relevances, some of which refer to the whole situation. If the man enters a ship's cabin, the type "cabin" is completely compatible with the type "coiled rope." The experience "object-in-this-cabin's-corner" can with high credibility be interpreted as a "coiled rope," namely, as a "coiled-rope-in-the-cabin." The man in the example often may have had such experiences and may be quite familiar with them. In this case it is even very probable that the object in the corner, even if it could not be unequivocally determined in the first perception (as was also the case for the other objects in the room), would be experienced through routine coincidence. The theme of attentiveness would not have to intrude at all. This is so even if the theme, because of other reasons here, had been brought into relief as needing to be explicated. If, for example, the man had taken a child with him and the child had asked him: "what is there?," the interpretation "a coiled rope" would present itself with the greatest "self-evidency." It should be noted that due to the relatively slight determinability of the object in the first perception, the chance is always on hand that in the course of further experience and with closer determination of the theme this interpretation may need to be revoked. Only no occasion or motive for further explication is on hand if the interpretation had a high credibility from the beginning. That means that in this case the interpretation is only revoked if additional *thematic* relevances intrude ("the coiled rope" moves by itself) which are incompatible with the original interpretation.

We now follow the situational dependence of interpretational relevance through a further variation of the example. Let us assume that the man had not entered a ship's cabin, but rather the room of a friend who is a sailor by profession. Since on the basis of his prior experiences the man does not enter rooms (including those occupied by sailors) with the *automatic* expectation of finding a coiled rope among the objects in the room, the tables, chairs, etc., no routine coincidence takes place. The object in the corner forces his attention. By adverting to the theme, a coincidence again takes place with certain elements of knowledge: the type "coiled rope" contains no determinations which would be incompatible with the actually present, perceivable, interpretatively relevant determinations of the object. At the same time, the determinateness of the type is sufficient (one does not need to worry about a coiled rope) to solve the present problem—the case presupposed that the interpretation is sufficiently credible. What credibility does this have? The man has already been in this room once, but saw no coiled rope. In his experience it is not usual for sailors to bring coiled ropes home. On the other hand, however, many people bring everything conceivable home;

perhaps it happens now and then that they bring home coiled ropes. Since sailors in their profession handle coiled ropes, the probability of sailors bringing home coiled ropes is perhaps greater than for other people. In short, the interpretation "coiled rope" is compatible with the theme and has, in addition, within the typical total situation, a certain credibility sufficient under the circumstances. What does under the circumstances mean? Let us assume, somewhat artificially, that the only other possible interpretation would be "harmless snake" (in a country in which there are no poisonous snakes), though this interpretation appears somewhat less credible (the house is in an area in which there are no snakes found anyway). Although the man thus would not be subjectively sure that it was just a matter of a coiled rope, none of the other less credible possibilities of interpretation is threatening. Even if the interpretation should turn out to be false, no special measures are required. Although the interpretation "coiled rope" still contains the proviso that further determinations of the object could turn out to be incompatible with the type "coiled rope," the credibility of this first interpretation is sufficient under *these* circumstances.

Let us vary the example still further. Let us assume that it is a question of a room with which a man has been familiar for some time. The total situation is changed. He knows with absolute assurance that he himself did not bring a coiled rope home, and that it is most improbable that other persons could have gained access to his room. This up to now has happened only once—and that intruder was a robber, who took something with him and surely did not leave a coiled rope behind. The theme, though, is compatible in its actual determinateness with the type "coiled rope." That means that this interpretation is in principle "possible." But it has a very small credibility in the present total situation. What happens now? Basically, it is again conceivable that the man could shove the problem to the side unsolved. This possibility is, given the circumstances adduced in the total situation (unfamiliar object in his own unlit room), extremely unlikely. Let us assume with Carneades that the man is of an anxious sort. Then it would be inconceivable that he would shove this problem to the side. The solution "coiled rope" had little credibility, and the problem is therefore not solved. He looks for other interpretations, which are at least as compatible with the actually present determinations but can in addition possess a higher credibility in this situation. We will ignore the fact that an anxious man, who notices an unfamiliar object in his own unlit room, probably does not begin with the interpretation "coiled rope," if more threatening possibilities of interpretation are compatible with the theme. Given two interpretations as "equally compatible" with the thematic relevances, the sequential order of mental arousal is connected with another relevance structure yet to be discussed, namely, motivational relevance. Therefore let us assume that the man would not have taken the interpretation "coiled rope" as a solution to the problem because of its slight credibility. Other interpretations compatible with the theme are also offered, for example "rolled-up snake." But this interpretation also does not have a very high credibility, since the room was locked. And let us further assume that no other interpretations are compatible with the theme. Thus we have again come to a situation in which type typifications "snake" and "coiled rope" are "possible" ($\pi\iota\theta\alpha\nu\acute{o}\nu$), that is, both interpretations are compatible with the actually present determinations of the theme. This corresponds to the situation that Carneades characterized with the expression $\pi\epsilon\rho\iota\sigma\pi\alpha\sigma\tau\sigma\varsigma$ ("bent" or "twisted"). What happens now?

The interpretatively relevant determinations of the theme are first compatible with two types stored in the stock of knowledge. But both contain more determinations than were perceived in the actual theme up to now. The interpretative relevances in the *theme* do not suffice in the choice between the two interpretatively relevant typifications being offered. If we ignore the total situation, the two interpretations are "equally possible." The stock of *knowledge* as such would indeed suffice for the solution of the problem; it is the object of *experience* which is not sufficiently determined. The problem, therefore, can only be solved when one determines aspects of the theme that were not immediately grasped or could not be grasped in the original situation. The process of explication ($\pi\epsilon\rho\iota\acute{o}\delta\epsilon\upsilon\sigma\iota\varsigma$) must be pushed on ahead until determinations are found in the theme which are compatible with the interpretatively relevant determinations of type A but not of type B. One has to achieve better illumination, or take a stick and hit the object. If, then, in better lighting a typical snakeskin pattern is noticeable on the object, or if the object begins to move "by itself," the further determinations are compatible with the type "snake" but not with the type "coiled rope," which from then on loses all credibility.

A few generalizations can be derived from the different variations on the example. First, the same holds for interpretational relevance as for thematic relevance: it does not exist in isolation. Rather, both form a coherent structure. This holds good for both correlates of interpretational relevance: for the interpretationally relevant aspects of the actual experience that have been brought thematically into relief, as well as for the interpretational schemata that had been developed in the stock of knowledge on the basis of prior experiences sedimented according to their typical aspects. These sedimentations (and the structure of the stock of knowledge in general) refer to the history ("biography") and the conditions for the acquisition of knowledge. In other words, one has "learned" to interpret. This naturally holds good not only for explicit problem explications, but also for interpretative processes in the prepredicative sphere. In contrast, the present use of the interpretational schemata is situationally conditioned, so that the grasping of the situation in its typicality is on the other hand a function of the present state of knowledge and thus of the subjective structure of the interpretational relevance.

From this it is now completely clear why at least the wide-awake, normal adult experiences nothing, including what he sees in a dark corner, as a simple something. In the interplay of thematic and interpretative relevances, the elements brought into relief and the flow of experience are "from the very start" grasped by their type. Even if the man in Carneades' example vacillates between the interpretations "snake" and "coiled rope," it never occurs to him that it could be an elephant, a table, etc. In general, the structure of interpretational relevance is determined by the principle of compatibility: compatibility between the current theme (its determinations that are presented as "typical") and the interpretational schemata in the stock of knowledge—but compatibility also between the interpretational schemata in their relation to one another; and frequently more than one schema is interpretatively relevant. Thus an object can be interpreted as a Scotch pine, a tree, or also possibly "more of a shrub than a tree," but not as a telephone pole. The ordering of the schemata, typifications, and elements of knowledge in general, according to decreasing and increasing consistency, has already been described in the analysis of the structure of the stock of knowledge.[93] Here, only the conclusion is to be drawn: "motivated" acts of explication are also not absolutely "free." Rather, they are "prescribed"

93. See Chap. 3, A, 3, d.

by the situation and the current theme as well as by the current state of knowledge and the ordering of the interpretational schemata in the stock of knowledge.

Before we conclude the analysis of interpretational relevance, we must still clarify what is meant by the statement that in doubtful situations one "chooses" between different interpretations. Does this involve an oscillation between two different themes? This seems to be assumed by many authors, including Husserl.[94] The matter may be otherwise. If a theme is constituted as problematic, it remains in the grasp of consciousness. If one proceeds to an explication, the direction of attentiveness changes only insofar as the elements which were up until now in the thematic field are not brought within the core of experience. In the interpretative processes different schemata or typifications are "held up." But the attentiveness is not directed first to schema A and then to schema B, but rather to the relation (measure and coincidence) between the *object preserved as the theme* and schema A, and then schema B. One could also speak of particularized subthematizations which are in the foreground of attentiveness in "comparisons" between the main theme and the two interpretational schemata. Obviously it can also happen that the main theme is abandoned. In this case it is no longer a question of a uniform process of explication, but rather of theme change.

4. MOTIVATIONAL RELEVANCE

a. The project of action (motivation in the in-order-to context)

That there is a third relevance structure, namely, motivational relevance, besides the other two, has already become clear. Thus, in the description of thematic relevance, "prompt" advertences to the theme and its "weight" were discussed. In this regard, it also had to be pointed out that thematizations are related to the mastery of the situation and to the biographically conditioned aspects of "personality." The interwoven character of thematic and motivational relevance is clearly demonstrated by hypothetical relevances. In the analysis of interpretative relevance it was further shown that the flow of experience is not interrupted and that the coincidence automatically remains between the theme and the elements of knowledge as long as this

94. [Husserl, *Ideen I*, §§ 106–7.]

process suffices for routine mastery of the situation. Finally, we saw that the processes of explication proper are pressed to the point where the problem is "solved," that is, until the actually present "interest" in the situation is satisfied—ignoring cases where the problem is not covered over by new, "more urgent," or "more important" problems. All these statements clearly refer to the fact that thematic as well as interpretative relevances are indissolubly bound up with the motivational bind.

Furthermore, however, the basic distinction between "imposed" and "motivated" forms of interpretative and thematic relevance already points to the role given to motivational relevance in the context of relevance structures. Certainly, the question arises here whether motivational relevance as such should be distinguished as a separate structure or simply treated as a basic aspect of the arrangement of "motivated" and "nonmotivated" levels of relevance in thematization and interpretation. And, further, if one may already speak of motivational relevance as a separate structure, is it not then ridiculous to distinguish two levels by analogy to the other two relevance structures? Only systematic investigation, which again confronts the example of Carneades, can give an answer to these questions. Here we want to anticipate the result of this investigation and establish that it is indeed justified to speak of one's own structure of motivational relevances and that two forms of this structure are found, a "free" and a "bound." The first is the chain of motivations determined by the project for future action; the second is the biographical "attitude" determined by sedimented motives.

In Carneades' example, the man saw himself faced with two interpretations. These appeared equally credible on the basis of the previous, interpretatively relevant thematic material. Consequently, he could not be satisfied in the actually present situation. (Here we must introduce a consideration. It was established earlier that interpretations are not undertaken until one can "agree with" the result of explication. In principle, one can do this on all levels of credibility, as they were distinguished by Carneades. One has a greater amount of interest in subjective certainty if one must decide between the alternatives "coiled rope/snake" than if the alternatives are "coiled rope/crumpled suit.") In the present example, the man is thus "interested" in being able with subjective certainty to "agree with" one of the two alternatives. A well-founded decision is "important" to him. The expressions "interest" and "important" obviously do not here refer to the structure of thematic relevances: the theme has not changed; it has brought nothing "new" into relief. However, neither are these expressions based on the structure of interpretative relevances: all available, existing material was evaluated, and it was in just this way that the man reached two similarly credible interpretations. Thus the expressions must refer rather to the structure of motivational relevances. An interpretative decision is *motivationally* important for the man. That means that it is relevant for his conduct, for his action, finally for his manner of living.

As the man entered the room, he wanted to go to sleep there. The need for sleep is imposed on the man, thanks to his worldly situated, living body. While sleeping, he wants to be routinely protected from rain, cold, and other possible disturbances and dangers. Therefore he wants to sleep in a room. At the moment in which he meets the unfamiliar object, the accomplishment of his (more or less) vital intention is interfered with. If it were only a question of a coiled rope, there would then be no reason not to carry out his intention. He could consider it a "false alarm." If the situation should involve a potentially dangerous snake, going to sleep would be connected to danger, in which case the man would have to change his intention. His projected act, the decision to act either thus or so, requires an interpretative decision. In this example, the importance of the motivation for the interpretative decision is based on a project for future action. We can formulate this in general terms: the motivational importance consists of decisions which are in the meaning-context of plan hierarchies. That is, motivational relevance puts conduct in the current situation into a meaningful relation with life-plans and daily plans, in the case of both routine prior decisions and "extraordinary" decisions.

Let us look more closely at the motivational importance of the interpretative decision in the example of Carneades. Of the two interpretations being offered as similarly credible, one is motivationally irrelevant. Coiled rope is in the present situation neither dangerous nor otherwise "interesting." In case the man could agree that this interpretation was well founded, that would mean that the interference with the original intention to go to sleep (and the interruption of the routine flow of experience by the unfamiliar object) was "superfluous," "unjustified." "Snake" is on the contrary dangerous, and the interruption of the routine would in this case be "justified." The man would have to give up or at any rate alter his original intention. Other projects for acts would have to be worked out.

But in the current situation such a decision still lies in the future. Now both interpretations are still equally possible.[95] The danger is at the moment only hypothetical. Here, still a further consideration must be injected. Naturally, one can so conduct himself *before* an interpretative decision between two alternatives in such a way that he simply avoids the posited hypothetical danger. The man could leave the room at once after he notices the unfamiliar object in the corner. Since he must, as he knows, sleep somewhere, he can try to spend the night with a friend. But the friend lives at the other end of the city, and it's quite far. And the friend, so he suspects, would spread the story. They would laugh about his timidity. This further development of the example is enough to show that one cannot, without limit, simply avoid hypothetical dangers. Sometimes a posited hypothetical danger necessarily will encounter a hypothetical danger which is posited as greater; one avoidance maneuver collides with the other. Expressed formally: the levels of urgency and importance and the principle of "first things first," conditioned by the situation (finitude, corporeality, etc.) of man in the world, determine the plan hierarchies for action and conduct in the course of the day and in the course of life. Given these plan hierarchies, one cannot avoid all possible, merely hypothetical (in principle an unlimited number of) dangers. One must make conduct-guiding, interpretative decisions which are oriented on the one hand by the stock of knowledge, above all by the typifications it contains concerning the probability of certain events, as for example dangers ("there were last year so and so many victims of traffic accidents"). But, on the other hand, the decisions are determined by superimposed plans ("I cannot remain holed up in my room just because streets are 'dangerous' to cross").

In general, therefore, great motivational importance accrues to interpretative decisions of this kind. If that does not also apply in every individual case (one time at least one also can probably run away from simply hypothetical snakes), it holds good, at least in most cases, for routine, ongoing, vital, everyday decisions ("Is it already time to go to sleep?," "Is there a spice in this soup that doesn't agree with me?," "There have already been very

95. See also the expositions concerning hypothetical relevance, Chap. 3, B, 2, c.

many accidents with this airline. Should I fly with it?," "One can risk this glacier descent only when the weather is good. Will it stay good?," etc.). In doing so, it need not at all be expressly formulated that superimposed plan hierarchies "are hidden behind" such decisions ("I have to eat," "I want to make the descent," etc.).

The man in Carneades' example, therefore, must decide whether the possibility that a snake is involved is actually the case. In order to be able to make a well-founded decision, he has to acquire additional, interpretatively relevant material. In order to acquire this, he has to change the situation, that is, his possibilities for observation in the situation. To this end, he has to have an effect on the object in question, in a way that allows new aspects to emerge. That is, he has to touch the object—the hypothetical snake—since he knows on the basis of the typification sedimented in his stock of knowledge that "real" snakes begin to move after they are touched. In order to touch the object, he has to use a stick—in order not to lay himself open to the hypothetical danger of a bite by the hypothetical snake. In order to be able to use a stick in this way, he has to move his arm in a way that is habitual, has to open and close his fingers in the habitual way, etc. We need not further develop the example to illustrate the intimate interdependence of the specific elements of knowledge, skills, and knowledge of recipes which are at the basis of every action.[96] Every "in-order-to" in these sentences reveals a link in a chain of motivational relevances. In this chain, what should be done motivates what "first" must be done as its presupposition. This chain of motivations, therefore, at the same time leads "backward" from "later" to "earlier": from the goal of an act, through the mediate stages of the project, to the beginning of the act.

We can therefore say that the goal of the act (in our example, the acquisition of additional interpretative material) motivated the act in the phases of its duration. At the beginning of our descriptions we said that the interpretative decision is motivationally important for future conduct (if snake . . . then avoid). How do these two statements relate to one another? What is motivated in the temporal structure of the flow of experience and what is motivating? Without making a prior decision about temporal or "causal" priority, we may say that the relation of

96. See Chap. 3, A, 1, c.

motivating and motivated elements is reciprocal. We have only demonstrated one chain of motivation, in which the relevance of one link for the other takes place "at the same time" but with the "opposite" relevance relation. This motivational chain can nevertheless be seen from two different temporal perspectives. In order to enlarge on this point we must briefly anticipate the analysis of action in the life-world.[97]

We said that the goal of an act motivates the projection of the act in its various phases, including its beginning: that is, the goal of the act precedes the actual action. The act ensues in order to reach the goal. This goal is a result of the act, a future state of affairs which is actually anticipated, that is, is a fantasied *modo futuri exacti*. As soon as this goal is given, then, as was explained in the example, the interlocking links of the chain can be traced back: from the interpretative decision "back" to the movement of the hand which grasped the stick. When we formulate it: the goal of an act motivates the act; we change places, strictly speaking, with a phase of the flow of experience, which precedes the completion of the act.

If we turn back to the resulting act and scan its course, the motivational chain appears to us in another time perspective. This holds as well, moreover, for the case where to a certain extent we "stand still" in the course of the act, yet before its goal is reached, and look back to its just-past phases. Let us assume that in the example of Carneades one of the man's acquaintances had entered the room after he did. Just as he held out the stick, he was interrupted in the execution of his project with a question as to what he was doing there. The conversation could have developed approximately this way: "I am going to hit that object with this stick." "Why are you doing that?" "Because I want to see whether that object begins to move." "Why do you want to see that?" "Because I want to know whether it is a snake." In short, the chain of motivations, which we originally described with in-order-to sentences, could have all its members expressed in because-sentences. Both sentences are based on the goal of an act as the motivating element and apprehend the partial acts or the individual phases of an act as motivated elements. Although the one-sentence form seems to be "teleological" and the other "causal," the sentences are equivalent in meaning. The difference exists purely and simply in the time-perspective in which

97. See Chap. 5 [Vol. II].

the chain of motivation is examined. What is "teleologically" relevant when seen from the beginning, is presented from the end as "causally" relevant. This consideration brings us back, therefore, to the earlier statement that the relation of motivating and motivated elements in the chain is reciprocal. It should be added that sentences about this kind of "causal" context can in principle be translated into sentences about motivational contexts, as on the other hand sentences about "free" results can be transcribed into "causal" sentences of this kind. This naturally holds good only so long as it involves human action in the narrower sense, that is, in the sense of planned conduct.

A further consideration is necessary here. It was just determined that chains of motivation are expressible in in-order-to sentences or "counterfeit" because-sentences (this is how we want to characterize those because-sentences which can be transcribed into in-order-to sentences). Does that mean that the previous analysis of the motivational context is essentially dependent on the data of a certain language, the expression of a certain relative-natural world view? We can answer the question negatively, but not unqualifiedly. In the question, two different moments should be separated from one another. One need not go any further into the trivially self-evident fact that every analysis, even an analysis of prelinguistic structures of experience, is formulated linguistically. Yet a certain linguistic "entanglement" of the analysis is unavoidable, since there is no language "as such" but rather only concrete languages with semantic and syntactical peculiarities. Another consideration is more important. As we have seen, action as planned conduct has a syntactical structure, which only "disappears" in completely routinized action. Thus one can speak of action in the pregnant sense, in contrast to "simple" conduct, only in respect to people who are socialized and consequently capable of language. That means that lifeworldly action is bound *empirically* not only to language "as such" (as a presupposition of syntactical projects for acting) but also to a certain language with its semantic and syntactic forms. Viewed formally, action is founded on the temporal structure of the flow of experience. It is *essentially* independent of the peculiarities of a concrete language. This justifies our negative response to the stated question.

A certain limitation must now be added. The time-perspectives of experience in the natural attitude find various expressions in different languages, or different relative-natural world views.

This is sufficiently verified by linguistic and ethnologic material. The linguistically objectivated time-perspectives decisively influence the usual *thinking* about the courses of acts and the chains of motivation. Everyone is socialized in such forms of habitual thought. As a consequence he has at his disposal linguistically objectivated forms of habitual thought about time-perspectives, which are to a certain extent "detached" from the basic temporal structure of the flow of experience, the courses of acts, and the chains of motivation involved in them. With the help of such forms he can explicate his own action just like the action of his fellow-men. Along with this there is the possibility that typical styles for considering courses of acts and contexts of motivation will be developed within social groups and societies which are confronted by typically similar situations and undergo a typically similar fate—as, for instance, predominantly "teleological" or predominantly "causal," typically "dynamic" or typically "static." Such styles of consideration can therefore vary historically from one relative-natural world view to another. They can also be socially distributed within a society, as for instance according to social strata and various institutional provinces.

b. The biographically conditioned nature of the attitude (motivation in the because-context)

Until now only one form of the context of motivation has been described: the reciprocally relevant chain of courses of acts or partial acts, motivated by the goal of the act. This form of the motivational context is, as we have seen, expressed in in-order-to sentences, but it can also be formulated in because-sentences if the time-perspective in which the chain of motivation is observed becomes displaced. The because-sentences which can be expressed by in-order-to sentences we characterize as "counterfeit." But have we exhaustively described all the possibilities of the motivationally relevant context? Are all because-sentences, in which this relevance is expressed, transcribable into in-order-to sentences?

Let us again return to the example of Carneades. We said that the interpretative decision (snake or coiled rope), acting as a goal for the act, motivated the acts (lifting up the stick, striking the object, etc.) which are necessary in order to collect new interpretatively relevant material (object moves/object doesn't move). This interpretative decision, as we said, is relevant for the future conduct of the man; it is for him immediately or mediately "vital." All these sentences obviously underlie a certain way of considering things. We have not concluded the situation as not yet definitively past, but rather as changeable; we have considered it as "manipulable" within certain limits. Correspondingly, the conduct of the man appears determinable by him, as well as codeterminable within the limits of his lifeworldly situation. His conduct appears, therefore, as potential action. If we look at the same situation, the same conduct of the man, from the vantage point of the past, the situation no longer appears "obvious," the conduct no longer a project in the future. Rather, the situation appears to us as conditioned by already past experiences. What was "free" in relation to the future horizon has changed into "bound" from the vantage point of the past.

If we bring this method of consideration to the example, we can say that the man wants to know whether the object could be a snake, because he is afraid of snakes. If we here try to express the sentence with an in-order-to sentence, we stumble over an obvious absurdity. It is senseless to say that the man fears snakes in order to want to decide whether the object is a snake or a coiled rope. Although such a translation fails, there is still a question of motivational relevance whose structure is distinguished from the one described before. If he did not fear snakes, he would hardly be interested in an interpretative decision. Thus we are, for instance, not very interested in deciding whether a tree, which we see among other trees from the train while passing by, is a silver fir or a Douglas fir. But we are almost always interested in deciding whether the insect which has just landed on our arm is a mosquito or a "harmless" insect.

Where does the difference lie in the previously discussed form of the motivational context? The chain of motivation was apprehended there as determined by the goal of the act; there, the goal of the act itself appears as motivated. Actually, it is also here a question of a displacement of the time-perspective; at any rate, displacement is not now freely available. The fear of snakes in any case "precedes" the project for an act, not to mention the course of the act. That is also the reason why a transcription into an in-order-to context is impossible here. We want to characterize such motivational relevances as "genuine" because-contexts.

But what is this fear of snakes? How is it present in consciousness, and how can it operate as a motive? And, how did it originate in the first place?

Before the man entered the room, he thought of the prior

conversation with his friend. In no case did he think of snakes, and not at all of the fact that he fears snakes. Snakes and fear of snakes are not continually in his consciousness, neither as a theme nor in the thematic field including all other themes in the flow of experience. The man does not think he will see a snake in every unfamiliar object, nor do all Objects of experience by their meaning refer to snakes; they are not, so to speak, "snake-like." Nor does the man go around looking in every corner and under all the beds to see whether there could be any snakes there. In what way, then, are "snakes" and fear of snakes "cogiven" in his consciousness?

"Snake" is a type stored in his stock of knowledge, which was formed in sedimentations from previous experiences. In certain situations, the type can be actualized, "awakened" by the interpretative relevance of certain thematic elements which stand in relief. Just as with other specific elements of knowledge and the stock of knowledge, this type is also "cogiven" to a certain extent in every experience, but in a "neutralized" form. It is brought into consciousness not through other typical objects (for example, elephants), but rather only in reciprocal relation with typical, interpretatively relevant elements which stand in relief in the actual theme.

What is the status of the fear of snakes? It is not a specific element of knowledge like the type "snake." It is rather a "syndrome," which comes from various elements. The syndrome contains typical expectations concerning hypothetical events which appear more or less "vital" ("it will bite me—I will die"). The expectations are therefore bound up with typical "frames of mind," whose intensity is determined by the limits of the life-worldly situation (finitude, "first things first," etc.), and of the biographically conditioned plan-hierarchy of the manner of living. Consequently, the intensity of the "frame of mind" is coupled with the different degrees of importance and urgency. The expectations, related to hypothetical events, are at the same time "solutions" to typical projects for an act ("run away immediately"). It need hardly be stressed that the projects for acts, for their part, presuppose different skills and recipes, either immediately or mediately. Such a "syndrome" consisting of expectations, hypothetical relevances, plans for acts, skills, and other elements of habitual knowledge, as well as of "frames of mind," we will characterize with the expression "attitude." Although the different elements of an attitude belong to various dimensions of the stock of knowledge—and are interwoven with thematic and interpretative relevance structures—we can say that an attitude is motivationally an entirely habitual possession. What that means will be best clarified by an investigation of the circumstances under which attitudes are activated.

The attitude (fear of snakes) is activated whenever the interpretation "snake" becomes actually present with subjective certainty, either through automatic coincidence between the theme and the element of knowledge (type "snake") or through more or less explicit processes of explication ("this animal here is a snake"). It is activated as well when the interpretation has a hypothetical character ("it could be a snake"). The attitude is therefore "already there" but is only activated under typical circumstances. The motivationally habitual possession is coupled with explicit elements of knowledge, or thematic and interpretative relevances. Even here the relation is *reciprocal*. We have just said that the attitude is activated by the interpretation. Vice versa, however, the attitude is also motivationally relevant to the degree of credibility requisite for an interpretation—in the present example, to the point where the man agrees with the interpretation "snake" or "coiled rope." Further, the attitude is already included in the formation of the alternatives of explication: "coiled rope/snake," instead of "coiled rope/rumpled suit." Thus we could imagine the extreme case of a person who "sees snakes" everywhere, where the thematic determinateness of the Objects of experience did not positively exclude this possibility, given his state of knowledge ("house," "elephant"). But from this it follows that, depending on the motive, the attitude is even involved in the constitution of the theme, and above all in bringing the unfamiliar into relief against a background of the familiar.

An attitude, therefore, is ready under typical circumstances to put into motion typical ways of conduct, as well as typical in-order-to chains of motivation—and, indeed immediately, without having first to "plan." If, for example, the man in the example traveled in a country where he knew there were no snakes, then objects which previously always awakened the type "snake" could even here call "snake" to mind, and the attitude "fear of snakes" could be coupled with it. Since the application of the type comes into conflict with the superimposed typifications ("country without snakes"), he naturally would subsequently remove the credibility from the interpretation and at the same time again "neutralize" the attitude. With this, it is especially clear that attitudes are closely coupled with specific elements of knowledge, and that they necessarily are in relation to other elements of knowledge in the structure of the stock of knowledge.

The man in the example can be compared with a general who has an over-all plan *a* with tactical projects 1, 2, 3 ready for the strategic situation *A*, and for the strategic situation *B*, he has ready plan *b* with projects 4, 5, 6. According to the situation, he can put immediately into gear plan *a* or plan *b*, quasi-automatically. The comparison is imperfect if one looks a little more closely. First, the attitude in its entirety is not a "plan" but rather, as we have already said, a stratified "syndrome." This "syndrome" was not worked out by the general staff in explicit acts of thought; rather, it is the "result" of heterogeneous experiences which have been sedimented in various levels of consciousness and are interwoven with one another. Second, the man in the example has to master not only snake situations, as the general has war situations, but also a manifold number of the heterogeneous situations of everyday life. In spite of his fear of snakes he is not "adjusted" to "snake situations" in the same way that the general is to war, although he is in a certain sense "always prepared" for snakes.

Up until now we have tried to show how an attitude is activated. An apparently related, yet basically different, question is how an attitude enters into consciousness. Here it involves again the already frequently mentioned distinction between "living-in-the-relevances" and "looking-at-the-relevances." It is in principle possible for an attitude to have been developed and to be motivationally efficacious without ever having been reflectively grasped as such. Indeed, every element of the stock of knowledge refers to originary situations of acquisition and thus to former "problems." As has been shown,[98] sedimentations of experience can be overlaid in the stock of knowledge by experiences which follow them. In this way, in any case, they become inaccessible to the immediate grasp of reflective consciousness. This especially holds true for elements of habitual possession founded on habitual knowledge. In addition, attitudes are not typically constituted in a "single" experience, and so no specific situation of acquisition is present for memory. Therefore, attitudes frequently contain no specific memory of the situation of acquisition, are usually very difficult to thematize, and are only accessible with difficulty

98. See, above all, Chap. 3, A, 2, d.

by reflective consciousness. Yet they work "unconsciously" as "motives" in the form of specific because-contexts.

So it happens that the actor himself is in no way in a privileged situation for discovering attitudes "on his own," as is the case for motivational chains in an in-order-to context. Rather, motivations in a because-context can also be adequately grasped by attentive observers of the typical conduct of fellow-men in typical situations. We add to this the fact that one is more frequently *motivated* in the life-world of everyday life to uncover such because-contexts in fellow-men than in himself, since one can pragmatically orient his own conduct to such knowledge. Thus it often happens that as an onlooker one often uncovers in his fellow-men motivational contexts of this variety, of which the fellow-man himself was not conscious. Finally, through painstaking interpretation of such motivational contexts, through the systematic accumulation of knowledge, and through generalizing typifications, some people can also be brought to a certain expertise concerning human motivation. An important basis for the predilection of social-scientific thought for such quasi-causal motivational contexts (excluding methodological considerations) is to be sought in this circumstance.

We have in Carneades' example a case in point, in which the attitude (fear of snakes) is subjectively thematizable. The man need not be able first to "explain" how it is that he fears snakes; he knows that he is afraid of them. Under certain circumstances, he can reflect about his fear and even try to reconstruct the "history" of his attitude. For, like all habitual possessions, like all components of the stock of knowledge as such, every attitude has its "history." It is a biographical datum. We want to reconstruct it to elucidate the prior example and thereby at the same time proffer an answer to the question posed at the beginning about the origin of attitudes.

The child who grew up to be the man in the example had at one time gone walking with his father in the woods. At that time, snakes were still unknown to the child. There were already typifications within his stock of knowledge by means of which, according to certain form- and movement- characteristics, he could have described a snake as an animal, even if not as a snake. A general attitude toward animals had already developed: up to then, animals that had appeared in his life were not all dangerous, most of all those that were especially small, and which were tame. Further, lived experiences of animals had at that time already lost their fundamental novelty, were routinized and in general unproblematic. As the child went walking in the woods, he saw an animal that seemed partly typically similar to animals he knew, partly novel. So he gave it his attention and went up to it. Then his father cried out fearfully, ran to the child, and pulled him back forcibly. He taught the child that snakes can be poisonous (the father knew that not all snakes are poisonous, but he thought it prudent to imbue the child with a general aversion to snakes), that their bite was dangerous. Further, he taught the child certain rules of conduct, which were already known to the child in their typicality from earlier encounters, at least in an opposite form ("you do not need to run away from chickens"). So, for the child, explicit elements of knowledge were bound up with in-order-to motivational chains, skills, knowledge of recipes, and at the same time with a certain "frame of mind."

The expressions of the attitude are derived from the originary situation of acquisition. In our example they reach from "all-snakes-are-dangerous-have-almost-stepped-on-one-father-terribly-frightened-highly-dangerous-run-away-immediately," to "poison-ous-snakes-are-dangerous-if-poisonous-snake-better-not-go-close," to "in-this-area-there-is-only-one-kind-of-poisonous-snake-better-not-walk-to-this-others-are-harmless-and-useful." Various attitudes, which range from panicky fear to neglecting caution, obviously correspond to these various formulations.

Two further considerations should be added here. First, there are no "isolated" attitudes. The originary situation of acquisition already put the experience in relation to other attitudes and elements of knowledge. The child had, for example, already had unpleasant experiences with other animals that had been characterized by the father as harmless. His warning was all the more effective in this case. If, on the contrary, the child had typified the father as unnecessarily concerned, the warning would have been ordered in a completely different context. Second, changes in attitude which are derived from subsequent relevant experiences must be considered. The child, for example, is later ridiculed by his playmates for his anxiety when they, as a matter of course, put blind worms in their pocket, while the child himself runs away trembling. On the other hand, the child may have disregarded the rules set down by his father and may have barely missed being killed as a result of a snake bite. The attitude "fear of snakes" was developed (and modified) in all such thematic, interpretative, and motivational variations of the originary situation of acquisition, as well as of the subsequent experiences. The attitude functions in a corresponding fashion as a because-motive in an actually present situation.

With that, we are at the end of our analysis of biographically conditioned, motivational relevance. There remains only the question of how justified the division is between the "free" project and the "bound" attitude. We have drawn this division quite sharply: "genuine" because-statements, so we said, cannot be transcribed into in-order-to sentences. It is a question of basically different methods of consideration and not only displacements of the time-perspective. But are we not indeed concerned with the same phenomenon?

Fear of snakes is a "genuine" because-motive for the goal of an act—namely, the interpretative decision between "coiled rope" and "snake." Transferring the statement into an in-order-to context appears ridiculous. Vice versa, it also appears senseless to maintain that the fear of snakes functions as a "genuine" because-motive, for example for the swinging of the stick. Thus it first appears as if our question had a simple answer: the project, and with it the course of an act, is motivated by the goal of the act, while the latter is motivated by means of the attitude. Does this then mean that the attitude, and therefore the "bound" form of the motivational relevance, acquires an essential priority, and that therefore the "freedom" of the project is at the same time an illusion of the method of consideration? Or can one more or less flatly reverse things with the assertion that every attitude is the "result" of "free" projects and that motivational "causality" has nothing to do with human action?

Both ways of expression absolutize a mode of consideration. If we say that the goal of an act is motivated by the attitude, this only holds true as long as we grasp an act's course in isolation. Every specific goal of an act is, when closely inspected, only a partial goal. Every partial goal, however, is in an in-order-to context with superimposed goals: interpretative decision (snake/coiled rope), in order to be able to go to sleep without worrying, to sleep in order to be rested the next day, to be rested in order to be able competently to finish an important job, etc. In short, plans are imbedded in plan hierarchies, which finally refer to the limits of the human situation in the life-world. This means that either immediately, or at least mediately, all conduct can be ordered in contexts of "free" motivational relevance. Vice versa, however, in principle every act and all conduct have a "history." A "first" project is—as long as we are satisfied with the description of the life-world—unimaginable. Fundamentally, all conduct and every act can be understood in contexts of "bound" motivational relevance. Only, this statement may not be interpreted as if because-contexts were in a certain sense more "Objective," as if they involved a "more real" variety of "causality" because of the previously discussed reasons (accessibility by the observer, by the social scientist).

5. THE INTERDEPENDENCE OF THE RELEVANCE STRUCTURES

The structures of thematic, interpretative, and motivational relevance are, as we have seen, interdependent. In the particular descriptions of these structures the results of a systematic analysis of the interconnection of these structures repeatedly had to be anticipated. This lack of an analysis can now be rectified. Two related questions should serve as clues. How do the relevance structures function in the constitution of an experience, of conduct? And, correspondingly, how do they function in the activation of the stock of knowledge at hand in the mastery of an actual situation? And further, how do the relevance structures function in the sedimentation of an experience as an element in the structure of the stock of knowledge?

An experience is originarily constituted in the turning of one's attention to a well-circumscribed theme within the actual situation. In general terms, this is the condition for the acquisition of knowledge. The analysis of thematic relevance has shown that a theme can intrude on one's attentiveness, that it is "imposed" within the actual situation. This can occur when the unfamiliar is brought into relief within the framework of the familiar, as a result of "leaps" from one province of reality with finite meaning-structure to another, or as a result of changes in the tension of consciousness in the flux of experience within the same province of reality, or when attention is socially imposed.[99] On the other hand, however, advertence to the theme can be "motivated." This occurs particularly in "abrupt" changes of focus when approaching more or less unfamiliar situations, in routine interruptions and resumptions of the courses of acts within the daily plan, and

99. See Chap. 3, B, 2, a.

in the development of themes within the framework of a "program of work."[100]

From what has been said, the interdependence of the three relevance structures clearly results in the originary constitution of an experience. Motivational relevances in the form of attitudes influence the initial determination of the situation and accordingly "direct" the attention (ignoring "motivated" advertences). Motivational relevances, especially in the form of chains of in-order-to motivations, play an important role in "abrupt" anticipations and in theme changes, especially in routine theme change in the framework of "programs of work." Further, it is clear that a theme as such is never brought into relief as such without typifying determinations of some kind; here, therefore, interpretative relevances function. And with theme development the difference between thematic and interpretative relevances can be maintained only for purposes of analysis.

A theme being developed from this can routinely coincide well enough with the elements of knowledge which are, with regard to the predominant attitude and to the chains of in-order-to motivation in the course of the act, sufficiently determined.[101] If, on the other hand, a routine coincidence does not occur with the elements of knowledge, which are on hand with sufficient determinateness and familiarity in the stock of knowledge, the current theme is experienced as a problem requiring explication. In other words, a motive for explication of the current theme arises. This motive can be derived from a specific attitude (fear of snakes) or can be related to the motivational chain of a specific project for an act (how do I chop down this tree?). The motive for explication can also be of a general kind, if it can be traced back to a cessation in the lifeworldly idealizations. If, for example, the automatic protensions or explicit expectations which characterize a phase of the flux of experience are radically disappointed in subsequent phases, as if they were "exploded," then the lifeworldly idealization of the "and-so-forth" which is at the basis of these events, comes to a standstill. We can recall here the example of the mushroom-front-side and mushroom-hind-side used in the first chapter. Even if no specific (mushroom-related) attitude and no specific (mushroom-related) projects for an act result, the current experience (of the mushroom) becomes problematic.

100. See Chap. 3, B, 2, b.
101. See Chap. 3, B, 3, a.

We can best characterize the nonspecific attitude which functions as a motive for the cessation of this idealization with the expression "curiosity." It is derived from an interest in maintaining the lifeworldly idealizations. Analogously, this is also the case for the idealization "I-can-always-do-it-again." This is based on skills, on conduct which is determined by knowledge of recipes, on routinized in-order-to chains of motivation in general. If an unforeseen resistance arises in the use of the skills or in the completion of routinized in-order-to chains, "if it doesn't go as it should," "if things don't work out," one is interested in restoring the routine, "to put things in order"—completely without regard to the specific, actual interest in the mastery of the situation. This interest motivates, according to what it concerns, "experiential" modes of conduct, a "straightening out" of certain members in the in-order-to chain of motivation, or also, to some extent, "training by conditioning," in the case of skills. If we look at the situation from the vantage point of the past, we experience a problem, generally stated, as requiring an explication on the basis of specific or even general attitudes. If we look at the situation from the point of view of "openness" to the future, we can correspondingly show that a problem develops as a result of the orientation of the experience or conduct according to a specific project for an act or also according to the capability of any acting whatever.

The problem requiring explication is interpreted, in that what thematically is actually brought into relief is "compared" with the "available" elements of knowledge ("results" of the interpretation of earlier problems) themselves. To be articulated with reference to specific "problems of conduct" means: one tries to overcome resistances in the course of an act by means of "available" alternative skills, recipes, or even "experimental" modes of conduct. On the one hand, the processes of explication consist of theme development, subthematizations, and the "motivated" procurement of interpretatively relevant material which was not yet accessible in the situation in which the theme originated. On the other hand, the processes of explication consist of "feeling out" more or less relevant elements of knowledge (typifications, schemata of interpretation). The interpretation may be pursued until the unfamiliar is sufficiently familiar, that is, until the unforeseen resistance is satisfactorily overcome. The expressions "sufficient" and "satisfactory" obviously refer to the prevailing, actually present motive of explication. The processes of interpretation, however, can also be interrupted even before satisfaction of the current motive for explication, therefore before the problem is "solved." This is the case if "more important" or "more urgent" problems are introduced into the flux of experience. It is a question of problems induced by attitudes (i.e., which are oriented to plans) which in the hierarchy of motivational relevances are superimposed on the attitudes (or plans) to which the "old" problem is related. This way in which new problems are introduced can, of course, be "imposed" or can be connected with the routinized motivational contexts of the daily plan and manner of living.

In short, in the development of a problem requiring explication as well as in the direction that the explication takes, and in the conclusion or discontinuance of the processes of explication, it is clearly apparent that the structure of motivational relevance is most closely interwoven with the structure of interpretational relevance. That every interpretation presupposes prior thematizations, and that on the other hand in the course of an interpretation new themes can be drawn into the flux of experience, hardly needs to be stressed.

And what of the sedimentation of experience in the stock of knowledge? Experiences which are not presented as problems requiring explication introduce no new elements of knowledge into the stock of knowledge. Also, they do not change the relevance structures or elements of knowledge (typifications, schemata of interpretation) which share in their constitution. In any case, they do not expressly change the determinations of the elements of knowledge in question. In contrast, they "confirm" the typical applicability of these elements of knowledge and corroborate the efficacy of the relevance structures. That means that the determinations of the affected elements of knowledge (for example, characteristics of a type) become more familiar and more unquestionable. And for another thing it means that skills become better coordinated and that recipes become more taken for granted, attitudes more "firm," and in-order-to chains of motivation more "automated." In other words, experiences which are routinely deposited in the stock of knowledge contribute toward the routinization of explicit elements of knowledge, the extension of the province of habitual knowledge, and the strengthening of already existing routines. Finally, this process has repercussions for thematic relevances, which are at the basis of such experiences: the latter forfeit more and more of their "well-circumscribed" character, and can sink entirely into the background of the completely familiar and be taken for granted in the flux of experience.

It is otherwise with problematic experiences requiring explication. Every interpretation, whether concluded or interrupted, whether "definitive" or "provisional," led to a "result." This result adds "new" elements to the stock of knowledge or changes those elements already on hand. Since one cannot establish an "absolute zero" for the state of knowledge, even "new" elements of knowledge may be considered as variants of the elements of knowledge already on hand. In any event, it is the case that the relevance structures, which proved efficacious in the application of certain elements of knowledge in the constitution of a problematic or unproblematic experience, also determine the sedimentation of the experience concerned in a corresponding "place" in the structure of the stock of knowledge—that is, in a set of types, interpretational schema, a recipe for conduct, a routinized in-order-to motivational chain, attitude, skill, etc. This general statement naturally does not apply in the *same* way to unproblematic and problematic experiences. The former need no further elucidation beyond what has been said; but the latter require a more detailed account. The distinction between the polythetic constitution of an experience and the monothetic grasp of its meaning is useful here. It has already been pointed out repeatedly that the polythetically constituted meaning of experiences can be subsequently grasped in a monothetic grip. Let us apply this to our problem. The processes of explication which lead to an interpretative "result" have an obviously polythetic character; the relevance structures that take part in them operate step by step. Accordingly, what stands out as thematically relevant in a given phase of the acquisition of knowledge can be presented in subsequent phases as "unessential," for example as determinations which may be freely varied, contrary to the original assumption inherent in a type. Attempts at interpretation which appear in one phase of the processes of explication to lead to a problem's solution, can be presented in subsequent phases as "blind alleys." In short, the *relevances efficacious in a given phase of the acquisition of knowledge can be presented in later phases as irrelevant*. In this case, they are overlaid by the relevances which have preserved their "validity" up to the "last" phase. Only the latter show the result of explication, its "place" in the structure of the stock of knowledge.

This circumstance has further consequences. The application of the result of explication as an element of knowledge in the mastery of an actually present, typically similar situation is determined only by those relevance structures which concern the end result of the explication, its monothetic meaning, and not by all the relevance structures which are more or less at the basis of the polythetic process of explication. This holds true as well for reflexive advertence to the meaning of an element of knowledge, in the natural attitude as well as in the more or less theoretical attitudes. The "valued" relevances have been skipped over and no longer emerge "by themselves." Yet the motive for an attempt at polythetic reconstruction of the *acquisition of knowledge* is usually absent. Considering this "overlaying," it can be left an open question how far such reconstructions are at all possible by means of the "last valid" relevance structures. In any case, what has become irrelevant is "dead ballast."

Strictly speaking, one must distinguish the following levels of operation for the interdependent relevance structures. *First,* the thematic relevances which in connection with the structures of interpretative and motivational relevance determine the originary constitution of an experience. *Second,* the motivational relevances which in connection with the structures of the thematic and interpretative kinds can make an experience problematic. *Third,* the interpretative relevances which in connection with the structures of thematic and motivational relevance determine the "direction" of the processes of explication. *Fourth,* the motivational relevances which in connection with the structures of the interpretative and thematic relevance cause the conclusion or discontinuance of the processes of explication. *Fifth,* the three mutually interdependent relevance aspects not "devalued" in the course of explication which guide the sedimentation of the result of the explication in the structure of the stock of knowledge. *Sixth,* the relevance structures which bring about the application of the sedimented element of knowledge in the mastery of new actually present situations, whereby the circle has been closed and we are again at the first point. And if we want to use the distinction between "living-in-the relevances" and "looking-at-the-relevances," we have lastly to add those relevance structures which are prominent in consciousness' reflective grip on an "already constituted" element of knowledge.

With these expositions, the closely interwoven character of the three relevance structures is once more made clear. That none of the three is due a priority of any kind has already been sufficiently stressed and is strengthened by these statements. It would be senseless to say that in the flux of experience any one of the three relevance structures is efficacious "first." Only in reflection can one or the other come up "first," in which case it can be grasped as the "fundamental" relevance, while both of the others appear as conditioned through it. To draw the conclusion that an "essential" priority accrues to it is unwarranted. Without going into a criticism of positions (such as that of pragmatism, operationalism, or even ethical idealism), let it be noted that these positions can be characterized by the fact that they determine such priorities all too readily.

[C] TYPICALITY

1. STOCK OF KNOWLEDGE, RELEVANCE, AND TYPICALITY

THERE HAS ALREADY BEEN quite a bit said about the connection between the familiarity of the elements of knowledge and the types included in the stock of knowledge.[102] But an exact analysis of typicality could not then be offered. The relevance structures at the basis of the stock of knowledge and its set of types had not yet been investigated. Only now, after the analysis of the former, can the discussion of typicality again be taken up.

The two chief forms of familiarity have been distinguished. On the one hand, there is familiarity, which rests on the fact that objects, persons, etc., are recognized again, and indeed as the "same" ones which have already been given in earlier experiences. This form of familiarity rests, as was expressed, on the "concrete sector of memory." On the other hand, there is a form of familiarity in which objects, persons, properties, events are not grasped as the "same," but as "similarly" determined, previously experienced objects, persons, properties, or events, whereby the relevance structures predominant in the current situation do not demand any determinations transcending this "similarity." This form of familiarity therefore rests on the set of types in the stock of knowledge. New experiences are determined by means of a type constituted in earlier experiences. In many situations of

102. See Chap. 3, A, 3, b, ii.

daily life the type is sufficient for the mastery of the current situation. Naturally, the "concrete sector of memory" and the form of familiarity which rests on it are grounded in the set of types in the stock of knowledge. This is the case because the objects, persons, etc., recognized again were once experienced "for the first time." Obviously, in doing so they were not grasped merely in their factual existence, but rather, at the same time, in their typical being-thus-and-so as well. Following this summary of the previous description of the relation of typicality and familiarity,[103] the relation of typicality to the other dimensions of the structure of the stock of knowledge, and above all to the determinateness of elements of knowledge, must be investigated. But first the question must be raised as to what a type is, how it arises, and what connection it has with relevance structures.

Every type in the lifeworldly stock of knowledge is a meaning-context "established" in lifeworldly experiences. Otherwise expressed, the type is a uniform relation of determination sedimented in prior experiences. This statement must now be expanded in detail.

Like elements of knowledge in general, the type is constituted as a "unity" of determinations, in an "originary" situation of acquisition. What was said about the genesis of elements of knowledge as such, and what was brought out about the relevance structure lying at the basis of this genesis, naturally also hold true for typifications. The situation of acquisition is determined by motivational relevances. The individual enters the situation with a particular attitude, and his experiences are incorporated into the chain of motivation of a specific in-order-to context. In the situation of acquisition, a theme is brought into relief. This can routinely be brought into coincidence with interpretatively relevant elements of knowledge, and the situation can be routinely mastered, in which case grasping of the core of experience occurs by means of determinations in "automatic" processes. But if, due to the reasons already given,[104] no routine coincidence occurs, a problem results. In the processes of explication that are then initiated, possibilities of determination are grasped which were not yet in the grasp of consciousness in the thematic field, that is, in the thematically relevant inner and outer horizon of the core of experience. This is the case only inso-

103. *Ibid.*
104. See Chap. 3, B, 3.

far as they appear interpretatively relevant in the current situation, according to the prevailing state of knowledge. The processes of explication, as has already been brought out in the analysis of interpretative relevance, result therefore in a "simultaneous" and reciprocal relation between what has been brought into thematic relief and the possibilities of determination which are relevant for mastery of the situation and which have in earlier experiences been deposited in the stock of knowledge. If an adequate coincidence occurs between these two aspects of interpretative relevance, a problem is "solved."

Through every "problem's solution" something "new" becomes consequently something "old." The "old" consists of the possibilities of determination already on hand in the prevailing stock of knowledge in an established, interpretatively relevant context (four-footed, wags its tail, barks). The "new," on the contrary, consists in the active seizing of the possibilities of determination which were originally "hidden" in the theme—which had been neglected and which were proven in the current situation to be interpretatively relevant ("bites"). The "new" determination enters into the relation of determination; a meaning-context is "established" between those determinations which were earlier relevant and those which are now becoming so: a type is constituted ("dog": four-footed, wags its tail, barks, bites).

In other words, a type arises from a situationally adequate solution to a problematic situation through the new determination of an experience which could not be mastered with the aid of the stock of knowledge already on hand. Here that means: with the aid of an "old" determination relation. We can therefore imagine a type to be like a line of demarcation which runs between the determinations explicated on the basis of the "hitherto existing" relevance structures (which are in a meaning-context) and the, in principle, unlimited possibilities for the determination of experience. The meaning-context of determinations is "established" through the predominant thematic and interpretative relevances in the situation of acquisition acting in unison with the motivational relevances. From this it follows that there can be no types as such, rather only problem-oriented types. Every type contains a reference to its constitution, the "originary" problem state, which in turn had been constituted by the three relevance structures acting in unison. Accordingly, every type has a "history," which reaches from the "originary" situation of acquisition to the current application. Before we explicate this point more fully, another fundamental implication of the prior analysis must be pursued.

In the constitution of a type, a stock of knowledge must already be presupposed, however impoverished this may be. The descriptive analysis cannot be driven to an "absolute-zero" state of knowledge. One can only theoretically construct such a state. But it should also be considered that no experience can be thought of as "pretypical." Rather, we must, with Husserl, construe experience and type as "equally originary." [105] Thus every type is, strictly speaking, only a variation on typifications already on hand, however plain and ill-defined they may be (e.g., edible/ unenjoyable; painful/pleasurable; etc.). Such variations can be trivial and can only lead to a higher degree of determination for the type already on hand. They can also lead to a division of the type into subtypes. We can really only speak of a "new" type when the original relation between possibilities of determination is dissolved and a novel meaning-context between "already" typical possibilities of determination is established.

A further implication of the previous analysis is that there can be no "definitive" types in the lifeworldly stock of knowledge. Every type formed in an "originary" problem state is employed in further routine situations and problem states. If it continues to show itself to be adequate for the mastery of the situation, it can be *relatively* "definitive." It changes over into the province of habitual knowledge, and its application can become completely "automatic."

Here we must indicate the relation of the set of types to the dimensions of the structure of the stock of knowledge. We have seen that the types stored in the stock of knowledge are directly connected with the degrees of determination in the elements of knowledge. The relation of the types to the levels of credibility has in any case already been discussed. Now it need only be added that typifications of complex kinds, thus types as relations of determination, can also be more or less credible, and that they are in relations of compatibility with one another. The more credible a type is, the more often it will be "confirmed" and the more compatible it is with other types and elements of knowledge, and the more "definitive" it is as well. Hence, for us, typifications like "tree," "dog," etc., are relatively "definitive." But even relatively "definitive" typifications can be presented afterward as

105. [Husserl, *Erfahrung und Urteil*, § 83 a and b.]

"provisional," and indeed in a double sense. First, a type which has up to now proven true again and again may appear in a new problematic situation as insufficiently determined. And second, the relation of determination, even of relatively definitive types, may have to be resolved, or partially resolved. At some time our ancestors had to change radically the type "whale" (containing the determination "fish"). But even in the prevailing given state of a subjective lifeworldly stock of knowledge some typifications carry the subscript of provisional. Indeed, in the originary constitution of the type, some determinations of the meaning-context may appear less credible, or be brought into question in subsequent experiences. In the event that no decision about the interpretative relevance reaches such a determination, or in the event that the questionable determination can achieve no higher degree of credibility, the type certainly need not be discarded in its entirety. Its use, however, contains the subjectively graspable significance of "being provisional."

2. TYPICALITY AND LANGUAGE

Up to now the role of language has been neglected in the consideration of the constitution and structure of typicality. This was justified insofar as type-constitution, as well as type-structure, is in principle conceivable without language, as in a certain sense "prelinguistic" experiences can also be conceived. This is valid in a twofold manner. First, the founding relations are such that the structure of language presupposes typification but not vice versa. Second, empirical-genetic typifying schemata can also be positively demonstrated in children who do not yet talk.

The above says nothing fundamental about the relation of language and type. Everyone is born into a situation in which the language, more exactly, a certain language, is already given to him as a component of the historical social world. The language is something that the child has to learn. It is transmitted to him by fellow-men, first by those in especially immediate relations of lived experiential nearness.[106] The language is a system of typifying schemata of experience, which rests on idealizations and anonymizations of immediate subjective experience.[107] These

106. See Chap. 4, A, 1, b.
107. See Chap. 4, B, 1 and 2.

typifications of experience detached from subjectivity are socially objectivated, whereby they become a component of the social a priori previously given to the subject. For the normal growing person in the natural attitude, typification is most closely entwined with language. The main aspects of this entwining can be briefly described.

The relevant schemata of experience predominant in a society, or relative-natural world view, are "imitated" by the arrangement of language into semantic-syntactic fields. The language "contains" within one homogeneous objectivating medium the results of type-constitution and type-variation that have been accumulated over many generations and demonstrated to be trustworthy. Every type finds a "place value" in the semantic arrangement of the language by means of linguistic objectivation. That means that the types are embedded in a type-context, which is still more extensively detached than the individual type from subjective immediate experience. At the same time, this embedding means that type-constitution and variation is cumulative *within* the system; that is, the change of "place value" which affects one type has consequences for the "place value" of other types within the system. For the type included in the subjective stock of knowledge this has decisive consequences. Surely during the development of the child there are prelinguistic typifications. Surely for the adult there are also typical determinations, which operate in subjective experience without being linguistically objectivated. The capability of forming reciprocally dependent types in a succession of stages presupposes language as a socially objectivated system of meaning. Processes of explication which are expressly undertaken are impossible without semantic ordering and the infinite syntactical possibilities for combination in the language.

By far the largest province of lifeworldly typifications is linguistically objectivated. Whatever is typically relevant for the individual was for the most part already typically relevant for his predecessors and has consequently deposited its semantic equivalents in the language. In short, the language can be construed as the sedimentation of typical experiential schemata which are typically relevant in a society. Change in the meaning of a language can be seen as a consequence of changes in the social relevance of given experiential schemata. Many of these become irrelevant and disappear from the "living" language; new schemata become sufficiently relevant for individuals, for groups, classes, etc. This causes the formation of new fields of meaning, that is, the remodeling of those which are already more on hand.

It is clear that, to a large extent, a historically pregiven language relieves the individual of the burden of independently forming types. In language, as a pregiven element of the biographical situation, the world is pretypified. The possibility of separate type-constitution remains unchallenged. But even here language plays a decisive role, since it establishes the developed types through objectivation of sounds and through embedding in semantic "matrices." The reciprocal relation of language and typification is an important factor in the formation of customary thought and conduct.

The originary formation of language is thus unthinkable without the subjective capability for type-constitution. It fundamentally presupposes this. At the same time, however, a historically pregiven language is of decisive significance in the subjective origin of types, in that on the one hand it contains already constituted types, which are learned, while on the other hand it stabilizes independently formed types. We can accordingly say that the semantic arrangement of a language corresponds to a great extent to the typically relevant experiential schemata dominant in a society. Therefore it also corresponds to a great extent to the set of types included in the subjective stock of knowledge of the individual socialized in this society and language.

3. THE ATYPICAL

Indeed, in the formation of every well-circumscribed experience what is thematically brought into relief is grasped in its typical determinateness. One could, strictly speaking, imagine a "first" experience only as completely atypical, while an already typifying grasp enters into all "consequent" experiences through comparison with the remembered determinations of the "first" experience. The distinction between typical and atypical experiences, events, acts, etc., which we meet in the natural attitude, is not nonsensical. It is, though, so ambiguous that the problem of the atypical in the life-world demands a short discussion.

First, we can speak of the atypical if thematic relevances intrude in the experiential flow of attentiveness, for which there is no equivalent in the typifications already sedimented in the prevailing subjective stock of knowledge. That is, as was demonstrated in the analysis of relevance structures, coincidence between the actual theme and the potentially relevant elements of knowledge does not occur sufficiently for the mastery of the situation in question. Obviously, at this point typical determinations (e.g., qualities of forms, temporal order, etc.) are also grasped in the theme (events, objects, etc.). These determinations just do not suffice for grasping the current theme in its concrete context while doing justice to the situation. The reason for this is that in the stock of knowledge no determination-context established in prior experiences, no type in the narrower sense, can be found that could achieve an interpretative coincidence with the concrete context of the actual thematic relevances. Thus, the theme (the event, the object, etc.) in its present actuality is experienced as atypical. It is clear that the experience is atypical only in relation to the prevailing state of the biographically articulated stock of knowledge. But the theme remains fundamentally typifiable. If the atypical experience is made the theme of the acts of explication, a determination-context, a type, can be "established" which is "suitable" for the concrete theme and which suffices for mastery of the current situation. If, for example, something which on the basis of its typical form, mobility, etc., is grasped as an animal comes toward me, the type "animal" is not sufficient. Although the determinations "four-leggedness" and "horns" are grasped, I cannot order the animal in any subtype on hand in my stock of knowledge (buffalo, cow, etc.), since it contains a determination inconsistent with the subtypes on hand (covered with scales). However, I cannot be satisfied with the superior "animal," since I also do not know whether the animal is dangerous or not. The animal is "atypical," that is, it does not correspond to a situationally suitable type established in prior experiences. It is also clear that a form of hypothetical relevance is present here: the "atypical" animal could be dangerous, therefore I am motivated to conduct myself as if it were dangerous, until I can make the interpretative decision whether it is actually dangerous or not. If I experience in the subsequent acts of explication that it is a question of a completely harmless animal of a known species, the animal will no longer appear to me as "atypical" in the future.

Second, we can speak of a less "radical" kind of the atypical. Let us assume that a theme (object, event, etc.) is grasped not only in some typical determinations, but rather in a determination-context until now grasped as adequate (e.g., as ocean plant). Unforeseen characteristics come into the actually present theme, which is first perceived as a typical representative of this species, the characteristics being atypical in relation to the former determination-context. Here two principal possibilities must be distinguished. In the first place, the atypical determinations can be consistent with the already instituted type (e.g., the ocean plant changes its color in a short time under the influence of the sun). In this case, the already instituted type is enriched only by new typical determinations ("many ocean plants change their color under the influence of the sun"). In the second place, however, the atypical determination can be inconsistent with the already instituted determination-context ("the object moves by itself"). In this case the prior determination-context must be radically changed ("there are a few plants that move by themselves"), which means that the conditions for consistency are themselves modified. There is one further possibility. If the conditions for consistency in the current state of knowledge must be seen as unchangeable, the determination-context instituted earlier is dissolved and a new one is reconstructed (the type "ocean plant" no longer includes the subtype, in which I until now ordered it, and to whose representatives I ascribed mobility). The "line of demarcation" between determination-contexts is therefore displaced because mobility is radically "atypical" for one type, that is, inconsistent with it, but not for another.

The type is, as was brought out, a determination-context, in which irrelevant possibilities for determination of concrete experiences were *suppressed*. Every concrete experience must consequently contain "atypical" elements. Add to this that every experience enters the flow of experience at a unique place and is consequently "unrepeatable," thus already exhibiting "atypical" characteristics. In the natural attitude, in which the pragmatic motive predominates, these "atypical," namely, unique and unrepeatable aspects of experiences, are in general of no interest. Rather, the correspondence between the actual concrete experiences and the typical determination-context itself is typically relevant. But in the routine of everyday experiencing, especially in "exceptional situations" and above all in transitions to other provinces of reality with finite structures of meaning, in particular the religious, I depend on the uniqueness and unrepeatability of the experience, but not on its typicality. As a further complication, certain biographical "solitary happenings" can be socially typified. That is clear, for example, in *rites of passage*. What is not repeatable in the subjective biography can be socially pre-typified.[108]

4. TYPICALITY AND PREDICTION

In the natural attitude the lifeworldly stock of knowledge serves above all the purpose of determining and mastering actual situations. As the analysis of the relevance structures which determine the constitution and structure of the stock of knowledge has shown, this involves either the routine employment of habitual knowledge sedimented from past experiences or the explication and re-explication of past experiences and situations. The current stock of knowledge consequently operates either as an "automatic" pattern of conduct or as an explicit interpretational schema. The determination and mastery of actual situations also involves an orientation to the future. We have not up to now systematically examined the role of the stock of knowledge in this process. Only in the description of relevance structures, above all in the analysis of the in-order-to motivational context, was the future orientation of everyday conduct referred to in some aspects. But now, after we have investigated the set of types included in the stock of knowledge, we can treat the question of how knowledge about future events comes about in the natural attitude of daily life.

First, two aspects of this question closely related to one another must be separated. *Why* one anticipates future events and why one is interested in anticipating certain experiences and situations as possible or impossible, probable or improbable, is a question that fundamentally refers to the subjective relevance system, which guides the individual into the natural attitude of daily life. We already touched on this question in the analysis of hypothetical and motivational relevance. The unchangeable givens of the world, the "causal" contexts of "Objective" relations, are subjectively experienced in the realization of plans as hindrances or as means to ends. As a "province of applicability" for the idealizations of the "and-so-forth" and the "I-can-always-do-it-again," these relations take their place in the subjective plan-

108. See Chap. 2, B, 6.

hierarchies in the form of knowledge about the unfeasible and the imposed, about limiting conditions and possibilities for action, about presuppositions of the feasible and the achievable. In the framework of these limiting conditions one is under pressure of various urgencies (which are determined by the pragmatic motive which is predominant in the natural attitude); one is above all interested in the prediction of one's own acts, more exactly, in the *result* of one's intentions. But since one's own acts are embedded in the act-contexts of fellow-men and in the imposed consequences of "natural" events, one is at the same time interested in the prediction of social and natural relations which are more or less outside the control of one's own action.

What is anticipated and *how* it is anticipated are questions that must be answered with the aid of a closer investigation of the structure of the stock of knowledge and its set of types. Before we turn to the problem of prediction in the proper sense of the word, we want to remember that every experience is "future-oriented." With reference to Husserl's analysis of inner-time consciousness, it has already been stressed in the description of the temporal structure of the flux of experience that every actual phase of inner duration also contains, besides retentions of just-elapsed phases, protensions of future phases. These protensions are never completely empty of content. Rather, they are more or less specific on the basis of the lifeworldly idealizations; that is, they are filled with automatic typifications which are derived from the province of habitual knowledge. As has already been brought out, as long as the automatic protensions are not "refuted" in the future flow of experience, no cessation takes place in the routine flow. It is self-evident that the "content" of the protensions consists of typifications, not of anticipations of unique and unrepeatable events, lived experiences, etc. The protensions are more or less undetermined in spite of their "fullness of content," and the uncertain aspects of the protensions are for their part "filled in" with the "unique" and unrepeatable aspects of the concrete, actual experience. If one is speaking of a "refutation" of protensions, this thus refers to "atypical," "unexpected," but situationally relevant thematic relevances of actual experience.

Automatic protensions are not really "predictions." The latter presuppose syntactical acts of thinking, whose "content" is derived from explicit elements of the stock of knowledge. It hardly needs to be stressed that prediction is founded on protensions, that the typifications used in prediction are grounded in automatic typifications. As in automatic protensions, so also in explicit predictions, the "unique," unrepeatable aspects of future events are not grasped, but only the possibility, probability, etc., of typical sequences, typical relations, typical methods of acting, etc., coming true again.

It is obvious that experiences, strictly speaking, cannot be repeated. There cannot be two "identical" experiences, since every experience necessarily has a "unique" biographical expression. Two experiences "similar" in their typicality are already different solely in their biographical "place value," according to whether they are embedded earlier or later in the flux of experience. They are necessarily in a different meaning-context. Even if we disregard all other possible changes in the stock of knowledge and the "becoming older," the second experience is differentiated from the first by the fact that it can be brought to coincide with the interpretatively relevant aspects which were sedimented from the first experience in the stock of knowledge. The second experience can be recognized as "similar" to the first one through this. At the time of the second experience, a stock of knowledge is therefore available which differentiates it, by means of the element E if not after all by means of something else, from the stock of knowledge which was available at the time of the experience E.

Naturally, what has been said about experiences in general also holds good for acts. If we consider two "similar" acts, Hx_1 and Hx_2, the following is to be noted: Hx_1, which began in the situation Sx_1, leads to the result Rx_1. If the "similar" act Hx_2 is begun, the situation Sx_2 necessarily diverges from Sx_1 in that the stock of knowledge in it contains the element of knowledge: Hx_1 in Sx_1 led to Rx_1. This knowledge was not on hand in Sx_1. In Sx_1 the knowledge that "typical act" Hx leads to "typical result" Rx had perhaps been socially transmitted, without having been confirmed in one's own experiences. Perhaps one observed that fellow-men, who carry out typical movements in water, swim. One carries out the "same" movements in the expectation of achieving the "same" result. If this expectation has once been confirmed, one goes in the water the second time with a specific new element of knowledge. Another possibility, however, is that the special act H_1 was not at all begun with the knowledge Hx (Hx_1, Hx_2, Hx_3, etc.) leads to Rx (Rx_1, Rx_2, Rx_3, etc.), but rather in the expectation that it would lead to the result Ry_1. After the completed act, it turns out that it led to the result Rx_1. In S_2, in contrast, Ry is no longer expected, but rather Rx. Otherwise expressed, Ry is the in-order-to motive in S_1, but in S_2 the in-order-to motive is Rx. The situation S_2 is consequently determined differently. The history of "unintended" discoveries and inventions offers many examples of such situations.

The praxis of everyday life is characterized in general by one being interested not in the uniqueness of S_1, R_1, H_1, E_1, but rather in the typical repeatability of S, E, H, R. In the sedimentation of S, E, H, R in the stock of knowledge, the typical, in principle "repeatable," aspects of S, E, H, R (namely, Sx, Ex, Hx, Rx, or Sy, Ey, Hy, Ry) are in general interpretatively relevant. By means of the idealizations of the "and-so-forth" and the "I-can-always-do-it-again," not unique but typical situations, experiences, acts, and results of acts are then predictable. If indeed these then take place, they can either be "atypical" (neither Ex nor Ey, etc.), that is, they disappoint the expectation, or they can confirm the expectation in its typicality so that the necessarily "unique" aspects of the concrete experience, situation, etc. (E_1, E_2, H_1, H_2) can be disregarded.

Let us summarize. By means of the typifications included in the stock of knowledge and on the basis of the idealizations of the "and-so-forth" and the "I-can-always-do-it-again," the stock of knowledge makes possible the orientation of the flux of experience toward the future. Every current situation or the conduct in it has a future horizon which is automatically filled with typical and typically relevant contents. The stock of knowledge functions as a routine schema for conduct. Further, the act is also oriented toward the future, whereby typical courses of acts and results of acts are established as possible, probable, or also as subjectively certain. At the same time it should be stressed again that in daily life nothing can be predicted just as it indeed happens. What happens could never have been exactly predicted. But since under the dominance of the pragmatic motive, this kind of exact prediction is in general irrelevant, while just the typical and typically repeatable aspects of experience and of action are of interest, prediction of the "future" in the natural attitude is possible and—in spite of its chance character—"successful."

[A] THE SUBJECTIVE STOCK OF KNOWLEDGE AS SOCIALLY CONDITIONED

I. THE ELEMENTS OF THE BIOGRAPHICAL SITUATION ALREADY SOCIALLY ON HAND

a. The social structure "behind" the earliest we-relations

THE FACT THAT the everyday life-world is not a private, but rather an intersubjective and thereby a social reality, has a series of extremely important consequences for the constitution and structure of the subjective stock of knowledge. Because an individual is born into a historical social world, his biographical situation is, from the beginning, socially delimited and determined by social givens that find specific expressions. From the beginning, the subjective structures of relevance are developed in situations which are intersubjective, or at the least they are mediately put into socially determinate meaning-contexts. This is of special significance for the constitution of the subjective interpretational relevances, or for the set of types and motivational relevances. The sedimentation of specific elements in the subjective stock of knowledge is socially conditioned, indeed in a twofold manner. First, the occurrences of the sedimentation of experience are indirectly and also socially determinable, since they are based on the socially conditioned, subjective relevance structures. Second, the specific elements of knowledge, the typical "contents" of the subjective stock of knowledge, are not for the most part acquired through processes of explication, but rather are derived socially. That is, they are taken from the "social stock of knowledge," namely, from the socially objectivated results of Others' experiences and explications. The larger part of the stock of knowledge of the normal adult is not immediately acquired, but rather "learned." [1] These different aspects of the socially conditioned and determined nature of the subjective stock of knowledge must be examined more closely. Let us now consider the elements of biographical situations which are already socially given.

As is discussed in other passages,[2] the biographical situation is delineated from the beginning. Certain elements of the world-structure are irrevocably imposed on the individual. A historical social structure, which has a specific relative-natural world view, is ingredient in the elements of the biographical situation already on hand. Mediate and immediate social relations are in part unambiguously institutionalized and in part molded by meaning-contexts, which are for their part socially objectivated in speech and institutions. However, not only is the social world in the narrower sense laid out and typified, but so also is reality in general (above all the daily life-world, yet not only it, but also the other provinces of finite meaning-structure). The customary attentional advertences and interpretational schemata for nature, society, and conduct in general are objectivated in language and are more or less firmly institutionalized in the social structure. All this demands a still more exact analysis. Here we are interested in how this social a priori, already given in the biographical situation, is subjectively experienced.

The historical social structure is already "causally" presupposed in the earliest experiences of the child. We do not need to discuss this circumstance further at this point; it is obvious that the social structure (mother, provider, protector, teacher, etc.) always serves a function in the survival of the human child. But the historical social structure is not only "causally" presupposed in the earliest experiences of the child, it is also included in them as a meaning-context. Also, we can hardly discuss the pure "presocial" experiences of a child who has not yet learned to speak. It is of course permissible to speak of presocial elements in the founding structure of all experience. But from an empirical-

1. [Alfred Schutz, *Reflections on the Problem of Relevance*, ed. Richard M. Zaner (New Haven: Yale University Press, 1970), pp. 84–85.]
2. See Chap. 2, B, 6, and Chap. 3, A, 1, a.

genetic perspective it is only possible to demonstrate presocial experiences, interpretational schemata, and acts when one more or less artificially abstracts from the intersubjective and social meaning-context of the flux of experience. It is crucially significant here that the self, on which the conscious unity of subjective experiences and acts is based, becomes educated through intersubjective events and thereby presupposes a historical social structure. This must be elaborated in greater detail.

The explicit reference of every experience, of every act, back to an experiencing and acting self, presupposes two things. First, it presupposes the automatic syntheses inherent in the temporal phases of inner duration, or to be more exact, the processes of intersubjective mirroring. These processes make possible a *mediated* comprehension of the self—mediated through the immediate experience of an Other, who experiences the developing self immediately. Further, "responsibility" for one's own acts, both past and present, is "imposed" on the individual by means of the Other. The personal identity of a self can first be expressed as a consequence of such "responsibility," the explicit context of which connects past, present, and (in subjective derivation) planned acts, and therefore presupposes the "presocial" temporality of the flux of experience. But this first comes within conscious grasp as the individual is reproached by Others. And just as the flux of experience is binding on a socially originating personal self, so also is a disassociation (for instance, like that which is an ingredient possibility in "irresponsible" fantasy and in dream worlds) hindered in the everyday life-world by social control.

From these considerations it follows that we can analytically imagine "presocial" experiences, but that they stand in a social meaning-context, since they are necessarily bound to a personal self. To be sure, we may not consider the child who is not yet in the earliest we-relations as provided with such a self. One may assume that the degree of consciousness, clarity, and determinateness of the earliest social encounters is relatively low. One may also assume that such encounters do not initially appear in sharp distinction from "nonsocial" experiences. Nevertheless, the child is already concerned with them as a kind of we-relation. What is given are the immediacy of the experience of the Other and the reciprocal attentional advertence. The social relation is in a certain sense already reciprocal for the child before the development of a personal self. The reciprocity with which we are concerned is, of course, in a certain sense "imposed" on the child. The one confronting him (e.g., his mother) always conducts herself in such a way as to presuppose a certain reciprocity on the part of the child. At first it may only consist of a quasi we-relation. But one of the partners always conducts himself as if it were a genuine we-relation. After all, such a quasi we-relation can also exist, for example, between an old maid and her canary, with the difference that the complete reciprocity of a genuine we-relation does not result. The reciprocity of the we-relation is therefore "forced" on the child through the Other. It is a socially pregiven element of his biographical situation. But on the other hand, it also depends on his "presocial" subjectivity. This means that it is also based on the structural "abilities" of the child. It must once again be stressed that the "presocial" conditions of subjective experience, of acquisitions of knowledge, and of the personal self are really only conditions with which the intersubjective mirroring is necessarily associated. Only in this multifaceted process of experiencing the Other, and the self by means of the experience of the Other [3] does the identity of the child unfold.

The fellow-men who come in contact with the child in the earliest we-relations have themselves developed a personal self through early we-relations with Others and have modified, differentiated, and consolidated this in a later we-relation. Their action is determined by social institutions, their experiences stamped by the relative-natural world view, their knowledge derived extensively from the "social stock of knowledge." Thus, with respect to the child they conduct themselves in ways which are determined by social institutions (marriage, fatherhood, etc.), and the child is apprehended by them in socially derived typical forms (such as first-born, son, blessing of God, crutch, etc.).

From the earliest we-relations, the child is included in a reciprocal motivational context whose structures of relevance (goals, means, attitudes) are socially delimited as being prescribed and sanctioned in a taken-for-granted way. Thus the child first of all experiences the historical social structure, which is a component imposed on his biographical situation, in the form of immediate we-relations. Through events of intersubjective mirroring he "learns" relevant aspects of the social structure, and he "internalizes" the relative-natural world view. All of his experiences, including those of a "private" nature, are embedded

3. See also Chap. 2, B, 5, b.

in intersubjectively relevant, socially determined, and predeline-
ated contexts of motivation and interpretation.

There is still one thing to be added. Although a concrete historical social structure lies "behind" the we-relations, even "behind" the earliest we-relations which are especially important for
the development of a personal self on the part of the child, these
relations are not exhausted in their "representation" of the social
structure. They are indeed socially, but not unalterably, determined. As there are "good" and "bad" fathers, so there are also
(to be sure, structurally predetermined) degrees of variation of
the subjective conduct within these relations. And finally, the
specific meaning of every we-relation is naturally "unique" in its
special biographical articulation (for the child as well as for his
partners), with all its socially predetermined typicality.

b. *Language and the relative-natural world view in the earliest we-relations*

A thorough description is needed of the constitution of language in we-relations and the structure of language as a socially
objectivated system of signs, including the relation of language
to the life-world's typicality.[4] We will limit ourselves here to uti-
lizing the results of those analyses for the problem which concerns us here—the role that language plays as an element
already on hand in the biographical situation. Let us first recall
what language does for the individual.

Every language conforms to a determined relative-natural
world view, and the inner form of language agrees with its
fundamental meaning-structures. The semantic and syntactic
structure objectivates typical experiences and the results of their
explication by the members of a society. This presupposes different forms of detachment (idealization and anonymizing) from
immediate subjective experiences. It is exactly in this way that
language can function as a socially objective system of signs and
as a component of the "social-historical a priori," as a "model" for
"everyone's" subjective experiential structures. More exactly, it
can function as a coherent manifold of "regional models" (fields
and provinces of meaning) for the experiences of typical members of society. The semantic and syntactic structure of language
indicates the typical attentional advertences (thematic rele-

4. See Chap. 3, C, 2.

vances), models of explication (interpretational relevances), and patterns of "because-" and "in-order-to" contexts (motivational relevances) present in subjective experience. Language determines what is usually differentiated in the subjective experience of a typical member of society, and which potential differences are disregarded. It determines which objects, properties, and events are routinely related to each other, and which belong to heterogeneous provinces of meaning, systems of classification, etc.; which goals are binding generally or only under special circumstances, and which are approved, disapproved, or tolerated; which are desirable and praiseworthy, etc.; which typical means lead to such goals; and finally, which typical moments of typical experiences are conjoined with typical attitudes. In short, the meaning-structures of the everyday life-world, of the "world of nature" as well as of "society," are indicated and expressed in language along with the line of demarcation between these two provinces which can be shifted from one relative-natural world view to another. The same applies to the other provinces of reality having a finite meaning-structure, if not to all to the same extent.

The child does not meet this linguistically indicated and stabilized reality in one thrust: the child has experiences before the acquisition of a language which surely are not exhausted in their concrete actuality, and in which typifications and schemata of explication are often already included. In a certain sense, therefore, he indeed has prelinguistic experiences. As has been stated, these are interwoven very closely with the earliest we-relations. Even before the acquisition of language, even before the actual meeting with the grammatically indicated and consolidated reality, language appears to the child as an element of the we-relation which is already on hand. The fellow-men, to whom the child stands first in quasi and then in "genuine" we-relations, speak. From the start, language for the child, as the speech of his fellow-men, is interwoven with their facial expression, gestures, and their typical conduct. This means that within the we-relation, language is bound up from the first with typical contexts of experiences and acts (no matter how rudimentary this involvement may be at the prelinguistic level). In the immediacy of the we-relation, the meaning of linguistic signs refers first to experiences in the current situation, to the natural and social environs. On the one hand, the development of these meanings presupposes the typifications and schemata of experience, which are already at least partly established prelinguistically. But on the other hand, it presupposes the processes of intersubjective mirroring in the we-relation, in which language itself is constituted through intersubjective mirroring, the "socializing" of subjective indications and different forms of detachment from immediate experience. While we should not engage here in a detailed analysis of the acquisition of language, it might be pointed out that the same processes which are "phylogenetically" operative in the social constitution of language are also presupposed in a modified form in verbal "ontogenesis," in the subjective acquisition of language. Since language is interwoven in the very beginning of the earliest we-relations and in the processes of intersubjective mirroring to which it gives rise, language for the child appears as an element of direct experience of the fellowmen, as an element of immediately given social reality. The consolidation and structuring of "prelinguistic reality" (i.e., of reality-oriented typifications and prelinguistic schemata of experience) takes place in specific and concrete we-relations, in agreement with the semantic and syntactic structural ensemble of language, or of the relative-natural world view. The permeation of subjective structures of relevance by language and the consequent indirect influence of even the self-generating type-formation and explication also take place in specific, concrete we-relations. And the same applies to the transference of the linguistically objectivated "social stock of knowledge." We will later be concerned in some detail with an important consequence of this state of affairs.

For the present, we will maintain that the relation of language to experiences which transcend the immediate natural and social environs presupposes an original relation to immediate experiences that have been molded by the concrete we-relation. Further, it presupposes that this relation is built up upon them. The concrete reality of the we-relations is the social basis for the individual learning a language as a system of meanings referring to "any reality whatever." After language is acquired as a coherent semantic-syntactic structure, it becomes to a great extent independent of the concrete we-relation and of the immediacy of experience (the extent to which this is the case can vary from one language to another). Language can then provide knowledge about realities which not only transcend the current experience of the individual, but also are practically, if not also in principle, inaccessible to him. Language thus provides knowledge that has its origin in the experiences and explications of ancestors or contemporaries. And finally, language can provide knowledge that refers to provinces of meaning which are in principle inaccessible in immediate experience.

We can thus say that the reality to which the child gradually awakens and grows is "filtered" and consolidated by means of language, in accord with the meaning-structures of the relative-natural world view. This awakening growth depends on a "factual" social reality of the concrete we-relation which is first prelinguistic but which then becomes increasingly permeated by language. The typical meaning-structures of the normal adult's experience are essentially determined by language (and consequently by the relative-natural world view of a society). Insofar as language becomes habitual to the individual, he can make routine distinctions between what is and is not worth noticing, between the obvious and the problematic, between what is worth communicating and what must be communicated. At the same time, he no longer needs, for the most part, to engage in independent explications of problems and self-generating type-formations. As a result, the subjective experiences of different members of a society are stabilized, so to speak, around the "median values" for typical experiences in a relative-natural world view. Through the stabilization of experiences that occurs around these "typical median values" and arises through objectivation in language, subjective experiences become comparable to each other in the subjective flux of experience and in the biography of the individual. These experiences can then form the basis for explicit plans of acts and explicit interpretations of the past. From this point on, the results of explication are communicable and can become parts of a cumulative social stock of knowledge.

We must now anticipate a detailed analysis of the social distribution of knowledge with respect to a point which has already been important in the previous discussion. It is obvious that the given social structure and its factual, "causal" givenness condition the meaning-structures that prevail in a relative-natural world view as well as the typical contexts of experience and act that are molded by them. They differ from one relative-natural world view to the other, and they can change historically. They are also differentiated within a given society. The *typical* contexts of experience and act would be the same for all members of a society only where there were no divisions of labor, no differentiation of roles, and thus only in a society having no social structure in the proper sense. Only in such a "society" would the social stock of knowledge be distributed in a completely homogeneous way. As a thought experiment, one can perhaps imagine such a "society." In contrast, all historical societies were characterized by a differentiation of roles and a heterogeneity in the distribution of knowledge, however minimal these were. The typical structures of experience are not the same for all members of society, but in their turn show a social distribution, since they are conditioned by various roles which are socially objectivated and in part also institutionalized (as well as being conditioned by the determinations of the situation dependent on them). Thus, for example, what is taken for granted in a society of hunters can be problematic for farmers; what for women is worthy of communication can usually remain unnoticed by men, etc. Not only are the typical contexts of experience and act distributed socially, but so also is the knowledge relevant in them, as are their corresponding linguistic structures (above all vocabulary, semantic arrangement, and also syntax and morphology, such as the general style of language).

As a result, the meaning-structures of the relative-natural world view and their corresponding linguistic structures are not accessible to all children in the same way. The social distribution of knowledge and language determines the concrete "contents" of the earliest we-relations in which the child grows up. It is not *the* language, but a definite version of language (e.g., dialect, the language of a caste, etc.), which the child finds to be his "mother tongue," the taken-for-granted and habitual possession of the Others relevant for him. We need not go into the multiplicity of empirical variations which can function concretely as a "filter" for the appropriation of language and of the relative-natural world view (e.g., the historically pregiven amount of variation between the socially distributed versions of language, agreements, or departures in the versions of language which are expressed by the Others relevant for the child, not to mention the special problem of bilingualism, etc.). In any case, the meaning-structures of the life-world, as they are expressed in a relative-natural world view, are obtained through a definite version of a definite historical language, the version being "filtered" through we-relations. Language and the relative-natural world view as elements of the biographical situation which are socially already on hand can be considered only in terms of this historical specificity.

2. THE SOCIAL DEPENDENCY OF THE SUBJECTIVE RELEVANCE STRUCTURES

a. *The dependence of subjective relevances on what is given in the social situation*

The subjective relevance structures which operate in the flow of experience and in the acts of a normal adult in the everyday life-world are in many ways socially conditioned. The different forms of such social dependency can be arranged into two main classes: the actually present dependence of the subjective relevance structures upon the prevailing data of the social situation, and the social character of the subjective relevance structures in the biography of the individual. We will treat the second main form, the "socialization" of the relevance structures, in the next section. Here we begin with an examination of the first main form.

The normal adult's course of experience in the everyday life-world is determined through a succession of social situations. This succession is unbroken, since the everyday life-world is an essentially social reality. "Nonsocial" situations do not appear in it, but rather can be only construed as theoretical borderline cases. The social character of everyday situations is not the same throughout. The differences in the sociality of a situation are determined by two principal, mutually interwoven dimensions: by the *formal* arrangement of subjective experiences of the social world into provinces of mediacy and immediacy, and through the prescribed levels of anonymity in the relative-natural world view which accompany the *meaning* of subjective experiences in the social world.[5]

In some situations, the individual has immediate relations with his fellow-men, while in others the meaning of his conduct is simply based on the most anonymous social data. But immediate social relations can also be variously graduated according to their meaning. When fellow-men are grasped with the greatest concreteness and fullness of symptoms, the relation can be characterized by advertence to the subjective meaning of the experiences of the Other, as for instance is typically the case in making love. In we-relations, on the other hand, attention can be directed

5. See Chap. 2, B, 5.

to the Objective meaning of the acts or communications of the Other, as for example in a purposively oriented conversation. The meaning which accompanies the inclusion of the partner in the immediate social relation can be individualized ("my old friend X") or highly anonymous ("cigarette salesman"). Further situations in which Others are immediately given can be unilateral and not reciprocal (as is the case in the social relations just mentioned). In simple "imaginings," attention can also be directed to the subjective meaning of the experiences of Others, for instance to the observation of the facial expressions of a person who believes himself to be unobserved. Or, attention can be directed to the Objective meaning of his conduct, as for example to the observation of enemy troops marching through an advanced outpost.

But the various social situations in which Others are not immediately apprehended are also differentiated according to both their "mediacy" and the levels of anonymity accompanying their apprehension. Thus, for example, the fullness of symptoms in which the Other is given diminishes, according to whether one is concerned with the exchange of letters, with news which is obtained through a third person, etc. In order to illustrate the variations of anonymity, we need only think of the difference between the exchange of letters between two married people and a business letter, or a last will and testament which refers to later generations, stock transactions, judicial decrees, etc.

Moreover, it should be remembered that social situations either arise solely out of simple attitudes or contain various forms of social actions. Social attitudes can be related, on the one hand, to a concrete individual ("my absent father"), or also to different degrees of anonymous social groups, roles, institutions, social objectivations, etc. (aversion to lawyers, fear of the police, respect for the Napoleonic Code, preference for Italian, etc.). Social action, moreover, exhibits a similarly complex structure. It can be mediate or immediate, unilateral or reciprocal, recurring once or regularly, referring to a concrete individual or to anonymous representatives of social givens.

Therefore, social situations are, as was stated at the beginning, determined by the formal arrangement of subjective experiences in the social world and by the prescribed, typical meaning-structures of social conduct and action in the relative-natural world view. The later circumstance is derived from the "socialization" of the interpretational and motivational relevances and what is connected with them: the experiential schemata and the models of explication, typifications and classifications, as well as the because- and in-order-to contexts. In contrast the formal arrangement of subjective experiences in the social world determines the limits and the forms of the actual dependence of subjective relevances on what is given in the prevailing social situation.

When the individual enters into a situation, he brings with him a biographically modeled, and to a large extent socially derived, stock of knowledge, and consequently a greatly "socialized" system of interpretational and motivational relevances. On the other hand, in the situation he meets actually present social givens which are, in a certain sense, "forced" on him. There are two aspects to differentiate here: intersubjective thematic relevances, so to speak "socialized" in the current situation, and social givens in the narrow sense, as for example fellow-men, institutions, etc. Let us examine these aspects more closely.

Only in the we-relation do the partners share the same spatial and temporal sector of the life-world. Consequently, only in the we-relations are the thematic relevances which are "imposed" on one also "imposed" on the other. The "same" events, objects, etc., force themselves on the attention of one person as on the other. The perspectives of apprehension in which the thematic relevances are presented are not, though, strictly speaking, identical. As a result, the biographically modeled interpretational and motivational relevances which both partners "bring into" the we-relation cannot be identical, although they are sufficiently congruent with regard to the similar "socialization" of the partners for the determination and management of the situation. In principle, the "same" events, objects, etc., can consistently have a different meaning for each of the partners. To be able to speak of the "same" thematic relevances, one must fall back on the identity of the limiting conditions for the situation of man in the life-world: his live corporeality, temporality, etc. The more the interpretational and motivational relevances of the partners vary in the we-relation, the more the meaning of the specific situation, of events and objects, differs from the two, and therefore the more important the common imposed character of the situation's thematic relevances becomes. This is so for the following reason: the animate organism of the other partner is also given to each participant in the we-relation, along with the commonly pre-given events, objects, etc. That the subjective thematic relevances are also thematically relevant to the other can be read in the partner's organism, which is a field of expression for the greatest fullness of symptoms. The subjective thematic relevances of both partners are interwoven in the processes of intersubjective mirroring and themselves become "intersubjective." No matter how one or another person may explain the meaning of an event, an object, etc., the basic meaning "already given to us both," "relevant for us both," has been constituted in the contemporary relation to the theme and to the Other.

But this also results in the role which intersubjective thematic relevances play in the "socialization" of the interpretational and motivational relevances. Even if we assume that the latter context, in which a particular theme is first given to partners in a we-relation, is different, not only is the attentional advertence (to the "same" theme) coapprehended in the processes of intersubjective mirroring, but so also is the kind of grasping and, at least in rudimentary form, the kind of interpretation on the part of the partner. This is the presupposition for each "originary" socialization of the interpretational and motivational relevances, insofar as this presupposition goes beyond the identity (conditioned through the limitations of the human situation in the lifeworld) of subjective relevance structures. Although the individual for the most part appropriates socially approved typifications, motives, etc., via language, from a relative-natural world view, the learning of a language (as the "originary" constitution of a language) already presupposes a community of relevance structures that goes beyond this basic identity of the lifeworldly situation. It is exactly this community which is constituted in the (under prelinguistic circumstances) processes of intersubjective mirroring that refer to a theme which is commonly already on hand. Besides, naturally intersubjective thematic relevances can be used again and again in the verification of the congruence of the schemata of experience and explication "brought into" a we-relation by the partners. This plays an important role, especially in situations where (for one reason or another) language "breaks down."

Since the intersubjectivity of thematic relevances is dependent on the formal arrangement of subjective experiences in the social world, it also has significant relevance for the "socialization" of the interpretational and motivational relevances. Beyond this, it also determines the mode of givenness of the Other in social situations and even conditions the actual dependency of subjective relevances on social givens in the narrow sense. The meaning that accompanies the experience of the latter is indeed *relatively* independent of the mediacy or immediacy of experience. A friend remains a friend whether he is absent at the moment or not, even if on the other hand a friend whom one has not seen in twenty years is no longer "the same" and the relation to him is, as a result, necessarily modified, even in its meaning. In any case, the mode of givenness of the Other is always subjectively relevant in the current situation. The immediately given Other is "problematic" in a pressing fashion as a contemporary or even as an ancestor or successor. He immediately motivates the conduct in the current situation, no matter how "short-term" the conduct and unimportant the meaning of this conduct in the total biography of this individual may be. If one is bumped by someone in a crowd on the street, this is usually unimportant, but it urgently calls for moving aside, an apology, or the like. The Other is, we could say, a social given in the narrow sense, which is thematically "imposed." "In the long run," the conduct of the individual is naturally much more decisively and enduringly determined by the *meaning* of the experience than by the Other's mode of givenness (for example, orienting a career of many years to the "honor of the family").

The subjective relevances in the current situation of the normal adult are thus dependent on social givens. But the interpretations and motives that have been "socialized" in the course of the biography play a decisive role in determining and mastering the situation. The "socialized" interpretational and motivational relevances again refer in turn to "originary" situations of acquisition based on intersubjective thematic relevances and formed by immediate social givens.

b. The "socialization" of the motivational and interpretational relevances

We have described in what way the subjective relevances are dependent on the social givens of the current situation. It was then pointed out that the individual in the situation confronts socially conditioned, thematic data, but enters the situation with a "socialized" store of interpretational and motivational relevances, this stock being, in general, already extensive. What this means for the individual must be more fully developed.

The individual never enters the situation "completely" and

never grasps its thematic data in their absolute, actually present uniqueness. He brings to the situation definite attitudes, plans, designs of acts, as well as a stock of preformed typifications and explications; in short, he enters the situation with a system of interpretational and motivational relevances. Not only how he grasps the thematic data, but also to a certain extent what he grasps in general of the thematic givens within the situation, depend on this system.[6] The subjective system of relevances "brought with" him conditions what is experienced in the current situation as obvious and routine or as problematic and needing explication and mastering.

The attitudes, plans, typifications, models of explication, etc., in short, the subjective system of interpretational and motivational relevances that is effective in the current situation, naturally have a "prior history." As has been said previously, it has been acquired in a succession of prevailing, actual situations. As we said then, these situations have been either social or at the least socially conditioned. This means that this subjective system of relevances has a "social" prehistory.

In the strict sense of the word, there is not a "self-sufficient" system of interpretational and motivational relevances, in any case not in the everyday life-world. This does not mean that all these relevances are "social" in the same way. It is true, they all have a "social" prehistory. But there are also those among them that stand out as being "socialized" in the pregnant sense of the word. Three circumstances that we want to examine more closely in the following paragraphs play a decisive role here: the varying "social" character of the *situation* of acquisition; the "social" character of the *processes* of explication or, more exactly, of explication; and the varying *origin* of the acquired element of knowledge, viz., of relevances.

The social character of the situation in which these relevances are developed extends from situations in which the Others are immediately given, to situations in which merely the results of the Others' acts are given, to situations in which the meaning of subjective experiences (in memories, attitudes, explications) is only mediately directed to Others or to the results of their acts. However, not only the situation as such, but also the processes in which these relevances are constituted within this situation can be distinct with regard to their social character. In various

6. See Chap. 3, B, esp. § 5.

situations—also in those in which Others are immediately given —step-by-step subjective explications and the polythetical sedimentations of attitudes can be effected without immediate reference to the explications and motivations of Others. In other words, interpretations and motivations can be developed in "independent" polythetical phases. But on the other hand, they can be developed in the subjective completion (after the fact) of the explications and motivations of Others. And finally, they can get to the state where only the monothetic meaning of the attitudes and motives of Others is taken over.

Although there are numerous transitions and intermediate stages, we can determine the three most important main forms of the "sociality" of the motivational and interpretational relevances. First, there are explications and motives which have indeed been developed in socially conditioned situations, but in "independent" polythetical processes and without immediate reference to the explications and motives of Others. Second, there are explications and motives which have been constituted in social situations (in the narrow sense) in the polythetical (after-the-fact) completions of those of Others. Third, there are explications and motives which consist in the acceptance of the monothetical meaning of the attitudes and results of explications of Others. We can therefore speak of "independent," "empathetic," and "socialized" interpretations and motives. Only the latter interest us here, since the problems that are connected with the first have been more closely examined, partly in the formal analysis of relevance structures,[7] and partly in the analysis of the immediate experiences of the Other.[8]

The "socialized" interpretational and motivational relevances are derived from the typical, linguistically objectivated interpretations and motives predominant in the relative-natural world view. In general terms, these involve attitudes, patterns of acts, typifications, models for explication, etc., which were originally constituted in the subjective experiences of Others. While they contain a basic reference to a subjective polythetical constitution, their monothetic sense is "Objectively" determined: in systems of signs, above all in language (and here especially in the semantic arrangement of language) and in patterns of acts., viz., in the institutionalized "explanations" and legitimations of pat-

7. See Chap. 3, B.
8. See Chap. 2, B, 5, b.

terns of acts. The Others, whose results of experience and explication are "objectivated," can as easily be fellow-men as mere
contemporaries or ancestors. We need not here consider whether
the individual who accepts the results of the experience and explication of Others apprehends these Others as concrete fellow-
men (e.g., one's own father, whose greed one appropriates for
himself, the father having acquired it in the poverty of his
youth), or only apprehends them on different levels of anonymity
(e.g., "the nobleman" whose "duties" are compelling, or the
"vernacular" whose "wisdom" one takes for his own, not to mention the typifications set up in language, e.g., the concepts of
judicial language). It is crucial that the interpretations and motives which concern us here are not the result of "independent"
experiences and explications, nor are they "empathic" ex post
facto completions of the experiences of fellow-men in we-relations. Rather, they are in one way or another socially "objectivated" and thus function for the individual as a part of the social
a priori.

The "socialized" relevances in question are "learned." As was
made clear in a previous section,[9] the earliest we-relations are of
fundamental significance in the learning processes. The child
learns specific elements of knowledge and the relevance structures basic to these chiefly in events of intersubjective mirroring.
"Behind" the Others who meet the child in the earliest we-relations, there is always a specific social structure. The meaning-
structures of the relative-natural world view, language, the
elements of the social stock of knowledge, and likewise the relevance structures involved therein are accessible to the child at
first only through a "filter" of Others. The fundamental relevances
which the child obtains in the earliest we-relations are thus not
only socially "objectivated," but also to a certain extent "filtered"
through the social structure.

An additional consideration must be brought in here. In the
appropriation of the fundamental interpretational and motivational relevances, the "filter effect" is compelling. That is, we
could also say that it is biographically imposed upon the child.
But even in subsequent learning processes and in later social
relations the "filter effect" remains effective. It is, though, in
principle possible that the effect be diminished to a certain degree, that it no longer be imposed in the same compelling fashion.

9. See Chap. 4, A, 1.

After learning a language, and after consolidating a personal structure, the individual can appropriate definite elements on hand in the social stock of knowledge (e.g., models of explication). He can do this in subjectively motivated "acts of choice" and "learning processes" which are *relatively* independent of specific fellow-men and what is immediately socially given. It is obvious that this independence from the social "filter effect" can only be relative, and that the degree of independence is for its part socially-historically conditioned. We cannot take up this problem here, but we do want at least to lay out some of its important dimensions. The relative degree of independence from the social "filter effect" is dependent, for example, on whether the society into which the child is born knows how to write or not. But even when one is dealing with an advanced culture, the opportunities of learning to write are unevenly distributed. Further, the degree of independence is connected with the existence in the society under consideration of specialized institutions for the transmission of knowledge. And if these exist, it depends upon how autonomous these institutions are in relation to other provinces of institutions. The predominant processes of socialization in different societies typically lead to different levels of "individualization," which again is related to the typical possibilities of "distancing" oneself from one's roles in a given social structure. All these factors are in a causal context with two historically changeable dimensions of social structure: the division of power (i.e., the relations of authority) and the division of labor.

In summary, the subjective relevance system generally has a "social" prehistory which contains "independent" as well as "empathic" and "socialized" interpretational and motivational relevances. The latter are derivations of the relevance structures predominant in the relative-natural world view, structures which are "filtered" through a specific historical social structure.

Since the "independent" and "empathic" relevances genetically play the larger role, and are the presupposition for the appropriation of "socialized" relevances, they occupy a broader area of the everyday relevance system of the normal adult. The routines for mastering life (from skills to knowledge of customs which are typically necessary for the members of a certain society) are socially objectivated in typical forms. The Others who confront the child in his earliest we-relations consider them to be "obvious" to any educated person, and they are thus imparted to the child. We need not here consider whether the routines must be acquired step by step by the individual, perhaps through an "empathic" assimilation of social models (as for instance a typical style of walking), or through more or less conscious learning processes (as for example recipes, homespun wisdom from proverbs, etc.). In any case, all routines contain typical relevance structures. These are taken over whether or not the relevances themselves come into conscious awareness. Through the appropriation of "socialized" routines, what is socially presented as obvious or taken for granted is delimited from what, for the individual, is socially presented as problematic. But typical models for explicating that which is problematic are also taken over. Thus, the typical solutions to problems and the typical conditions under which a problem can be regarded as solved are socially derived, along with the typical determinations of that which is problematic.

The subjective relevance system of the normal adult is thus extensively "socialized." But it must not be forgotten that this is biographically stamped on his entire being, completely apart from the "independent" relevances. It is, indeed, extensively "socialized" and shows extensive, typical similarities with the subjective relevance systems of fellow-men and contemporaries. In social relations, such similarities are presupposed, so to speak, until further notice, and provide the basis for intersubjective understanding, for adequate explications of the conduct between fellow-men, etc. But since the subjective relevance systems are biographically modeled, they naturally cannot be "identical." They are the "unique" possession of the individual, and whenever the individual turns to his own relevances they appear to him in this "uniqueness." Seen from the outside, the result of the socialization of subjective relevance structures is the typical similarity in the conduct of contemporaries who are understood as typical. Seen from the inside, such similarities are accidental. The socialized man is "unique."

[B] THE ORIGIN OF THE SOCIAL STOCK OF KNOWLEDGE

1. THE SUBJECTIVE ORIGIN OF SOCIAL KNOWLEDGE

BEFORE WE BEGIN TO DESCRIBE the structure of the social stock of knowledge, we must ask ourselves how it ever happens that these stocks of knowledge are developed. It need hardly be stressed that we do not want to be concerned here with the formulation of historical-causal hypotheses or schemata of meaning. That task comes within the province of the empirical sociology of knowledge. Rather, we are interested in the basic question of what the general presuppositions are for the constitution of a social stock of knowledge. We thereby reverse the order of questioning by which we investigated the social dependency of subjective knowledge. In that inquiry we simply joined the prior givenness of a social stock of knowledge to the subjective biography, without looking at the problems hidden behind such an acceptance. It will be our task now to bring just these problems to light. Here the results of the prior inquiry will be especially useful.

We have found that the subjective stock of knowledge consists only in part of "independent" results of experience and explication. It is predominantly derived from elements of the social stock of knowledge. Furthermore, the "independently" acquired elements of knowledge are also embedded in the whole context of an extensively "socialized" subjective stock of knowledge, since the most important relevances of interpretation and motivation are "socialized" (completely apart from the fact that the development of the subjective stock of knowledge is from the beginning conditioned by a "factual" social structure). Consequently, one cannot actually speak of absolutely "independent" elements in the stock of knowledge of the normal wide-awake adult.

Despite this empirical priority of the social stock of knowledge in relation to any particular subjective one, the subjective acquisition of knowledge is still the origin of all social knowledge. There is in principle no difficulty in imagining a subjective stock of knowledge which would simply consist of "independent" sedimentations of experience and explication. In the formal analysis of the subjective acquisition of knowledge, the prior givenness of a social stock of knowledge and the "socialization" of subjective elements of knowledge can be bracketed without thereby distorting the basic forms of the subjective acquisition of knowledge.[10] Such a hypothetical stock of knowledge acquired altogether "independently" would surely be indescribably inadequate in comparison with the knowledge of a normal adult (even

10. See Chap. 3, A, 2.

if it is the knowledge of the "dumbest" member of the "most primitive" society). Yet a subjective stock of knowledge independent of the social one is conceivable without contradiction. In contrast, to imagine the latter as developed independently of the subjective acquisition of knowledge is sheer nonsense. At most, one can speak with an analogically transferred meaning (easily leading to error) of social experiences, that is, of experiences by a society. One can seek the origin of the social stock of knowledge, more exactly, of the elements that form it, only in subjective experiences and explications. But this means that in the last analysis the social stock of knowledge points back to "independent" experiences and explications. This is the case regardless of to what extent the situations in which the experiences and explications occur are conditioned, if not by "society" in the full scope of the concept, then at least by means of whatever is "factually" given in a social way.

Once we have established the fundamental priority of the subjective stock of knowledge (and finally of the knowledge based on "independent" experiences), in contrast to the social stock of knowledge, we must stress that in its actual development things are otherwise. The subjective elements of knowledge which enter into the social one are only to a small degree "independently" acquired—and this only in the restricted sense of the "independence" previously indicated. Whenever we take on such a minimal social stock of knowledge (and that by definition happens in every human society), most of the subjective elements of knowledge that enter into its further development are derived from the prevailing, already given state of this stock of knowledge. It hardly needs to be stressed that such socially derived elements of knowledge can be modified in more or less "independent" processes of explication. They can, for example, be "improved" before they are channeled back into the social stock of knowledge.

Once the previous analyses exhibited the nearly complete social dependency of the subjective stock of knowledge, it was necessary to bring out the fundamental priority of "independent" experiences and explications in the constitution of the social stock of knowledge. This, however, should not be an occasion for false conclusions. Despite the fundamental priority of the subjective acquisition of knowledge, the social stock of knowledge may in no way be understood (even if only formally) as the "sum" of subjective stocks of knowledge. One need only ask "which stocks of knowledge?" in order to see that such a view must lead to insoluble difficulties. The social stock of knowledge contains not only "more" than the subjective, but also "more" than the "sum" of them. This will become clear in the following examinations, especially in the analysis of the structure of the social stock of knowledge and the social division of knowledge.[11]

Here it must be added that the social stock of knowledge also contains "less" than any particular subjective stock of knowledge. Thus, for example, the subjective stock of knowledge can contain elements which have been sedimented out of "novel" experiences and therefore could "still" not be incorporated in the social stock of knowledge. Moreover, the former contains elements which do not fulfill the presuppositions for the acceptance of subjective knowledge in the latter. It also contains elements which refer back to the biographical "uniqueness" of subjective experiences, and elements which evade an objectivation in language.

Through these considerations we confront a question that will occupy us in the next section: What are the presuppositions for the acceptance of subjective knowledge into the social stock of knowledge? The answer to this question will allow us to describe the basic forms of those processes by which subjective elements of knowledge are transferred to the latter.

2. PRESUPPOSITIONS OF THE SOCIALIZATION OF SUBJECTIVE KNOWLEDGE

a. "Objectivations" of the subjective acquisition of knowledge

The general and fundamental presupposition for the acceptance of subjective elements of knowledge into the social stock of knowledge is their "objectivation." This expression is meant to characterize, in general, the embodiment of subjective processes in the objects and events of the everyday life-world. Accordingly, all acts that gear into the latter, as well as their "results," would be understood as "objectivations" insofar as they can be traced back to these acts. Also to be characterized in this manner are forms of expression in the broadest sense: gestures, facial expressions, etc. At this juncture we are interested only in those "objectivations" that are indeed grasped and interpreted by

11. See Chap. 4, C.

Others as indications of subjective processes. Among these we are chiefly interested in those which can be interpreted by Others as "objectivations" of subjective explications, or of subjective results of explications of generally subjective knowledge. When, for example, A observes how B sneezes, the sneezing is indeed an expression of subjective processes, if we follow this concept far enough, but it hardly can be construed as an "objectivation" of subjective knowledge. A univocal and sharp line of distinction cannot be drawn, since all experiences can be sedimented as subjective knowledge. In other words, no experience is in essence definable as "unproblematic."

As will be shown in the following, we can differentiate various levels of "objectivation" according to whether they are concerned either with continuous "objectivations" pertaining to the subjective acquisition of knowledge, or with those already on hand as indications of subjective knowledge, or with "translations" of subjective knowledge into the sign system. We want to begin with a description at the simplest level.

Let us assume that A is wandering in a region unknown to him and must cross a river. If he were completely left to his own devices, he would have to undertake a series of steps in order to find out at which places the river is too deep to be waded, where it has the appearance of being shallow, etc., until he could decide to try his luck at one place or another. Then he would have to turn around in the middle of the river, because the current in the vicinity of the other bank has dug too deep a channel. After all these deliberations and attempts, he would finally make it to the other shore and know where the river could be forded. If he should return to the same river, he would be aided by this "independently" acquired knowledge. But let us now assume that A notices on his arrival at the river that B forded the river at a certain place. He notes the place where B began, observes B as he goes across and comes safely to the other bank. Thereby A saves himself a series of "independent" steps; he can replace them through observation of the appropriate steps undertaken by B.

We have intentionally begun with this simple example, for here it is relatively unimportant in which subjective meaning-context the crossing of the river exists for B, and it is already clear that it makes no difference whether we think of B as a man or a horse. Further, the example is so chosen that it cannot create a problem of "false" interpretation. On the other hand, it is unimportant whether we assume that B already knew where to find a ford, thereby, strictly speaking, acquiring no "new" knowledge, or whether he himself had to initiate the processes that characterize the acquisition of new knowledge.

But now let us take an example that illustrates the same level of "objectivation," but where matters are a bit more complicated. If A would like to find out whether the water in a pot is hot or cold, he can reach a decision between the two possibilities by means of a series of "independent" steps. When he sees, however, how B sticks his finger into the water and immediately takes it out again with a painful expression on his face, he can interpret the connection between the act of B and his facial expression as an indication that B found the water hot. He can therefore accept his observation of B's acquisition of knowledge as a substitute, or to be more exact, as a substitute for various "independent" steps in his own acquisition.

By means of the common features in the two examples, we can obtain a general characterization of this "objectivation." On this level, it is not a subjective element of knowledge as such, but rather the event of the subjective acquisition of knowledge, which is "objectivated" in the continuous events of the everyday life-world. The events are observed by an Other, and then interpreted in such a way that they are taken as "independent" steps in his own processes of acquisition. We can therefore say, only in a quite restricted sense here, that A has taken over an element of knowledge from B. If we may be allowed in this connection to repeat a concept we used in the analysis of relevance structures: A "takes over" from B certain steps in the inspection of a problem, but he must himself interpret the "saved" steps by means of more or less explicit analogical conclusions. Here we will maintain that we are at this level of "objectivation" already concerned with a "social derivation" of knowledge, even if limited.

From the foregoing it clearly follows that transference of knowledge on this level of "objectivation" is indissolubly bound to the concrete situation. The "acceptance" of knowledge by A presupposes a similarly synchronized interpretation of the observations of the "continuous objectivations" (of B's flow of experience). Further, depending upon the context of the problem, a greater or lesser congruence of the subjective relevances of A and B is presupposed. To put it concretely, in many problematic situations a horse can furnish "independent" steps in the explication of a problem, while in others this can only be done by a man similarly built, talented, etc.

On this level of objectivation, it makes no real difference whether B knows that his behavior is observed and interpreted by A. Naturally, if B is motivated to acquire the knowledge that A has in mind concerning him, and to impart it to A, he can consciously direct the "objectivations" of his subjective processes. For example, he can try to facilitate for A the interpretation of "objectivations" by intentionally exaggerating them. But on the other hand, he can also try to hinder A's attempt to acquire knowledge of his behavior by limiting or concealing the "objectivations" of his subjective processes and thus obfuscating their meaning. He can even attempt to lead the other astray by placing "false" objectivations before A in anticipation of typical interpretations. B can, for example, if he is malevolent, control his facial expression, even if he has scalded himself, in the hope that A will also scald himself. Therefore, on this level of "objectivation," if A and B are in a we-relation, the motivated exchange not only of "correct" but also "false" knowledge is in principle possible. This is the case no matter how much the exchange of "false" knowledge may be so limited that A and B have the same immediate access to the other components of the situation.

b. "Objectivations" of subjective knowledge in indications

On the first level of "objectivation," A interprets a continuous series of events as alluding to the "simultaneously" occurring acquisition of knowledge by B. In the typical case, A and B therefore come to typically similar knowledge in similarly synchronized processes of interpretation, so that A can use B's conduct and actions as substitutes for "independent" steps of explication (in the context of interpretation with the other immediately grasped components of the situation). On the second level, there are elements of knowledge already fully constituted and embodied in the events or objects of the everyday life-world. These "objectivations" are interpreted by Others as an indication of definite knowledge.[12] It is in any case not possible to draw a sharp line

12. [See the discussion of indications in *Collected Papers*, Vol. I: *The Problem of Social Reality*, ed. Maurice Natanson (The Hague: Nijhoff, 1962), pp. 310–11; also *The Phenomenology of the Social World*, trans. George Walsh and Frederick Lehnert (London: Heinemann Educational Books, 1972), p. 119.]

between the two levels of "objectivations," since transitions are possible without further ado. Let us assume that A does not see how B puts his finger in the pot filled with water, but that he only notices B standing next to the pot and blowing on his finger with a pained expression on his face. He can still bring the indications into an interpretative context along with the other components of the situation, and decide that the pot most probably contains hot water, although he has not participated in the individual phases of B's cognitive acquisition. In general, an adequate interpretation becomes more difficult when fewer components of the original situation are available to A. The interpretation will be more difficult the greater the disparity between the knowledge B originally acquired and the indication to be used for interpretation. The second level of "objectivation" is also relatively dependent on the situation, although in comparison with the first level there is a certain independence from the situation of acquisition.

Let us return to the first example and vary it a bit. Suppose we again assume that A comes to a river with which he is unacquainted and looks for a place to cross. After some consideration, he begins to cross the river at a certain place. Then he notices that B is waving to him energetically from the other bank, pointing to another place. A can explain B's motions as an indication that B knows something that is possibly relevant for A, and that B is trying to inform him of it. In connection with the previous situation and its components, he comes to the conclusion that it most probably concerns some knowledge of the problem of crossing the river. It is therefore really immaterial whether B has only just acquired this knowledge, whether he has possessed it awhile, or even whether he acquired it "independently" and simply has only taken it over. It is not the acquisition of knowledge but its results that are "objectivated" in indications. Thus the transfer of knowledge, its "objectivation" in indications, is already detached from the original situation of its acquisition. But the interpretation of indications by an Other, the acceptance of "objectivated" knowledge (as was previously indicated), is still more or less strongly connected to the immediate apprehension of the components of the original situation relevant to the constitution of the epistemic elements.

The acquisition of knowledge on this level of "objectivation" is not necessarily dependent upon the fact that the one whose knowledge is "objectivated" in indications consciously posits these indications. From B's gestures, facial expressions, and other such components of the situation relevant to the interpretation, A can infer some particular knowledge B has, even if B believes himself to be unobserved. In principle, it thus suffices if A can interpret certain events or circumstances as indications of certain definite knowledge on the part of B, whether or not B is motivated to posit these indications.

In any case, a reciprocal motivation for both positing and interpreting indications already accompanies those instances which are more important for the social acquisition of knowledge on this level of "objectivation." It was for this reason that this level was chosen as an illustrative example, in which indications were posited by B in "objectivating" acts (waving). But what was established concerning the first level applies with special force here: when B knows that A is interpreting his behavior as an indication of some knowledge, he can overemphasize, hide, or feign such indications. When, for instance in a poker game, B picks up the cards dealt him and his eyes light up, A can take this as an indication that B has gotten a good hand. But if B anticipates this, he can put on a "poker face" or let his eyes light up if he has gotten a poor hand. There can be further deceptive maneuvers on top of this: a double, triple, etc., bluff. The more the cognitive element is detached from the situation of its original acquisition by B, the more inaccessible the components of this situation are for A, then in general the simpler it is for B to hide this knowledge or to convey "false" knowledge to A.

We do not want to anticipate too far in advance the course of the analysis, above all the investigation of the processes of socializations. But here we must insert a reflection concerning the role of "objectivations" in the structure of the social stock of knowledge on both levels previously discussed. We have established that "objectivations" on these levels are still extensively bound to the situation (or more exactly to the situation of acquiring knowledge), even though a certain detachment of the transmission of knowledge from the situation of its acquisition can enter here. Consequently, idealized ("abstract") and anonymous knowledge cannot be socialized by means of such "objectivations." On the contrary, such "objectivations" are of the greatest importance for the socialization of other elements which belong to the stock of knowledge. If we do not want to limit unduly the concept of the social stock of knowledge to explicit knowledge or "higher forms of knowledge," we can also speak of socialized skills, or in any case of social components of skills. But in a certain sense, skills can be taken over by Others without necessarily presupposing an explicit, for example, linguistic, acquisition of knowledge. What has been said in general about "objectivations" on the first two levels applies here. Thus, for instance, A can observe how B swims. If he then tries to imitate B, he has already saved himself various "steps" in the "independent" acquisition of knowledge. A no longer needs to experiment with various alternative combinations of movement. Or, if A notices how B makes an ax, he can himself produce an ax, by imitating the "best method" of ax-making that he has just observed.

Whenever skills (and, more generally, "objectivations" on the presymbolic levels) are taken over by Others, the basic presupposition for socialization is already present. We will still have to investigate what this means. But we can already ascertain that the explicit transmission of knowledge (e.g., "objectivations" on the level of sign systems) is not necessarily presupposed. "Objectivations" on these presymbolic levels can be incorporated as such in the "possessions" of a group or a society. As "traditions" of certain skills, and more generally as recipes for conduct, they constitute a component of the social a priori. Everyone who is born into a society takes such traditions over with a high degree of taken-for-grantedness, just because he does not need to learn them explicitly. Even though explicit transmission is not necessarily presupposed in the acceptance of knowledge "objectivated" on these levels, it must be noted that the typical acceptance of socialized skills, modes of conduct, and "traditions" usually takes place in an interweaving of imitative acceptance of recipes "objectivated" in the conduct of Others, "independent" steps of acquisition, and explicit transmission of knowledge on the linguistic level.[13] Thus, for example, a typical style of walking, a typical style of work, and a typical style of art contain these components of cognitive acquisition in different proportions.

In general, when we spoke of "traditions" in the previous discussion, we did not want to anticipate an analysis of the problems of the "social duration" connected with the socialization of knowledge. Above all we need not always think of the long-term components of the social store of knowledge, since something

13. [For a discussion of the acquisition of recipes, see *Collected Papers*, Vol. II: *Studies in Social Theory*, ed., with an introduction, by Arvid Brodersen (The Hague: Nijhoff, 1964), p. 95.]

similar also holds good for short-lived "fads" (e.g., a certain style of tying a tie).

"Objectivations" on the presymbolic levels can also play a subordinate but not unimportant role in the transmission of explicit elements of the social stock of knowledge. This is especially true in the province of practical recipes for mastering everyday situations. In the acceptance of such recipes, the observation and imitation of skills and examples of conduct (which are "objectivated" again and again in relations with Others) enter into the learning of explicit rules by means of proverbs, maxims, etc. Even in the appropriation of "higher forms of knowledge," "objectivations" can play a certain role on the presymbolic levels.

Finally, it should be noted that such "objectivations" have a decisive meaning for the early stages of the "socialization" of the child. Before a child has learned a language, explicit and more or less "abstract" (idealized and anonymous) elements of the social stock of knowledge cannot be explicitly transmitted to him. But they can be re-concretized for him on the presymbolic levels of "objectivation." Apart from that fact, such "objectivations" naturally play a mediating role in the learning of language itself, viz., in the appropriation of language's quasi-ideal and anonymous matrices of meaning.

c. Products as "objectivations" of subjective knowledge

We define "objectivation" as the embodiment of subjective processes in everyday occurrences and objects. Up until now, we have only described "objectivations" in the form of lifeworldly occurrences, and have passed over the possibility of "objectivations" in lifeworldly objects. In other words, until now we have limited ourselves to the description of the "objectivation" of subjective processes in acts and forms of expression. In the following, we will turn to the embodiment of subjective processes in the "results of acts."

The obtaining of subjective knowledge from Others on the two levels of "objectivation" previously described did not presuppose the historical pregivenness of a system of signs nor the intersubjective constitution of signs. However, it did presuppose that the positing of "objectivations" done by one person and their interpretation done by an Other occurred "at the same time." On the first level of "objectivation" this involves the embodiment of the subjective stock of knowledge in lifeworldly events which save the Other "independent" steps in the acquisition of knowledge through similar synchronized processes of interpretation. On the second level of "objectivation" there were certain subjective elements of knowledge which were embodied in lifeworldly events and were interpreted by the Other as indications of certain elements of knowledge. The second level was thus characterized by a certain detachment of the transmission of knowledge from its original acquisition. Yet on both levels of "objectivation" cognitive acquisition necessarily requires that the one from whom knowledge is accepted and the one who accepts knowledge stand in a we-relation, or in any case that one is able to immediately observe the Other.

But when we look at the possibility of the "objectivation" of subjective processes in objects instead of in occurrences in the everyday life-world, this condition does not hold good. When subjective processes are "objectivated" not in forms of expressions or in acts but rather in the "results of acts," the interpretation of "objectivations" (and therewith the acceptance of subjective knowledge through an Other) is not bound to the present of the one whose subjective processes have been embodied in this way. But what does it mean when we say that these processes can be "objectivated" in the "results of acts"?

It is a basic fact that acts which gear into the everyday life-world change it. Some acts of this kind can change the life-world in such a minimal way that the change remains unnoticed, at least to routine observation. Some acts, on the other hand, leave behind traces in lifeworldly objects which are also apprehendable through everyday attentional advertences. We can formally describe all such traces as the results of acts, no matter whether they are the central goal, the secondary goal, or even an attendant circumstance of the action. All such actional results can be interpreted as "objectivations" of action. From determinate changes in lifeworldly objects, one can infer back to a determinate action and from this to certain subjective processes, above all to determinate subjective knowledge.

The interpretation of the results of acts as "objectivations" of subjective processes in general, and of subjective knowledge in particular, naturally does not require that the process of interpretation occur at the same time as the course of the action. In this case, therefore, in order for A to be able to accept knowledge from B, he need no longer be his fellow-man; the interpretation is no longer bound to the immediate pregivenness of the Other. No temporal limit exists in principle for the taking over of the knowledge, except only a technical one—namely, the natural or artificial enduring of objects in which acts have been impressed. By means of "objectivations" of this kind, knowledge can be conveyed not only to contemporaries but also to successors.

It need hardly be stressed that the development of examples used for interpretation (interpretational relevances by means of which the results of acts can be interpreted completely independently of the course of the act) originates from situations in which the connection between the course of the act and the result of the act can be immediately observed. That is to say, the interpretation of the results of acts as "objectivations" of subjective processes fundamentally presupposes the interpretation of acts and forms of expression in we-relations or situations of immediate observation.

We have already said that we wish to characterize all changes in lifeworldly objects brought about by human acts as "objectivations," viz., as the "results of acts," no matter whether these changes are simply circumstances accompanying the action, or are themselves the result of a motivated action. But a distinction is still to be made between such results of acts. The mere attendant circumstances or "traces" of an action can indeed, as "objectivations" of subjective processes, convey knowledge to Others. They are, however, of much less significance in the socialization of knowledge than motivated changes, which we will term "products." It will therefore be enough for us to illustrate the first case only briefly, in order to proceed to a more careful description of products.

If A gets lost in the woods, he may suddenly stumble onto footprints that lead in a certain direction. It is obvious to A that the footprints were left by a person walking. He has observed how such a person, B or himself, left prints in the soft earth. He can explain the footprints as the results of an act, in the sense of the "accompanying circumstances" of a certain action. The possibility does arise that B, who left the footprints, was himself lost. In that case the footprints are only the "objectivations" of B's acquisition of knowledge. For that reason, A does not know whether for B (and, indeed hypothetically for A) that search for knowledge was successful. But if there is a beaten path, then A will decide that it most probably will eventually lead to a human settlement, and that the print therefore "objectivates" a certain part of B's knowledge which is relevant for A. In this case it is all the same whether B wanted to leave the prints or not; they convey knowledge to A. However, we can already see from this example that the delineation of motivated products is not sharply drawn. We need only change it slightly and assume that we are dealing with a cultivated path found by A; then we have already stepped over the dividing line to products.

Let us begin with a description of products. It must be stressed that we are interested in products only in a very restricted context—namely, only insofar as it can be said that they "objectivate" subjective knowledge and convey it to others. This limitation is important. We can differentiate three main forms of products: marks,[14] tools, and works of art. It is clear that a comprehensive investigation of these forms will lead us on the one hand to the empirical problems of technology, and on the other to the theoretical and historical problems of art.

Marks are the results of acts established by the one acting in order to hold onto a definite element of knowledge and to remind one of this. If someone goes through difficult terrain and wants to make sure that he will find his way back, he can notch the trees while underway. It is clear that the limit for "objectivations" discussed earlier is flexible. For example, a man may make sure that he leaves clear footprints. Although these are only "attendant circumstances" of his action, they can serve him as marks. The same generally holds good for the interpretation of these marks made by Others. Thus we have already seen how "tracks," for example, footprints, can be interpreted. If someone else traverses the same countryside and comes upon the hatchings, they can also serve as marks for him.

What was said in general about the development of interpretative models for "objectivations" of the results of acts, and their detachment from the course of acts (namely, that they refer back to the situations of the immediate observation of the connection between the act and its result), is especially true for marks. From this it follows that such interpretative models are invested with various grades of probability. Whether the interpreter will be able to accept a specific interpretation with more or less subjective security depends on whether he can bring the marks into a sensible relation with the other components of the situation (that is, it depends upon how simply he can resolve an association between typical marks and typical "problems about

14. [Schutz, *Collected Papers*, I, 308–9.]

markings"). If one gets lost in an underground labyrinth, but then discovers a string fastened to the wall, he will follow this with confidence on the basis of the interpretation: "Someone probably knew the right way out of the labyrinth and most likely marked it by means of this string." On the other hand, if someone finds a handkerchief with a knot in it on the street, he knows that this knot was supposed to remind someone of something, but from this knot he can acquire no relevant knowledge about this "someone." The enormous quantity of typical "problems about markings," for which a knot can serve as a typical mark in contrast to the example of the regular notching of trees, does not allow a specific interpretation without some further point to grasp onto. In the last example, we can see that still another fact plays a role in the interpretation of marks. If one recognizes the handkerchief as the property of a close friend, who continually forgets the birthdays of his wife and children, one can assign a specific interpretation to the knot with a certain degree of likelihood. We can say in general that the further removed a mark is from the original situation of its establishment, or the less at hand the relevant components of the original situation are for the interpretation, or the more anonymous the one who made the mark is for the one who interprets it, then so much the less can the mark convey specific knowledge.

When, though, typical marks are socialized for typical "problems about markings," that is, when the interpretation of them is standardized, we have already crossed over the boundary of presymbolic "objectivations." In any case, such "marks," then, have the function of signs, even if they are not yet elements of a developed system of signs. When systems of socialized "marks" are developed, the use of this expression is already misleading. In this case, one is concerned with signs that find their "objectivation" in the results of acts, thus in lifeworldly objects, in contrast to language, which is embodied in forms of expression. Just for this reason, "systems of marks," such as writing, can serve for the "translation," into a more "stable" medium, of "systems of signs" which have been "objectivated" originally in forms of expression, such as language. At this point the level of presymbolic "objectivations" is naturally left behind. We will return to this later.

Tools, like all products, are also "objectivations" of subjective knowledge. As will be shown later, they differ in essential ways from marks (as well as from works of art). Marks are motivated products, with the motive of "objectivating" for the subject a determinate subjectivated element of knowledge. In this way, as we have shown, such "objectivations" can also, under certain circumstances, be interpreted by Others. On the other hand, tools are objects in the everyday life-world which are used in acts that change it. In a borderline case, they do not themselves need to be the results of acts. Rather, it suffices that they are built in as useful means in the typical courses of acts. The normal situation (the way in which one typically imagines a tool) is that the life-worldly object is itself produced or made, and thus can be characterized as the result of an act. Being the result of an act, the tool itself then stands within the typical course of an act. We can consider tools as "objectivations" of component parts of in-order-to contexts, above all those associated with skills that have become routine. The motive that lies behind the making of the tool is consequently not an objectivation of knowledge in a literal sense, nor an "objectivation" of a skill. In principle, one can infer from a tool that has been considered as a result of an act, back to the act and to the knowledge that is embodied therein. The interpretation of a tool essentially refers to its function in an in-order-to context (to a skill), while the specific producer can in principle remain anonymous. All that is presupposed for an adequate interpretation is that A, who apprehends the tool as an "objectivation," has mastered a similar everyday problem to that of B, who produced the tool, and that the problem is presented to A in a similar "functional chain." In this case he can apprehend and accept the tool as a "solution."

In everyday life, a tool is very seldom interpreted as an "objectivation" of specific elements of knowledge. The reason for this is that the use of tools with the skills pertaining to them is in general socialized and routinized, while the obtaining of specific elements of knowledge finds "more appropriate" media. From the fact that such interpretations are in principle possible, one can see that in the absence of other "objectivations," as for example in the absence of historical inscriptions, etc., archaeology uses just such interpretation of tools as the most important evidence for the reconstruction of the social stock of knowledge ("culture") of prehistorical societies.

It is different with works of art. They are indeed products in the strict sense of the word. They are, however, differentiated from marks as well as from tools in an extremely important way. Only in a theoretical, limiting case can one imagine that the motive for the creation of a work of art is that it should be an "objectivation" only for the producer, as is the case with marks, or that it be imbedded in purely pragmatic "functional chains" in the everyday mastery of life, as is the case with a tool. Nevertheless, one can conceive of works of art that overlap with marks and with tools. The essential factors that characterize a product as a work of art are precisely that a work of art is created as an interpretation for Others, and that it "objectivates" the "solution" of problems in everyday products. These factors refer to the relation between everyday and non-everyday levels of reality. Nothing more can be said about this here, since a theory of symbols would have to be developed in order to allow further analysis. We must be content at this point to establish that works of art, like marks and tools, can be interpreted as "objectivations" of subjective knowledge, but of a knowledge that presents attempts to solve the problems transcending the everyday life-world.

d. "Objectivations" of subjective knowledge in signs

The previously discussed levels of the embodiment of subjective processes in indications and products had one thing in common, despite all the various differences in the form of "objectivation." The dependence of our interpretation upon a situation strongly limits the possibilities of transmitting knowledge. "Objectivations" can indeed be interpreted as indications of subjective knowledge, detached to a certain extent from the situations in which this knowledge was originally acquired. The interpretation of products can even be accomplished in the absence of the producer. In these levels of "objectivation," the transference of subjective knowledge necessarily presupposes a far-reaching agreement between (1) the structures of experience and relevance, out of which the one who originally acquires the knowledge develops a specific element of knowledge and (2) the structures of experience and relevance of the Other, who interprets certain of the former's "objectivations" of subjective processes as indications of a specific element of knowledge. The problem whose solution is "objectivated" in determinate indications or products must from the beginning be presented in a similar way to the one who takes over the solution, through an interpretation of this "objectivation" as it is presented to the one who had originally found the solution. That one can interpret such "objectivations" as indications useful for problem-solving is to a great extent dependent on the fact that in the interpretative situation the "same" elements are given as in the original problematic situation. Therefore, on these levels of "objectivation" subjective knowledge, which has by "anonymization" and "idealization" been detached from the spatial, temporal, and social stratification of everyday experiences, cannot be transmitted to Others.

This radical limitation does not affect the possibilities of the conveying of knowledge on the level of "objectivation" (which will now be discussed), in which subjective knowledge is "translated" into signs. On this level, subjective knowledge can be transmitted to Others, though it is detached from the spatial, temporal, and social stratifications of experiences out of which it had originally become sedimented. Interpretation is here to a great extent independent of the previously given elements of the interpretational situation and the relevance structures of the actually present experiences of the interpreter. Thus knowledge can be gained which is only hypothetically relevant for him. By means of signs, "attitudes to problems," not only "solutions to problems," can be transmitted.

As previously stressed, the transmission of subjective knowledge on the presymbolic levels of "objectivation" presupposes only a certain degree of agreement between the structures of experience and relevance of the one who produces the "objectivations" and those of the one who interprets them. It does not, however, presuppose that both already have an area of knowledge in common before the transmission of a specific element of knowledge. In contrast to this, transmission of subjective knowledge through signs always presupposes common knowledge; he who "objectivates" his knowledge in signs and he who interprets them must be familiar with the same system of signs. Only then does something correspond to the processes through which the former translates back into his subjective knowledge.

When we ask ourselves how subjective knowledge can be passed on to Others by means of signs, we necessarily come to the problem of the intersubjective constitution of signs. Or, when we wish to bracket this problem, we come to the problem of the historical pregivenness and the subjective appropriation of a system of signs. These problems will be examined later.[15] Here we can only indicate the main results of these investigations.

15. See Chap. 6 [Vol. II].

We have already said that subjective knowledge (which is to a great extent freed from the stratification of immediate experiences in the everyday life-world) can also be transmitted through systems of signs. It must be remembered that a far-reaching detachment of subjective experiences from the spatial, temporal, and social stratifications of everyday experiences is just what the constitution of systems of signs presupposes. This detachment ("anonymization" and "idealization") has its origin in the processes of intersubjective mirroring. Due to this detachment, "objectivations" of subjective processes (and even those that refer to *commonly* experienced objects) are *on their part* commonly experienced in the spatial and temporal community inherent to the we-relation. It is thus that intersubjectively valid and reciprocally interpretable "objectivations" can develop. *In principle*, one can imagine the development of such symbolizable "objectivations" in each "genuine" we-relation. But in historical reality, things are not so. Each individual finds ready, completely developed systems of signs already present. Historical systems are an "imposed" element of the biographical situation; they form an essential component of the social a priori into which every individual is "born." One need only add that the subjective *appropriation* of historical systems of signs naturally also occurs through processes of intersubjective mirroring (above all, in the earliest we-relations).

Let us illustrate these considerations with the help of a modification of our previous example. If A wants to cross the river at a place with which he is completely unacquainted, he looks for a suitable crossing. He can try to find it in "independent" steps in the acquisition of knowledge. He can observe how someone else looks for and finds the crossing, and then he can follow him. He can be apprised of it by means of the forms of expression of an Other (waving, yelling, etc.). He can also find posts driven into the river at certain intervals and decide that someone probably crossed the river with their help. In any case, it is clear that the problem of crossing the river in a region with which A is completely unacquainted first occurs when A comes to the river, that is, when the problem becomes actually relevant. Further, he can take over B's knowledge concerning the crossing only when he observes B actually using this knowledge, or when B's products can be brought into the current situation in an unambiguous relation to the problem of crossing the river.

But let us assume that A and B meet in a hotel that is ten

kilometers from the river (of whose existence A still is not aware, but whose crossings B knows exactly). Let us further assume that from the direction of A's approach B gathers that A probably will come across the river and that B for certain reasons would like to save A an hour's search for the crossing. Since neither the river nor the crossing are "on hand" in the current situation, the possibility of his sharing his knowledge by means of presymbolic "objectivations" is completely excluded. If A and B by their meeting possess no common system of signs, then B would have to walk to the river with A in order to impart his knowledge to him. In the then actually relevant problematic situation he could transmit his knowledge to A by means of "objectivations" on the presymbolic plane, for instance, by showing A the crossing. Let us assume that B knows of a second river which A will probably come across in the course of his wandering. Then, by referring to the actual river and to visible bends in the river, groups of trees, etc., he can try to draw up a primitive cartographical system with A, thus "scrutinizing," too, the way in which A interprets it. With the help of such a primitive system of signs he could then try to inform A of the crossing in the next river, thus transmitting to him "idealized" and "anonymous" knowledge that is only hypothetically relevant for him.

But if A and B bring with them congruent interpretational schemata for symbolizable "objectivations," if they, for instance, speak a common language or (which would suffice in this example) if they have a command of a limited cartographical system, then A can find out from B not only the nature of the problem but also its solution. B need only tell him that he, A, will come across a river and that he can wade across this river only at a certain place, namely, where three weeping willows stand next to the second bend in the river after the river comes from the hills to the plain. The constellation of quite anonymous and idealized constitutions of types (bends in the river, weeping willows, three, second, etc.) is detached both from the concrete surroundings and actually present relevances of the situation in which A and B presently find themselves (e.g., hotel) and from the persons A and B. For A, the constellation of signs as such is significant. He can transform the significant matrices of the system of signs into subjective knowledge, even if he does not know B, has never seen the river, and does not intend to go walking in this direction.

It is hard to imagine adequately the motivation to produce a system of signs, just as it is also difficult to illustrate the processes of constitution themselves. Therefore, in our example we only said that, through intersubjective processes, A and B develop a primitive cartographical "system" limited to a narrow province of application. But let us take a somewhat romantically simplified, though quite descriptive, example of "speech construction." When a man and a woman, belonging to two different tribes, bringing different ("independently" acquired and socially transmitted) subjective knowledge with them, and speaking different languages, are driven onto an island, it does not require any special fantasy to imagine the motivation to produce a common language. Here we are not concerned with the intersubjective constitution of a system of signs *ex nihilo*, rather "only" with the construction of a common language. Although the linguistic means that have been "brought along" may play an important role, the intersubjective processes, the "objectivation" of common experiences, etc., are decisive. Naturally, after they have created a common language for themselves, they can share not only newly acquired but also previously acquired, not only actually but also hypothetically relevant knowledge.

We can thus summarize: the transmitting of subjective knowledge that is largely detached from the stratifications of subjective experiences involved in the acquisition of knowledge, and from the current relevance structures of the situation in which the knowledge is transmitted, presupposes that knowledge of the "same" system of signs was brought into the situation in which knowledge is transmitted, or that in the situation a common system of signs is created. Given these presuppositions, subjective knowledge can be translated into the "idealizing" and "anonymous" interpretative matrices of a system of signs, and it can be again transformed into subjective knowledge by means of an appropriately meaningful retranslation.[16]

It was shown that "objectivations" can also be unmotivated on the presymbolic levels (i.e., that the motive which accompanies "objectivation" can be something other than that of transmitting knowledge).[17] On these levels, though, the interpretation of "objectivations" and consequently the acceptance of knowledge is, of course, also motivated. On the level of "objectivations" of subjective knowledge in signs, both the transmission of knowl-

16. [See the discussion of the function of signs in *Collected Papers*, I, 321–23.]

17. See Chap. 4, B, 2, a, b, and c.

edge and the acceptance of knowledge are motivated. That is, the positing of signs is, for the one who posits them, within the subjective in-order-to or because-context pertaining to the transmission of knowledge. And the interpretation of these signs is in this context concerned with the acceptance of knowledge for the one who interprets the "objectivations." (We will not here consider exceptions such as a monologue which is overheard.) This has consequences for both the positor and the interpreter of signs. The former assumes that the Other will interpret the "objectivations" in accordance with the meaning of the "Objective" interpretative schemata of the system of signs. But he also assumes that the Other will do this in typical ways, and that the same will hold true for typical subjective deviations from the "Objective" schemata of interpretation. The better he knows the Other, the better he can anticipate the Other's typical "retranslations." Such knowledge enters into the original acts of positing signs and can change these according to the subjective in-order-to or because-contexts in which they occur. He who interprets the signs knows, on the other hand, that the "objectivations" are the motivated acts of the positor, who "controls" what he communicates and how he communicates it. The communication of knowledge on this level thus has the formal structure of a reciprocal social action.

A further consideration must be included. Even on the pre-symbolic level, "objectivations," if they are motivated, can lead to certain anticipations of their interpretation by Others. This can lead to motivated "overstatements" as well as motivated "deceptions." In the transmission of knowledge on the level of the systems of signs the possibility of motivated construction and transmission of "false" knowledge takes the place of more or less conscious control of "objectivations" (e.g., the control of facial expression). The further removed the transmitting is from the acquisition, and the more detached the transmitted knowledge is from the stratifications of immediate lifeworldly experience, then the more the transmitted knowledge evades an everyday, pragmatic reconsideration by the one taking over the knowledge. This is a circumstance not without relevance for the character and social function of "special knowledge."

These considerations touch on a problem which we can only indicate here. First, it should be noted that the fact of translating subjective knowledge into quasi-ideal and anonymous categories of meaning in a system of signs necessarily has as its consequence a "falsification" of this knowledge. The polythetical construction inherent in the acquisition of knowledge and the specific temporal dimension of subjective knowledge are "overcome." The alternatives and blind alleys of the acquisition fall away. The unique biographical constellation of the subjective meaning-structures in which the subjective elements of knowledge are embedded are bracketed out. The subjective meaning-contexts are largely "replaced" by the "Objective" meaning-context pertaining to the system of signs. The latter belongs, however, to a historical-social level of reality which transcends the individual (the one who posits the signs and the one who interprets them). Everyday, pragmatic criteria for scrutinizing knowledge lose their significance for the one who has appropriated this reality, for whom the reality is a matter of course. On the presymbolic level of "objectivation," a lifeworldly, pragmatic criterion for the differentiation between "correct" and "false" knowledge can be set up as obvious. But on the symbolic level of "objectivation," subjective knowledge is placed in relation to historically matured "ideal" dimensions of reality, to which the everyday, pragmatic concept of "accuracy" or "falsity" is no longer applicable. Since we cannot go into this problem here, we only want to note that the social dissemination of "false" knowledge rests on the same *formal* presuppositions: of anonymity, ideality, historicity of the symbolizable stratum of reality, and above all naturally of the language.

As a consequence of its translation in an anonymous system of signs, subjective knowledge itself is rendered anonymous. When A takes over from B an element of knowledge "objectivated" in signs, he grasps it in this "Objective" sense, this anonymous meaning, but he still knows of its origin in B's subjective experiences. The element of knowledge in question can be passed on from A to C, D, E, etc., without its "Objective" sense as a transmitted element of knowledge being essentially changed, although its origin for C, D, E, etc., can be completely anonymous. If, on the other hand, the specific origin of a certain element of knowledge is to be established, then a specific act of "historization" is necessary. That is, a specific assertion about its origin is required, which makes use in turn of the temporal, spatial, and personal possibilities of categorization, which are invested in the sign system's matrices of meaning. ("My friend told me that . . . " "Loki taught our forefathers the art of forging metal.") It hardly need be stated that such "historizations" may correspond to "facts," but they can also be legendary or fictive. ("Nikola Tesla discovered the light bulb," "Moses received the Ten Commandments on Mount Sinai.") Such "historizations" originate from socially conditioned motives. Where these do not exist, the knowledge "objectivated" and socialized in signs assumes the anonymity of something linguistically taken for granted, for example, that of a routinely employed semantic organization, the anonymity of a proverb, a recipe. ("Everyone knows that . . . " "One has maintained that since time immemorial.")

The "idealization" and "anonymization" of subjective knowledge (which necessarily occur in the "objectivation" of subjective knowledge in the categories of meaning within a system of signs) play a decisive role in the embodiment of subjective results of experience and explication in the social stock of knowledge. The "Objective" meaning belonging to elements of knowledge can be transmitted to Others relatively independently of the biographical uniqueness of its acquisition. Others can grasp the "Objective" meaning of transmitted elements in relative independence of their unique biographical situation. The meaning of transmitted knowledge is largely independent of the concrete relevance structures and the limiting spatial, temporal, and personal conditions of the acquisition, the transmission, and the taking over of knowledge. The "idealization" and "anonymization" of subjective knowledge in the course of its "objectivation" in a system of signs is thus the presupposition for the social accumulation of knowledge. The latter, *relatively* independent of "place and time," is the condition for the development of "higher forms of knowledge," that is, for the development of systems of explicit elements of knowledge on a higher level of "ideality."

In order to emphasize a further aspect of the "objectivation" of subjective knowledge in systems of signs, we must anticipate the analysis of the socialization of knowledge. Symbolized "objectivated" knowledge can, depending on its socialization, preserve either the specific authority of a legendary (e.g., "historical") origin or the anonymous authority of our "forefathers" (e.g., "everyone"). It is thus, as we have shown, that knowledge comes to have an overwhelming and at the same time taken-for-granted independence, which in the end is based on the subjective results of experience and explication, but which contrasts with the individual and the subjectivity of his experiences and situation. It hardly need be stated that the social validity of such "objectivated" knowledge can outlast its original social relevance. This fact is of decisive importance for the development of traditions and, following from this, for the development of a historical social reality as such (i.e., of a relative-natural world view). This reality, which is inserted between a (hypothetical) presocial individual and·a (hypothetical) presocial reality, has barely any traces of its subjective origin.

We must once again return to the fact that the individual who has acquired a historical system of signs, and especially a language, can "objectivate" this in his subjective and indeed "independently" acquired knowledge. More exactly, this observation holds good only for subjective knowledge, which does not transcend the categories of meaning in the system of signs on hand. In this connection, it is clear that the regularly repeated "objectivations" of already socialized knowledge (e.g., in the processes of socialization) do not interest us. Here, there is obviously no "problem of objectivation," but rather a problem concerning the institutionalized transference of knowledge. Even "new" knowledge may be new only in "content" and contain no problems as far as the "possibilities of objectivation" in the categories of meaning in the system of signs then on hand are concerned. This is the rule for "new" knowledge that is relevant for overcoming problems in the everyday life-world. Such knowledge can, for the most part without difficulties, be passed on to Others by means of the system of signs on hand, in a way adequate for practical everyday goals.

But "new" knowledge can be "objectivated" only with difficulty, even when it is only relatively atypical with reference to the categories of meaning of the system of signs that is on hand. The routine possibilities for objectivation within the latter do not suffice in order to transfer "new" knowledge adequately. The system of signs can, however, contain nonroutine "possibilities of objectivation." Their use demands creative acts in which the individual's new knowledge and the society's history (which is sedimented in the system of signs) work together. Let us consider here the nearly inexhaustible possibilities for the formations of analogies, metaphorical expressions, etc, "on hand" in a differentiated system of signs such as a language.

Beyond this, however, radically atypical and, truly, essentially "novel" knowledge can lead to changes in the system of signs now on hand; in borderline cases it can lead to the constitution of new signs and systems of signs. We can once more use changes in language as an example. These changes can range from the change of meaning in individual words, through the formation of new words, to the development of new provinces of meaning (e.g., "technical languages," etc.). Even the apprehension of nonroutine "objectivations," for instance the understanding of an analogy, demands the reperforming of the original "creative" act. This naturally holds good all the more when it concerns the taking over of "new" knowledge "objectivated" in "new" signs. In general, let it be noted that essentially "novel" knowledge has its origin mainly in experiences which refer to non-everyday realities. If we want to pursue the problem of the "objectivation" of essentially "novel" knowledge further, then we must, before anything else, consider the role of mythological, religious, poetic, and (on certain historical levels of the development of "higher forms of knowledge") philosophic and scientific "advances" in the non-everyday dimensions of reality.

Now to summarize. The basic presupposition for the incorporation of subjective knowledge into the social stock of knowledge is its "objectivation." Subjective knowledge can be "objectivated" on different levels, depending on how tightly its transference is bound to the acquisition of knowledge, depending on whether subjective knowledge is embodied in lifeworldly processes or objects, and whether or not subjective knowledge is translated into an idealizing and anonymizing system of signs. The social stock of knowledge contains elements of various levels of "objectivation." It includes skills (such as a typical gait, style of work, etc.) which in the conduct and action of Others are pre-given to the individual as models. It contains products, recipes, and explicit elements of knowledge. The latter are "objectivated" in systems of signs, especially in language. Systems of signs, again especially language, are for their part a component of the social stock of knowledge and are the "medium" for the "objectivation" of explicit elements of knowledge. They are thus the presupposition for the social cumulation of knowledge and for the development of "higher forms of knowledge."

3. THE SOCIALIZATION OF "OBJECTIVATED" KNOWLEDGE

a. *Social relevance of knowledge*

Subjective knowledge must be "objectivated" in some form before it can enter into the social stock of knowledge. But its "objectivation" is not enough to incorporate it into the social stock of knowledge. One should consider that only a fraction of all the subjective results of experience and explication is "objectivated." But only a fraction of that subjective knowledge that was somehow "objectivated" also enters into the social stock of knowledge. Besides the basic presupposition, namely, the "objectivation" in some form, still other conditions must obviously also be fulfilled before subjective knowledge becomes a component of the social stock of knowledge. Thus the question that we must now ask ourselves is how it happens that determinate subjective elements of knowledge are socialized following their "objectivation," while others are not. To find an answer to this question we must first consider which relevance structures lie at the basis of an original "objectivation" of subjective knowledge as well as at the basis of the subsequent acceptance of the "objectivated" knowledge.

As has been shown, the subjective acquisition of knowledge is determined by subjective (although extensively socialized) relevance structures. On the other hand, the "objectivation" of such acquired knowledge can be unmotivated on the presymbolic level of the "objectivation," i.e., the motive for the "objectivation" may be other than that for the transference of knowledge. Only its acceptance (i.e., the interpretation of the "objectivation") is in principle already motivated on this level. That means that those who interpret grasp the "objectivation" as an embodiment of actually or hypothetically relevant knowledge. The acceptance of knowledge on the presymbolic level depends on the typical similarity of problems; that is, it presupposes that the context of the problem for the one who in "independent" steps found the "solution" to the problem is the same as for him who accepts the "solution."

This also applies to the transfer of subjective knowledge through signs—with one important difference: the transference is, as we have said, "reciprocally" motivated. The typical motive for the original "objectivation" is the transference of one's own knowledge to Others. More precisely, the transference is the typical in-order-to motive for "objectivation," irrespective of what the because-context may be in which the transference occurs (e.g., worry about an Other, duties to Others, working together on certain problems, etc.). It hardly need be stressed that the in-order-to and because-contexts pertaining to the transference of knowledge are extensively socialized and derived from an existing social structure (mothers, teachers, etc.). Not only is the acceptance of knowledge dependent upon the symbolic level of "objectivation," but the original "objectivation" depends on the typical similarity of the problems. He who transmits his subjective knowledge to Others assumes on the basis of his knowledge about a certain Other or about typical Others that the element of knowledge in question is, or will be, just as relevant for them or their typical problems as it was for him.

We can say that on all levels of "objectivation" the acceptance of "objectivated" knowledge depends on the typical similarity of subjective relevance structures, and further that on the symbolic level the transference of knowledge depends on one's *granting* the typical similarity of subjective relevance structures. Knowledge that presents "solutions" for typically similar problems for one person as well as for the Other is intersubjectively relevant. (As will be shown later, it is at least in its inception already socially relevant.)

Let us try to illustrate these considerations by returning to an example that we have already used repeatedly. B meets A and tells him where he can best cross the river. B acquired this knowledge "independently"; it offers him the solution to a problem that was already relevant. He assumes that the "same" problem will also be relevant for A if he continues in this direction. And, because for some reason he wants to convey the knowledge to A, he supplies A with his "solution." We could cite countless because-contexts as examples: because he has a friendly disposition, because he is interested in tourist travel, because A is his nephew, etc. A and B now share a certain element of knowledge that has the "same" typical relevance for them. The solution of the problem was "objectivated" and taken over. Can we here already speak of a social stock of knowledge? Although two formal presuppositions for the sociality of elements of knowledge are already fulfilled, we are not able to use this concept here because A and B do not form a "society," and because the example concerns only a single element.

But, on the other hand, it is impossible to add a quantitative criterion to the two formal presuppositions for the sociality of an element of knowledge. How many people must share an element of knowledge, how many elements of knowledge must be involved, before we can speak of a social stock of knowledge? There are languages spoken by a few dozen people, there are societies in which only a "few" elements of knowledge belong to the general public. This naturally does not mean that quantitative questions are not very important for causal-historical analyses in the empirical sociology of knowledge. Thus, for instance, population size, population density, density of communication, etc., to select only a few factors of this kind, undoubtedly bear in a certain way upon the differentiation of the stock of knowledge, and upon its social distribution. But with the help of another example that we already have used earlier, we want to show now that the sociality of elements of knowledge cannot be adequately determined on this basis.

We had assumed that a man and a woman from different races and without a common language were stranded on a desert island. Each brings with him a different stock of socialized interpretational and motivational relevances. But a "common" fate is imposed on them. A wide range of typical problems confronts them both. Whoever "independently" finds the "solution" to a definite everyday problem (or has already "brought" it with him) can transmit it to the other person. This will probably first involve "objectivations" on the presymbolic level. In the course of continuing we-relations, due to compelling motives and with the help of the two languages "brought with them," a common language will develop in which they can share relatively "ideal" and "anonymous" knowledge with each other. Thus, we now have a "society" consisting of two people: a "common fate," i.e., typically similar problems, a factual social structure, in this case limited to the we-relation, a common language, and a common stock of knowledge.

This common stock of knowledge is primarily concerned with "common" and typically similar problems. It is, then, "generally valid," although the general public here consists only of two persons. Besides the elements of knowledge which both share, each has a stock of subjective knowledge that is not "objectivated," partly because it may not be easy to "objectivate," but also partly because it is related to problems relevant only for one and not for the other. To take an example: there are problems relevant only for the woman as woman and only for the man as man. There is no urgent reason to convey the existing "solutions" to these problems. On the basis of *common* relevances a common quasi-social stock of knowledge is formed for subjective elements of knowledge. The fact that this is not simply the sum of subjective elements of knowledge is especially clear in this example.

The concept of the social stock of knowledge still seems to be out of place in the description of this example. But in no way does this depend on either the size of the "society" or the quantity of its common elements of knowledge. The reason that we characterize the latter as quasi-social is to be found in the fact that this "society" has no "history," if one does not want this expression to mean the intersecting of the biographies of A and B. When they die, their common knowledge will die with them. The solutions to problems acquired by them could not be taken over by others. Rather, these must once again be "independently" acquired. But when we speak of a social stock of knowledge, we think principally of the transference of knowledge over generations. Of course, it must be stressed that no usable quantitative criterion can be established here.

Let us return to our example, and assume that C comes to A and B: the couple have a child. In contrast to A and B, the child brings no socialized motivational and interpretational relevances with him, nor does he have knowledge of a system of signs. The language and the (quasi-) social stock of knowledge of the parents given to him in advance fill this role. They are components of what is for C already a historical-social a priori. A and B have an urgent motive to transmit their knowledge to C, that is to say, insofar as they assume that the problems confronting them will also confront C, and thus that the "solutions" will also be relevant for C. On the other hand, C appropriates this knowledge in his earliest we-relations. Since these processes were extensively discussed elsewhere,[18] we can be content here to draw attention to the fact that the social structure lying "behind" C's earliest we-relations is nothing other than the structure of the we-relations between A and B. We still wish to add that this structure must necessarily be changed by the arrival of C and the new relevances arising from this fact. This is a question that must lead to an analysis of the institutionalization of action. We merely want to consider here what it means when we say that the knowledge had by A and B is passed on to C.

We have already said that not everything relevant for A need also be relevant for B. Knowledge exclusively concerning the relevance structures of one or the other alone will typically be not at all "objectivated" and will not enter into their common stock of knowledge. There can also be knowledge relevant for and common to them but not relevant for C, i.e., considered by them to be irrelevant for C. In this case no motive arises to trans-

18. See Chap. 4, A, 1.

mit this province of the common stock of knowledge. As an example, we can cite "solutions" to the relation between A and B which come from the particular way in which it is viewed by each. But they can consider other "solutions" to this relation to be "solutions" to typical problems arising in the relation between man and wife, and consequently pass them on to C as hypothetically relevant for him.

But there can also be knowledge that does not belong to their common stock of knowledge, because it was considered by A as irrelevant for B or vice versa, but it is now deemed by one or the other as hypothetically relevant for C. To give an example: "solutions" of problems relevant for A as a woman were looked on by her as irrelevant for B, the man, but as hypothetically relevant for C, the daughter. This knowledge is, so to speak, for the first time "objectivated" and transmitted to C. In this way, a certain differentiation of the social stock of knowledge already enters in: knowledge belonging to A and B and C, knowledge belonging to A and B, knowledge belonging to A and C, etc. This differentiation obviously touches on certain anonymizing typifications. Some elements of knowledge were taken as typically relevant for A and B, others as typically relevant for people of type A and type B, some as typically relevant for people of type A and type C, some knowledge on the other hand as typically relevant for people of types A, B, and C, and finally other knowledge as typically relevant for "everyone." We have already extensively discussed the problem raised here in the analysis of the social distribution of knowledge, only from another viewpoint.[19]

b. *Social transference of knowledge*

However small and simple a "society" is, it provides against the "dying out" of knowledge relevant for it. That is, there is an initial differentiation of knowledge according to which knowledge is (or is considered to be) relevant for certain typical problems and for certain typical persons. In the example previously used (a society of A, B, and C), the social relevance and transference of knowledge are still immediately bound to the subjective motives of A and B, and their subjective viewpoint as to what could present typical problems for C. It is this circumstance that differentiates the "society" in the foregoing example from historical societies. In the latter, socially relevant knowledge is for the most part independent of subjective viewpoints and subjective

19. See Chap. 3, C.

relevance structures. What the typical problems are, whose typical problems are involved, who has to transmit the solutions, and to whom the solutions are transmitted are for the most part predetermined in historical societies. The answers to these questions are themselves elements of the social stock of knowledge. By this means the transference of socially relevant knowledge is anchored in the social structure.

The "social structure," in which knowledge was transmitted in the previous example, was limited to the structure of the we-relations among A, B, and C. Indeed, a certain differentiation with regard to the transference of knowledge follows from this structure. Thus, "generally valid" knowledge (knowledge that presented the solutions to problems relevant as much for A as for B and for C) was taken over by C in social relations with A or B. But knowledge relevant for people of types A and C, but not B, was taken over by C in social relations with A, as on the other hand knowledge relevant for people of types B and C, but not A, was taken over by C in social relations with B. Even in this simple social structure there is thus an initial independence of the relevance and "validity" of knowledge from the highly specific, "unique" social relations among A, B, and C. Relevance and "validity" are related to certain typifications (people of type A, B, C). Inherent in this is the tendency for the association of provinces of knowledge in social roles. This association is the prerequisite for binding the *transference* of knowledge to social roles. But in this example both the motive for the transference as well as the typifications of the Other (C), which are at the basis of the assumptions of the hypothetical relevance of an element of knowledge for C, are still essentially determined by the subjective relevance structures, i.e., by the motivational and interpretational relevances.

But how are the processes of taking over knowledge presented to C? The typifications used by A and B in comprehending C naturally determine their behavior in relation to C. Consequently, these typifications are "read off" by C from the behavior of A and B: the typifications in the processes of intersubjective mirroring are transformed into facets of C's self-typification. Foreign typifications at the basis of the transference of knowledge from A and B to C (i.e., his earliest we-relations in general) thus play a decisive role in the development of C's self-image. But at the same time, these typifications also transfer to C an initial knowledge about the arrangement of the social world. For these typifications (insofar as they are grasped by C) already contain a rudimentary anonymization of A and B (and naturally also of C). They are thus in principle available to be comprehended by D, E, F, etc. C grasps himself as typically similar to Others (and as typically in need of definite knowledge) or as typically different from Others. For C it is obvious that determinate problem solutions are relevant for people of a definite type. C further experiences that determinate needs for knowledge are typically satisfied by certain persons (fathers, mothers, etc.). It becomes taken for granted that determinate knowledge is to be passed on to definite people. The insight into the hypothetical relevance of determinate elements of knowledge for definite Others and the motive to transmit knowledge, is for C, strictly speaking, no longer "independently" but rather socially derived. Add to this the fact that the *How* of the original acquisition of knowledge (from A and B) forms a precedent-setting case for C, through which the ways and means of further transmission of knowledge to D, E, F, etc., is predetermined.

With these considerations we have reached the transition to the question concerning the social transmission of knowledge in historical societies. For in these the transmission of socially relevant knowledge is already to a great extent independent of subjective relevance structures (typifications and motives for transmission of knowledge) and constitutes a taken-for-grantedness firmly anchored in the social structure. What is socially relevant, for whom it is relevant, and to whom and how it is to be transmitted belong to the stock of "socialized" interpretational and motivational relevances. Certain provinces of the social stock of knowledge are seen as typically relevant for determinate, more or less "anonymous," social roles, and passing on the pertinent knowledge is bound up with them. That means, therefore, that the social stock of knowledge of a historical society contains a "socialized" system of hypothetical relevances related to the "problem's solutions" that have ripened within it. Thus, not only the "problem's solution" but also the passing on of the "problem's solutions" has a connection with social roles.

The earliest we-relations have decisive importance for the transference of "universally valid" knowledge. "Everyone" learns a language by means of these, and at the same time learns certain "general" skills and standards of conduct. The earliest we-relations are typically determined by the structure of the kinship system. For the child the family is typically the first immediately experienced social reality—a comprehensible reality already conditioned by the total social structure "behind" the family.[20]

The transmission of a broad province of the basic elements of the social stock of knowledge, for the generally relevant problem solutions, is bound to the social roles within the family. Besides language and general skills and standards of conduct, knowledge is also transmitted within the family, knowledge relevant for the problems that are essentially bound to biographically "imposed" roles, such as roles associated with sex. Thus, typical mothers transmit specific, different "problem solutions" to their daughters.

Here we must proceed with caution. Historical social structures and relative-natural world views are extraordinarily variable, and indeed not only in the "content" of the stock of knowledge, but also in the way the transmission of knowledge is anchored in the social structure. The importance of the family in the transmission of basic elements of social knowledge (which coincides with the decisive role of the family in the early "socialization" of the person) is as good as universal, although even here there are exceptions. Still, "universally valid" provinces of knowledge, such as those bound up with "imposed" roles, can be transmitted beyond the family structure. Thus, for example, essential aspects of knowledge relevant for sex-linked roles are transmitted in some societies through male leagues, in others through more or less informal groups of the same age. And in modern societies with general compulsory schooling, broad provinces of "generally valid" knowledge are passed on by means of specialized institutions for the transference of knowledge, such as grammar schools.

Knowledge relevant for problems that are not essentially bound up with biographically "imposed" roles (which is indeed the case with many professions in relatively simple societies) is usually transmitted by means other than kinship institutions. In general, one can say the following: where solutions to socially relevant problems are precipitated as routine forms of acts, which in turn are bound to an institutionalized structure of roles, the transference of knowledge is then also typically institutionalized and routinely taken over by certain role-bearers. Thus, there are teachers and masters, "noncommissioned officers of development," and "officers" in the province of religious, commercial,

20. See Chap. 4, A, 1, a.

and political institutions. It is worth noting that although we are concerned here with the transmission of knowledge bound up with certain roles, this is not necessarily the exclusive function of such social roles. The development of social roles whose exclusive function is the transmission of knowledge is not entirely universal. An institutionalized establishment of the independence inherent in the transmission of knowledge occurs only under determinate social-historical circumstances. The clarification of the causes and conditions of such development falls within the province of the empirical sociology of knowledge. For here also, the proposed limitation relative to the anchoring of the transmission of knowledge in the family holds good. The extraordinarily wide historical variability of the institutionalized transmission of knowledge permits only the *formal* determination that in every historical society the transmission of socially relevant knowledge becomes independent of the subjective relevance structures, and that it is routinely anchored in the social differentiation of roles on the basis of "socialized" relevance structures. Determinations proceeding from this in the form of "causal" hypotheses must prove themselves through ethnological and historical material.

c. *The social accumulation of knowledge*

The anchoring of the transmission of socially relevant knowledge in the social structure guarantees its maintenance over generations. But what happens to elements of knowledge (after they are "objectified" in intersubjective processes) which are passed on routinely within the social structure on the basis of their social relevance?

The first and originally "objectivated" solution of a problem was still largely dependent on the subjective relevance structures of the individual. But the "objectivation" into signs already submits the solutions to an initial anonymization. The repeated use of the elements of knowledge in question in typically similar (but not completely identical) problem situations by people to whom the problem is presented in a typically similar (but not completely identical) fashion, steadily wears away the remaining subjectively conditioned moments of the problem's solution. In the course of the social transmission of the latter, a certain "improvement" in the solution takes place (in any case, with respect to its social relevance). Let us assume, for example, that the original problem was to kill some wild animal. The original solution may have presented itself to two hunters in this way: one will lie in wait while the other drives the game into the trap. When this solution is transmitted to other people, they first want to imitate the original solution exactly. In the course of repeated use it occurs to someone to make use of the size of the participating group of, say, twenty people in order to surround the game so that it cannot go anywhere save into the trap. From then on, the modified solution, "battue in large groups," becomes a permanent component of the social stock of knowledge. The production of tools is another example effectively illustrative of the "improvement" of elements of knowledge over a great number of generations. The subjective forms of the "original" tool, which are only accidentally related to the general applicability of tools, are worn away until a social style of the "best" form of tools is developed.

The "improvement" of elements of knowledge in the course of their social transmission conflicts with another condition associated with their maintenance in the social stock of knowledge: the "rigidity" of the original fixation. A social stock of solutions to typical problems has above all the function of relieving the individual from wide provinces of "independently" acquired knowledge. There is normally no reason for the individual to seek other and "better" solutions to a problem that is already "solved," a problem whose "self-evident" solution was socially derived. Its social demonstration tends to hinder "independent" modifications, that is, the acceptance of modifications in the social stock of knowledge. The degree of "rigidity" (or reciprocally of "openness") is connected with the social structure and general characteristics of the relative-natural world view, and can only be ascertained in comparative historical and ethnological studies. In order to illustrate the problem, one may think, for instance, of the conservatism characterizing the use of a plow form in a society, or on the other hand of the rapid spread of electricity as an everyday natural occurrence.

It must finally be stressed that we are speaking here only of solutions to everyday problems. The radical shifting of perspectives, problems "being stood on their heads," which characterizes religious, philosophic, as well as scientific thought under certain circumstances, is foreign to the natural attitude. Radical shiftings of this sort can, however, mediately infiltrate into the everyday stock of knowledge of a society from every province of thought and knowledge.

The maintenance of elements of knowledge in a social stock of knowledge (irrespective of certain modifications and "improvements") presupposes two things. *First,* the social chain of transmission, i.e., the social structure, must remain preserved in its essential features. If radical changes affect the social structure (an event linked with far-reaching changes in the social stock of knowledge), the chain of transmission can be interrupted for certain elements of knowledge and even for whole provinces of knowledge. These then sink into oblivion. Knowledge, though, can naturally be "rediscovered" if the knowledge in question is, in addition to being passed on in oral tradition, also fixed in a fashion independent of an uninterrupted social chain of transmission (e.g., in the form of inscriptions, texts, etc.). But in that event it has ceased to be the taken-for-granted property of the individual socialized in the relative-natural world view. There is still another possibility to be mentioned. Given a certain complexity of the social structure, definite elements and provinces of knowledge can be taken out of the "official" transmission in the social structure, and thus can be passed on underground in peripheral social groups or strata. The history of ideas offers abundant examples of such underground traditions of knowledge.

The *second* presupposition for the maintenance of elements of knowledge in the social stock of knowledge is the continuing relevance of the problems whose "solutions" are presented by these elements. When the problem ceases to be socially relevant, the solution becomes pale and is, in the typical case, taken out of the social stock of knowledge. If roe disappear from the environment of a society, there is no reason to transmit knowledge concerning the deer hunt.

But a restriction must be considered here. What has been said holds good above all for the expressly pragmatic techniques of mastering everyday problems in life. The more it involves knowledge concerning non-everyday provinces of reality (e.g., religious knowledge), the more probable is the retention of this knowledge, though probably in changed, possibly mythological form. Notice further that it is conceivable that knowledge, which has become irrelevant from one viewpoint, is routinely passed on, since a social apparatus for its transmission is on hand. Only if there appear explicit, socially relevant motives for the removal of this knowledge from the social stock of knowledge, and if they prevail vis-à-vis the "Establishment," if a "reform" or "revolution" takes place, does this knowledge disappear from what is routinely passed on. The transmission of socially irrelevant knowledge (if we consider the concept of relevance narrowly and pragmatically) is connected with a factor which we discussed earlier. When the original element of knowledge is fixed historically or mythologically, it typically occupies an important place in the hierarchy of the stock of knowledge. Even if, considered strictly pragmatically, it has become socially irrelevant, it remains meaningful for what is taken for granted and the consciousness of tradition in this society. It may therefore continue to be preserved in the routine transmission of socially relevant knowledge.

But we must return to our main theme. The social stock of knowledge transmitted to the individual relieves him of the necessity of "independently" solving a whole series of important everyday occurrences. As a consequence of this, the individual has in principle the possibility of turning toward "new" and thus not-yet-solved problems that are also perhaps not even recognized. This is not just the case for "new" problems in everyday life. More importantly, such an unburdening allows one to turn to non-everyday problems.

Making use of this opportunity to acquire new knowledge "independently" is in turn socially conditioned. Because the prevailing social stock of knowledge frees every individual from finding "independent" solutions to broad provinces of typical everyday problems, one could in principle assume that new elements always flow out of subjective, more or less "independent" solutions to "new" problems, into the stock of knowledge. (One must add that the necessity to labor works against this: problems must not only be solved but also must be effectively mastered again and again.) The increase of new knowledge, the massing of knowledge in the social stock, is as a historical process dependent on the prevailing social structure as well as on the prevailing basic dimensions of the relative-natural world view. The historical processes in the accumulation of knowledge can produce extraordinarily wide differences both in the tempo of the massing and in the meaning-structures that are "amassed."

Let us take two extreme examples: a completely stable social stock of knowledge in a society in which all problems have been already "definitively" solved and in which "independent" advances in its acquisition do not occur; and on the other hand, a social

stock of knowledge built from the ground up, anew, from generation to generation. It is obvious that these extreme examples are
theoretical constructions. No society, no matter how "primitive,"
has an absolutely fixed stock of knowledge; no society, no matter
how revolutionary in its self-transformation, builds a new stock
of knowledge from the ground up. Different societies (i.e., types
of societies) can come close to one or the other limiting case. One
compares, for example, the development of the stone ax or the
formation of "folk wisdom" over countless generations with the
extraordinarily fast change of wide provinces of "healthy human
understanding" under the influence of technological revolutions
in the last centuries.

One of the most important tasks of the empirical sociology of
knowledge is the examination of structural factors (e.g., the
density of communication) and the dimensions of the relative-
natural world view (e.g., the religiously strengthened "fixity" of
some traditions), which play a decisive role in the historical processes of the accumulation of knowledge. A fundamental fact can
be seen in all historical variations: as soon as a social structure
provides for the routine transmission of socially relevant knowledge, then the principle of the division of labor is embodied in
the social stock of knowledge within a *historical* dimension, as a
"division of labor" between generations.

d. Concerning the development of higher forms of knowledge

The analysis of the social relevance of knowledge demonstrated that besides knowledge relevant for "everyone," knowledge relevant only for problems connected with specific social
roles is also incorporated in the social stock of knowledge.[21] But
while it turns out that generally relevant knowledge is routinely
transmitted to "everyone," [22] knowledge relevant for specific social roles is routinely transmitted only to the "role-holder" concerned. In short, no matter how simple one imagines the structure of a society to be, a constitutional analysis of social stocks
of knowledge shows that these must necessarily exhibit a certain
differentiation. In this connection one might again add that
ethnology knows of no society so "primitive" as to possess a completely "homogeneous culture," i.e., an absolutely undifferentiated
stock of knowledge.

21. See Chap. 4, B, 3, a.
22. See Chap. 4, B, 3, b.

Indeed, when we speak on this level, with regard to a differentiation of the social stock of knowledge, we mean only that the *routine* transference of determinate elements of the stock of knowledge is differentiated. But it must be established that, on this level, the whole stock of knowledge is still fundamentally accessible to "everyone." This first form of differentiation is important here insofar as it constitutes the basic presupposition for the specialization of knowledge and the development of "higher forms of knowledge."

We now want to inquire into the further presuppositions for specializations of knowledge. It is easy to find an abstract answer to this question: the historical process of accumulating knowledge. It is in any case clear that generally relevant knowledge exhibits only comparatively slight, and then only extremely slow, changes. Knowledge of universal relevance is highly anonymous and presents solutions to problems that must be mastered again and again by "everyone" in the routine of daily life. In a given society, the "scope" of such problems remains comparatively unchanged.

It is a different matter with the differentiated provinces of the social stock of knowledge. Here the acquisition and transmission of knowledge are within institutionalized purposes and meaning-contexts. Role-specific knowledge is thus much more inclined to a certain systematization and (we want to use the concept here with caution) "rationalization" than is "common sense." The relation of means to end is more clearly circumscribed in role-specific problems. Solutions to problems can in general be learned and passed on in an explicit way. Thus there is a greater chance for such solutions to come within the grasp of reflective consciousness. And, finally, while generally relevant knowledge can be passed on from "everyone" to "everyone," role-specific knowledge is passed on from specific role-bearers to other specific role-bearers. Thus the opportunity arises for institutionally isolating that knowledge. We will soon return to this point. But first it must be established that the historical processes of accumulating knowledge tend in general to enrich the differentiated provinces of the social stock of knowledge more than those having universal relevance.

Generally relevant knowledge in the social stock of knowledge is obviously knowledge that "everyone" *can* in principle learn. This circumstance is connected with the relative invariability of the "range" of "common sense." The accumulation of differentiated knowledge in the social stock has as a consequence the fact that certain provinces of knowledge are no longer surveyed by "everyone." Not only is "everyone" not motivated to learn certain role-specific knowledge; not only is all differentiated knowledge not routinely transmitted to "everyone"—but in addition, more and more tedious and complicated processes of learning are requisite for assimilating the knowledge. Thus, one person can learn only one, and another person only another, differentiated province of the social stock of knowledge. Formally expressed: the social distribution of knowledge is necessary because of the accumulation of differentiated knowledge. It makes no difference here whether the learning of specific knowledge is socially conditioned, whether it is concerned with socially "imposed" roles, or whether the choice of roles and the learning of role-specific knowledge remain left to subjective motives. This is a "structural" problem that finds different "solutions" in different types of societies. In any case, the *routine* transmission of this knowledge is anchored in the prevailing social structure.

A further circumstance follows from this. Since specific knowledge (e.g., its application) is anchored in the social structure, "everyone" need not learn it in order to share in the pragmatic utility of the problem's solution. When a problem confronts the uninitiated, for the mastery of which his own knowledge does not suffice, he need only turn to one who is initiated (the smith, the physician, etc.). The presupposition here is only that, "where" specific knowledge can be consulted, such knowledge is a component of general knowledge. But since such knowledge obviously is generally relevant, it is objectivated and routinely transmitted to everyone. Conversely, knowledge about the possibility of consulting specialists about specific problems functions as a further motive for leaving differentiated provinces of knowledge to "specialists." [23] And for their part, the "specialists" become the uninitiated in other problem areas, if they are not completely relieved by society's division of labor of the solution (i.e., the everyday mastery) of certain "general" problems, such as the search for nourishment. If the latter obtains, they can be dedicated all the more intensively to their "specialty." This in turn accelerates the further accumulation of knowledge in differentiated provinces of knowledge.

The "relief" of which we were just speaking has its institu-

23. See Chap. 4, D, 2, b.

tional basis in the division of labor, viz., in the differentiation of roles which divides labor. This, though, leads in turn to the institutional anchoring of differentiated provinces of knowledge: its acquisition, transmission, and cultivation are connected exclusively or almost exclusively with specific social roles. Indeed, this provides the basic condition for a further systematization of different provinces which is decisive for the development of higher forms of knowledge. Knowledge which is connected with specific social roles, which is borne by these roles, and whose further transmission is part of the range of tasks that belong to them, can be freed from the immediate context of acts involved in the concrete solutions to problems: it can become the Object of reflection. Certain solutions to problems can be grasped as concerned with problems that possess a typical relation. They can be examined with regard to their compatibility and thus can be ordered in more or less systematic meaning-contexts. The further this (institutionally established) systematization progresses, the more the related elements of knowledge unequivocally form a delimited province of knowledge whose inner meaning-structure gains a certain autonomy vis-à-vis other provinces. As a consequence, such a province of knowledge develops, to a certain extent, its own logic and its own methodology, just as it must also have its own "pedagogy" (because of the requisites of the role-bound transmission of knowledge).

With this we have cited all fundamentally necessary presuppositions for the development of higher forms of knowledge. It is clear that, up to a point, it will be arbitrary at which level of a given historical development one may speak of higher forms of knowledge. As soon as the basic presuppositions are fulfilled, a province of knowledge becomes separated and attains a certain autonomy in its meaning-structure. But it can be left to social-historical analysis to decide whether it will use the formation of an unequivocal theoretical attitude out of the more or less "de-pragmatized" act-contexts of knowledge as the primary criterion of separation and autonomy—or whether it will rely on institutional criteria. Thus, does one talk of higher forms of knowledge in the case of the thought of the pre-Socratics, or only after the creation of the Academy? It hardly needs to be stressed that in the systematization of a province of knowledge, in the "pedagogy" of the knowledge concerned, etc., the existence of a written tradition plays an important empirical role as against simply an oral one.

To speak of a certain "de-pragmatization" of knowledge and the formation of a theoretical attitude does not yet, by any means, imply the development of purely theoretical knowledge. The anchoring of even extensively systematized provinces of knowledge in the social structure stipulates, to begin with, that knowledge is detached only incompletely from the immediate act-context and the necessities of its use in concrete situations. Thus "specialists of knowledge" remain throughout just "specialists of acts," as it were "general practitioners," to stay with the example used previously. On the other hand, however, the processes of institutional specialization, the separation and systematization of provinces of knowledge, and the inception of a theoretical attitude, which have been discussed, are the basis for the further possibility of historical development: the separation of knowledge from action, of theory from practice. The detachment of theoretical areas of knowledge from lifeworldly act-contexts, the progressive de-pragmatization, is a highly specific social-historical process, which is due to the institutional, economic-political establishment of the "theory" and "self-regulation" of the history of ideas. The dialectic between institutional and intellectual conditions is clear in the role of the Alexandrian library during the blossoming of knowledge in the Hellenistic age. But it must be stressed that the "applicability" of theoretical knowledge must still be presupposed in principle, even if a series of institutionalized levels is inserted between knowledge and use ("applied scientists," "practitioner," etc.).

Here we must add that in the course of the development of higher forms of knowledge a certain separation arises between the "technique" of mastering everyday (in the narrower sense) pragmatic problems and the provinces of knowledge related to non-everyday levels of reality. The kind and degree of this separation are, doubtless, variously expressed (one thinks, for instance, of the practical and religious moments in Pythagorean thought as compared to the conception of mathematics after Newton). In addition, the dividing line between everyday and non-everyday levels of reality is drawn differently in different societies. It is clear that in "primitive" societies a more or less systematized "technique" (the hunt, farming, conduct of war) is in a stricter meaning-relation to non-everyday levels of reality (e.g., mythology, magic). It is even questionable whether such meaning-relations have been completely abolished in modern society, in spite of the "rationality of goals" in its institutions and the separation of the areas of competency of technology, science, and religion.

We must be satisfied here with having shown the general relation between, on the one hand, the differentiation of knowledge in the social stock of knowledge, in the historical processes of the accumulation of knowledge, and the institutionalization of specialties of knowledge; and, on the other hand, the development of higher forms of knowledge. An examination of the interweaving of these factors in concrete historical processes and the testing of causal and functional hypotheses concerning the development of higher forms of knowledge in various societies belongs to the domain of the empirical sociology of knowledge. Let us merely touch on a few of the problems not yet sufficiently explained. What limitations are imposed by the oral tradition on the tempo of the accumulation of knowledge and on the systematization of provinces of knowledge? What are the minimal economic presuppositions for the institutionalization of the specialized transmission of knowledge, for the formation of schools, etc.? What role is played by writing in the fixation of "scientific" traditions? What relevance do ecological (tempo of communication!), political (e.g., dynastically promoted "writing of history"!), etc., moments have in the development of higher forms of knowledge?

[C] THE STRUCTURE OF THE SOCIAL STOCK OF KNOWLEDGE

1. THE SOCIAL STOCK OF KNOWLEDGE AND THE SOCIAL DISTRIBUTION OF KNOWLEDGE [24]

SEDIMENTED SUBJECTIVE EXPERIENCES form the *subjective* stock of knowledge in the life-world. The former are conditioned by the stratifications of the life-world, and the sedimentation of experiences in the stock of knowledge results from subjective relevance structures. The structure of the subjective stock of knowledge is determined by the processes of the acquisition of knowledge.[25] The arrangement of elements in the former, according to different grades of credibility, familiarity, consist-

24. [See *Collected Papers*, II, 120–34.]
25. See esp. Chap. 3, A, 2, b.

ency, and accuracy, refers back on the one hand to the limitation of, and on the other hand to the unity of, a subjective stream of experience and biography.

The *social* stock of knowledge refers back only mediately to the subjective acquisition of knowledge.[26] The elements of the social stock of knowledge obviously arise from the processes inherent in the subjective acquisition of knowledge. But the incorporation of subjectively acquired elements in the social stock of knowledge presupposes intersubjective processes of objectivation and the expression of social relevances. And, the historical accumulation of knowledge is dependent on institutionalized processes in the transmission of knowledge. The development of a social stock of knowledge is thus in no way analogous to the development of a subjective one. In view of the previous analyses, it may appear unnecessary that we here stress this point again. It is, though, important to keep in mind a related circumstance: the *structure* of the social stock of knowledge does not have dimensions corresponding to those of the subjective stock of knowledge. Because the structure of the former, which is developed through the processes of the historical accumulation of knowledge, is determined by the institutionalized processes in the transference of knowledge, it corresponds to the prevailing social distribution of knowledge.

These considerations present a fundamental problem. The description of the subjective stock of knowledge and its structure could in general refer to the characteristic features of subjectivity. The processes and structures described directly depend on the temporal, spatial, and social accumulations of subjective experiences in the life-world. They depend on the structure of subjective relevances, on the unity of the flow of experience, and on the finitude of a biography. But as was just stated, the structure of the social stock of knowledge depends only mediately on the characteristic features of subjectivity; it cannot be directly derived from them. Its structure depends, first, on the characteristic features of intersubjectivity, namely, on the conditions of communication—that is, of the objectivation and interpretation of knowledge. Thus in the following discussion, we will see to what extent it is possible to deduce the structure of any social stock of knowledge "whatever" from the conditions for the genesis of any of them "whatever." Second, the structure of historical

26. See Chap. 4, B, 1.

stocks of knowledge is derived from specific historical processes of accumulating knowledge and from its institutionalized transmission. The questions concerning how elements objectivated in the social stock of knowledge are apportioned in any given society, and which concrete elements are routinely transmitted to certain institutionally fixed types of persons ("holders" of specific roles) can only be answered within the framework of the empirical sociology of knowledge. We must be content here to develop the formal types for the social apportionment of knowledge from the general conditions for the genesis of any social stock of knowledge "whatever." Thus, we intend to mark out the spectrum of variation in the structural differentiation of historical stocks of knowledge as conditioned by the accumulation of knowledge.

2. FORMAL TYPES OF THE SOCIAL DISTRIBUTION OF KNOWLEDGE

a. The impossibility of a uniform distribution

Let us now try to construct a formal type of the distribution of knowledge, corresponding to certain assumptions of the natural attitude. In another place [27] we examined the fact that the experience of fellow-men and of the social world proceeds on the whole from the general thesis of the reciprocity of perspectives: I assume that fellow-men are "essentially" similar to me, fundamentally experience the world in the same way that I do. The implication of this thesis which interests us here is the assumption that fellow-men know the same things I do and vice versa. Now, what structure must a social stock of knowledge have in order to correspond to these assumptions, not only approximately or sufficiently for certain practical purposes, but exactly?

If A is to know the same as B, C, etc., B the same as A, C, etc., C the same as A, B, etc., the "range" of the social stock of knowledge must be identical with the "range" of subjective stocks of knowledge. What presuppositions must be fulfilled for the development of such a completely, uniformly distributed social stock of knowledge? First, all subjectively acquired knowledge must be socially relevant. This could only be the case if all problems imposed on A were also imposed on B, C, etc., if all problems imposed on B were also imposed on A, C, etc. Second, the condi-

27. See Chap. 2, B, 5, a.

tions of communication in space and time must be disregarded: objectivation of knowledge and interpretation of objectivation must be fully congruent in order to avoid "changes" in the element of knowledge in the course of its being passed on. Third, the consequences of biographically conditioned, subjectively different sequences of acquiring knowledge must be excluded from the "content" and distribution of the elements of the social stock of knowledge. And fourth, the possibility for the further accumulation of knowledge must be completely eliminated: the ability to absorb further knowledge is not limitless as a consequence of the necessities of praxis, of the continual routine mastering of the recurring, already "solved" problems of daily life. After the common social stock of knowledge has attained a certain "range," all further acquisition of knowledge must be curtailed, as long as we do not add the still more unrealistic assumption that every further acquisition brings with it a corresponding jettisoning of "old" elements in the stock of knowledge, which is matching, simultaneous, and identical for everyone.

It is therefore clear that the construction of a completely similar distribution of knowledge is based on untenable assumptions. The assumption of an undifferentiated "presocial nature" of man is contrary to reality. No matter how the differences between man and woman, young and old, strong and weak, etc., may be socially expressed, we cannot assume that all problems are imposed on them in the same way, nor that the "same" problems are presented to them in an identical fashion. Moreover, the exclusion of a social expression of the different relevances contradicts the results of the analysis of the social accumulation of subjective experiences from the life-world. It contradicts as well the results of the analysis of subjective relevance structures. The exclusion of the biographically conditioned sequences of acquiring knowledge, and of the intersubjective conditions for its communication, is in contradiction to one of the essential presuppositions for the development of any social stock of knowledge whatever. The same holds good for the assumption which would exclude the necessary effects of the transference of knowledge to its accumulation.

From this we must conclude that a completely uniform social distribution of knowledge cannot exist. But for a moment let us disregard the fact that the assumptions at the basis of the construction of such a type for the distribution of knowledge are as unrealistic as they are incompatible with the conditions for the development of any social stock of knowledge whatever. Thus, even the construction of such a type itself contains the tendency to a lack of uniformity in the distribution of knowledge, however insignificant it may be. As soon as A acquires an element of knowledge and transmits it to B, then the "same" element of knowledge that is "independently" acquired by A is for B "socially derived." Also, A's subjective stock of knowledge is different from B's in respect to "identity of content." Objectivation and interpretation of all further elements of knowledge thus necessarily depend on the subjective stocks of knowledge and relevance structures that are differentiated, however insignificantly. Nevertheless, the "identity" of elements of knowledge sufficient for most practical purposes depends on the processes of idealization and anonymization. These, though, presuppose the intersubjective conditions of communication and an, at least, minimal differentiation of social relevances. In any case, absolutely homogeneous knowledge is therefore unimaginable.

b. Simple social distribution of knowledge

As was just shown, the assumptions which would have to be posited as the basis of a completely uniform distribution of knowledge in society are untenable. If we attempt to construct the formal type of a social distribution of knowledge characterized by the least possible unevenness, we can, however, proceed from those assumptions. They are to be relaxed gradually, solely in order to take into account the basic data of subjective experience in the life-world and the conditions for intersubjective communication—and until they are consistent with the structural presuppositions for the genesis of a social stock of knowledge. As soon as this is the case, they can be held as the valid assumptions at the basis of the simplest case of the social distribution of knowledge.

First, a differentiation in the "presocial nature" of man, no matter how minimal, is to be taken as established. We need not be concerned here with the question regarding the ontological status of this differentiation. The problems involved in the live corporeality of man that are contained in that question belong, in any case, to the area of inquiry of philosophical and biological anthropology. It is sufficient for our purposes that we have established that a differentiation in the "presocial nature" of man is a given component of the life-world, which may be taken as a start-ing point for the expression of relatively simple differences in social relevances. It hardly needs to be stressed that "biologically" established social relevances are not simply reducible to biological differences. In the present context all that is significant for us is that the simplest differences in social relevances are founded on "presocial" differentiations of some sort. Of many possible con-crete examples, only the one nearest at hand will be advanced: the manner in which differentiated social relevance structures for men and women are marked out.

It is further taken as given that the temporal and biographical differences in subjective streams of experience codetermine an individual perspective in what are otherwise extensively "social-ized" relevance structures—relevance structures on the basis of which experiences are sedimented in the subjective stock of knowledge. There, differences play a role in the processes by which elements of the social stock of knowledge are transmitted. They are socially relevant and are themselves in a certain sense "socialized": learning sequences are embedded in social rele-vance-contexts. The processes of transmission are differentiated in the dimension of *social* time and with reference to socially cut-lined, biographical categories. An obvious concrete example is the socially determined conjunction of age levels with learning sequences (i.e., socially defined, not "biographical" or "psycho-logical" categories).

And, as a last point, one must abandon the assumption of a complete rupture of the accumulation of knowledge. In the con-struction of the formal type or model of a simple social distribu-tion of knowledge, we may assume that knowledge is accumu-lated only very slowly. Accordingly, we may suppose that the specialization of knowledge is only of small proportions and de-velops no quasi-autonomous "higher forms of knowledge." From this follows a circumstance of the greatest importance in the characterization of a simple social distribution of knowledge: all knowledge matured in the social stock of knowledge is in principle accessible to everyone. More exactly: there is nothing in the *structure* of the knowledge that would stand in the way of its acquisition by anyone. If we do not consider institutional bar-riers, which more or less (for reasons having nothing to do with the structure of knowledge as such) stand in the way of the ac-quisition of certain knowledge by particular social types (e.g., secret knowledge), the uneven distribution of knowledge is still based exclusively on the social differentiation of routine processes of transmission.

With the construction of this formal model, we proceed, so to speak, from the fact that not all problems are imposed in the same way on all people and that they cannot be imposed on everyone at the same time. If this occurs within social relevance structures in even a simple form, a differentiation of the routine transference of the "problem's solution" is thereby determined: first, according to the socially defined types of persons for whom the solutions are relevant, and second, according to socially defined temporal-biographical moments. A social stock of knowledge, which did not at least exhibit an unevenness of distribution of its elements in these two dimensions, would be quite unimaginable.

Let us then try to illustrate, with the help of the previously mentioned concrete examples, such a conceivably simple, social distribution of knowledge, taking into account what is fundamentally given in subjective lifeworldly experience, and the presuppositions of intersubjective communication. The basic reserve of the social stock of knowledge consists of elements relevant for everyone. These elements are routinely transmitted to "everyone," and the routine transference is institutionally secured. The processes of transmission are, in a way (again institutionally secured), temporally and biographically graduated, for example according to the levels of age ("youth" and "adult"). At every given point of time all "normal adults" possess, therefore, all those elements of the social stock of knowledge that are socially established as relevant for "everyone." Young people, in contrast, possess only one part of the supply of such elements of knowledge, which is also socially established. But at the same time the youth know that they will in the course of their biography acquire the generally relevant elements of knowledge still unavailable to them, and indeed at a point in time that is likewise socially established. Depending on the relative complexity of the knowledge to be acquired, depending on the extent to which essentially necessary sequences of learning must follow upon one another, there will be relatively short preparations for initiation that institutionally prescribe transitions (e.g., puberty rites), or relatively tedious teaching and learning periods.

Further, there are, in this social stock of knowledge, elements relevant only for men and others relevant only for women. The one type will routinely be transferred only to men, the other only to women. Thus "normal men" should be in possession of both generally relevant knowledge and that relevant only for men. Moreover, "normal women" should likewise be in possession of generally relevant knowledge and of that relevant only for women. But since the socially prescribed temporal-biographical differentiation of processes of transmission holds good also for the "masculine" and "feminine" elements, a further aspect is added. At any given point in time, strictly speaking, only "normal adult men" are in possession of the elements of knowledge relevant for everyone as well as those relevant only for men, while "normal young men" possess only the socially prescribed components of the general supply of elements of knowledge as well as those relevant for men. The same obviously holds good also for young and adult "normal women."

Though we have used obvious (and, empirically, probably also the most important) concrete examples of divisions according to age and differences according to sex, it must be stressed that a generally valid *material* determination of the provinces of the social stock of knowledge is not possible. It can probably be said that the conditions which are the basis of a simple social distribution of knowledge determine the arrangement of the social stock of knowledge into "general knowledge" and "special knowledge." But what belongs to the latter classification in one society can be general knowledge in another. And, what at a given point of time is specific in one society can also become general knowledge without changing to a more complex type of social distribution of knowledge, and vice versa.

Even when we use the more general categories developed in the analysis of the subjective stock of knowledge, we come up against the impossibility of a material determination of the structure of the social stock of knowledge. General as well as special knowledge can include skills, usages, recipes, and explicit elements of knowledge. Surely there are definite skills, practical knowledge, and knowledge of recipes that belong almost universally to "normal" general knowledge: walking, typical orientations in time and space, "generally valid" norms of conduct. By means of language they form the basic reserve of everyone's relative-natural world view. But beyond this nothing can be said, if one does not want to venture into the sphere of activity belonging to the empirical sociology of knowledge. And it surely need not be stressed that historical and ethnological material affords enough of the multiplicity which belongs to the province of special knowledge of skills, usages, and recipes.

There is another consideration which must again be taken up in the analysis of the subjective correlates of the social distribution of knowledge.[28] General knowledge is routinely transmitted to everyone, special knowledge only to determinate social types, but *fundamentally* all knowledge is accessible to everyone. Even if there is not a motive for "everyone" to learn special knowledge, even if institutional barriers oppose such an acquisition, "everyone" knows, in simple social distributions of knowledge, which social types are in possession of which forms of special knowledge. In other words, the social distribution of special knowledge is in turn an element of knowledge belonging to general knowledge. Thus, in simple social distributions, reality and above all the social world still remain relatively surveyable by "everyone."

c. Complex social distribution of knowledge

In the above description a distinction was made between general knowledge that is evenly distributed, and special knowledge that exhibits a role-specific, and thus uneven, distribution. Equality or inequality of distribution was thus at the same time a criterion distinguishing general and special knowledge. If the formal type of a complex social distribution of knowledge is to be characterized in this way, that is to say, if a certain "inequality" is similarly manifest in the distribution of general knowledge, then one must explain in greater detail what is meant by such an "inequality."

Let us remember that general knowledge consists of the socially objectivated solutions to such problems as are relevant for "everyone." But what does "everyone" mean here? It hardly need be stressed again that problems confronting "everyone" also appear individually in the meaning-horizon of a "unique" biography. The typical, socially objectivated solutions to problems that are taken over by the individual thus necessarily undergo certain idiosyncratic variations within his "unique" subjective meaning-context. In addition, the transmission of the elements in the social stock of knowledge takes place in concrete social relations, which for the individual occur within the meaning-horizon of

28. See Chap. 4, D.

"uniqueness." This is also a source of the "idiosyncratic" modifications of typical solutions to problems. But all this only means that absolute equality in the distribution of the elements in the social stock of knowledge is in principle impossible—a circumstance already referred to. But as long as one is concerned only with "idiosyncratic" modifications which occur only "after" the subjective acquisition of the socially objectivated elements of knowledge, these remain essentially meaningless for the structure of the social stock of knowledge. There we would be justified in saying that the simple social distribution is among other things characterized by the fact that general knowledge is evenly (more exactly: relatively equally) distributed. Here, the unavoidable inequalities in the distribution of general knowledge are not role-bound but rather (with reference to the social structure and the structure of the social stock of knowledge) can be considered "accidental."

Such purely "accidental" variations in general knowledge (such as remain irrelevant for the structure of the social stock of knowledge) can be assumed for extremely simple forms of society. Only in societies with extremely simple divisions of labor, and without established social strata, are the problems that are imposed on "everyone" also presented to everyone in essentially similar apprehensional perspectives and contexts of relevance. But as soon as the division of labor is even a little bit further developed, and as soon as social levels are established, the perspectives in which the "same" problems are apprehended decline. This is not the progressive differentiation of special knowledge that obviously accompanies the progressive division of labor. Rather, what occurs here is that similar "biographies" (i.e., similar biographical categories of subjective experience) develop in the course of the progressive division of labor. These biographies form the basis for more or less unified apprehensional perspectives. These perspectives which are conditioned by the social world are in part socially established, as for instance in the common relevance structures of more or less well-defined social levels. The transmission of elements of general knowledge is differentiated accordingly. The basic aspects of this state of affairs were already pointed out in the analysis of the "filter effect" of the social structure "behind" the earliest we-relations.[29]

29. See Chap. 4, A, 1, a.

Language offers an obvious example of the differentiated versions and transmission of general knowledge. As a component of the general knowledge of every society, language can be relatively equally distributed, because subjective variations in the form of idiosyncratic usages remain socially irrelevant. Given a certain complexity in the social structure, language is converted into socially conditioned, socially established, and socially transmitted "versions": as dialect, courtly language, "social dialect," etc. But the same holds true in other provinces of general knowledge—ranging from skills, as for instance the style of walking peculiar to a class (e.g., of the soldier, the city dweller, etc.), to explicit elements and provinces of knowledge, as for instance "religious knowledge" (the Catholicism of the rural population, the Catholicism of the intellectuals, etc.).

It is clear that here one is not concerned with specialized knowledge which is role-specific, but rather with general knowledge, even if this occurs in socially differentiated "versions." One is still concerned with solutions to generally relevant problems whose basic features are present everywhere. Only in this restricted sense can one speak of an "inequality" in the social distribution of general knowledge. But it is just this "inequality" which is one of the most important characteristics of the complex social distribution of knowledge.

The latter involves a further partitioning and "specialization" of special knowledge. In comparison with a simple social distribution of knowledge, this can be regarded first of all as simply a quantitative difference. Through progressive partitioning and "specialization," the various provinces of special knowledge gain a certain, albeit limited, "autonomy." The various provinces of special knowledge become progressively further "removed" from general knowledge. The distance between "laymen" and "experts" becomes greater. On the one hand, relatively involved, more or less tedious, meaningful presuppositions (learning sequences) come to precede the acquisition of special knowledge. On the other hand, even the transmission of special knowledge depends increasingly on role-specific prerequisites. This is tantamount to saying that the various provinces of special knowledge are "specialized" as meaning-structures, as well as that the transmission of knowledge is itself institutionally specialized.

From this it follows that the acquisition of special knowledge necessarily becomes more and more a "career." Above and beyond institutional barriers, the finitude of the individual biography prevents the learning of special knowledge in its totality. We are not referring here to the fact that the acquisition of special knowledge in its totality is improbable in the concrete case, since hardly any motive exists for it in a society with a division of labor, or the fact that institutional barriers allow only certain typical, socially determined persons to acquire determinate provinces of special knowledge. Indeed, it is of significance that, given a complex social distribution of knowledge, special knowledge (in its totality) is no longer *in principle* accessible to "everyone."

From this there is a further consequence, characteristic of complex social distributions of knowledge. The fact that there are different provinces of special knowledge is a part of general knowledge. The factual social distribution of special knowledge is no longer a part of the supply of "equally" distributed general knowledge. Furthermore, in general, even the knowledge of the outlines of the structure of special knowledge and its basic content becomes more indistinct. This means, first, that the social stock of knowledge in its totality can no longer be surveyed by the individual and also, second, that this lack of an inclusive view is itself variously "distributed" within the society. What repercussions this has for the social structures is a question of the greatest interest for the empirical sociology of knowledge. Here it can only be pointed out that knowledge can become more and more of a power factor in complex social distributions of knowledge. Groups of "experts" form one of the institutional catalysts of power concentration. On the other hand, there is always the possibility of a conflict between different groups of "experts" in a struggle for a "power monopoly." A further epistemo-sociologically relevant possibility associated with the highly complex social distributions of knowledge is that some "experts" become, socially, nearly completely invisible.

The main characteristics of a complex social distribution of knowledge are "inequality" in the distribution of general knowledge, progressive partitioning and specialization of special knowledge into various, more or less "autonomous," provinces, and the corresponding institutional specialization of the transmission of special knowledge. The unsurveyability of the social stock of knowledge in its entirety is a further subjective correlate. Since in that case we can also speak of a complex social distribution of knowledge even where fully developed, higher forms of knowledge are lacking, a brief indication of the relation of higher forms of knowledge to such a society will suffice. In the comments concerning higher forms of knowledge,[30] it was shown that the separation of elements of knowledge into "autonomous" provinces of meaning and their institutional specialization conceals within itself the possibility for progressive "de-pragmatization" and "theoretization." If, therefore, the formal type or model of the complex social distribution of knowledge does not necessarily include the ready availability of higher forms of knowledge, then at least the basic presuppositions for the development of these forms are already on hand in this type of distribution of knowledge. If, then, higher forms of knowledge do in fact develop, it must first be noted that these exhibit a role-specific social distribution, in general analogous to the distribution of highly specific, relatively "autonomous" provinces of special knowledge, and that the transmission of higher forms is institutionally quite specialized. If indeed a high degree of "autonomy" is reached—which is only the case given very definite socio-historical presuppositions—the higher forms of knowledge form "ideal meaning-contexts," structures of "pure knowledge." To a certain extent these can become detached from the social structure and can become relatively independent of the routine institutional transmission of knowledge. This by no means implies that higher forms of knowledge are not conditioned, objectivated, as well as transmitted socially. But in their historical "special destiny" as "pure knowledge," they again become accessible to "everyone." The individual who re-enacts the meaningful "learning sequences" can grasp the Objective meaning of this "pure knowledge," even if he is generations removed and within the most different, socially conditioned, subjective relevance-contexts. We cannot go into here either the questions concerning the social perspectives through which the Objective meaning of "pure knowledge" is apprehended, or the forms of objectivating knowledge which this involves. These questions belong within the provinces of competence of empirical sociology (e.g., the, as it were, Pierian accessibility to "texts"). Furthermore, it hardly needs to be stressed that these observations neither indicate a theory of a "free-floating intelligence" nor necessarily grant a special ontological status to the "ideal meaning-contexts."

30. See Chap. 4, B, 3, d.

3. CONCERNING CHANGE IN THE SOCIAL DISTRIBUTION OF KNOWLEDGE

The description of the formal types of social distribution of knowledge is especially relevant within the framework of the present investigation. It illuminates important social presuppositions required for the development of typical similarities and typical differences in subjective stocks of knowledge.[31] But in addition, the formal types of the social distribution of knowledge can even have a certain heuristic value for the empirical sociology of knowledge. If they are to serve as "models" for the analysis of concrete structures in the social stocks of knowledge, they must be fitted into the "causal" explanatory schemata for the historical reciprocity between social structures and social stocks of knowledge. To go into the questions connected with this would naturally go far beyond the compass of the present investigation. The previous formal analysis can, however, serve as a starting point for some general considerations concerning the dynamics of change in the social distribution of knowledge. These can then have a certain relevance for the empirical sociology of knowledge.

It is obvious that the "proportion" of general to special knowledge is changeable. In simple social distributions of knowledge, general knowledge takes in a much broader province of the social stock of knowledge than does special knowledge. In any case, the historical accumulation of the latter is in a necessary, even if in no way simple, relation to the prevailing quantity of general knowledge.

Apart from that, the "content" of general as well as of special knowledge changes. For example, to establish that in a nomadic tribe the knowledge of a (pragmatically oriented) plant-classification system belongs to general knowledge, but reading and writing belong to special knowledge, while things are just the reverse in a modern industrial society, is just as trivial as to establish a "line" from Babylonian astrology to modern astronomy by means of a history of ideas. But how such a change in "content" is connected to the change in the "proportions" of general and special knowledge, and through what "causal" relation such a change is connected to change in social structure, is a matter to be re-

31. See also Chap. 4, D.

searched much more systematically by the sociology of knowledge.

What is straightforward, general knowledge in one generation and routinely transferred to "everyone" can sooner or later appear in strikingly different "versions" conditioned by the social structure. This knowledge can later become special knowledge, which is now transmitted only within a social class, a sect, etc. And on the other hand, "new" problems can crop up which potentially affect "everyone," but whose relevance is not yet grasped by "everyone." The "solutions" involved may then be socially stabilized as special knowledge belonging to a group of experts. Under what conditions does this special knowledge become general knowledge? Certain institutions can limit the development of the former into the latter, can make it impossible, or promote it. But this development can also involve an automatic trickling-through of this knowledge from one social class to the other. What motivations underlie the "Objective" meaning of knowledge, what follows this or the opposite dynamics? Obviously, one can go no further with categories such as "intellectual development," "regression," etc.

To conclude, still one particular problem must be mentioned. The differentiation of "versions" of general knowledge can, given certain socio-historical presuppositions, progress to the point where broad provinces of general knowledge finally become the special property of social groups, classes, etc., often in the form of "ideologies." If, in a borderline case, the province of common knowledge and common relevances shrinks beyond a critical point, communication within the society is barely possible. There emerge "societies within the society." Whether one can then still speak of a common society naturally depends not only on the structure of the social stock of knowledge but also on the factual social structure. But, above all, it depends on the distribution of power. In general, in modern industrial societies such a differentiation of the "versions" of the common good arises between the most varying ideological points of view, and is usually presented as a "social," indeed "political" problem. For that reason, an attempt is frequently made to guarantee an "equal" transmission of the essential provinces of the common good and to guarantee the "same" access to different provinces of special knowledge. This is done by creating highly specialized institutions of transmission, thereby minimizing the "filter effect" of the family.

[D] THE SUBJECTIVE CORRELATES OF THE SOCIAL STOCK OF KNOWLEDGE

1. THE SOCIAL STOCK OF KNOWLEDGE AS A SUBJECTIVE POS-SESSION, AS AN IDEAL MEANING-STRUCTURE, AND AS AN OBJECT OF SUBJECTIVE EXPERIENCE

WE HAVE DISCUSSED various aspects of the relation between the social and the subjective stock of knowledge, as a basic dimension of the dialectic between man and society. After an analysis of the presuppositions and basic structures of the subjective, the origin of the social stock of knowledge in subjective knowledge was described. Then it was shown how the elements of the social enter the subjective stock of knowledge. But there is still one question to answer: how is the social stock of knowledge presented in subjective experience?

First, it should be noted that the essential elements of the former do not appear as such in the latter. That is, they do not appear at all as Objective social data, as aspects of the factual social structure, as "conventions," etc. Rather, they are for the individual a taken-for-granted possession, a component of his subjectivity. The habits derived from the social stock of knowledge are his habits, the explicit elements of knowledge taken over from it are his knowledge, the relevance structures originating from it function as his motives and categories of explanation. Since this point was extensively examined in the previous analysis, we do not need to go into it any further. We can be content to stress that for the normal adult in the natural attitude of daily life the social stock of knowledge is divested of its social character, insofar as it has entered into the subjective stock of knowledge. It appears in the form of a taken-for-granted subjective possession.

However, certain provinces of the social stock of knowledge, as for instance the quasi-autonomous structures of the special and, above all, the higher forms of knowledge, can confront the individual as more or less ideal systems. This is so even when they are taken over in the subjective stock of knowledge as explicit. This point as well has already been extensively discussed. We only want to emphasize that such quasi-autonomous, more or less ideal, meaning-structures appear to the individual in a manner divested of both their social as well as their subjective character. The degree of ideality possessed by a mode of appearance is historically variable. It depends equally on the history of ideas in that province of knowledge and on the structural conditions involved in freeing knowledge from the social structure. Thus, language can appear as subjective possession and as something socially given. But given determinate conditions, it can also appear as an ideal system, depending on the historical (and biographical) situation of the individual. One can think of the "increase" in the ideality of geometry, to introduce another example. Above all, the history of Occidental ideas includes many examples of the development of higher forms of knowledge into meaning-structures which appear only as "pure" ideality, as "spirit" freed from society and subjectivity. Finally, the social stock of knowledge has a mode of appearance in subjective experience, which refers expressly to the social nature of knowledge: the subjective analogues of the social distribution of knowledge. Everyone, that is, every normal adult, knows that his knowledge is not "complete," and he knows that he knows some things better than others. This consciousness of not knowing, and of knowing with varying quality, is the basic correlate of the social distribution of knowledge. We now ask what experiences correspond to this knowledge, in order to turn our attention toward the description of the specific expression of this knowledge in its relation to the social distribution of knowledge.

The biographical course of the subjective acquisition of knowledge includes (even if we leave out of consideration the fact that a large part of the subjective elements of knowledge is socially derived) in its meaning-horizon the implication that the acquisition of knowledge is really never "definitively" closed. New problems arise for which new solutions must be found. Further, some situations demand that elements of knowledge already sedimented in the stock of knowledge must be modified. For example, they must be transformed into higher degrees of clarity. This implication, necessarily on hand in the meaning-horizon of the subjective acquisition of knowledge, can lead to the conscious recognition that one does not know everything and that even that which one knows could be inadequate. Indeed, this insight thus arises in subjective experience as such.

Something further must be added to this. The acquired knowledge is only in part "independently" acquired. It is, to a great extent, socially derived. The individual knows that he learned it from Others. Since essential elements of the subjective stock of knowledge were transmitted by certain people, these fellow-men are necessarily grasped by the individual as people who know "more" or know "better," at least at a point in time immediately preceding the subjective appropriation of the knowledge in question. Such experiences are naturally most prevalent in the earliest we-relations. The "omniscience" of the parents is typically a part of the early phases of socialization. But even when the level of knowledge of the parents is reached, normal adults cannot deny the possibility that other fellow-men, in one way or another, know "more" or "better." This possibility is confirmed repeatedly in concrete social situations. This proves true in a marked way for the subjective appropriation of certain provinces of special knowledge. Everyone finds out not only that he can learn something about definite things from definite fellow-men, but also that he must often do so. It is an especially frequent experience that what one knows only in outline particular fellow-men may know more clearly, more surely, and with less contradiction. In other words, elements that belong to one's own knowledge by acquaintance are at hand for certain fellow-men in the form of knowledge through thorough familiarity. In short, the processes of socialization, primary as well as secondary, lead to the view that the "what" as well as the "how" of knowledge is socially distributed. This view, although in different degrees of clarity, is an inevitable component of subjective experience in the everyday life-world.

We must now find out what specific expressions this subjectively fundamental correlate of the social distribution of knowledge receives. After all, as was shown, knowledge concerning the social distribution of knowledge is not entirely the result of an implication contained in the meaning-horizon of the subjective acquisition of knowledge. Rather, it is also derived from the subjective experiences of determinate fellow-men. For this reason, knowledge about this social distribution must already consist of specific elements of knowledge, namely, of typifications which concern the relation of one's own knowledge and non-knowledge to that of determinate fellow-men. And further, we must remember that knowledge about the social distribution of knowledge is *socially* relevant. It is therefore objectivated in every society and routinely transmitted to the individual. This knowledge is in no way a simple and undifferentiated element in the meaning-horizon of the subjective acquisition of knowledge. Nor does it remain limited to the typifications of individual fellow-men. Rather, it consists as well of patterns for interpretation that are based on the typical possession of typical knowledge on the part of typical members of society.

In every society the normal adult knows that he possesses typical elements of knowledge which are likewise possessed by typical fellow-men. Referring to this, he grasps himself as typically similar to them. But he also knows that he possesses other typical elements not yet possessed by other typical fellow-men (e.g., children) or probably never to be possessed by determinate typical fellow-men (e.g., women). Further, he knows that typical fellow-men (e.g., the elders) possess typical elements of knowledge which he knows in a more or less uncertain fashion, but with which he is not yet familiar—and that typical fellow-men (e.g., the shaman) possess typical elements of knowledge of which he has heard, whose "use" he may have observed, but which he will hardly ever be able to acquire. Fellow-men are thus typified with relation to possession as well as to the mode of possession. And the individual knows not only that he grasps his fellow-men in this manner, but that he is also correspondingly viewed by them in a form related to his own typical knowledge.

In order to delineate this situation still more precisely, we will return to the difference between general and special knowledge. Since the former is acquired by "everyone," we can say that elements of it can be grasped as not yet acquired; still, they have the status of being fundamentally acquirable. Thus, there is no occasion for a socially relevant differentiation of fellow-men in respect to their possession of general knowledge. The only thing relevant is a typification of the levels of acquisition. Surely, that should not mean that individual differences are not in principle on hand, even in the appropriation of general knowledge, nor that they are not grasped as such.

Special knowledge puts a different light on the matter. Determinate provinces of special knowledge may appear to the individual as "in principle" inaccessible, for specific reasons that concern individuals (the blacksmith's art for the one-armed man), or because of insurmountable institutional barriers (secret knowledge). The individual may already have acquired other provinces of special knowledge, or may take it as obvious that he will yet acquire them (e.g., the son of the smith, the art of forging in societies with inherited professions). On the other hand, other provinces may be grasped as in principle accessible; yet the individual may consider it improbable that this will lead to his betterment, since people of his kind in this society typically do not acquire knowledge of this sort.

A form of apprehending others as well as oneself is developed in an essential connection to special knowledge, a form which is of prime social relevance: the typical differentiation of specialists vis-à-vis laymen. Everyone knows that for problems of type A there are typical people in possession of the relevant special knowledge: specialists of type A. With problems of type A everyone else is a layman. Furthermore, everyone knows that for problems of type B there are specialists of type B, while all the others, including the specialists of type A, are laymen. Individual fellow-men can therefore be grasped as specialists of type A, or if that is not the case, as laymen, just as the individual experiences that he is grasped by fellow-men in a corresponding fashion, and just as he himself can finally also grasp himself. An essential dimension of the experience of others and the experience of self consists of typical connections between being an expert and being a layman.

Moreover, the knowledge of the typical circumstances under which the specialists' knowledge can be transmitted belongs to the type "specialist." When the special knowledge under consideration is "in principle" inaccessible, it is of special importance to know under what typical circumstances this knowledge will be *applied* to one's own advantage. Also, the impulse to learn special knowledge which is accessible in principle is diminished as soon as it becomes typically possible for laymen to participate in its "results." That holds in any case as long as one can satisfy the conditions set by the specialists. Thus a typification concerning the motives of specialists also belongs to the type "specialist."

Let us summarize. The social stock of knowledge appears as a taken-for-granted subjective possession, as an element of subjectivity. Determinate areas of the social stock of knowledge can be presented in subjective experience as ideal meaning-structures. In subjective knowledge about the social distribution of knowledge the social stock of knowledge appears in its specifically social character. From this perspective, considering the form of specialization and the role of being a layman, the social stock of knowledge determines a further essential dimension of the apprehension of oneself and of others—and thus of orientation in the social world in general.

2. CONCERNING THE HISTORICAL CHANGE IN THE SUBJECTIVE CORRELATES OF THE SOCIAL DISTRIBUTION OF KNOWLEDGE

a. The subjective correlates of the simple social distribution of knowledge

Knowledge concerning the social distribution of knowledge is a component of the social stock of knowledge. It is thus for its part socially distributed. And, since the social distribution of knowledge changes historically, the knowledge concerning it also changes correspondingly. For this reason the subjective correlates of the social distribution of knowledge assume various historically conditioned forms. Therefore, we cannot be satisfied with the description of the basic characteristics of the subjective correlates of the social distribution of knowledge. Indeed, in every society the individual will grasp typical differences between specialists and laymen. And in every society this will be a moment of the experience of self and others, and a moment of orientation to the social world in general. The current historical expression of the social distribution of knowledge determines the forms and the content of being a specialist and of being a layman, and their significance for orientation in the social world. With historical change in the structural bases for the social distribution of knowledge, the basic characteristics of the subjective correlates to the latter express themselves in various ways. It hardly need be emphasized that an investigation of the historical multiplicity of these expressions would exceed the scope of the present work. This is rather one of the tasks of the empirical sociology of knowledge. We will confine ourselves to developing the implications of the ideal-typical difference between simple and complex social distributions of knowledge relevant to the present problem.

Let us begin with an inspection of the simple social distribution of knowledge. This was characterized by "uniformity" in the distribution of general knowledge, by the absence of a multiplicity of developed and quasi-autonomous provinces of special knowledge, and by only a trivial degree of specialization of its institutional basis. Which subjective correlates have these characteristics?

Every normal adult is in full possession of general knowledge. The individual differences in general knowledge are only minor: in any case they have hardly any *social* relevance. Every normal adult can be considered typically to be highly competent. Further, since only a relatively limited portion of the social stock of knowledge consists of special knowledge, all problems which have the status of being able "in principle" to be mastered are also typically mastered by everyone. The lifeworldly reality is relatively easy for everyone to survey; orientation (but not necessarily life) in the social world is *relatively* unproblematic. If we did not want to limit the concept of the specialist to experts in the different areas of special knowledge, we could say that in the province of use of general knowledge everyone is a specialist.

There are only a few specialists in the prevailing sense of the word (e.g., shaman and smith). Consequently, only a few individuals in this society can be specialists and laymen at the same time (e.g., the shamans in relation to the art of forging). The majority of the members of society are only laymen. However, it is important to notice that the laymen understand themselves and others expressly as laymen only in a few, sharply defined, social relations, viz., problem situations. Only rarely in the routine of daily life do problem situations arise in which the factor of being a layman is prominent. Therefore, competence in general knowledge must play a predominant role in the apprehension of oneself. There is an exception: viz., the encounter with the few specialists whose specialty stands out sharply. Here laymen find themselves in a situation typically similar to that of the specialists who are socially visible in a pre-eminent fashion. With them, they partake of typically similar social relationships. Everyone has in essence the same knowledge about specialists: who they are, what their "province of jurisdiction" is, what typical motivational structures one can ascribe to them. Everyone knows when, where, and how one turns to specialists. In other words, knowledge concerning the social distribution of knowledge is relatively uniformly distributed, and correspondingly the subjective correlates of the social distribution of knowledge are expressed in a typically similar way for the majority of the members of society.

The contours of knowledge are identical for the "mere laymen"; only those belonging to the few specialists vary. The acceptance on the part of the individual that fellow-men are "the same" as he, is repeatedly substantiated in social relations, as an important consequence of the fact that the socially conditioned relevance structures of "mere laymen" are so similar (if we leave the social expression of biographical categories and the difference between the sexes out of consideration). Only the specialists are not "the same"; their "difference in kind" is thus more sharply outlined.

A simple social distribution of knowledge thus has, as we have shown, important consequences for the apprehension of self and others and for subjective orientation in the social world. On the other hand, the historically specific forms of the apprehension of self and others obviously have repercussions for the social structure and the distribution of knowledge. Again, investigation of such repercussions is a problem for the empirical sociology of knowledge. For instance, it is concerned with the question of the extent to which the absence of a socially stabilized and relevant differentiation of knowledge, in conjunction with the strongly expressed "difference in kind" of the specialists who monopolize special knowledge, influences the distribution of power in society among "mere laymen."

b. The subjective correlates of the complex social distribution of knowledge

An important characteristic of the complex social distribution of knowledge is the socially conditioned disproportion in the distribution of general knowledge: a complex social structure, especially in the form of highly developed political and economic institutions, conditions the stabilization of social strata related to authority and business, and of relevance structures specific to social strata. From these arise differentiated versions of general knowledge. We add to this the fact that the transmission of differentiated versions is anchored primarily in the social stratification. This means that not everyone is introduced to the "same" general knowledge, but rather learns the version belonging to the class into which he was born. These versions are valued differently in the society at large. They must not under any circumstances be considered to be "of the same value." This fact naturally has important consequences for orientation in the social world, as well as for the assessment of oneself and others.

Apart from socialization in different versions (which are not typically seen to be "of equal merit"), social structure and social stratum condition socially relevant differences in the subjective acquisition of general knowledge. While with simple social distributions, differences in competence with general knowledge are of an essentially individual nature, in the complex social distributions the typical chances for access to general knowledge depend on the social structure and social stratum. Such differences of competence are thus "socially caused," and as "socially imposed" characteristics play an important role in the apprehension of oneself and others, above all as a central moment of rank and class typifications, e.g., the "language" (vocabulary, grammar, accent) of farmers, townspeople, aristocracy, etc. How strongly the differences of competence with general knowledge are expressed naturally depends on the extent and nature of structural limitations on the access to the transmission of general knowledge.

Thus, characteristic typifications of oneself and others, and evaluations of oneself and others, are developed from the experience of socially conditioned and socially relevant differences in competence with respect to general knowledge, and from an understanding of the differentiation of the latter into versions which are not "equivalent." While these generally have less direct repercussions on the social structure (than do the typifications of self and others with regard to being a specialist and being a layman), they are not without significance for subjective orientation in the social world. Above all, it is important that the individual can only assume the "equivalency" of the relevance structures of his fellow-men in a conditioned fashion, subject to recall. This state of affairs is still further augmented by the multileveled relation between being a specialist and being a layman which exists with complex social distributions of knowledge.

The more that general knowledge is divided into different versions, the more difficult it is for the individual to survey general knowledge in its entirety (and its province of use: the core of everyday reality). To this is added the fact that the degree to which one can survey reality is socially distributed. This statement is based only on social reality as a whole. From within the differentiated "partial worlds," a comparison of competence with general knowledge is inadmissible. Within his "world" the farmer may be just as competent, or even more so, than the city dweller is within his.

Let us turn to the subjective correlates concerning the characteristic configuration of complex social distributions of knowledge, a configuration of comparatively specialized provinces of special knowledge which are relatively independent of each other. The structural basis of this development is the progressive division of labor. But the more division of labor in a society, the more everyone becomes a specialist in a certain area of special knowledge relevant for complexes of acts in one of the various institutional provinces of the division of labor. While in simple social distributions of knowledge "mere laymen" are numerically dominant, their number is increasingly diminished by the progressive division of labor, until for all "normal adults" the statement holds that everyone is at the same time not only a layman but also a specialist.

An important consequence of the progressive division of labor is a shift in the proportions of general and special knowledge within the social stock of knowledge. With the expansion of special knowledge, the importance of being a specialist increases as a dimension of the typification of self and others. But with a progressive division of labor not only is the proportion of general and special knowledge shifted in the social stock of knowledge, but the structure of specific knowledge is also changed. The latter is composed of a multiplicity of heterogeneous provinces whose meaning-structures cohere loosely, if at all. It is "in principle" impossible to acquire expertise in all areas of special knowledge.

Furthermore, as a consequence of the quasi autonomy of the areas of special knowledge, of the institutional restriction of the province of application of individual areas of knowledge, and of the historical accumulation of knowledge within the areas, the complexity of the meaning-structures can increase within every province of special knowledge. Correspondingly, the character of expertise is changed. Indeed, everyone is a specialist in one way or another. But for the majority of society's members, the expertise is limited to the complexes of acts which are ever more strongly, institutionally specialized through the progressive division of labor. Action in the different institutional provinces increasingly requires the appropriation of special knowledge; correlatively, the province of application is limited to the individual areas of special knowledge. Although the latter may still possess homogeneous meaning-structures, it is only specific subprovinces of special knowledge relevant for limited complexes of acts which are transmitted to the majority of society's members. In general, specialists, that is (as one should perhaps phrase it instead) "sub-" specialists, no longer survey their own area of expertise in its entirety.

A survey of the entirety of an area of special knowledge requires relatively lengthy and specialized processes of learning, in which the meaning-structures of the area are grasped more and more systematically. In other words, a "theoretical" education is needed. Expertise is thus differentiated within a given area of special knowledge. "Partial" and "complete" expertness do not have the same social relevance and, socially, are evaluated differently. Traditional classifications of expertness are developed, whose primary criterion is the range of the applicability of the knowledge. But since the range of applicability depends on the systematization of the area of knowledge as well as on the "length" of the education, expertness can become "professionalized." Its classifications are arranged according to the already existing classifications of the significance of institutional provinces vis-à-vis one another (e.g., blacksmith's art versus hunting, or religion versus economics). Levels of competence are thus socially strengthened and even under certain circumstances institutionalized, for instance in professional organizations. There are naturally different levels of competence in expertness, even in simple social distributions of knowledge. But there, they are predominantly of an individual nature (good blacksmith, bad blacksmith), as far as they are not based upon relatively simple biographical categories which typify the steps in the acquisition of special knowledge (e.g., a young apprentice shaman). In complex social distributions of knowledge, transmission and acquisition of special knowledge are in general extensively specialized institutionally, and the place of experts is "attested to" in quite anonymous institutional categories (officer of the Marine artillery).

Expertness is differentiated not only according to the traditional significance of the institutional province, to which the present area of special knowledge is related, but also according to the function of the respective act-complex in the institutional province and according to the degree of socially "verified" competence in special knowledge. There develops a network of the typifications of oneself and others which are related to special knowledge: a socially stabilized, anonymous "scale of the prestige of occupations," which is for the most part detached from the individual. This plays a central role in subjective orientation in the social world and decisively influences the formation of the subjective self-image. It need hardly be stressed that this state of affairs, which was originally conditioned by the progressive division of labor, social stratification, and the structure of special knowledge, has its own repercussions on the division of labor, social strata, and special knowledge.

Surely, if there are socially conditioned differences between experts in the same area of special knowledge, with respect to competence and their ability to survey the area of knowledge, this is all the more the case for those who are not experts in a given area. In general, the areas of special knowledge are not at all surveyable by laymen. Knowledge is typically limited to formulas for those situations in which the application of special knowledge, the consultation with experts, is relevant. Thus, everyone typically knows that there are physicians to whom one should turn when one is sick. But some may know further that they must go to internists in some cases, to surgeons in others. Although in its differentiation special knowledge is no longer surveyable as a whole by anyone, the *relative* survey of the province of expertness is socially distributed. Above all, two factors play a role here: the arrangement of institutions, viz., the appropriate arrangement of special knowledge (one understands something of the related field, but nothing of unrelated areas), and the social stratification (a certain orientation in the province of expertness within a society typically belongs to the "refined" versions of general knowledge).

We touch here on a further problem. As a consequence of quasi autonomy, inner differentiation, and accumulation of meaning-structures which accompany the stratification of expertness, the gulf between layman and expert increases. But at the same time the "applications" and "consequences" of special knowledge take hold more and more deeply in the daily life of laymen, frequently even in a more incisive fashion. Let us take an example from the modern world. The effects of technology illustrate most forcibly the state of affairs. Everyone uses electricity: one pushes a button; one does not stick his finger in the socket. But few "understand" what electricity is; the majority can hardly repair a defective light-switch themselves. One drives a car without being a car mechanic, not to mention knowing the laws at the basis of the internal combustion engine. But this is not the case just in the province of technology. One puts money in banks without being an economist; one votes without being a political expert, etc. All these examples illustrate the unusual connection of two factors: the growing gap between expertness and the lack of it, and the growing, almost continuous dependence of the layman on the expert.

In subjective experience, this state of affairs is reflected in a multileveled union (which does not exist at all in simpler social distributions of knowledge, or only in an incipient way) of lack of knowledge, half-knowledge, and knowledge of "power" and dependence. Everyone is at the same time a layman and an expert, and is thus given the chance to grasp consciously the gap between expertness and the lack of it. But when this is the case, a strong impulse arises to diminish the dependence on experts in areas where one is a layman, but which reach decisively into daily life. The acquisition of all such special knowledge is typically impossible. But at the same time it is in principle possible to acquire the "perspectives," the main methods, and the basic presuppositions of individual areas of special knowledge. This is enough in order to enable one to turn to the "correct" experts, to form a judgment concerning contradictory experts, and to make more or less well-founded decisions for one's own actions. Thus, we should deal here with a type of orientation in the everyday life-world lying between expertness and the lack of it. Let us call this type the "well-informed." This type is differentiated from the layman above all by the fact that he is not ready unreflectively to accept dependence on the judgment of the expert; on the other hand he is differentiated from the expert by the absence of specific explicit knowledge in the area in question.

In complex social distributions of knowledge, the subjective orientation in the total social reality can thus be apprehended ideally-typically by means of three types: the layman, the well-informed, and the expert, where expertise includes further socially defined degrees of competence. The concrete relation of these types to one another, and the consequences of this relation for apprehending oneself and others, are determined by means of the social structure and the structure of the social stock of knowledge.[32]

32. [Chap. 4 ends here. Chaps. 5 and 6 will be included in Vol. II.]

Index